BLACK & DECKER®

THE COMPLETE GUIDE TO EASY WOODWORKING PROJECTS

50 Projects You Can Build With Hand Power Tools

CREATIVE PUBLISHING international
CHANHASSAN, MINNESOTA
www.creativepub.com

Contents

CREATIVE PUBLISHING international

18705 Lake Drive East
Chanhassen, Minnesota 55317
1-800-328-3895
www.creativepub.com

Printed on American Paper by: R. R. Donnelley

10 9 8 7 6 5 4 3 2 1

President/CEO: Michael Eleftheriou
Vice President/Publisher: Linda Ball
Vice President/Retail Sales & Marketing: Kevin Haas

Executive Editor: Bryan Trandem
Creative Director: Tim Himsel
Managing Editor: Michelle Skudlarek
Editorial Director: Jerri Farris

Editor: Karen Ruth
Copy Editor: Tracy Stanley
Senior Art Director: David Schelitzche
Mac Designer: Jon Simpson
Project Manager: Julie Caruso
Studio Services Manager: Jeanette Moss McCurdy
Photographer: Tate Carlson
Scene Shop Carpenter: Randy Austin
Director of Production Services & Photography: Kim Gerber
Production Manager: Kim Gerber

THE COMPLETE GUIDE TO EASY WOODWORKING PROJECTS
Created by: The Editors of Creative Publishing international, Inc.,
in cooperation with Black & Decker. Black & Decker® is a trademark of
The Black & Decker Corporation and is used under license.

Library of Congress
Cataloging-in-Publication Data

The complete guide to easy woodworking projects :
50 projects you can build with hand power tools.
p. cm.
Includes index.
ISBN 1-58923-093-0 (soft cover)
ISBN 1-58923-184-8 (hard cover)
1. Woodwork–Patterns. 2. Power tools. I. Title: At head of title: Black & Decker. II. Black & Decker Corporation (Towson, Md.) III. Creative Publishing International.

TT180 .C695 2003
684'.08–dc21

2003040975

Portions of *The Complete Guide to Easy Woodworking Projects* are taken from the Black & Decker® books *Decorative Accessories; Kitchen Accessories; Maximizing Minimal Space; Easy Wood Furniture Projects.* Other titles from Creative Publishing international include:

The New Everyday Home Repairs; Basic Wiring & Electrical Repairs; Building Decks; Home Masonry Projects & Repairs; Workshop Tips & Techniques; Bathroom Remodeling; Flooring Projects & Techniques; Customizing Your Home. Carpentry: Remodeling; Carpentry: Tools • Shelves • Walls • Doors; Exterior Home Repairs & Improvements, Home Plumbing Projects & Repairs; Advanced Home Wiring; Advanced Deck Building; Built-In Projects for the Home; Landscape Design & Construction; Refinishing & Finishing Wood; Building Porches & Patios; Advanced Home Plumbing; Remodeling Kitchens; Finishing Basements & Attics; Stonework & Masonry Projects; Sheds, Gazebos & Outbuildings; Building & Finishing Walls & Ceilings; The Complete Guide to Home Plumbing; The Complete Guide to Home Wiring; The Complete Guide to Building Decks; The Complete Guide to Painting & Decorating; The Complete Guide to Creative Landscapes; The Complete Guide to Home Masonry; The Complete Guide to Home Carpentry; The Complete Guide to Home Storage; The Complete Guide to Windows & Doors; The Complete Guide to Bathrooms; The Complete Photo Guide to Home Repair; The Complete Photo Guide to Home Improvement; The Complete Photo Guide to Outdoor Home Improvement.

BOOKS
UNIVERSAL WORLD REFERENCE ENCYCLO-PEDIA

Introduction

Tired of searching for unique decorative accessories that won't break your budget? Looking for ways to use the space you have more efficiently? If you're eager to try your hand at woodworking, but don't have an elaborate shop, this is the book for you. Every one of the 50 projects presented here can be built with a few basic power tools.

For each of the 50 projects in this book, you will find a complete cutting list, a lumber shopping list, and a detailed construction drawing. Full-color photographs of major steps and clear, easy-to-follow directions will guide you through each project.

Because you want your finished project to look its best, a comprehensive set of finishing instructions is also included. We give you pictures illustrating the variety of products available for finishing your project—be it paint, stain or varnish—and directions for how to achieve the best possible results.

You don't need a lot of experience working with the hand tools and portable power tools used to make the furniture in this book. But if you haven't used any of the tools before, it is a good idea to practice using them on scrap wood before you tackle the actual projects.

Because you build the furniture yourself, you can select lumber and hardware to match a certain room decor or complement another furnishing. If you need to, you can also size the projects to fit in the exact space you need. The finishing information provided will let you create just the right accent.

Read the Woodworking and Finishing Techniques section to become familiar with the background information you'll need to be most successful in building your chosen project. The Materials section (pages 8-11) introduces the tools and materials needed for the projects. Woodworking Techniques (pages 12-15) introduces you to some simple, time-tested methods used by woodworkers everywhere, and Finishes (pages 16-39) gives you detailed how-to instructions for giving your project a beautiful protective coat.

WARNING
AVERTISSEMENT
100% PURE BRISTLE
MADE IN INDONESIA

Woodworking and Finishing Techniques

Here are some basic woodworking techniques and tips to get you started—and to help you finish your project well. You'll find information on choosing wood, types of materials, and how best to achieve a beautiful finish.

Materials

Tools You Will Use

At the start of each project, a set of symbols shows which power tools are used to complete the project as it is shown. In some cases, optional tools, such as a power miter saw or a table router, may be suggested for speedier work. You will also need a set of basic hand tools: hammer, screwdrivers, tape measure, level, combination square, framing square, compass, wood chisels, nail set, putty knife, utility knife, straightedge, C-clamps and pipe or bar clamps. Where required, specialty hand tools are listed for each project.

Circular saw to make straight cuts. For long cuts, use a straightedge guide. Install a carbide-tipped combination blade for most projects.

Drill for drilling holes and driving screws. Accessories help with sanding and grinding tasks. Use a corded or cordless drill with variable speed.

Jig saw for making contoured and internal cuts and for short straight cuts. Use the recommended blade for each type of wood or cutting task.

Power sander to prepare wood for a finish and to smooth sharp edges. Owning several types of power sanders is helpful.

Belt sander for resurfacing rough wood. Can also be used as a stationary sander when mounted on its side on a flat worksurface.

Router to cut structural grooves (rabbets) in wood. Also ideal for making a variety of decorative edges and roundover cuts.

Power miter saw for making angled cuts in narrow stock. Miter scales and a guide fence make it easy to set the saw quickly for precise angles.

Organizing Your Worksite

Working safely and comfortably is important to successfully completing your woodworking projects. Taking the time to set up your worksite before you begin will make your progress from step to step much smoother.

You will need a solid work surface, usually at waist level, to help you maintain a comfortable work angle. A portable work bench is sufficient for many of the smaller projects in this book. For larger projects, a sturdy sheet of plywood clamped to sawhorses will work well. In some cases you will need to use the floor for layout or assembly space.

Portable power tools and hand tools offer a level of convenience that is a great advantage over stationary power tools, but using them safely and conveniently requires some basic housekeeping. Whether you are working in a garage, a basement, or outdoors, it is important to establish a flat, dry holding area where you can store tools. Dedicate an area of your worksite for tool storage, and be sure to return tools to that area once you are finished with them.

It is also important that all waste, including lumber scraps and sawdust, be disposed of in a timely fashion. Check with your local waste disposal department before throwing away any large scraps of building materials or finishing material containers.

If you are using corded power tools outdoors, always use grounded extension cords connected to a ground fault interrupter circuit (GFCI) receptacle. Keep cords neat and out of traffic lanes at all times. Remember that most of the materials you will be working with are flammable and should be stored away from furnaces and water heaters.

Safety Tips

- *Always wear eye and hearing protection when operating power tools.*
- *Choose a well-ventilated work area when cutting or shaping wood and when using finishing products.*
- *Some wood sawdust is toxic—cedar especially—so wear an appropriate dust mask when sawing, routing and sanding.*

Materials Used in This Book

Sheet goods:
AB Plywood: A smooth, paintable plywood, usually made from pine or fir. The better (A) side is sanded and free from knots and defects.
Birch Plywood: A sturdy plywood with birch veneer on both sides. Excellent for painting but attractive enough for stain or clear finish.
Oak Plywood: A plywood with high-quality oak veneers. A workable, stainable product that blends well with solid oak lumber.
Pine Panels: Edge glued pine boards, cut and sanded. Usually $\frac{5}{8}$" or $\frac{3}{4}$" thick.
Lauan Plywood: A relatively inexpensive plywood with a smooth mahogany veneer on one side. The natural color varies widely.
Medium-Density Fiberboard (MDF): A smooth highly workable product made from compressed wood fibers.
Hardboard: A dense fiberboard with one hard, smooth side.
Melamine Board: Fiberboard or particleboard with a glossy, polymerized surface that is water resistant and easy to clean.
Tileboard: Vinyl sheet goods resembling ceramic tile.
Sheet Acrylic: Clear plastic product available in thicknesses from $\frac{1}{16}$" to 1".

Dimension lumber: *The "nominal" size of lumber is usually larger than the actual size. For example, a 1 × 4 board measures $\frac{3}{4}$" × 3½".*
Select Pine: Finish-quality pine that is mostly free of knots and other imperfections.
#2-or-Better Pine: A grade lower than select but more commonly available.
Red Oak: A common, durable hardwood, oak is popular for its color, straight grain and solid appearance.
Aspen: A soft, workable hardwood. Aspen is good for painting but should be sealed for an even stain.
Cedar: A lightweight softwood with a natural resistance to moisture. Smooth cedar is best for furniture.
Poplar: A soft light wood that is easy to cut and good for painting.

Other wood products:
Wood Moldings: Available in a vast range of styles and sizes. Most types of molding are available in a variety of woods.
Veneer Edge Tape: Self-adhesive wood veneer sold in $\frac{3}{4}$"-wide strips. Applied to plywood edges with a household iron.
Wood Plugs: $\frac{3}{8}$"-dia. × $\frac{1}{4}$"-thick disks with a slightly conical shape.

Fasteners and adhesives:
Wood Screws: Steel, zinc-coated steel, brass or brass-coated steel screws with a heavy shank and fine threads. Steel screws are stronger than brass but can stain acidic wood, such as oak, if exposed to moisture. The gauge number refers to shank diameter.
Deck Screws: Similar to wallboard screws, these have a light shank and coarse threads, making them ideal for fastening soft woods.
Finish Nails and Brads: Thin-shank, steel nails with a small, cup-shaped head. They are driven below the surface with a nail set.
Wire Nails: Small, steel nails with a flat, round head.
Wood Glue: Yellow (or "carpenter's") glue is good for indoor furniture projects. Application and drying time depend on the product.
Ceramic Tile Adhesive: Multipurpose thin-set mortar or latex mastic. Each is applied with a V-notch trowel.

Other materials:
Ceramic Floor Tile: Sturdy tile suitable in situations where durability is required. Available in sizes from 1 × 1" to 12 × 18".
Tempered Glass: Stronger than regular glass. Used for glass shelving.

Materials

Lumber: Redwood (A) and cedar (B) are warm-colored softwoods. Because of their attractive color and grain, they usually are left unfinished or coated with a clear finish. Pine (C) is an easy-to-cut softwood often used for projects that will be painted. Framing lumber (D) includes rough grades of softwood pine and fir. It is used for structural framing and utility shelving. Poplar (E), a light-colored hardwood with very straight grain, is an excellent wood for fine painted surfaces. Maple (F) and oak (G) are heavy, strong hardwoods with attractive grain patterns. They usually are finished with tinted oils or stains.

These easy woodworking projects vary considerably in size and style, but they can be constructed with materials available at any home improvement center. If you prefer to use unique woods or unusual moldings, you may need to visit a woodworker's supply store or large wholesale lumber yard to find them.

To save money, construct your projects using finish-grade plywood for the main body (carcass), then trim exposed areas with more costly solid woods and moldings.

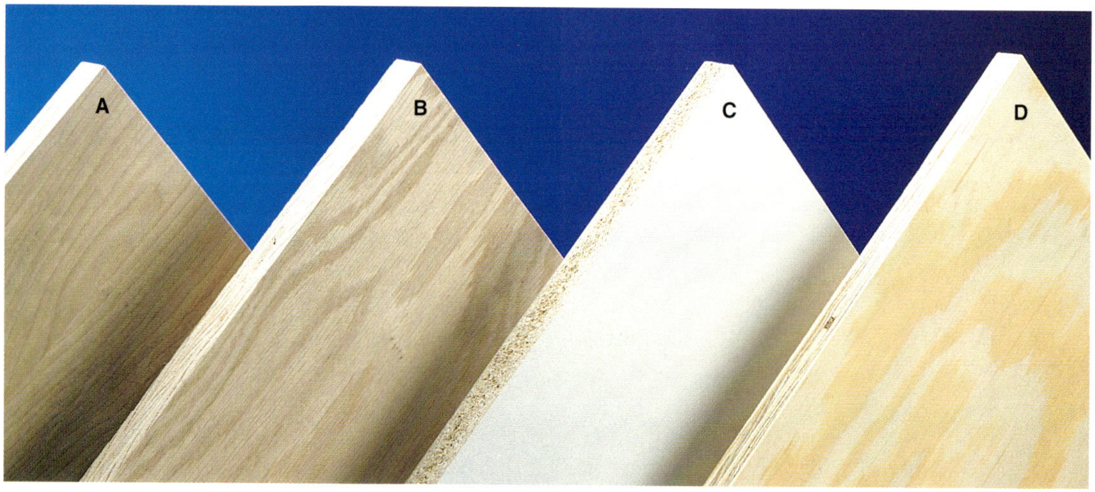

Sheet goods: Finish-grade plywood, including birch plywood (A) and oak plywood (B) are made from several layers of softwood veneer sandwiched between hardwood surface veneers. Finish-grade plywoods are used for exposed areas, and usually are edged with hardwood strips or moldings. Birch plywood frequently is used for surfaces that will be painted, and oak plywood is usually finished with tinted oils or stains. Particleboard (C), coated with a plastic resin called melamine, is used for making contemporary-style projects. Sanded pine plywood (D) is a good material for projects that will be painted or parts in hidden areas. NOTE: Most sheet goods are sold in 4 ft. × 8 ft. sheets, in ¼", ½", or ¾" thicknesses; some types also are sold in 2 ft. × 4 ft. and 4 ft. × 4 ft. sheets.

Trim moldings

Are both decorative and functional. They can be used to cover gaps around the base and sides of cabinets and shelves, to hide the edges of plywood surfaces, or simply to add visual interest to the project. Moldings are available in dozens of styles, but the samples shown here are widely available at home improvement centers.

Baseboard molding (A) is used to trim the bottom edge of a project along the floor line. Choosing molding that matches the baseboard used elsewhere in your home gives your project a custom look.

Hardwood strips (B) are used to construct face frames, and to cover unfinished edges of plywood shelves. Maple, oak and poplar strips are widely available in 1 × 2, 1 × 3 and 1 × 4 sizes.

Crown moldings (C, D) add a decorative accent to a project.

Cove molding (E) is a simple, unobtrusive trim for covering gaps.

Ornamental moldings, including spindle-and-rail (F) and embossed moldings (G, H), give a distinctive decorative look.

Door-edge molding (I), sometimes called cap molding, is used with finish-grade plywood to create panel-style doors and drawer faces.

Shelf-edge molding (J), sometimes called base cap molding, gives a decorative edge to plywood shelves.

Base shoe molding (K) covers gaps around the top, bottom, and sides of a project.

Woodworking Techniques

Cutting

Circular saws and jig saws cut wood as the blade passes up through the material, which can cause splintering or chipping on the top face of the wood. For this reason, always cut with your workpiece facedown.

To ensure a straight cut with a circular saw, clamp a straightedge to your workpiece to guide the foot of the saw as you cut **(photo A).**

To make an internal cutout in your workpiece, drill starter holes near cutting lines and use a jig saw to complete the cut **(photo B).**

A power miter saw is the best tool for making straight or angled cuts on narrow boards and trim pieces **(photo C).** This saw is especially helpful for cutting hardwood. An alternative is to use an inexpensive hand miter box fitted with a backsaw **(photo D).**

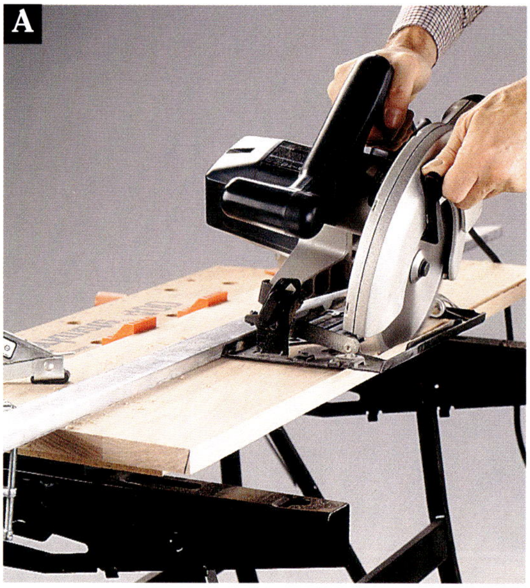

The foot of the circular saw rides along the straightedge to make straight, smooth cuts.

Make contoured cutouts by drilling starter holes and cutting with a jig saw.

A power miter saw is easy to use and quickly makes clean, accurate angle cuts in any wood.

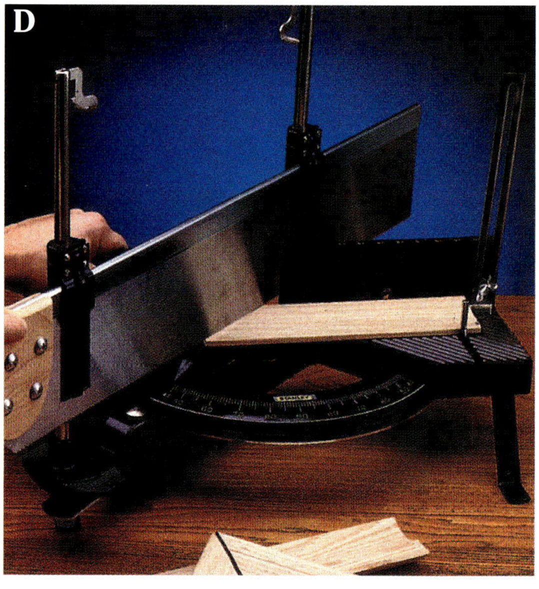

A hand miter box keeps your backsaw in line for making a full range of angle cuts.

Shaping

Create detailed shapes by drawing a grid pattern on your workpiece. Use the grid to mark accurate centers and endpoints for the shapes you will cut. Make smooth roundovers and curves using a standard compass **(photo E).**

You can also create shapes by enlarging a drawing detail, using a photocopier and transferring the pattern to the workpiece.

A belt sander makes short work of sanding tasks and is also a powerful shaping tool. Mounting a belt sander to your workbench allows you to move and shape the workpiece freely—using both hands **(photo F).** Secure the sander by clamping the tool casing in a benchtop vise or with large handscrew or C-clamps. Clamp a scrap board to your bench to use as a platform, keeping the workpiece square and level with the sanding belt.

To ensure that matching pieces have an identical shape, clamp them together before shaping **(photo G).** This technique is known as gang-sanding.

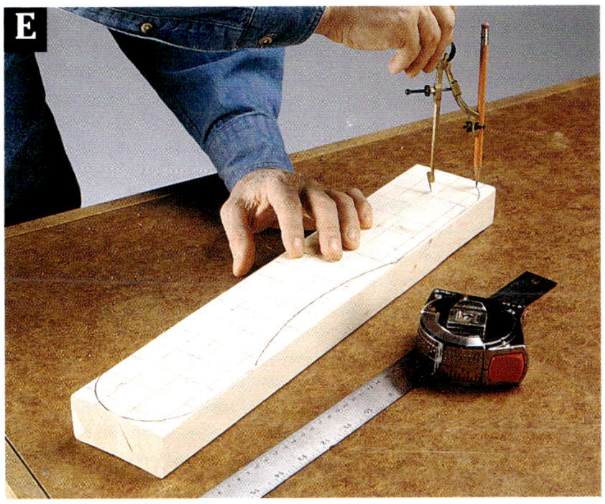

Use a square grid pattern and a compass to draw patterns on your workpiece.

Squaring a Frame

Squaring is an important technique in furniture construction. A frame or assembly that is not square will result in a piece that teeters on two legs or won't stand up straight. Always check an assembly for square before fastening the parts together.

To square a frame, measure diagonally from corner to corner **(photo H).** When the measurements are equal, the frame is square. Adjust the frame by applying inward pressure to diagonally opposite corners. A framing square or a combination square can also be used to see if two pieces form a right angle.

Clamp a belt sander and a scrap board to the workbench to create a stationary shaping tool.

Gang-sanding is an easy method for creating two or more identical parts.

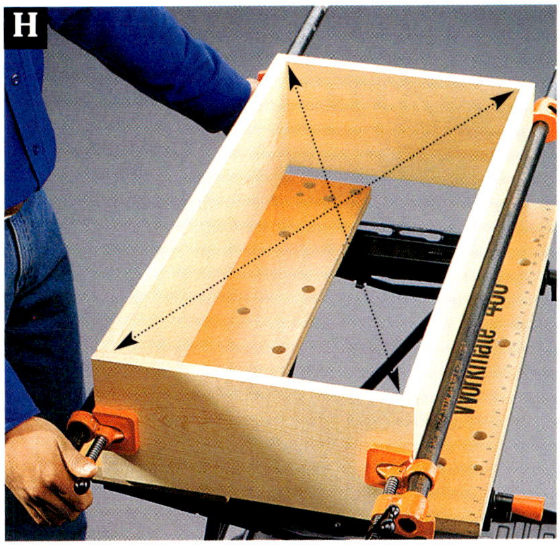

Clamp frame parts together. Then, measure the diagonals to check for square before fastening.

Piloting and Drilling

Pilot holes make it easier to drive screws or nails into a workpiece, and they remove some material and so keep the fastener from splitting the wood. If you find that your screws are still difficult to drive or that the wood splits, switch to a larger piloting bit. If the screws are not holding well or are stripping the pilot holes, use a smaller bit to pilot subsequent holes. When drilling pilot holes for finish nails, use a standard straight bit.

A combination pilot bit drills pilot holes for the threaded and unthreaded sections of the screw shank, as well as a counterbore recess that allows the screw to seat below the surface of the workpiece **(photo A).** The counterbore portion of the bit drills a $\frac{3}{8}$"-dia. hole to accept a standard wood plug. A bit stop with a setscrew allows you to adjust the drilling depth.

When drilling a hole through a workpiece, clamp a scrap board to the piece on the side where the drill bit will exit **(photo B).** This "backer board" will prevent the bit from splintering the wood and is especially important when drilling large holes with a spade bit.

To make perfectly straight or uniform holes, mount your drill to a portable drill stand **(photo C).** The stand can be adjusted for drilling to a specific depth and angle.

A combination pilot bit drills pilot holes and counterbores for wood screws in one step.

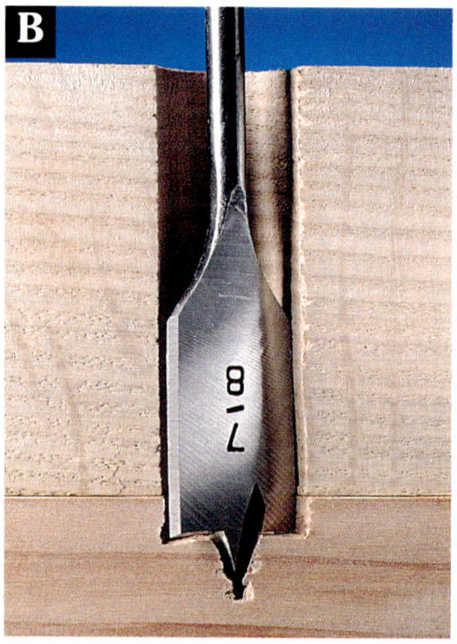

Use a scrap backer board to prevent tearout when drilling through a workpiece.

A portable drill stand helps you drill straight or angled holes.

Gluing

A gluing surface should be smooth and free of dust but not sanded. Glue and fasten boards soon after they are cut—machined surfaces, which dry out over time, bond best when they are freshly cut.

Before gluing, test-fit the pieces to ensure a proper fit. Then, clean the mating edges with a clean, dry cloth to remove dust **(photo D).**

Apply glue to both surfaces and spread it evenly, using a stick or your finger **(photo E).** Use enough glue to cover the area, with a small amount of excess.

Promptly assemble and clamp the pieces with enough clamps to apply even pressure to the joint. Watch the glue oozing from the joint to gauge the distribution of pressure. Excessive "squeeze-out" indicates that the clamps are too tight or that there is too much glue. Wipe away excess glue with a damp—not wet—cloth.

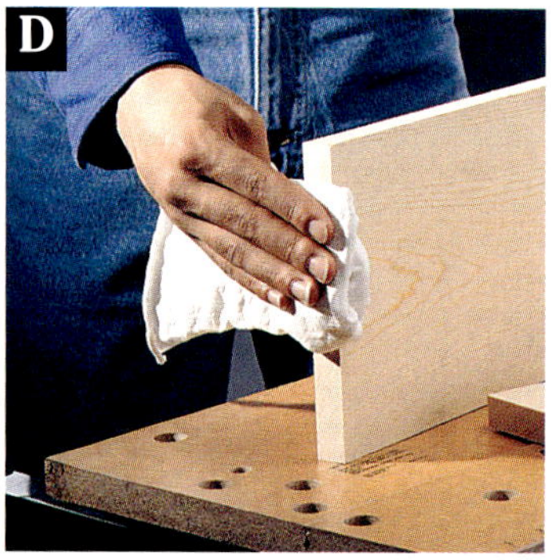

Clean the mating surfaces with a cloth to remove dust.

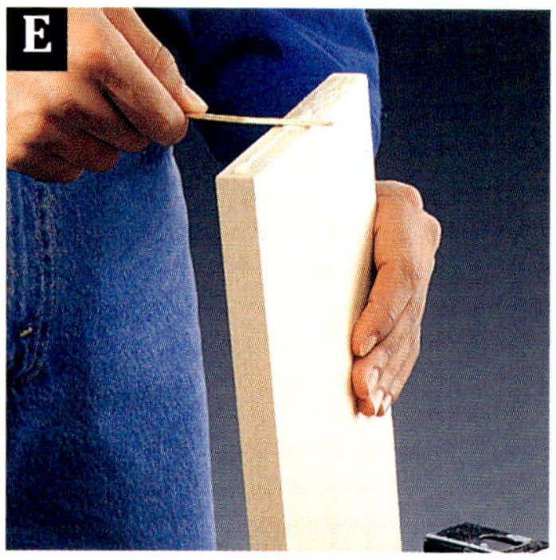

Spread glue evenly over the entire mating surface of both pieces.

Prepping Wood for Finishing Touches

Most projects require that nail heads be set below the surface of the wood, using a nail set **(photo F).** Choose a nail set with a point slightly smaller than the nail head.

Screws that have been driven well below the surface (about ¼") can be hidden by filling the counterbores with glued wood plugs **(photo G).** Tap the plug into place with a wood mallet or a hammer and scrap block, leaving the plug just above the surface. Then, sand the plug smooth with the surrounding surface.

Fill nail holes and small defects with wood putty **(photo H).** When applying a stain or clear finish to a project, use a tinted putty to match the wood, and avoid smearing it outside the nail holes. Use putty to fill screw holes on painted projects.

A power drill with a sanding drum attachment helps you sand contoured surfaces smooth **(photo I).**

Use a palm sander to finish-sand flat surfaces. To avoid sanding through thin veneers, draw light pencil marks on the surface and sand just until the marks disappear **(photo J).**

To finish-sand your projects, start with medium sandpaper (100- or 120-grit) and switch to increasingly finer papers (150- to 220-grit).

F

Set finish nails below the surface, using a nail set slightly smaller than the head of the nail.

G

Apply glue to wood plugs and insert them into screw counterbores to hide the screws.

H

Fill holes and wood defects with plain or tinted wood putty.

I

Smooth curves and hard-to-reach surfaces with a drum attachment on your power drill.

J

Draw pencil marks on veneered surfaces to prevent oversanding.

Selecting a Finish

A good finish both protects and beautifies wood. To achieve both goals, a finish is made up of several layers, each with its own specific purpose. Each element of a finish should be chosen carefully, according to the features of the wood, the function of the project piece, and your tastes. On new wood, apply a seal coat made of sanding sealer to create more even finish absorption and more consistent color. For a fine finish, some woods are best treated with grain filler instead of sealer (page 21).

The next layer is the color layer, which is usually created with wood stain or penetrating oil (pages 22 to 25). Color can either enhance or minimize grain pattern and other wood features, and it can beautify plain wood. With fine woods or to create a more rustic look, the color layer can be omitted. Dampen the wood surface with mineral spirits to see how it will look with a clear finish. To create a specific decorative look or to cover wood defects, apply paint as the color layer (pages 26 to 31).

Finally, a topcoat is applied to seal the wood and protect the finished surface from scratches and wear. Topcoats can be created with traditional finishing products, like tung oil, or more contemporary materials, like polyurethane (pages 32 to 37). A layer or two of well-buffed paste wax can be applied over most topcoat materials to create a glossy, protective surface that is easily renewed with fresh wax (pages 38 to 39).

When selecting a new finish, it helps if you know the wood species of your project. Softwoods, like pine, should always be treated with

A typical wood finish is composed of three basic layers: the seal coat, the color layer, and the topcoat.

sanding sealer or primer, for example. And open-grained hardwoods, like red oak or mahogany, look better when treated with grain filler. The finish samples on pages 18 to 19 show how some common finishes look on different woods.

As a general rule, base your finish selection on color. Simply choose a color you like, then select a coloring agent and a compatible topcoat. Consider use, as well. If the finished piece will be used by children or as a food preparation surface, use nontoxic water-based products to finish the wood. For more information on finishing products, refer to the sections indicated above.

Consider absorption rates. Some wood types absorb more finish materials than others, depending on the porosity of the wood grain. In the photo above, the same stain was applied to three different unsealed woods, resulting in three different levels of darkness. Sealing the wood or filling the grain minimizes this effect.

Highly figured wood, like the walnut shown above, usually is given a clear finish so the grain is not obscured. In some cases, however, tinted penetrating oil can be used to enhance an already striking grain pattern. Experiment with different coloring agents on a piece of similar wood or in an inconspicuous area of the project.

Use sanding sealer or grain filler for a fine finish. Sealing evens out the stain absorption rates, yielding a lighter, more even finish. Filling the grain creates a lighter finish that feels as smooth as it looks.

Consider combining colors to create interesting decorative effects. Contrasting stains and paints on the same piece can create a dramatic finish when used with good design sense.

Sample Finishes: Dark

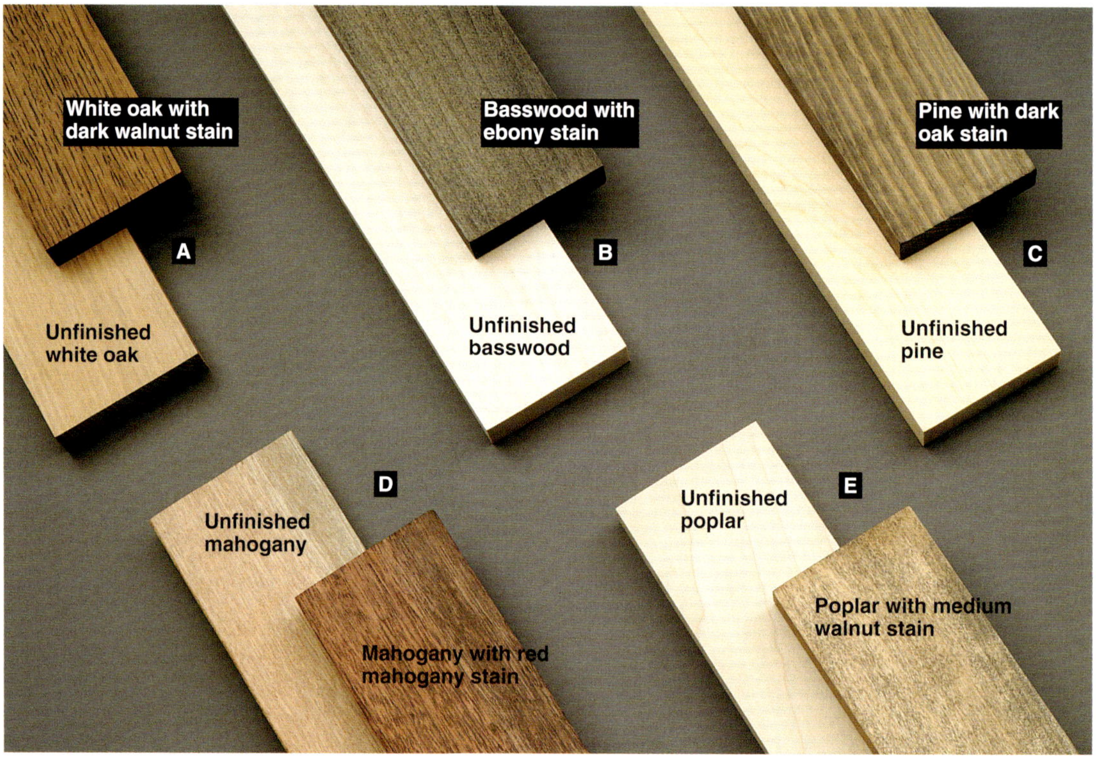

Use dark finishes to: enhance a distinctive grain pattern (A); add interest to plain wood (B); give a rich, formal look to softwoods (C); create a traditional finish (D); simulate the appearance of a finer hardwood on inexpensive wood (E).

Sample Finishes: Light

Use light finishes to: highlight subtle grain patterns (A); amplify attractive wood tone (B); modify wood tones to match a particular decor or color scheme (C); add a sense of depth (D); give unfinished wood a seasoned, antique appearance (E).

Sample Finishes: Clear

Clear finishes protect and seal wood while allowing the natural beauty of the wood to speak for itself. Choose clear finishes for exotic woods that are prized for their color or grain pattern, or for more common woods when a natural, rustic look is desired.

Sample Finishes: Painted

Painted finishes mask undesirable qualities, like old finish residue, and create decorative effects. Surface defects, like repairs, stains, knots, and holes should be filled with wood putty to create an even surface when painted. Man-made wood products, like plywood, also benefit from painted finishes.

Making Final Surface Preparation

Use a finishing sander on flat surfaces and specialty sanding blocks on contours.

Examine the workpiece with bright sidelighting during finish sanding to gauge your progress.

Use sanding blocks to handsand the entire workpiece with the finest-grit paper in the sanding sequence.

Finish Sanding

Ensure an even, quality finish for your woodworking project by carefully preparing the wood surface. Finish-sand with progressively finer grits of sandpaper, starting with 150-grit. Generally, hardwood requires finer-grit sandpaper than softwood. For speed and even results, use a power sander for the first stages of finish sanding. Use hand-sanding with the finest grit in the sequence so you do not oversand. Seal wood with sanding sealer to create more even finish absorption.

Finish-sand all surfaces with 150-grit sandpaper, following the direction of the grain. Use a finishing sander on flat surfaces and specialty sanding blocks on contours. When sanding hardwood, switch to 180-grit paper and sand again **(photo A).**

Examine the workpiece with bright sidelighting during finish sanding to gauge your progress. If shadows, scratches, or sanding marks are visible, more sanding is needed **(photo B).**

Your sandpaper will last longer and work better if you clean it regularly. Use a wire brush or rubber cleaning stick to remove sawdust and grit that can clog the sandpaper and cause burnishing of the wood surface.

Whenever you change sandpaper grits, wipe the wood surface clean using a cloth slightly dampened with mineral spirits. This removes dust and grit from coarser sandpaper that cause scratches when you continue sanding.

To decrease the chance of raising the wood grain during finishing, raise the grain during sanding by dampening the surface with a wet rag. Let the wood dry, then skim the surface with a fine abrasive pad, following the grain. The pad will pull out any raised fibers.

Use sanding blocks to handsand the entire workpiece with the finest-grit paper in the sanding sequence **(photo C).** Sand until all sanding marks are gone and the surface is smooth. If using sanding sealer, apply a coat now, then sand lightly with 220-grit when dry.

Applying Grain Filler

Especially when using oak, you will want to apply grain filler to guarantee a deep, smooth finish. Grain filler decreases stain absorption, which will result in a lighter finish. Sand, fill and stain small pieces of scrap wood to determine what your final finish will look like.

After finish sanding, use a rag or putty knife to spread a coat of grain filler onto the wood surface. With a polishing motion, work the filler into the grain **(photo D).** Let the filler dry until it becomes cloudy, usually about five minutes.

Remove excess filler by drawing a plastic putty scraper across the grain of the wood at a 45° angle **(photo E).** Let the grain filler dry overnight.

Lightly hand-sand the surface, following the direction of the grain, with 320-grit sandpaper **(photo F).** Clean thoroughly with a cloth dampened in mineral spirits before applying the finish **(photo G).**

Use a rag or putty knife to spread a coat of grain filler onto the wood surface.

Remove excess filler by drawing a plastic putty scraper across the grain of the wood at a 45° angle.

Lightly hand-sand the surface, following the direction of the grain, with 320-grit sandpaper.

Wipe the wood surface clean, using a cloth slightly dampened with mineral spirits.

A well-chosen, properly applied color layer is the most important component of an attractive wood finish.

Coloring Wood

There are several reasons to color wood. The most common reason is to enhance the appearance of the wood by showing off a fine or distinctive grain pattern or creating a beautiful wood tone. But stain and penetrating oil, the two most basic coloring agents, can accomplish more practical results as well. Using a dark color conceals uneven color in your wood and can blend together two or more different wood types.

When selecting a coloring agent for your project, you will find a vast selection of products to choose from. There are oil-based stains, water-based stains, wipe-on gel stains, penetrating oils, one-step stain-and-sealant products—the options seem endless. To sort through the many products and make the selection that is best for your project, start by finding a color you like. Then check the specific properties of the coloring agent to determine if it is the best general type for your project. Make sure it has no compatibility problems with the topcoat you plan to use, or with any sanding sealers or grain fillers (see charts, next page).

Whichever coloring agent you select, read the directions very carefully before applying it to the wood. Drying time, application techniques, and cleanup methods vary widely between products—even products that are similar. Also test the product on a wood sample similar to your project. When using a stain, apply enough coats to create the exact color shade you want (stain will become darker with each new coat that is applied). Keep careful records of how many coats you applied so you can refer to them when you finish the actual workpiece.

Penetrating Oil

Penetrating oil (often called "Danish oil" or "rubbing oil") delivers color deep into the wood for a rich-looking finish that can be buffed to form a protective surface.

ADVANTAGES:
- *easy to apply*
- *creates very even coloration*
- *does not "paint over" wood grain*
- *compatible with most topcoats*
- *penetrates deeper than stain for very rich color*
- *can be used without a topcoat*

DRAWBACKS:
- *may fade in direct sunlight*
- *limited range of colors*
- *cannot darken color with multiple coats*
- *toxic fumes; flammable*

COMPATIBILITY:
- *avoid using with oil-based polyurethane*

RECOMMENDED USES:
- *wood with attractive grain pattern*
- *antiques and fine furniture*
- *decorative items*

COMMON BRAND NAMES:
- *Watco® Danish Oil Finish, Deft® Danish Oil Finish*

Water-based Liquid Stain

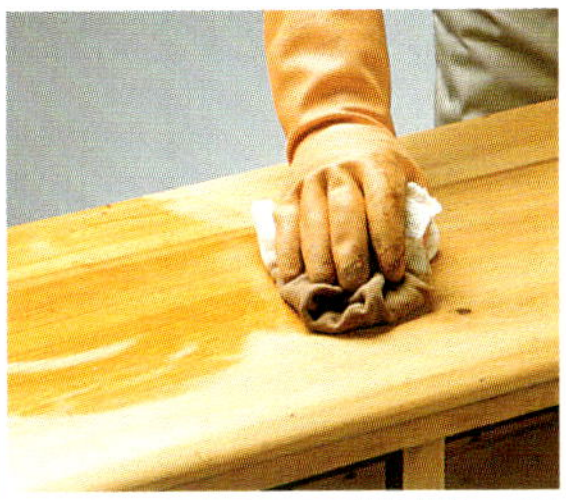

Water-based liquid stain is wiped or brushed on to create a color layer than can be darkened with additional applications.

ADVANTAGES:
- *easy to clean up, safe to use*
- *wide range of colors available*
- *can be built up in layers to control final color*
- *dries quickly*

DRAWBACKS:
- *can raise wood grain (requires sanding for an even surface)*
- *can chip or scuff if not properly topcoated.*

COMPATIBILITY:
- *bonds well with most topcoats*

RECOMMENDED USES:
- *floors*
- *woodwork*
- *previously finished furniture—can be "painted" on to cover color variations*
- *tabletops, eating surfaces, children's furniture and toys*

COMMON BRAND NAMES:
- *Carver Trip® Safe & Simple Wood Stain, Behr® Water-based Stain, Varathane Elite Wood Stain®*

Oil-based Liquid Stain

Oil-based liquid traditionally has been the most common type of wood stain, but its availability and popularity are declining due to environmental factors.

ADVANTAGES:
- *does not raise wood grain*
- *slow drying time increases workability*
- *permanent and colorfast*
- *can be built up to control color*
- *conditions and seals wood*
- *less likely to bleed than water-based stain*

DRAWBACKS:
- *harmful vapors; flammable; hard to clean*
- *regulated or restricted in some states*
- *decreasing availability*
- *unpleasant odor*

COMPATIBILITY:
- *can be used with most topcoats*

RECOMMENDED USES:
- *previously stained wood*
- *wood finish touch-up*

COMMON BRAND NAMES:
- *Minwax® Wood Finish, Carver Tripp® Wood Stain, Zar® Wood Stain*

Gel Stain

Gel stains, usually oil-based, provide even surface color that is highly controllable due to the thickness of the product. Gel finishes are growing in popularity.

ADVANTAGES:
- *very neat and easy to apply—will not run*
- *does not raise wood grain*
- *dries evenly*
- *can be built up to deepen color*
- *can be buffed to create a hard surface*

DRAWBACKS:
- *limited color selection*
- *more expensive than other stain types*
- *hard to clean up*
- *requires buffing between coats*

COMPATIBILITY:
- *can be used with most topcoats*

RECOMMENDED USES:
- *woodwork and furniture with vertical surfaces*
- *furniture with spindles and other rounded parts*

COMMON BRAND NAMES:
- *Bartley® Gel Stain, Behlen® Master Gel*

Applying Liquid Stain

The end grain of wood will absorb more color than the face grain, so seal all end grain and test the stain color before staining.

Oil-based or water-based stain in liquid form can be lightened by scrubbing, and it usually can be darkened by applying additional coats. Prepare for the stain, then stir the stain thoroughly and apply a heavy coat with a brush or cloth. Stir the stain often as you work **(photo A).** Let the stain soak in for about 15 minutes (see manufacturer's directions).

A

Prepare for the stain, then stir the stain thoroughly and apply a heavy coat with a brush or cloth. Stir the stain often as you work. Let the stain soak in for about 15 minutes (see manufacturer's directions).

B

Remove excess stain with a clean, lint-free cloth. Wipe against the grain first, then with the grain. If the color is too dark, try scrubbing with water or mineral spirits. Let the stain dry, then buff with a fine abrasive pad.

Remove excess stain with a clean, lint-free cloth **(photo B).** Wipe against the grain first, then with the grain. If the color is too dark, try scrubbing with water or mineral spirits. Let the stain dry, then buff with a fine abrasive pad.

Apply light coats of stain until the desired color tone is achieved, buffing with an abrasive pad between coats. Buff the final coat of stain before top-coating **(photo C).**

Applying Gel Stain

Creating consistent color is especially easy with gel stain, which clings to awkward surfaces without pooling.

Prepare for the stain. Stir the gel stain, then work it into the surfaces of the workpiece with a staining cloth, using a circular motion **(photo D).** Cover as much of the workpiece as you can reach with the staining cloth, recoating any areas that dry out as you work. Gel stain penetrates better if it is worked into the wood with a brush or rag, rather than simply wiped onto the wood surface.

Use a stiff-bristled brush, like a stenciling brush, to apply gel stain into hard-to-reach areas, where it is difficult to use a staining cloth **(photo E).**

Let the stain soak in (see manufacturer's directions), then wipe off the excess with a clean rag, using a polishing motion. Buff the stained surface with the wood grain, using a soft, clean cloth.

C

Apply light coats of stain until the desired color tone is achieved, buffing with an abrasive pad between coats. Buff the final coat of stain before top-coating.

Apply additional coats of stain until the workpiece has reached the desired color tone. Gel stain manufacturers usually recommend at least three coats to provide a thick stain layer that helps protect the wood against scratches and other surface flaws. Let the stain dry, then buff with a fine abrasive pad before applying a topcoat.

Applying Penetrating Oil

Prepare for the stain, then apply a heavy coat of penetrating oil to all surfaces, using a staining cloth. Wait 15 to 30 minutes, recoating any areas that begin to dry out. Apply oil to all surfaces, and let it soak into the wood for 30 to 60 minutes **(photo F).**

Wipe the surface dry with a clean cloth, rubbing with the wood grain. Apply another coat of oil with a clean cloth, then let the oil dry overnight. Two coats are sufficient in most cases, since further coats will not darken the finish color. Dab a few drops of penetrating oil onto a fine abrasive pad, then rub the surfaces until smooth **(photo G).** Let the oil dry for at least 72 hours before applying a topcoat. If you do not plan to topcoat the finish, buff with a soft cloth to harden the oil finish.

D

Gel stain penetrates better if it is worked into the wood with a brush or rag, rather than simply wiped onto the wood surface.

E

Use a stiff-bristled brush, like this stenciling brush, to apply gel stain into hard-to-reach areas.

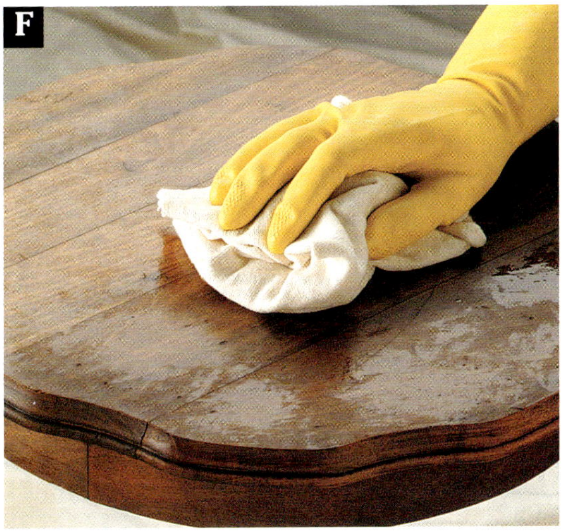

F

Wipe the surface dry with a clean cloth, rubbing with the wood grain. Apply another coat of oil with a clean cloth, then let the oil dry overnight. Note: Two coats are sufficient in most cases, since further coats will not darken the finish color.

G

Dab a few drops of penetrating oil onto a fine abrasive pad, then rub the surfaces until smooth. Let the oil dry for at least 72 hours before applying a topcoat. If you do not plan to topcoat the finish, buff with a soft cloth to harden the oil finish.

Painting Wood

Most woodworkers want to showcase the natural wood tones of their projects, so painting is a finishing option that is sometimes overlooked. However, there are many wood projects that are designed to be painted, including a number in this book. Painting surfaces also allows you to use less expensive woods, yet still have impressive results.

Use paint as an alternative to wood stain to give plain wood a splash of color or a decorative touch; or simply use it to hide wear, low-quality materials, or unattractive wood.

Furniture and woodwork generally should be painted with water-based or oil-based enamel paint except when using decorative painting techniques that call for flat wall paint. Enamel paint forms a tough, protective coat that resists moisture, chipping, and scratching. It is available in dozens of premixed colors, and in gloss and semi-gloss versions. Or, you can have special colors custom-mixed at a paint store.

Paint brushes for wood include straight trim brushes for flat areas, and tapered brushes for edges. Use synthetic brushes (nylon or polyester bristles) for both water-based and oil-based paint.

Water-based Paint

Water-based paint for wood is usually sold as "latex enamel" or "acrylic enamel." Because water-based paint can raise wood grain, use a water-based primer to prepare the wood, then sand the primed surface before applying the paint. The coloring agents in water-based paint settle quickly, so stir the paint often as you work.

ADVANTAGES:
- *safer for the environment*
- *less toxic than oil-based paints*
- *easy cleanup with soap and water*
- *dries quickly*
- *can be thinned with water*

DRAWBACKS:
- *raises wood grain*
- *scratches easily*
- *cleanup is difficult after paint dries*
- *softens with exposure to moisture*
- *cannot be applied in thick coats*

COMPATIBILITY:
- *will not adhere to most topcoats*
- *may be used over other water-based paints*

RECOMMENDED USES:
- *children's toys and furniture*
- *cabinetry*
- *woodwork*

Oil-based Paint

Oil-based paint (also called alkyd paint) dries to a harder finish than water-based paint and offers the best protection for wood that is exposed to wear. It is still the preferred paint type of most professional painters, but this preference is changing as water-based paints become stronger and more versatile. Use oil-based primer with oil-based paint.

ADVANTAGES:
- *hard, scratch-resistant finish*
- *unaffected by moisture*
- *does not raise wood grain*
- *dries to a very smooth finish*

DRAWBACKS:
- *releases toxic vapors*
- *slow drying time*
- *requires mineral spirits for cleanup*
- *use is restricted in some states*

COMPATIBILITY:
- *may be applied over varnish or oil-based polyurethane*
- *may be used over oil- or water-based paints*

RECOMMENDED USES:
- *stairs and railings*
- *floors and doors*
- *woodwork*
- *previously finished wood*

Stir paint with a mixing bit attached to a portable drill for fast, thorough mixing. Keep the mixer bit moving constantly. Repeatedly lower the mixer blade to the bottom of the can, then raise it to the top of the can to mix in settled pigment.

Strain paint to remove lumps, dirt, and other foreign materials. Commercial paint strainers are available, or you can make your own from cheesecloth or nylon stockings.

Applying Paint

Painting wood is very much like painting walls and other common do-it-yourself painting projects. Whenever you paint anything, preparation is critical. For wood, that means sanding the surface until it is flat and smooth, then sealing with primer so the paint absorbs evenly. Open grained hardwoods, like oak, must have the grain filled before painting unless you want to see the texture of the wood grain underneath the paint.

Although it is a different product, primer is applied using the same techniques as paint. In addition to sealing the wood, it keeps resins in the wood from bleeding through the paint layer. If the wood you're painting has highly resinous knots, like pine, you may need to use a special stain killing primer.

Cleanup solvents, thinning agents, drying time, and coverage vary widely from one enamel paint to another. Read the manufacturer's directions carefully. Most paints will be dry to the touch quite quickly, and are ready for a second coat in a short time period. Since you will be sanding in between paint coats, you will get the best results if you allow each coat to dry for 12 to 24 hours.

For best results, designate a clean, dust-free area for painting. Ideally you should sand in one area and paint in another.

Finish-sand the wood (page 20) and apply grain filler if necessary. Vacuum the surfaces or wipe with a tack cloth after you sand to remove

A

Finish-sand the wood.

B

Prime the wood with an even coat of primer.

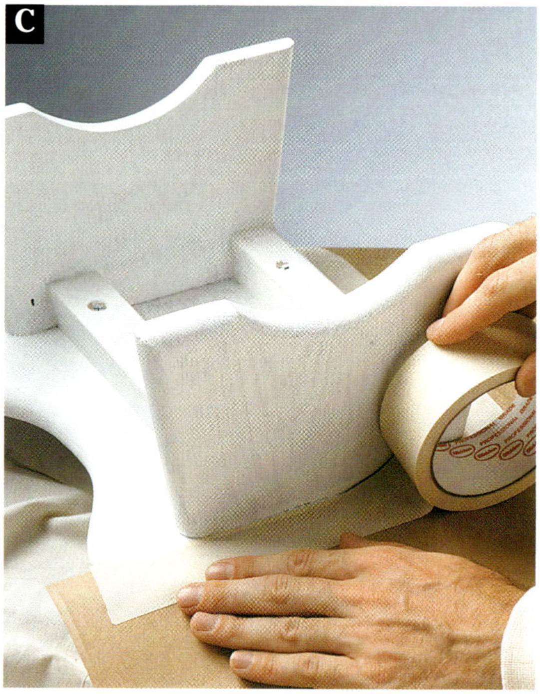

C

Mask any adjacent areas that will be painted a different color, using masking tape.

all traces of sanding dust from the workpiece **(photo A).**

Prime the wood with an even coat of primer **(photo B).** Use water-based primer with water-based paint, and oil-based primer with oil-based paint. Smooth out brush marks as you work, and sand with 220-grit sandpaper when dry.

Mask any adjacent areas that will be painted a different color, using masking tape. Press the edges of the tape firmly against the wood **(photo C).**

Apply a thin coat of paint, brushing with the grain **(photo D).** Heavy layers of paint will tend to sag and form an uneven surface. Loading your brush with too much paint will also cause drips to form on edges and around joints.

For a smooth surface that's free from lap marks, hold your paint brush at a 45° angle, and apply just enough pressure to flex the bristles slightly **(photo E).**

When dry, sand with 400-grit sandpaper, then wipe with a tack cloth. Apply at least one more heavier coat, sanding and wiping with a tack cloth between additional coats. Darker colors may require more coats than lighter colors. Do not sand the last coat.

Option: Apply clear polyurethane topcoat to surfaces that will get heavy wear. Before applying, wet-sand the paint with 600-grit wet/dry sandpaper, then wipe with a tack cloth. Use water-based polyurethane over latex paint, and oil-based over oil-based paint **(photo F).**

Apply a thin coat of paint, brushing with the grain.

For a smooth surface free from lap marks, hold your paint brush at a 45° angle, and apply just enough pressure to flex the bristles slightly.

Option: Wet sand the last coat of paint and apply clear polyurethane topcoat to surfaces that will get heavy wear.

Decorative Painting

Apply a creative touch to your project with decorative painting techniques. Antique finishes, stencils, and color washes give furniture and decorative items a rustic look. A handful of specialty paint brushes, some quality finishing materials, a few helpful tools, and a little creativity are all you need to create these unique painted finishes on your projects. With all of these techniques, it is best to practice on scraps before applying to your project.

Antique finishes re-create the look of worn paint. Finish sand the piece and apply a base coat of wood stain. If you use water based stain and water based paint, the stain may bleed through the paint. For certain colors this may be a desirable effect. To prevent bleed through, apply a topcoat of satin finish polyurethane. Allow the topcoat to dry and apply a layer of water-based paint. You may want to apply a second coat of paint in a different color, to enhance the illusion of age. Once the paint is dry, sand off randomly chosen areas of paint with 100-grit sandpaper, applying varying degrees of pressure to imitate natural wear **(photo A).** Sand the corners of the workpiece and any detail areas with 220-grit sandpaper, then wipe with a lint-free cloth and denatured alcohol to complete this vintage finish.

Stenciled designs add a bright, decorative touch to varnished or painted wood. Purchase ready-made clear acetate stencils at a craft store, or cut your own. Position the stencil on the wood, and secure it with tape. Stipple the wood by dabbing paint onto the surface through the stencil, using a stenciling brush **(photo B).** Acrylic craft paints are a good choice for stenciling, or you can purchase special stenciling paints. Allow the paint to dry before removing the stencil. If more than one color will be used, realign the stencil and apply each color, one at a time, starting with the lightest color. Allow the stenciled area to dry completely and topcoat with a clear finish for protection.

Color washes produce a thin, semi-transparent coat of paint on bare wood. Dilute water-based paint by mixing one part paint to four parts water (the more diluted the paint mixture, the thinner the paint layer will be). Brush the thinned paint onto the wood, working with the grain. Wipe the surface immediately with a lint-free cloth, removing paint until you achieve the desired color tone **(photo C).** Repeat the process to darken the color, if needed. Soften the look by scuffing the painted surface with a fine abrasive pad when dry.

Sand corners and high spots to create a worn appearance.

Use a special stencil brush to get the best results.

A color wash allows the wood grain to show through.

Protect your finish and wood with a topcoat layer, like the wipe-on tung oil being applied to this dresser.

Applying Topcoats

Topcoat finishes seal the wood, protect the finish from scratches and other wear, and increase the visual appeal of the wood. Because they dry clear, topcoats highlight the coloring and natural figure of the wood. For most projects, a topcoat of tung oil finish, polyurethane, or paste wax will give your wood the protection it needs and the finished appearance you desire.

When choosing a topcoat, consider durability, sheen, and compatibility with any coloring layers you use (see opposite page). Other factors, like drying time, ease of application and cleanup, and safeness, should also influence your choice. If possible, check samples at building centers or paint stores to see if a particular topcoat is suitable for your workpiece. Some one-step stain-and-seal products are also available. Test these products on scrap wood before using them.

Make tack cloths by moistening cheesecloth in mineral spirits. Apply a spoonful of varnish (or any other clear topcoat material) to the cheesecloth, and knead the cloth until the varnish is absorbed evenly. Make several tack cloths and store them in a glass jar with a lid.

Tung Oil Finish

Tung oil is extracted from the nut of the tung tree. Good for creating a matte or glossy hand-rubbed finish, tung oil products are available in clear and tinted form.

ADVANTAGES:
- *easy to apply*
- *flexible finish that resists cracking*
- *very natural appearance that makes minimal changes in wood appearance*
- *penetrates into the wood*
- *easily renewed and repaired*

DRAWBACKS:
- *not as durable as other topcoats*

COMPATIBILITY:
- *not compatible with polyurethane*

RECOMMENDED USES:
- *uneven surfaces like chairs and other furniture with spindles*
- *woodwork*
- *antiques*
- *wood with highly figured grain*

COMMON BRAND NAMES:
- *Minwax® Tung Oil Finish, Zar® Tung Oil, Tung Seal by McCloskey®*

Water-based Polyurethane

Water-based polyurethane is a popular topcoat because of its fast drying time and easy cleanup.

ADVANTAGES:
- *fast drying time*
- *easy cleanup*
- *nonflammable*
- *nontoxic*
- *impervious to water and alcohol*

DRAWBACKS:
- *can raise wood grain*
- *can have an unnatural "plastic" appearance*

COMPATIBILITY:
- *do not apply over other topcoats, or directly over commercial sanding sealer*

RECOMMENDED USES:
- *floors*
- *interior woodwork and furniture*
- *children's furniture and toys*
- *tabletops, eating surfaces*

COMMON BRAND NAMES:
- *EnviroCare®, Varathane® Diamond Finish, Carver Tripp® Safe & Simple, Zar® Polyurethane*

Oil-base Polyurethane

Despite the emergence of water-based polyurethanes, many refinishers still prefer oil-based polyurethane.

ADVANTAGES:
- *easier to get a smooth finish than with a water-base polyurethane*
- *forms durable, hard finish*
- *impervious to water and alcohol*

DRAWBACKS:
- *slow drying time*
- *disposal and use closely regulated in some states*
- *decreasing availability*
- *difficult cleanup*
- *toxic*
- *gives off unpleasant fumes*

COMPATIBILITY:
- *not compatible with other topcoats*

RECOMMENDED USES:
- *furniture*
- *surfaces where a very thick, durable topcoat is desired*

COMMON BRAND NAMES:
- *Defthane by Deft®, Heirloom Varnish by McCloskey®, Minwax® Polyurethane*

Paste Wax

Paste wax is natural waxes dissolved in mineral spirits or naphtha. It is favored for its handrubbed sheen.

ADVANTAGES:
- *easy to renew with fresh coats*
- *very natural appearance*
- *can be buffed to desired sheen*
- *can be applied over most topcoats*

DRAWBACKS:
- *easily scratched and worn away*
- *needs to be restored regularly*
- *water or alcohol spills will damage wax*

COMPATIBILITY:
- *No restrictions*

RECOMMENDED USES:
- *antiques*
- *fine furniture*
- *floors*

COMMON BRAND NAMES:
- *Antiquax®, Johnson & Johnson® Paste Wax, Minwax® Paste Finishing Wax*

Choosing and Using Topcoats

For safe use and low toxicity, water-based polyurethane is an excellent choice. Use it for children's furniture and toys, as well as for eating surfaces **(photo A).**

Choose the finish gloss that best meets your needs. Product availability has expanded among polyurethane products in recent years to include gloss, semi-gloss, and matte (or satin) sheens. Because of the expanding product lines, polyurethane-based topcoat products have almost completely replaced traditional wood varnish **(photo B).**

Stir topcoat finishes gently with a clean stir stick. Shaking the container or stirring too vigorously can create air bubbles that cause pockmarks in the finish when dry **(photo C).**

Wet-sand with a fine abrasive pad on the final topcoat layer to create a finish with the exact amount of gloss you want **(photo D).**

Transfer leftover topcoat materials to smaller containers to minimize the amount of air that can react with the product. Tung oil and polyurethane are especially susceptible to thickening when exposed to air **(photo E).**

Use water-based polyurethane for children's furniture and toys, as well as for eating surfaces.

Choose the finish gloss that best meets your needs.

To prevent bubbles, stir topcoats gently, and never shake.

Wet-sand to create the exact amount of gloss you want.

Store leftover topcoat materials in smaller containers to minimize thickening due to air exposure.

Applying Tung Oil Finishes

Tung oil is an extremely popular finish both for its easy application and its appearance. Several well-buffed coats applied with a clean cloth will form a suitably hard finish. With added coats and more buffing, you can achieve a glossy finish. Tung-oil-based products are suitable for most furniture, including antiques. Seldom sold in pure form, tung oil is usually blended with tinting agents or other topcoats, and is usually described by manufacturers as "tung oil finish."

Because tung oil forms a relatively thin coat, renew finished surfaces with a fresh coat of tung oil every year or so. Or, you can apply a protective layer of paste wax to guard the finish, and renew the wax topcoat periodically. Use lemon oil to refresh a tung oil finish without recoating.

Finish sand your project and clean the surfaces thoroughly with a cloth and mineral spirits **(photo A)**. Apply a thick coat of tung oil finish with a cloth or brush. Let the tung oil penetrate for 5 to 10 minutes, then rub off the excess with a cloth, using a polishing motion.

Use a paint brush to apply tung oil to very uneven surfaces. Because the excess tung oil is wiped off before it dries, there is no need to worry about drips or lap marks from brushes **(photo B).**

Buff the tung oil with a clean cloth after 24 hours, then apply additional coats as needed to build the desired finish. Three coats is generally considered the minimum for a good finish. Use a clean cloth for each application **(photo C).**

Let the finish dry completely, then buff it lightly with a fine abrasive pad **(photo D).** For a higher gloss, buff with a polishing bonnet and portable drill.

Tung oil is especially susceptible to thickening when exposed to air. Transfer leftover materials to smaller, air-tight containers to minimize the amount of air that can react with the product. Make sure you clearly label containers with the date and product.

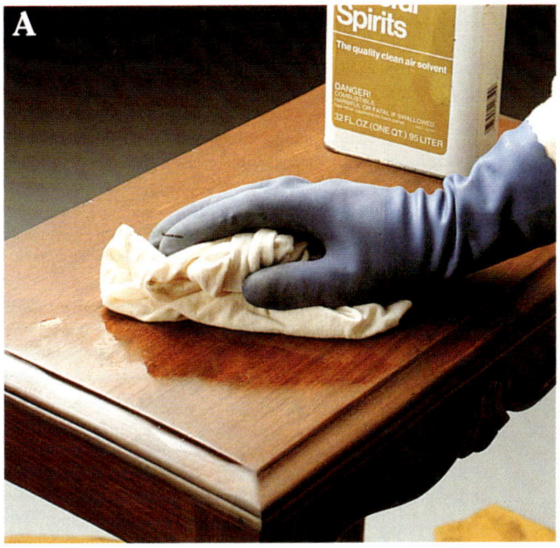

Clean the surfaces thoroughly with a cloth and mineral spirits.

Use a paint brush to apply tung oil to very uneven surfaces.

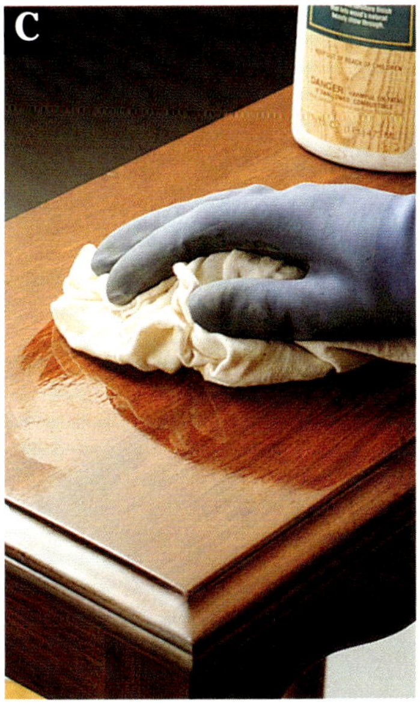

Buff the tung oil with a clean cloth after 24 hours, then reapply additional coats.

Let the finish dry completely, then buff it lightly with a fine abrasive pad.

Seal unstained wood. Check the product label for recommended sealer.

Apply a coat of polyurethane, starting at the top of the project and working your way down.

Applying Polyurethane

Polyurethane (often called polyurethane varnish or simply varnish) is a hard, durable topcoat material commonly used on floors, countertops, and other heavy-use surfaces. Available in both water-based and oil-based form, polyurethane is a complex mixture of plastic resins, solvents, and drying oils or water, that dries to a clear, nonyellowing finish.

A wide array of finishing products contain some type of polyurethane, which can causes a good deal of confusion. If a label uses the descriptive terms "acrylic" or "polymerized," the product is most likely polyurethane-based. Your safest bet in choosing the best polyurethane product for the job is to refer to the suggestions for use on the product label.

For safe use and low toxicity, water-based polyurethane is an excellent choice. Use it for children's furniture and toys as well as for eating surfaces.

Polyurethane products are available in a range of sheens. Choose the gloss level that best fits your project's intended use.

Hardening agents are available for some brands of water-based polyurethane for outdoor applications or high-traffic areas. Hardening agents lose their effectiveness quickly, so harden only as much product as you plan to apply in one coat.

Seal unstained wood with a 1:1 mixture of polyurethane and thinning agent (check product label), applied with a clean cloth or brush **(photo A).** Wipe off excess sealer with a clean cloth. Let the sealer dry. Wood that has been colored with stain or penetrating oil does not need a seal-coat.

Apply a coat of polyurethane, starting at the top of the project and working your way down. Use a good quality brush. When the surface is covered, smooth out the finish by lightly brushing in one direction only, with the grain. Let dry, then sand between coats using 600-grit wet/dry sandpaper **(photo B).**

Apply polyurethane in several thin layers for best results. Applying too much finish at once slows down the drying time, and causes running, wrinkling or sagging **(photo C).**

Brush out lap marks to create a smooth surface before the polyurethane dries. Small brush marks will show, but will blend together as the finish dries. Because it dries slowly, oil-based polyurethane gives you more time to brush out lap marks.

Examine the surface after each coat of polyurethane dries, using a bright side light **(photo D).** Wet-sand with a fine abrasive pad to remove dust and other surface problems, like air bubbles. After sanding, wipe the surface clean with a tack cloth.

Apply the second coat. To keep the finish from running, always try to position the workpiece so the surface being topcoated is horizontal **(photo E).**

C

Applying too much finish at once causes running, wrinkling or sagging.

D

Examine the surface after each coat of polyurethane dries, using a bright side light.

E

To keep the finish from running, always try to position the workpiece so the surface being topcoated is horizontal.

Applying Wax

Wax is an easily renewable topcoat that protects and beautifies wood. It is often applied over oil finishes and other topcoats to absorb small scratches and everyday wear and tear. Then, simply by removing the old wax and applying a fresh coat, you can create a new-looking topcoat without refinishing.

Paste wax is the best wax product for wood because it can be buffed to a hard finish. But other types of wax, like liquid wax, can be used for specific purposes.

Apply several coats of paste wax for best results. The hardness of a wax finish is a direct result of the thickness of the wax and the vigor with which it is buffed. Extensive buffing also increases the glossiness of the finish. For the hardest possible finish, choose products with a high ratio of wax to solvent (see label).

Apply a moderate layer of paste wax to the wood using a fine abrasive pad or a cloth. Rub the wax into the wood with a polishing motion **(photo A).**

Allow the wax to dry until it becomes filmy in spots **(photo B).** Gently wipe off any excess, undried wax, then allow the entire wax surface to dry until filmy (usually within 10 to 20 minutes). NOTE: Do not let the wax dry too long or it will harden and become very difficult to buff. Begin buffing the wax with a soft cloth, using a light, circular motion. Buff the entire surface until the filminess disappears and the wax is clear **(photo C).**

Continue buffing the wax until the surface is hard and shiny **(photo D).** Apply and buff another coat, then let the wax dry for at least 24 hours before applying additional coats. Apply at least three coats for a fine wax finish.

Buff wax to a hard, glossy finish with a polishing bonnet attached to a portable drill. Keep the drill moving to avoid overheating the wax **(photo E).**

Use liquid wax on detailed areas, where paste wax is difficult to apply. Apply the wax with a stiff brush, then buff with a soft cloth **(photo F).**

Apply a moderate layer of paste wax by rubbing the wax into the wood with a polishing motion.

Allow the wax to dry until it becomes filmy in spots.

Begin buffing the wax with a soft cloth, using a light, circular motion. Buff the entire surface until the filminess disappears and the wax is clear.

Continue buffing the wax until the surface is hard and shiny.

Buff wax to a hard, glossy finish with a polishing bonnet attached to a portable drill. Keep the drill moving to avoid overheating the wax.

Use liquid wax on detailed areas, where paste wax is difficult to apply. Apply the wax with a stiff brush, then buff with a soft cloth.

WARNING
AVERTISSEMENT:
Made in Mexico

Entryway Projects

Your home's entryway is a busy space. Building any one of these beautiful, hardworking furnishings will make your entryway more appealing and less cluttered. What could be nicer than coming home and being greeted at the door by charming furnishings you made yourself?

Kids' Coat Rack

Kids love using this monkey-topped coat rack, and you'll have fun building it.

PROJECT POWER TOOLS

Construction Materials

Quantity	Lumber
1	2 × 2" × 4' oak
1	1 × 6" × 2' oak
1	¾" × 2 × 2' birch plywood
1	1 × 3" × 4' oak

This stand is designed to hold eight coats or jackets, but kids will hang almost anything on the shaker pegs, including mittens, scarves, sweaters and pants. The decorative monkey acts as a motivator and reminder that it's more fun to hang your clothes on the stand than throw them on the furniture or floor. The monkey also gives you an opportunity to put your artistic talents to work. This popular stand is easy to construct and takes up little space, so it can fit in an entryway or bedroom with ease.

OVERALL SIZE:
58½" HIGH
16" WIDE
16" DEEP

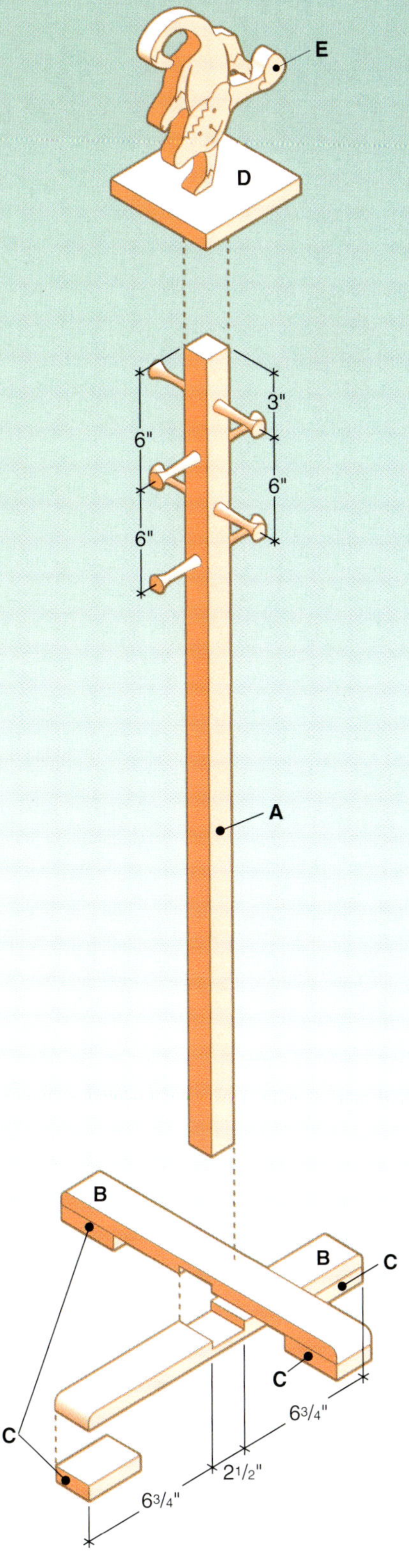

1" squares

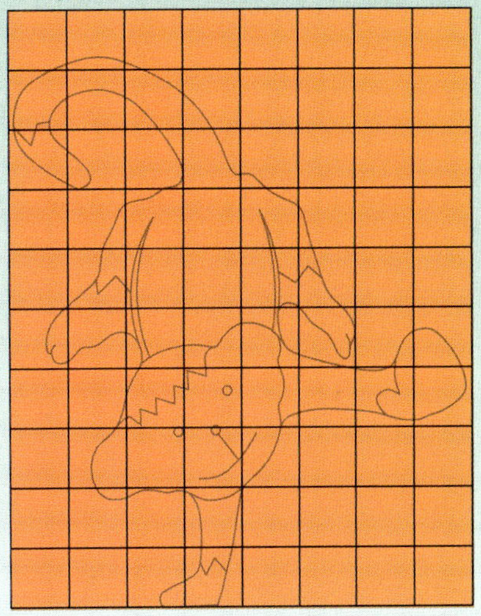

CUTOUT DETAIL

Cutting List

Key	Part	Dimension	Pcs.	Material
A	Post	1½ × 1½ × 46¼"	1	Oak
B	Leg	¾ × 2½ × 16"	2	Oak
C	Foot	¾ × 2½ × 3"	4	Oak
D	Platform	¾ × 5½ × 5½"	1	Oak
E	Monkey	¾ × 8 × 10"	1	Birch plywood

Materials: Wood glue, #8 × 1¼" wood screws, 4d finish nail, birch shaker pegs (8), finishing materials.

Note: Measurements reflect the actual thickness of dimension lumber.

Clean out the half lap joints with a chisel and a hammer. To ensure a tight fit, keep the edges square.

Mark and drill holes in the post to match the diameter of your shaker pegs.

TIP

To ensure accurate cuts, build a shooting board from a straight piece of 1 × 4" lumber about 24" long, and a smooth piece of ¼"-thick plywood about 6" wide and 24" long. Attach the 1 × 4" board along one edge of the plywood strip, using glue and screws. Then, run your circular saw along the 1 × 4" straightedge, trimming the plywood base to the exact distance between the edge of the saw foot and the blade. To use the shooting board, simply clamp it in place with the edge of the plywood along the cutting line, then run your saw over the plywood with the base of the saw tight against the straightedge.

Directions: Kids' Coat Rack

CUT THE COAT RACK PARTS.

1. Cut the post (A), legs (B) and feet (C) to length.
2. Align the legs side by side, and clamp together. Mark a 2½"-wide notch on each leg (see *Diagram*).
3. Build a shooting board (see *Tip*), and set the depth of the saw blade at ⅝" (allowing for the ¼"-thick plywood base, this will give you a ⅜"-deep cut).
4. Clamp the shooting board next to one side of the notch and make the first cut, keeping the saw base flat on the plywood and tight against the straightedge. Reposition the shooting board and cut the other side of the notch. Leave the shooting board in place after the second cut, and make additional cuts within the notch to remove the wood between the first two cuts.
5. Carefully clean any waste from the notch with a sharp ¾" chisel **(photo A).**
6. Test-fit the legs. If necessary, adjust the lap joint by chiseling, filing or sanding more stock from the notches.
7. Round off the top edges of the leg ends with a router or belt sander.

ASSEMBLE THE PARTS.

1. Glue and clamp the feet to the legs.
2. Position the post on the leg

Drill a pilot hole into the base of the monkey so it doesn't split when attaching it to the platform.

Attach the monkey to the platform using glue and a wood screw.

assembly by drawing intersecting diagonal lines across the notch, then aligning each corner of the post on one of these lines.

3. Drill two countersunk pilot holes through the bottom of the leg assembly, then attach the legs to the post with glue and wood screws.

4. Mark two peg holes on each side of the post (see *Diagram*). Carefully drill holes straight into the sides of the post, matching the diameter of the shaker pegs **(photo B).**

MAKE THE MONKEY AND PLATFORM.

1. Lay out the monkey pattern (E) on birch plywood (see *Diagram*), and cut out the pattern with a jig saw.

2. Use wood putty to fill any voids on the edges of the plywood.

3. Cut the platform (D) to size.

4. Drill a countersunk pilot hole into the bottom of the platform at the centerpoint for attaching the monkey. Drill two offset pilot holes in the top of the platform, about ¾" from the center hole. Counterbore one of these holes. Drill a pilot hole into the center of the monkey's paw **(photo C).**

5. Paint the monkey.

ASSEMBLE THE UNIT.

1. Attach the monkey to the platform, using glue and a wood screw **(photo D).**

2. Attach the monkey and platform to the post assembly with glue, a wood screw and a 4d finish nail.

3. Attach the shaker pegs with glue, and wipe off any excess.

APPLY FINISHING TOUCHES.

Sand the project smooth and apply oil or a clear finish.

TIP

For better control when painting faces and figurines, use latex paint as a base coat, and outline the pattern details with a permanent-ink marker. To protect your work, seal the monkey with a low-luster water-based polyurethane.

PROJECT
POWER TOOLS

Hallway Bookcase

A stable base that tapers to a low-profile top lets you add storage and display space in even the tightest quarters.

Construction Materials

Quantity	Lumber
2	1 × 10" × 8' pine
1	1 × 8" × 6' pine
1	1 × 6" × 6' pine
3	1 × 4" × 8' pine

Hallways are frequently underutilized areas of a home. The reason is simple—large furnishings would cramp the area. When foot traffic is heavy and space is at a premium, this hallway bookcase makes the most of the situation. Fitting flush against the wall, it allows you to store your books and display your knick-knacks without cluttering up the hall or consuming valuable floor space. The bookcase is tapered, so it is thinner at the top than at the bottom. This design reduces the chance of tipping and cuts down on space consumption. This bookcase is a very simple and inexpensive project to build.

OVERALL SIZE:
60" HIGH
36" WIDE
9" DEEP

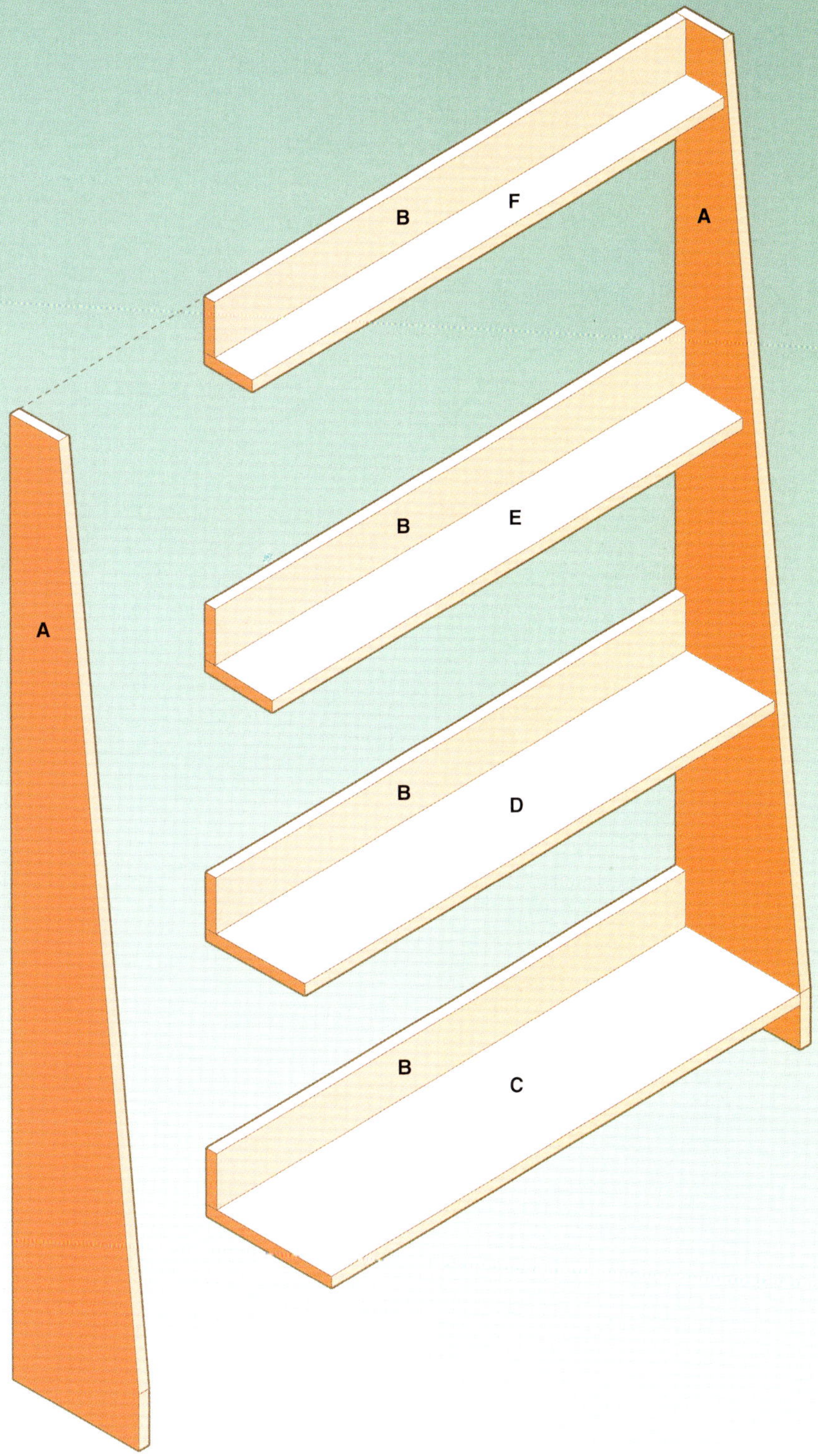

Cutting List

Key	Part	Dimension	Pcs.	Material
A	Standard	¾ × 9¼ × 60"	2	Pine
B	Spreader	¾ × 3½ × 34½"	4	Pine
C	Shelf	¾ × 9¼ × 34½"	1	Pine

Cutting List

Key	Part	Dimension	Pcs.	Material
D	Shelf	¾ × 7¼ × 34½"	1	Pine
E	Shelf	¾ × 5¼ × 34½"	1	Pine
F	Shelf	¾ × 3½ × 34½"	1	Pine

Materials: Wood glue, #8 × 2" wood screws, finishing materials.

Note: Measurements reflect the actual size of dimension lumber.

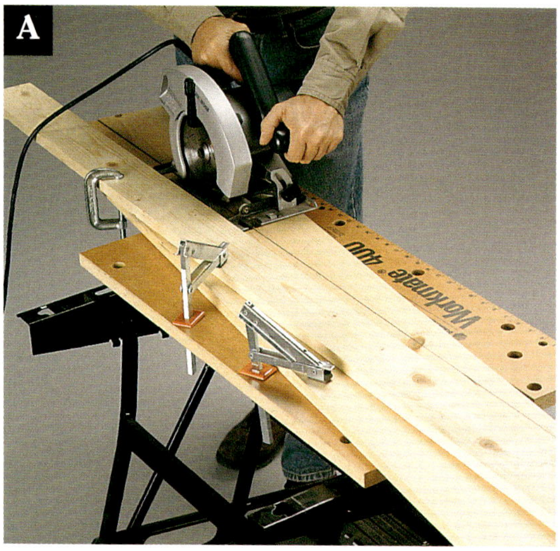

Clamp a straightedge to the standard, and make the taper cut with a circular saw.

Use a framing square to mark reference lines on the standards for shelf placement.

Directions: Hallway Bookcase

MAKE THE STANDARDS.
The tapered standards are wide at the bottom for stability and narrow at the top to conserve space in a busy hallway.
1. Cut the standards (A) to length from 1 × 10 pine boards.
2. Mark a point on the front edge of each standard, 3½" up from the bottom. Mark another point on the top of each standard, 3½" in from the back edge. Draw a straight line connecting these points to form a tapered cutting line for the standard.
3. Clamp a straightedge to the board, parallel to the cutting line, and cut the taper with a circular saw **(photo A).**
4. Sand the parts to smooth out any sharp edges or rough surfaces.

CUT THE SHELVES AND SPREADERS.
The shelves and spreaders are all the same length, but in order to conform with the taper in the standards, the shelves at the top of the hall bookcase are narrower than those at the bottom.
1. Cut the spreaders (B) and shelves (C).
2. Check the lengths again, and sand the parts to smooth out any rough edges.

INSTALL THE SPREADERS.
The spreaders help support the shelves while providing side-to-side strength for the bookcase. The spreaders also keep books and decorative objects from hitting the wall behind the bookcase or falling back behind the shelves and out of reach. Each spreader should fit flush with the back edges of the standards, directly above a shelf reference line.
1. Use a framing square and a pencil to mark reference lines on each standard, 3½", 20¾", 37½" and 56½" up from the bottoms **(photo B).** These reference lines mark the tops of the shelves. Make sure the shelf reference lines are the same distance from the bottom on both standards, or you may end up with sloping shelves.
2. Set the standards on their back edges so their outside faces are 36" apart. Position a spreader just above the bottom shelf reference lines.
3. Drill counterbored pilot holes through the standards and into the ends of the spreader.
4. Attach the bottom spreader with glue and #8 × 2" wood screws.
5. Attach the remaining spreaders in the same way, making sure the top spreader is flush with the top and back edges of the standards **(photo C).**
6. Check the bookcase to make sure it is square after the final spreader has been installed. Measure diagonally from corner to corner. If the measurements are equal, the bookcase is

TIP

Special tapered drill bits make drilling counterbores for screws a snap. Simply select a counterbore bit that matches the shank size of the screws you will use (usually #6 or #8), then drill a pilot hole for each screw with a plain twist bit. Counterbore the pilot holes, using the counterbore bit, to the correct depth for the wood plugs that will be inserted into the counterbores.

Fit the spreaders between the bookcase standards. Make sure the bookcase is square as you fasten them in place.

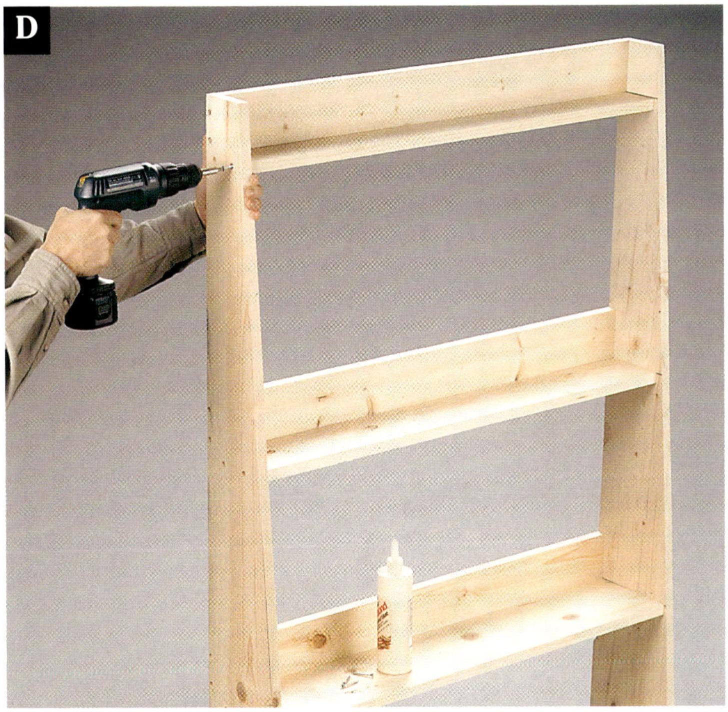

Drive wood screws through the pilot holes in the standards and into the ends of the shelves.

TIP

Anchor smaller furnishings to the wall in heavy traffic areas. In many cases, as with this open-back hallway bookcase, the exposed spreaders can be used as strips for screwing the project to the wall. For best results, drive screws into wall studs through the top spreader and at least one lower spreader. Counterbore the screws, cover the heads with wood plugs, then paint the plugs to match.

square. If the project is out of square, apply pressure to one side or the other with your hand or clamps to push it back into square before you fasten the shelves.

INSTALL THE SHELVES.

1. Position the bottom shelf between the standards. Make sure the top edge of the bottom shelf is butted up against the bottom edge of the bottom spreader and is flush with the reference line.
2. Drill counterbored pilot holes through the standards and into the ends of the shelf. Drill pilot holes through the shelf and into the bottom edge of the spreader. (Because the screw holes underneath the shelf will not be visible, you don't need to counterbore and plug them. Countersink them slightly so you can apply wood putty before finishing.)
3. Apply glue to the ends of the shelf and the bottom edge of the spreader, and attach the shelf with #8 × 2" wood screws. Attach the remaining shelves in the same way, working your way up the bookcase **(photo D).**

APPLY FINISHING TOUCHES.

1. Insert glued, $\frac{3}{8}$"-dia. wood plugs into all counterbored screw holes. Fill the holes on the bottoms of the shelves with wood putty.
2. Finish-sand the entire project with fine sandpaper.
3. Finish or paint the bookcase. We finished ours with a light, semitransparent wood stain and two light coats of water-based polyurethane to protect and seal the wood.

Umbrella Stand

Keep your umbrellas, canes and walking sticks within easy reach with this classic umbrella stand.

PROJECT POWER TOOLS

CONSTRUCTION MATERIALS

Quantity	Lumber
2	1 × 10" × 6' oak
1	¾ × ¾" × 4' oak cove molding
2	8 × 22" tin

This umbrella stand is the perfect rainy-day project. It easily holds up to six umbrellas, canes or walking sticks, so you'll never again have to search for these items on the way out the door. The umbrella stand is a natural in a hallway, entryway or foyer and a classy alternative to storing umbrellas in your closet.

Built from solid oak for sturdiness and good looks, the umbrella stand has miter-cut top trim and cove molding, and decorative diamond cutouts backed with tin panels. This project can be painted or finished with natural stain. Stain or paint the feet and trim so your umbrella stand blends in nicely with staircases or doors in your entryway.

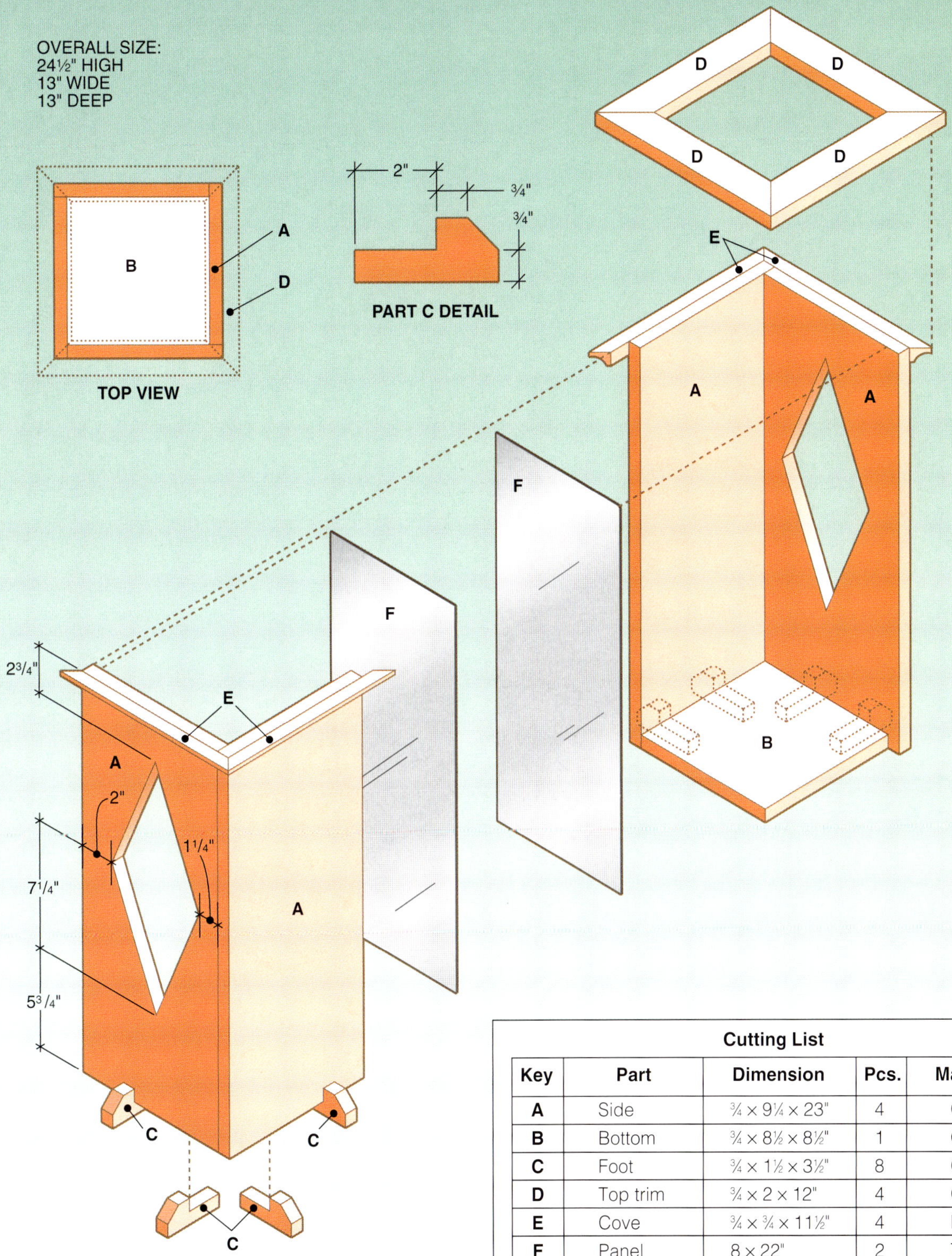

Cutting List				
Key	**Part**	**Dimension**	**Pcs.**	**Material**
A	Side	¾ × 9¼ × 23"	4	Oak
B	Bottom	¾ × 8½ × 8½"	1	Oak
C	Foot	¾ × 1½ × 3½"	8	Oak
D	Top trim	¾ × 2 × 12"	4	Oak
E	Cove	¾ × ¾ × 11½"	4	Molding
F	Panel	8 × 22"	2	Tin

Materials: #6 × 1¼" wood screws, #6 × ½" panhead screws, 2d and 4d finish nails, 16-ga. × 1" brads, wood glue, finishing materials.

Specialty tools: Aviation snips.

Note: Measurements reflect the actual size of dimension lumber.

Drill starter holes. Then, cut out the diamond shapes with a jig saw.

Use the diamond cutout as a guide when attaching the tin panel behind the cutout.

Directions: Umbrella Stand

CUT THE SIDES AND BOTTOM.

1. Cut the sides (A) and bottom (B) to size. Sand the cuts smooth with medium-grit sandpaper.

2. Draw the diamond on two side pieces. First, draw reference lines at 2¾", 10", and 17" down from the top and 5" in from the left side. On the 10" line, mark points 2" in from the left edge and 1¼" in from the right. Use these reference points to complete the diamond shape (see *Diagram*). NOTE: When the box is assembled, the diamonds will be centered side to side.

3. Drill starter holes, using a backer board to prevent splintering. Cut out the diamond shapes with a jig saw **(photo A).** Sand the cutouts smooth.

4. Cut the tin panels (F) to size with aviation snips. Position the tin panels on the inside face of each cutout side, leaving a ¾" space at the bottom and along the right edge for the bottom piece and adjoining side. Drill $\frac{3}{32}$" pilot holes, and attach the tin panel with ½" panhead screws. Drive screws at the corners and along the edges of the cutout. Use a cutout diamond section as a guide to position the screws **(photo B).**

Attach the cove molding to the sides with glue and 1" brads.

Use a miter saw to cut 45° angles on the top trim.

Attach the feet with 1¼" wood screws.

ASSEMBLE THE BOX.

1. Lay one of the plain sides on your worksurface. Butt a cutout side upright at a 90° angle against the left edge (make sure the tin panel is not covered). Drill pilot holes through the cutout side and into the edge of the plain side. Counterbore the holes ⅛" deep, using a ⅜" counterbore bit. Join the pieces with glue and 1¼" wood screws.

2. Rotate the assembly so the cutout is facedown. Butt the other plain side against the left edge. Drill pilot holes through the plain side and into the edge of the cutout side. Counterbore the holes. Attach the piece with glue and 1¼" wood screws.

3. Position the bottom piece inside the assembly, flush with the bottom edges. Drill pilot holes through the sides and into the bottom. Counterbore the holes. Attach the bottom with glue and 1¼" wood screws.

4. Rotate the assembly, and attach the remaining cutout side.

ATTACH THE COVE MOLDING AND TOP TRIM.

Miter the cove molding on the ends, and lock-nail the joints together to prevent separation (see *Tip*, page 150).

1. Cut the cove molding (E) to length, mitering the ends at 45° angles.

2. Position the molding so the top edges are flush with the tops of the sides. Drill 1/16" pilot holes through the molding, and attach the molding with glue and 1" brads **(photo C).**

3. Cut the top trim (D) to size, mitering the ends at 45° angles **(photo D).**

4. Position the trim so it overhangs the outer edges of the cove by ¼". Drill 1/16" pilot holes through the trim pieces. Attach them with glue and 4d finish nails. Lock-nail the mitered ends with 2d finish nails. Set all nails with a nail set.

CUT THE FEET.

1. Cut blanks for the feet (C).

2. With a jig saw, trim off the corners, and make the notches (see *Diagram*). Sand the cut edges smooth.

APPLY FINISHING TOUCHES.

1. Fill all nail and screw holes with wood putty. Sand the wood and finish as desired.

2. Mask the cove and trim, cover the tin panel with contact paper and paint the sides. When the paint dries, remove the paper and apply amber shellac to the tin.

3. Apply finish to the cove, trim and feet. Position two feet at the bottom of each side, 2⅛" in from the outside edges. Drill pilot holes and counterbore the holes. Attach the feet with 1¼" wood screws **(photo E).**

PROJECT
POWER TOOLS

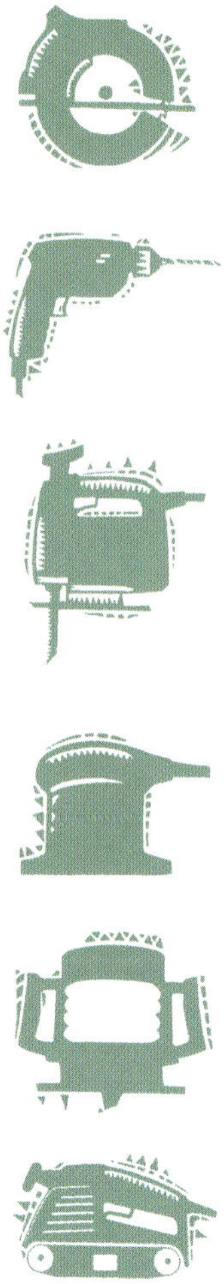

Mirrored Coat Rack

Nothing welcomes visitors to your home like an elegant, finely crafted mirrored coat rack.

Construction Materials

Quantity	Lumber
1	1 × 2" × 3' oak
1	1 × 3" × 4' oak
1	1 × 4" × 6' oak
1	½ × ¾" × 4' molding
1	¼" × 2 × 4' hardboard
1	⅛ × 15¾ × 24¾" mirrored glass

An entryway or foyer can seem naked without a coat rack and a mirror, and this simple oak project gives you both features in one striking package. The egg-and-dart beading at the top and the decorative porcelain and brass coat hooks provide just enough design interest to make the project elegant without overwhelming the essential simplicity of the look.

You can use inexpensive red oak to build your mirrored coat rack. Or, if you are willing to invest a little more money, use quarter-sawn white oak to create an item with the look of a true antique. For a special touch, have the edges of the mirror beveled.

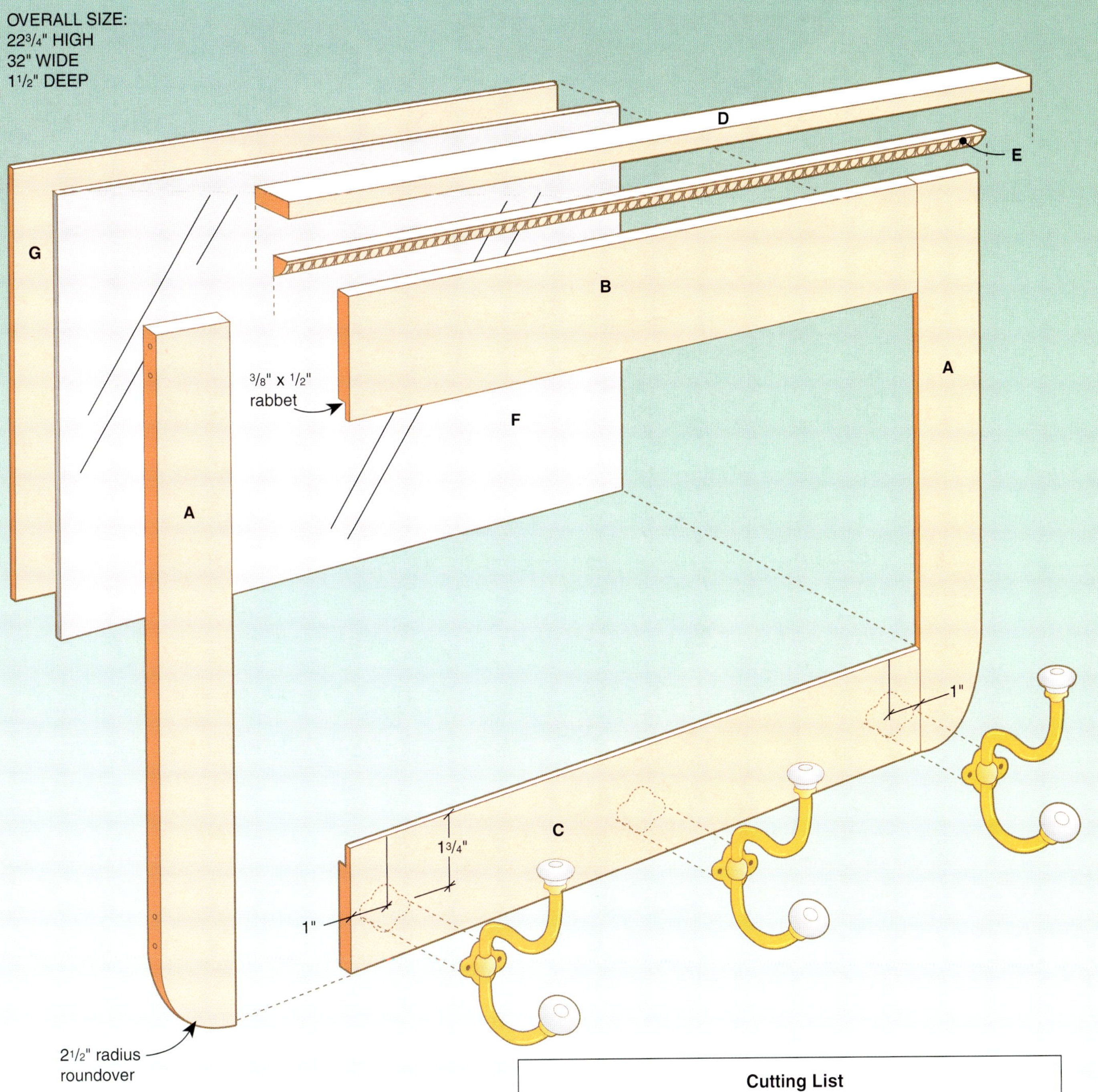

Cutting List

Key	Part	Dimension	Pcs.	Material
A	Stile	¾ × 2½ × 22"	2	Oak
B	Top rail	¾ × 3½ × 24"	1	Oak
C	Bottom rail	¾ × 3½ × 24"	1	Oak
D	Cap	¾ × 1½ × 32"	1	Oak
E	Molding	½ × ¾ × 29"	1	Oak
F	Mirror	⅛ × 15¾ × 24¾"	1	Mirror
G	Mirror back	¼ × 15¾ × 24¾"	1	Hardboard

Materials: #6 × 1½" wood screws, 16-ga. × 1" brads, coat hooks with screws (3), ¼ × 36" oak dowel, wood glue, finishing materials.

Note: Measurements reflect the actual size of dimension lumber.

Clamp the frame components together. Then, drill 3½"-deep guide holes for the through-dowel joints.

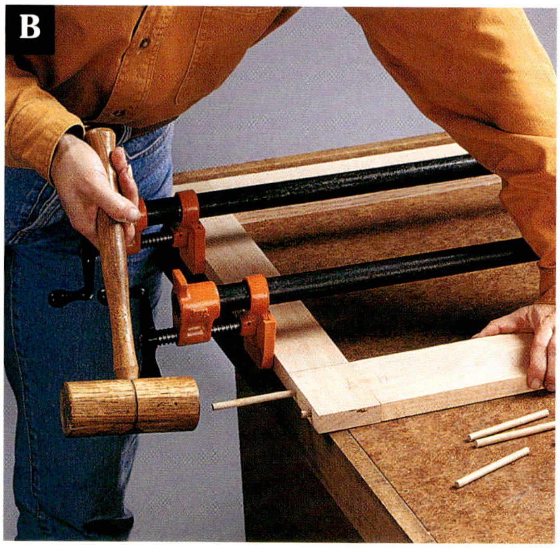

Drive glued 4"-long oak dowels into the guide holes to make the dowel joints.

Mount a belt sander to your worksurface, and use it to smooth the roundover cuts on the frame.

Directions: Mirrored Coat Rack

MAKE THE MIRROR FRAME.
Dowel joints hold the frame together.

1. Cut the stiles (A) to length. Cut the top rail (B) and bottom rail (C) to length.

2. Lay the rails between the stiles on your worksurface to form a frame. Square the frame and clamp with bar or pipe clamps to hold it together.

3. Drill two evenly spaced ¼"-dia. × 3½"-deep guide holes at each joint, drilling through the stiles and into the rails **(photo A).** Cut eight ¼"-dia. × 4"-long oak dowels. Unclamp the frame assembly, and squirt a little glue into each guide hole. Coat each dowel with a light layer of glue. Drive a dowel into each guide hole, using a wood mallet so you don't break the dowels **(photo B).**

4. When all joints are made, clamp the frame assembly together. Once the glue has dried, remove the clamps, and trim off the ends of the dowels with a backsaw. Sand them flush with the surface, and scrape off excess glue.

> TIP
>
> *Through-dowel joints are the easiest dowel joints to make—all you need is a good bar or pipe clamp and the ability to drill a reasonably straight guide hole. The visible dowel ends at the joints contribute to the traditional design of the project.*

ROUND OVER THE FRAME ENDS.

1. On the bottom end of each stile, draw an arc with a 2½" radius to mark the decorative roundovers. Cut along the arc line, using a jig saw.

2. Smooth the cut with a belt sander mounted to your worksurface **(photo C).**

DRILL MOUNTING HOLES AND CUT THE MIRROR RECESS.

1. Drill 11/64" holes through the fronts of the stiles, 6" down from the top, so you can attach the rack to a wall. With a counterbore bit, drill ⅜"-dia. × ¼"-deep counterbores for oak plugs to cover the screw heads after you

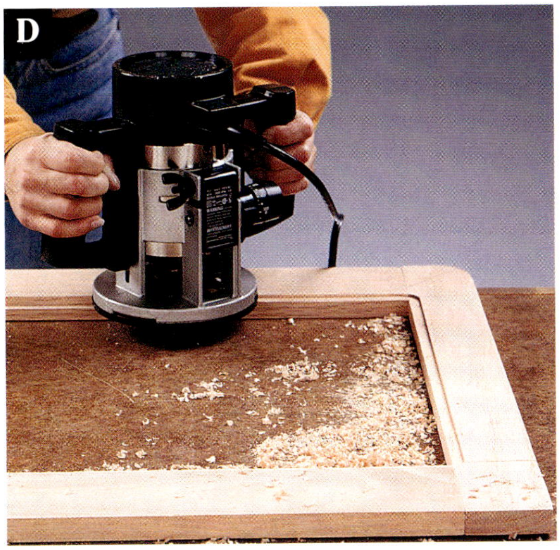

Use a router with a $\frac{3}{8}$" rabbeting bit to cut a recess for the mirror in the frame back.

Center egg-and-dart trim molding under the cap, and attach it with glue and brads.

Install the mirror and mirror back. Then, secure them to the frame with brads, using a brad pusher.

hang the coat rack.
2. Cut a rabbet around the back inside edges of the frame to make a recess for the mirror and back. Use a router and a $\frac{3}{8}$" rabbeting bit. Set the cutting depth of the router to $\frac{3}{8}$", then trim around the back inside edges of the frame **(photo D).** Reset the router depth to $\frac{1}{2}$", and make another pass around the edges to complete the rabbet. Square the grooves at the corners with a wood chisel.

INSTALL THE CAP AND MOLDING.
1. Cut the cap (D) to length.
2. Drill $\frac{3}{32}$" counterbored pilot holes through the cap and into the top rail. Attach the cap flush with the back edge of the rail, using glue and $1\frac{1}{2}$" wood screws. The cap overhangs the stiles $1\frac{1}{2}$" on each end.
3. Cut a piece of egg-and-dart style molding (E) to length. Sand a slight bevel at each end.
4. Attach the molding flush against the underside of the cap, centered side to side, using glue and 1" brads driven with a tack hammer **(photo E).** Drill $\frac{1}{16}$" pilot holes through the molding to prevent splitting. Set the nail heads, using a nail set.

APPLY FINISHING TOUCHES.
1. Fill the screw holes with oak plugs, and sand them flush with the surface.
2. Apply a finish. When it's dry, install the coathooks (see *Diagram*).
3. Set the mirror into the rabbet in the frame. Cut $\frac{1}{4}$"-thick hardboard to make the mirror back (G), and install it behind the mirror. Secure the mirror and mirror back by driving 1" brads into the edges of the frame with a brad pusher **(photo F).**
4. Hang the coat rack (see *Tip*). Fill the mounting screw holes with oak plugs. Sand them flush with the surface and touch up the area with finish. For a less permanant installation, use decorative brass screws that match the coathooks.

TIP

Try to hit a wall stud with the mounting screws when hanging heavy objects on a wall. Use toggle bolts to mount where no studs are present.

PROJECT
POWER TOOLS

Mitten Chest

This convenient mitten chest keeps your entryway clutter-free and stores hats and mittens right where you need them.

Construction Materials

Quantity	Lumber
1	¾" × 4 × 8' plywood
2	½ × 1⅜" × 7' stop molding
1	¼ × 15⁄16" × 7' corner molding
2	¾ × 1⅜" × 7' cap molding

This roomy mitten chest makes the most of valuable floor space in your entryway. It's large enough to hold all your family's mittens, hats and scarves. Move it to your den or family room, and this chest also makes a fine coffee table.

The mitten chest is a very simple project made from four plywood panels, top and bottom panels and some decorative trim molding.

For a neat, contemporary appearance, paint your mitten chest in soft pastel tones. Or try an antiquing technique to make it look like a family heirloom.

Another finishing option for the mitten chest is to line the interior with aromatic cedar liners to ward off moths and give your hand and head gear a fresh scent. Aromatic cedar liners are sold in 4 × 8 sheets or self-adhesive strips.

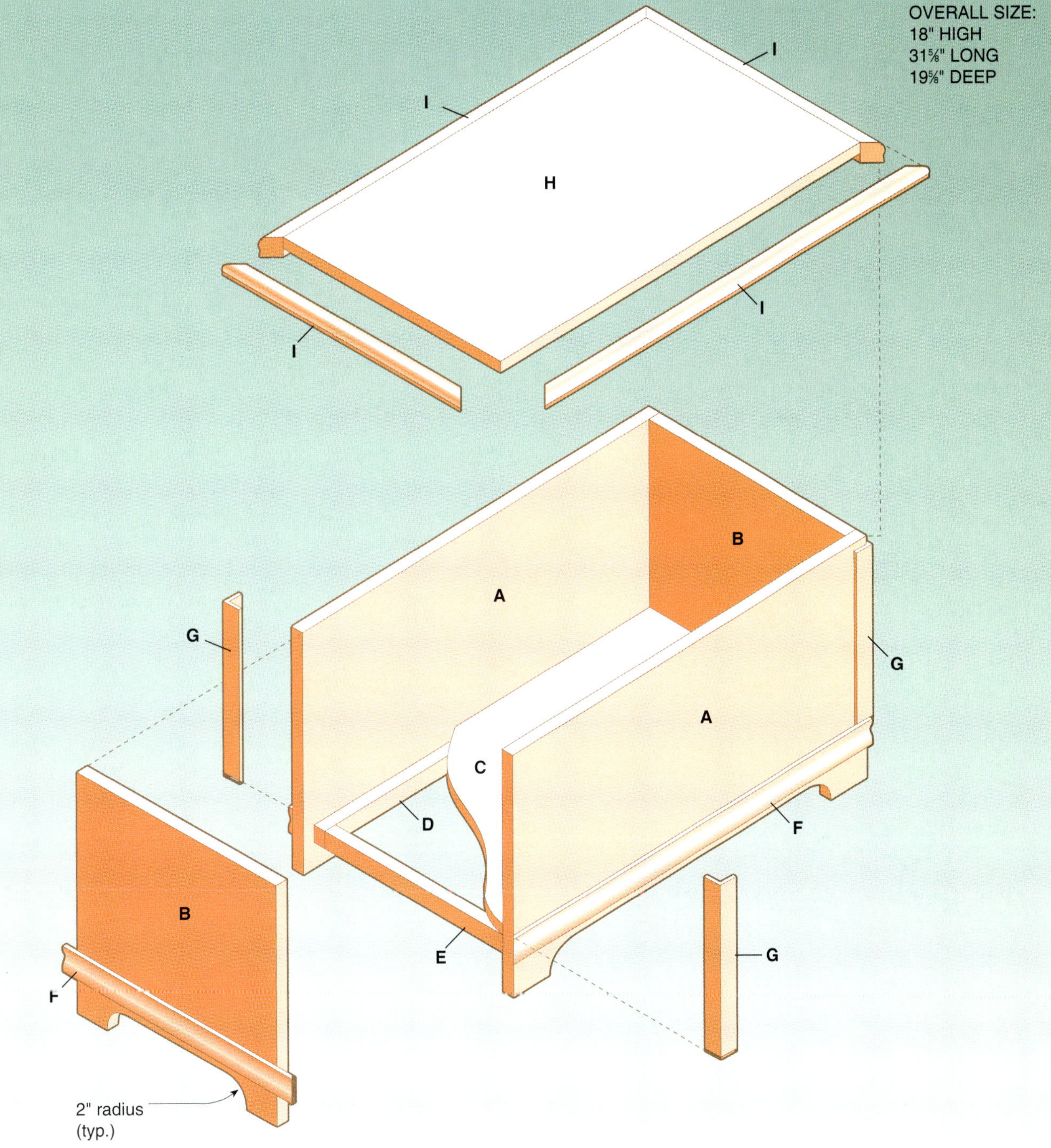

Cutting List

Key	Part	Dimension	Pcs.	Material
A	Side panel	¾ × 17¼ × 30"	2	Plywood
B	End panel	¾ × 17¼ × 16½"	2	Plywood
C	Bottom panel	¾ × 16½ × 28½"	1	Plywood
D	Side cleat	¾ × 1½ × 28½"	2	Plywood
E	End cleat	¾ × 1½ × 15"	2	Plywood

Cutting List

Key	Part	Dimension	Pcs.	Material
F	Bottom molding	½ × 1⅜" × *	4	Stop molding
G	Corner molding	¼ × 1⁵⁄₁₆ × 12"	4	Corner molding
H	Lid	¾ × 18⅛ × 30⅛"	1	Plywood
I	Top cap	¾ × 1⅜" × *	4	Cap molding

Materials: #6 × 1¼" and 2" wood screws, 16-ga. × ¾" and 1¼" brads, 2d and 4d finish nails, wood glue, finishing materials.

Note: Measurements reflect the actual size of dimension lumber.

*Cut to fit.

Use a jig saw and a straightedge as a guide to make the "kick space" cuts in the end and side panels.

Directions: Mitten Chest

MAKE THE SIDES AND ENDS.

1. Cut the side panels (A) and end panels (B) to size.

2. Draw cutting lines on the sides, 2" up from one long edge to mark the cutouts on the bottom edges of the sides. Use a compass to draw the curved lines at the ends of each cutout. Set the compass for a 2"-radius, and position the point of the compass as close as possible to the bottom edge, 5" in from the ends of the side panels. Draw the semi-circles. Clamp the sides to your worksurface, and make the cutouts with a jig saw, using a straightedge to guide the long, straight portion of the cut **(photo A).**

3. Draw the cutting lines 2" up from the bottom of each end panel. Set the compass for a 2"-radius, and position the point of the compass as close as possible to the bottom edge, 4¼" in from the ends of the end panels. Draw the semicircles, and make the cutouts with a jig saw and straightedge. Sand all edges smooth.

ASSEMBLE THE CHEST.

Attach cleats to the inside faces of the side and end panels. The cleats support the bottom panel of the chest, so it is important to attach them so their top edges are aligned and level.

1. Cut the side cleats (D) and end cleats (E) to size.

2. Draw reference lines on the side and end panels, 3½" up from the bottom edges and ¾" in from the side edges. Position the cleats so their top edges are

Center the end cleats over the kick spaces, leaving ¾" at each end where the side cleats will fit.

Draw opposite chest corners together with a bar or pipe clamp to keep the chest square.

Fasten the corner molding over the corners to conceal the joints and screw heads.

Attach the top cap around the perimeter of the lid. Drive nails in partially before positioning the strips.

flush with the reference lines. Drill 5/64" pilot holes through the cleats and into the panels. Counterbore the holes 1/8" deep, using a 3/8" counterbore bit. Fasten with glue and 1 1/4" wood screws **(photo B).**

3. Position the end panels between the side panels with the cleats facing in. Drill counterbored pilot holes through the side panels and into the end panels. Fasten with glue and evenly spaced 2" wood screws. Make sure the top and bottom edges are flush and the outside faces of the ends are flush with the side edges.

4. Cut the bottom panel (C) to size, and sand it smooth. Test-fit the bottom panel by setting it on top of the cleats. Remove the panel. Apply glue to the top edges of the cleats and along the underside edges of the panel, and reposition the panel inside the chest. Clamp diagonal chest corners with a bar or pipe clamp to hold the piece square while you fasten the bottom panel **(photo C).** To make sure you drive the screws directly into the bottom, mark the screw centerpoints 3 7/8" up from the bottoms of the sides and ends. Drill pilot holes through the sides and ends and into the edges of the bottom panel. Counterbore the holes. Attach with 2" wood screws.

ATTACH THE MOLDING.

1. Cut the bottom molding (F) to fit around the chest, mitering the ends at 45°.

2. Position the molding so the top edges are 4 3/8" up from the bottom edges of the sides and ends. Fasten it with glue and 4d finish nails, driven through 1/16" pilot holes. Apply glue, and drive 2d nails through the joints where the molding pieces meet to lock-nail the pieces (see *Tip*, page 150).

3. Cut the corner molding (G) to length. Use glue and 3/4" brads to fasten the corner molding over the joints between the end and side panels **(photo D).** Make sure the bottom edges of the corner molding butt against the top edges of the bottom molding. Sand the bottom edges of the corner molding to meet the bottom molding. Sand the top edges of the ends and sides to smooth the edges and corners.

MAKE THE LID.

1. Cut the lid (H) to size, and sand it smooth.

2. Cut four pieces of top cap (I) to fit around the perimeter of the lid.

3. Drill 1/16" pilot holes. Use glue and 4d finish nails to attach the top cap pieces, keeping the top edges flush with the top face of the lid **(photo E).** Glue and lock-nail the mitered corner joints. Set the lid into the top opening—no hinges are used.

APPLY FINISHING TOUCHES.

1. Use a nail set to set all nails and brads on the chest.

2. Fill all visible nail holes with wood putty and sand any rough spots smooth.

3. Finish-sand the entire chest. Finish as desired. We used two coats of glossy enamel because it is easiest to clean.

PROJECT
POWER TOOLS

Mission Window Seat

Curl up with a good book,
or just enjoy the view from this cozy window seat.

CONSTRUCTION MATERIALS

Quantity	Lumber
3	1 × 2" × 8' oak
1	1 × 2" × 6' oak
1	1 × 3" × 6' oak
4	1 × 4" × 6' oak
9	½ × 1¾" × 4' oak*
1	½ × 2¾" × 2' oak*
8	½ × 2¾" × 3' oak*
2	½ × 2¾" × 4' oak*
1	½ × 2¾" × 5' oak*
6	½ × 3¾" × 5' oak*
1	¾" × 2 × 6' oak plywood

*Stock sizes commonly available at most woodworking supply stores.

You'll find this Mission-style window seat to be an excellent place to spend an afternoon. Though it fits nicely under a window, the frame is wide enough so you won't ever feel cramped. The length is perfect for taking a nap, enjoying a sunset or watching children playing in the yard. Or perhaps you'd prefer to sit elsewhere to simply admire your craftsmanship from a distance.

The window seat uses oak for its strength and warm texture, and includes a frame face and nosing trim for a more elegant appearance. The rails are capped to make comfortable armrests, and the back is set lower than the sides so it won't block your window view. Though this project has many parts, it requires few tools and is remarkably easy to build. A few hours of labor will reward you with a delightful place to enjoy many hours of relaxation.

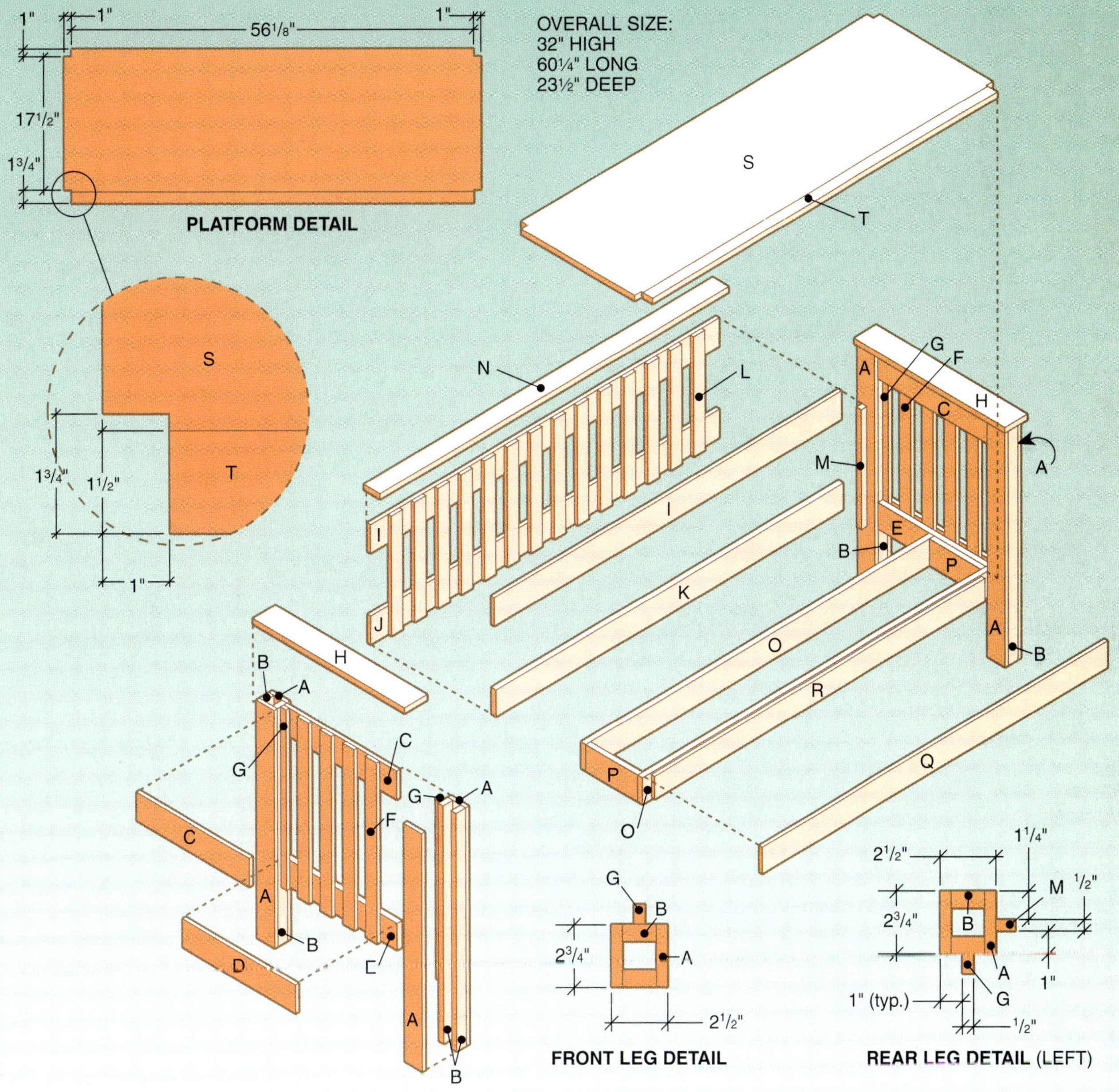

Key	Part	Dimension	Pcs.	Material
A	Wide leg piece	½ × 2¾ × 31¼"	8	Oak
B	Narrow leg piece	¾ × 1½ × 31¼"	8	Oak
C	End top rail	½ × 3¾ × 17½"	4	Oak
D	Outer bottom rail	½ × 3¾ × 17½"	2	Oak
E	Inner bottom rail	¾ × 3½ × 17½"	2	Oak
F	End slat	½ × 1¾ × 23¾"	8	Oak
G	End half slat	½ × ⅞ × 23¾"	4	Oak
H	End cap	¾ × 3½ × 23½"	2	Oak
I	Back top rail	½ × 3¾ × 54¼"	2	Oak
J	Outer bottom rail	½ × 3¾ × 54¼"	1	Oak

Cutting List

Key	Part	Dimension	Pcs.	Material
K	Inner bottom rail	¾ × 3½ × 54¼"	1	Oak
L	Back slat	½ × 1¾ × 15¾"	14	Oak
M	Back half slat	½ × ⅞ × 15¾"	2	Oak
N	Back cap	¾ × 2½ × 54¼"	1	Oak
O	Support side	¾ × 3½ × 54¾"	2	Oak
P	Support end	¾ × 3½ × 8"	2	Oak
Q	Frame face	½ × 3¾ × 54¼"	1	Oak
R	Spacer	½ × 2¾ × 52"	1	Oak
S	Platform	¾ × 18¾ × 56⅛"	1	Plywood
T	Platform nosing	¾ × 1½ × 54⅛"	1	Oak

Materials: #6 × ⅝", 1¼" and 1½" wood screws, 16-ga. × 1" brads, 3d finish nails, ¾" oak veneer edge tape (8'), ⅜"-dia. oak plugs, wood glue, finishing materials.

Note: Measurements reflect the actual size of dimension lumber.

Assemble the legs with glue and clamps, using wax paper to protect your worksurface.

Attach the end slats to the outer rails with glue and wood screws, using a spacer as a guide.

Directions: Mission Window Scat

For all screws used in this project, drill $\frac{3}{32}$" pilot holes. Counterbore the holes $\frac{1}{4}$" deep, using a $\frac{3}{8}$" counterbore bit.

ASSEMBLE THE LEGS.

1. Cut the wide leg pieces (A) and narrow leg pieces (B) to length.

2. Lay a narrow leg piece on your worksurface. Butt a wide leg piece against an edge to form an "L." Apply wood glue, and clamp the pieces together **(photo A).**

3. Assemble and glue together another "L" in the same fashion. Glue the two L-assemblies together to form a leg. Repeat to make the other legs.

BUILD THE END ASSEMBLIES.

To ensure that the end rails and slats remain square during the assembly process, build a simple jig by attaching two 2 × 2 boards at a 90° angle along adjacent edges of a 24 × 48" piece of plywood.

1. Cut the end top rails (C), outer bottom rails (D), inner bottom rails (E) and end slats (F) to length. Sand the pieces smooth.

2. Place a top rail and an outer bottom rail in the jig. Position two slats over the rails, $2\frac{5}{8}$" in from each end. Adjust the pieces so thc cnds of the slats are flush with the edges of the rails, and keep the entire assembly tight against the jig. Attach with glue, and drive $\frac{5}{8}$" wood screws through the slats and into the rails.

3. Using a $1\frac{3}{4}$"-wide spacer, attach the remaining end slats with glue and $\frac{5}{8}$" wood screws **(photo B).** NOTE: Make sure to test-fit all of the slats for uniform spacing before attaching them to the rails.

4. Position an inner bottom rail over the slats, $\frac{1}{4}$" up from the

> **TIP**
>
> *Take care to counterbore for all screw heads when building furniture that will be used as seating.*

Attach the end half slats to the legs with glue and wood screws.

Attach the lower inner rail with glue and screws and the upper inner rail with glue and finish nails.

bottom edges of the slats. Attach it with glue, and drive 1¼" wood screws through the inner bottom rail and the slats.

5. Place a top rail over the slats, and attach it with glue and 1" brads.

6. Repeat the process to build the other end assembly.

BUILD THE BACK ASSEMBLY.

1. Cut the back top rails (I), the outer bottom rail (J), the inner bottom rail (K) and the back slats (L) to length. Sand the pieces smooth.

2. Place a top rail and the inner bottom rail in the jig. Place two back slats on the rails, 2¾" in from each end. Adjust the pieces so the ends of the slats are flush with the edge of the top rail and overhang the edge of the bottom rail by ¼". Attach the pieces with glue, and drive ⅝" wood screws through the slats and into the rails. Test-fit the remaining slats, spacing them about 1⅞" apart. Attach them with glue and screws.

3. Position the outer bottom rail so the edge is flush with the bottom edges of the slats. Attach the bottom rail with glue and 1" brads.

4. Place the remaining top rail over the slats. Attach it with glue and 1" brads.

JOIN THE LEGS TO THE END ASSEMBLIES.

Half slats attached to the legs serve as cleats for attaching the end assembly.

1. Cut the end half slats (G) to size from ½ × 2¾" × 4' stock.

2. Place each leg on your worksurface with a narrow leg piece facing up. Center the half slat on the face of the leg (see *Diagram*), with the top ends flush. Attach the half slats to the legs with glue. Drive 1¼" wood screws, locating them so the screw heads will be hidden by the rails when the seat is completed **(photo C).**

3. Position an end assembly between a front and rear leg so the half slats fit between the rails and the top edges are flush. Attach the parts with glue. Drive 1¼" wood screws through the inner bottom rail and into the half slats, taking care to avoid other screws.

4. Attach the top rail to the half slats with glue and 3d finish nails driven through ⅟₁₆" pilot holes **(photo D).**

5. Repeat this process for the other end assembly.

Attach the support frame with glue, and drive screws through the support end and into the inner bottom rail.

Glue the platform nosing to the platform and hold it in place with bar clamps.

MAKE THE SUPPORT FRAME.

The support frame attaches to the inner bottom rails on the end assemblies and supports the seat.

1. Cut the support sides (O) and ends (P) to length.

2. Position the ends between the sides. Join the pieces with glue and 1¼" wood screws.

3. Lay one end assembly on your worksurface. Position the support frame upright so the front corner of the frame is tight against the front leg and the edges of the frame are flush with the edges of the bottom rail. Attach the support frame to the end assembly with glue and 1¼" wood screws **(photo E).**

4. Stand the window seat upright, and clamp the other end in position. Attach it with glue and 1¼" wood screws.

ATTACH THE BACK.

Like the end assemblies, the back assembly attaches to the legs with half slats.

1. Cut the back half slats (M) to size from ½ × 2¾" × 2' stock.

2. Measure 7½" up from the bottom on the inside face of each rear leg, and draw a horizontal line. Measure in 1¼" from the back edge of the leg along this line, and draw a vertical line upward.

3. Position a half slat against the leg so its rear edge is on the vertical line and its bottom edge is on the horizontal line. Attach the half slat to the leg with glue and 1¼" wood screws. Repeat this step with the other rear leg.

4. Slide the back assembly over the half slats so the top edges are flush. Attach with glue, and drive 1¼" wood screws through the inner bottom rail and into the half slats.

5. Drill $\frac{1}{16}$" pilot holes, and join the top rail to the back half slats with glue and 3d finish nails.

ATTACH THE CAPS.

Caps attach to the ends and back of the window seat to create armrests and a backrest.

1. Cut the end caps (H) and back cap (N) to length.

2. Center the end caps over the end assemblies, with the back edges flush. Attach the pieces with glue, and drive 1½" wood screws through the end caps and into the legs.

3. Position the back cap over the back assembly so the front edge is flush with the front edges of the legs. Attach with glue, and drive 1½" wood screws through the back cap and into the top rails.

Clamp the spacer and frame face to the support frame. Attach them with glue, and drive screws through the inside of the support frame.

Attach the platform to the rails, frame face and support frame with glue and wood screws.

MAKE THE PLATFORM.
The oak nosing and edge tape create the appearance of solid wood.

1. Cut the platform (S) and platform nosing (T) to size. Sand the top face of the platform smooth.

2. Glue the nosing to the front edge of the platform, leaving 1" exposed on each end. Clamp the nosing in place until the glue dries **(photo F).**

3. Use a jig saw to cut a 1 × 1" notch in each back corner of the platform and a 1 × 1¾" notch in each front corner to accommodate the legs (see *Diagram*). Apply self-adhesive oak veneer edge tape to the side and back edges of the platform. (Don't apply tape to the notches.) Lightly sand the edges of the tape.

ATTACH THE FRAME FACE.

1. Cut the frame face (Q) and spacer (R) to length.

2. Glue the pieces together, centering the spacer on the frame face. Clamp the pieces together until the glue dries.

3. Position the frame face assembly against the front of the support frame so the top edges of the face and support frame are flush. Attach with glue, and drive 1¼" wood screws from inside the support frame **(photo G).**

ATTACH THE PLATFORM.
Attach the platform to the support frame, frame face and bottom rails with glue and 1½" wood screws **(photo H).**

APPLY FINISHING TOUCHES.

1. Fill the screw holes with glued oak plugs. Sand them flush with the surface. Set all nails with a nail set, and fill the nail holes with wood putty. Scrape off any excess glue, and finish-sand the window seat.

2. Apply the stain of your choice and a coat of polyurethane.

3. Add seat cushions that complement the wood tones of the window seat and the decorating scheme of your room.

TIP

If you find nail holes that were not filled before you applied stain and finish, you can go back and fill the holes with a putty stick that closely matches the color of the wood stain.

Living Room Projects

Here are some great projects to customize your living room. You can display your collections on a rotating basis with the versatile collector's table or the space saving corner display stand. Make use of underutilized space by building a behind-the-sofa bookcase or mantel. Always wanted to add some vintage charm, but not willing to pay antique dealer prices? Try the wall-mounted knickknack shelf or the dry sink. From the two-tier bookshelf made without fasteners or glue to the picture frames that require precision cuts and joining—you're sure to find a challenging and rewarding project here.

PROJECT
POWER TOOLS

Two-tier Bookshelf

Here's a smart looking, easy-to-build project that requires no glue, screws or nails!

Construction Materials

Quantity	Lumber
1	¾" × 4 × 8' Baltic birch plywood
1	1" × 2' birch dowel

This two-tier bookshelf provides ample room for encyclopedias, dictionaries and other useful references. Its distinctive profile complements many decorating motifs, and with the right finish, it can become a vibrant accent piece. The bookshelf uses a joinery method, known as *pinned mortise-and-tenon*, that requires no glue, screws or nails. Instead, wedges hold the joints together. When moving or storing the unit, you can simply remove the wedges.

With the included plan for a mortising jig, you can easily make several of these bookshelves to give as gifts.

OVERALL SIZE:
26" HIGH
29¾" WIDE
12" DEEP

1" squares

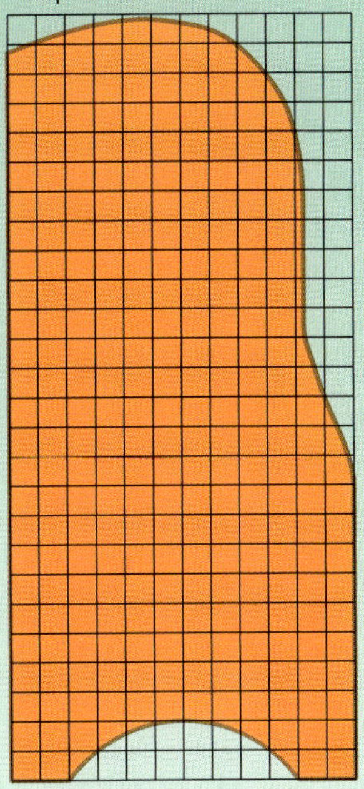

PART A PROFILE

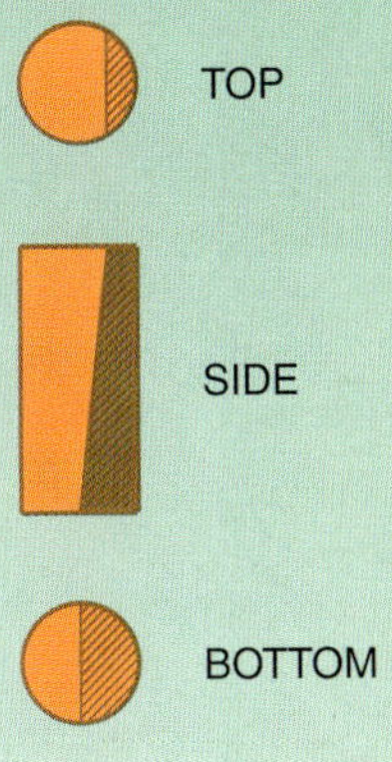

DOWEL DETAIL

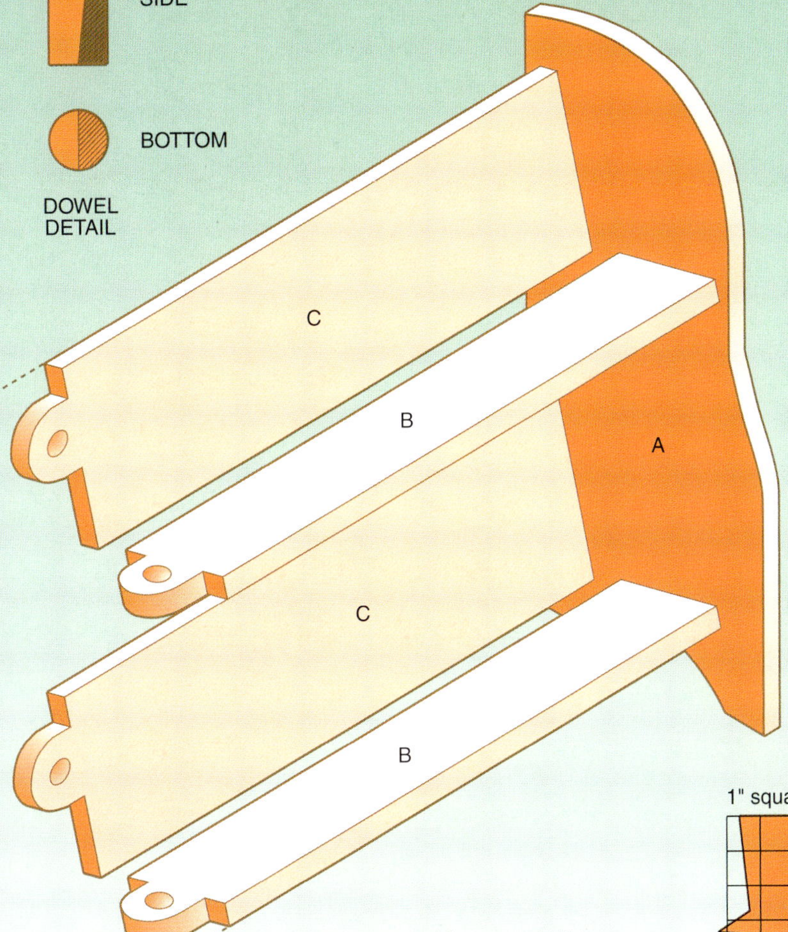

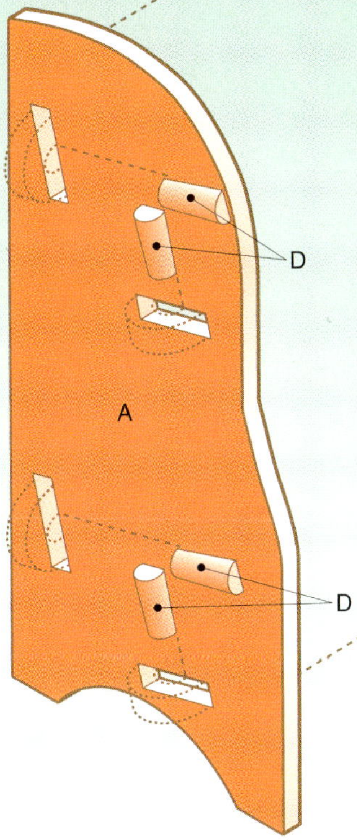

1" squares

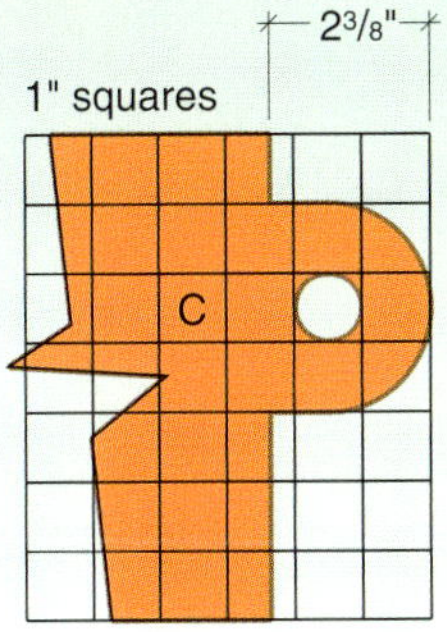

PART C DETAIL

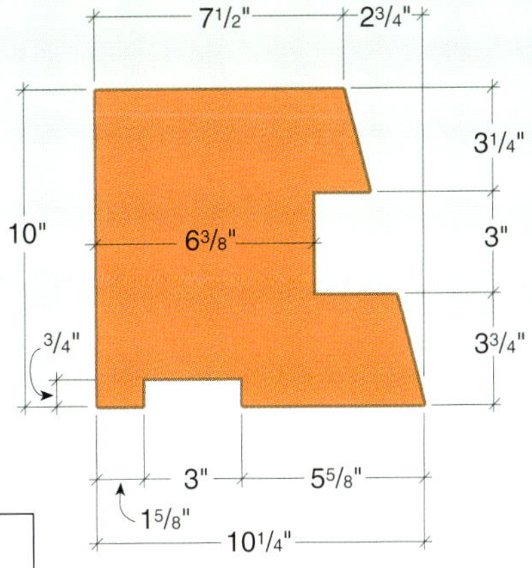

JIG DETAIL

1" squares

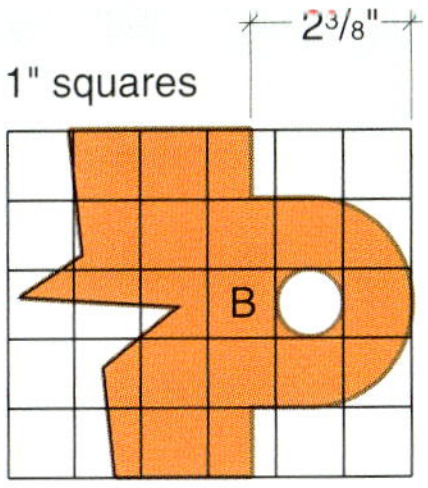

PART B DETAIL

Cutting List

Key	Part	Dimension	Pcs.	Material
A	End	¾ × 12 × 26"	2	Plywood
B	Shelf	¾ × 5 × 29¾"	2	Plywood
C	Back	¾ × 7 × 29¾"	2	Plywood
D	Wedge	1 × 2¼"	8	Birch dowel

Materials: Finishing materials.

Note: Measurements reflect the actual size of dimension lumber.

Directions: Two-tier Bookshelf

MAKE THE JIG.
A jig will help you accurately mark the location of mortises.
1. Cut a 10 × 10¼" blank from a scrap of ¼" material.
2. Measure and mark the diagonal line and the locations for the mortise guides (see *Diagram*). Use a jig saw to cut out the jig **(photo A).**

CUT THE ENDS.
1. Cut the ends (A) to size. Transfer the pattern (see *Diagram*), and cut with a jig saw.
2. Lay both ends on your workbench with the back edges together, forming a mirror image. Measure from the bottom back corners and mark reference points at ⅞" and 14¾" **(photo B).**
3. Lay out the mortises by positioning the bottom back corner of the jig at the first reference point, keeping the back edges flush. Outline the two lower mortises. Slide the jig up to the second reference point, and mark the two higher mortises **(photo C).**
4. Remove the jig, and draw lines to close the ¾ × 3" rectangles. Drill starter holes, using a backer board. Cut the mortises with a jig saw **(photo D).**

TIP

To yield an opening large enough to accommodate the tenons, make sure the mortises on your pattern are slightly oversized.

CUT THE SHELVES AND BACKS.
1. Cut the shelves (B) and backs (C) to size.
2. Lay out the profile for the tenons (see *Diagram*), and cut them out with a jig saw. Sand the edges smooth.

Use a piece of ¼" scrap plywood and your jig saw to create the mortising jig.

Mark reference points at ⅞" and at 14¾" along the backs of both sides as guides for positioning the mortising jig.

3. Drill wedge holes with a 1" spade bit. Use a backer board to prevent tear outs. Test-fit the tenons in the mortises. Adjust them if necessary.

MAKE THE WEDGES.
1. Cut 1"-dia. dowels to 2¼" lengths.
2. Measure from the edge, and mark reference lines across the top of the dowel at ¼" and across the bottom at ½".

Use the jig to mark the locations of both pairs of mortises. Then, flip the jig and mark corresponding mortises on the other end piece.

Drill pilot holes, using a backer board to prevent splintering, and cut the mortises with a jig saw.

TIP

When a project has modern lines, you can create a very interesting accent piece by applying an exotic-colored aniline dye. A rich burgundy or a bright green would create vibrant accents.

Connect the lines. Sand down the dowels to this line, using a belt sander clamped to your worksurface **(photo E).**

3. Assemble the shelves and backs between the ends, and test-fit the wedges. Disassemble the bookshelf for finishing.

APPLY FINISHING TOUCHES. Finish-sand the entire project. Then, paint or finish the bookshelf as desired. When the finish dries, assemble the pieces.

Sand the wedges to the lines, using a belt sander clamped to your worksurface.

Plant Stand

Our plant stand is a great way to display your favorite potted foliage. Build it for a corner in your sunniest room.

PROJECT POWER TOOLS

This plant stand is a perfect platform on which to set your favorite indoor plants. The simple lines and ceramic tile surfaces help focus the attention on the plants themselves, rather than on the stand. Make no mistake, however—our plant stand has a sleek design that fits nearly any environment or decor. Once you paint it, you can put it almost anywhere to showcase your plants. It's lightweight, so you can move it easily from place to place. But it's strong enough to support heavy pots easily.

The leg assemblies provide a sturdy base, while ceramic tile inserts on the shelf and top give our plant stand some weight and stability. It's perfect for a corner nook in a sun room or kitchen, and the tile pieces make cleaning up spills an easy task. What's more, the ceramic tile will not fall apart or rot due to moisture and aging. So, you are sure to enjoy this original and practical plant stand for many years.

Construction Materials

Quantity	Lumber
1	1 × 8" × 4' pine
2	1 × 3" × 10' pine
1	½ × 1" × 8' pine stop molding
1	½" × 2 × 2' plywood

OVERALL SIZE:
30⅜" HIGH
13¼" WIDE
13¼" DEEP

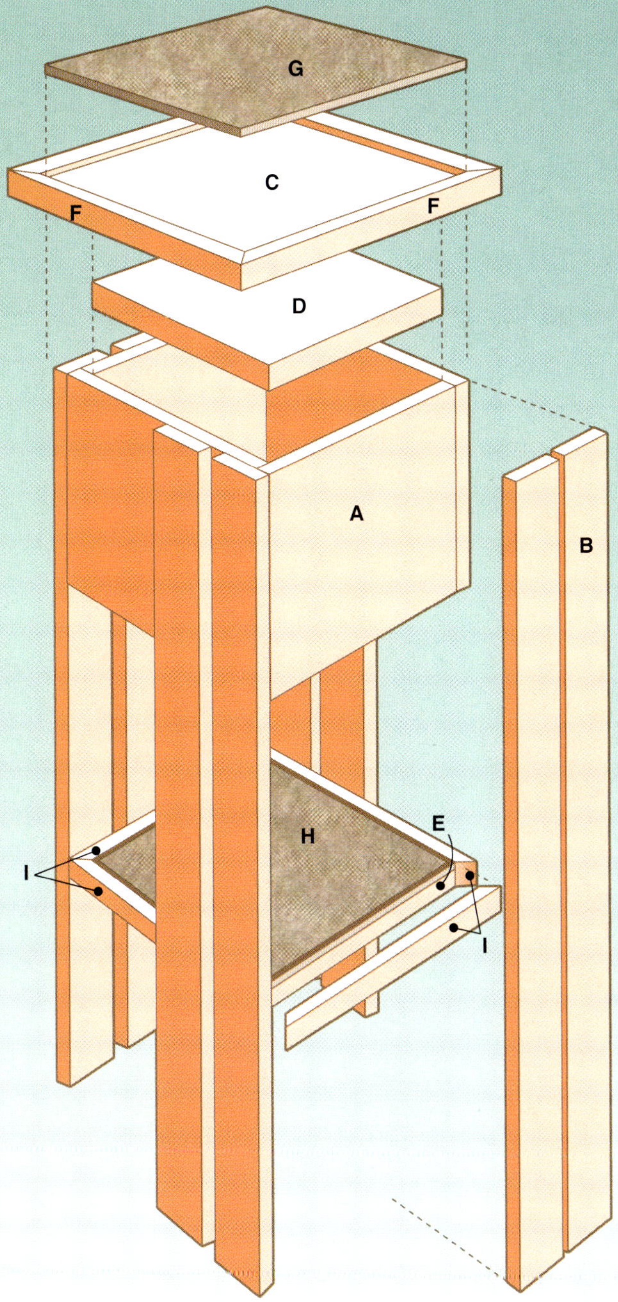

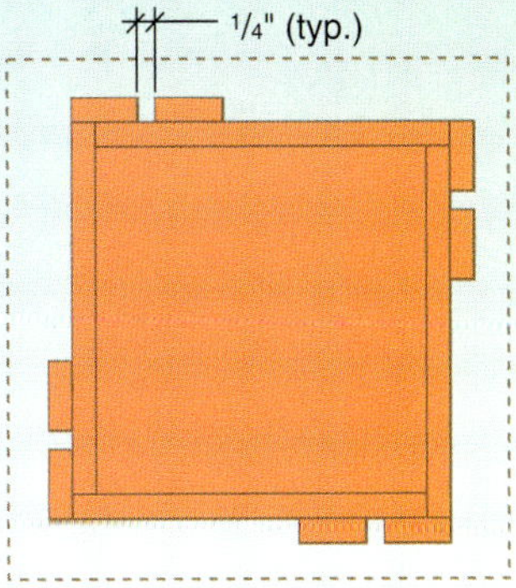

LEG LAYOUT DETAIL

Cutting List

Key	Part	Dimension	Pcs.	Material
A	Box side	¾ × 7¼ × 8"	4	Pine
B	Leg	¾ × 2½ × 29½"	8	Pine
C	Top tile base	½ × 12¼ × 12¼"	1	Plywood
D	Box top	¾ × 7¼ × 7¼"	1	Pine
E	Shelf	½ × 7¾ × 7¾"	1	Plywood
F	Top frame	½ × 1 × 13¼"	4	Molding
G	Top tile	12 × 12"	1	Ceramic
H	Shelf tile	7½ × 7½"	1	Ceramic
I	Shelf frame	½ × 1 × 8¾"	4	Molding

Materials: 1", 1¼" and 1½" deck screws, 3d and 4d finish nails, wood glue, finishing materials, ceramic tile, ceramic tile adhesive, tinted grout.

Specialty tools: V-notch adhesive trowel, grout float.

Note: Measurements reflect the actual size of dimension lumber.

A

Assemble the box using simple butt joints.

B

Place the top tile base and box top onto the box, and fasten them with screws.

C

Attach the leg pairs with glue and screws, obscuring the visible joints on the box.

D

Spread an even layer of adhesive over the shelf, and attach the tile.

Directions: Plant Stand

BUILD THE BOX.

Tile size varies from piece to piece, so measure your tile before cutting the top tile base (C). Allow a 1/8" gap for the grout joint between the tile and the top frame.

1. Cut the box sides (A), top tile base (C) and box top (D) to size. Sand with 150-grit sandpaper.

2. Fasten the sides with simple butt joints, which will be obscured by the legs. Drill 5/64" pilot holes. Counterbore the holes 1/8" deep, using a 3/8" counterbore bit. Use glue and 1½" deck screws to attach the sides together, making sure the edges are flush **(photo A).**

3. Center the box top on the bottom face of the top tile base. Fasten the pieces by driving 1" deck screws through the top tile base and into the box top.

4. Place the top tile base and box top onto the box **(photo B).** Drill counterbored pilot holes through the box sides and into the box top. Attach the box top with 1½" deck screws.

TIP

Ceramic tile is sold in both floor and wall styles. Floor tile is generally stronger and more scratch resistant.

ATTACH THE LEGS.

1. Cut the legs (B) to length.

2. Drill countersunk pilot holes through the legs and into the box sides. Fasten the legs to the sides with glue and 1¼" deck screws. Each outside leg is flush with the side edge and each leg pair has a ¼"-wide space between the pieces **(photo C).**

ATTACH THE SHELF.

1. Cut the shelf (E) to size.

2. Miter-cut the shelf frame (I) pieces to length.

3. Attach the shelf tile (H) to the shelf with tile adhesive **(photo D).** Spread the adhesive on the shelf, using a V-notch trowel. Press the tile into place, centered on the shelf, and allow to dry.

4. Fasten the shelf frame to the shelf with 3d finish nails. Align the top frame edges flush with the top face of the tile.

5. Attach the shelf to the legs by driving 4d finish nails through the legs and into the frame and shelf **(photo E).** The lower edge of the shelf should be 10" from the legs' bottom edges.

ATTACH THE TOP TILE.

1. Miter-cut the top frame (F) pieces to length.

2. Attach the top tile (G) to the top tile base with adhesive. Nail the top frame in place against the top tile base, keeping the top edges flush with the tile face **(photo F).** When driving the nails, be sure they line up with the top tile base, not the tile.

APPLY FINISHING TOUCHES.

1. Set all nails with a nail set, fill nail and screw holes with wood putty, and finish-sand all surfaces.

2. Prime and paint the plant stand. Coat it with two coats of satin-gloss polyurethane finish and allow to dry.

3. Mask the frame pieces with masking tape. Fill the gaps between the tiles and frames with tinted grout. Use a small grout float to pack the grout into the gaps. Smooth the joints with a damp sponge to remove excess grout.

(left) Use pieces of scrap wood as spacers, and attach the shelf with 4d finish nails.
(above) Install the top frame around the top tile base, using a lightweight tack hammer and 3d finish nails.

PROJECT
POWER TOOLS

Tile-top Coffee Table

The dramatic, contrasting textures of floor tiles and warm red oak will make you forget that this table is designed to create storage.

Construction Materials

Quantity	Lumber
1	¾" × 4 × 8' oak plywood
2	1 × 2" × 8' oak
2	1 × 4" × 8' oak
1	⅞ × ⅞" × 8' oak corner molding

Functionally, the trim size and the ample proportions of the storage shelf are the two most important features of this tile-top coffee table. But most people won't notice that. They'll be too busy admiring the striking tile tabletop and the clean oak lines of the table base.

Measuring a convenient 45" long × 20¼" wide, this coffee table will fit nicely even in smaller rooms. The shelf below is ideal for storing books, magazines, newspapers, photo albums or anything else you want to keep within arm's reach when sitting on your sofa.

We used 6 × 6" ceramic floor tiles for our coffee table, but you can use just about any type or size of floor tile you want—just be sure to use floor tile, not wall tile, which is thinner and fractures more easily.

After you've built this tile-top coffee table, you may like it so much that you'll want to build a tile-top end table to match.

OVERALL SIZE:
16" HIGH
20¼" WIDE
45" LONG

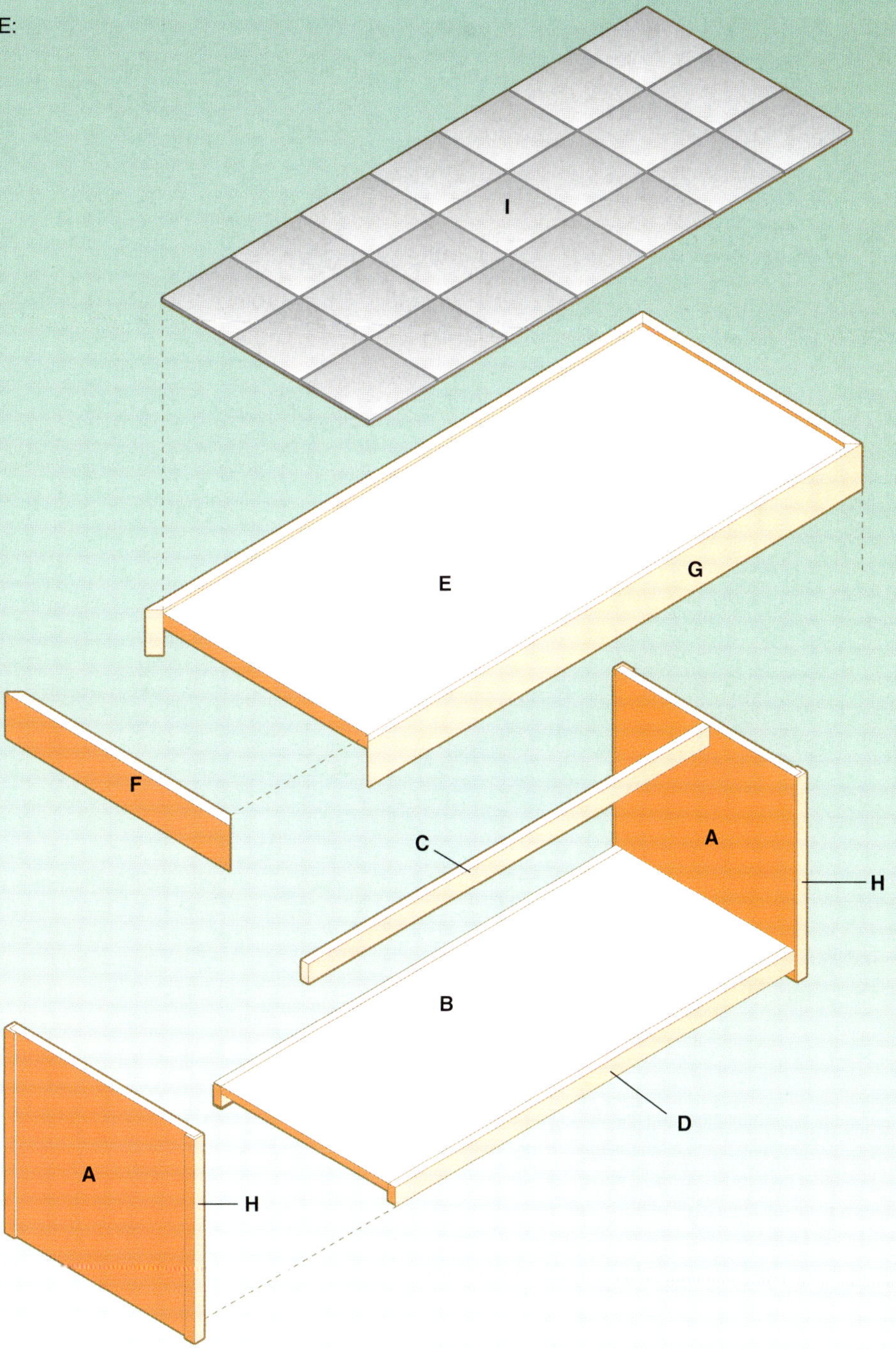

Cutting List				
Key	**Part**	**Dimension**	**Pcs.**	**Material**
A	Side panel	¾ × 16 × 15"	2	Plywood
B	Shelf panel	¾ × 14½ × 35"	1	Plywood
C	Stringer	¾ × 1½ × 35"	1	Oak
D	Shelf edge	¾ × 1½ × 35"	2	Oak
E	Top panel	¾ × 18¾ × 43½"	1	Plywood

Cutting List				
Key	**Part**	**Dimension**	**Pcs.**	**Material**
F	End skirt	¾ × 3½ × 20¼"	2	Oak
G	Side skirt	¾ × 3½ × 45"	2	Oak
H	Corner trim	⅞ × ⅞ × 15"	4	Corner molding
I	Table tiles	¼ × 6 × 6"	21	Ceramic

Materials: #6 × 1½" wood screws, 3d and 6d finish nails, ⅜"-dia. oak plugs, wood glue, finishing materials, ceramic tile adhesive, tinted grout, 3⁄16" plastic tile spacers, silicone grout sealer.

Specialty tools: V-notch adhesive trowel, rubber mallet, grout float.

Note: Measurements reflect the actual size of dimension lumber.

Fasten the shelf edges to the shelf panel with glue and 6d finish nails.

Secure the stringer in place with glue and screws.

Directions: Tile-top Coffee Table

Miter-cut and attach one skirt board at a time to ensure a proper fit.

ASSEMBLE THE TABLE BASE.

1. Cut the side panels (A) and shelf panel (B) to size using a circular saw and a straightedge as a cutting guide. Sand the faces of the plywood smooth with medium-grit sandpaper.

2. Cut the shelf edges (D) to length.

3. Fasten the shelf edges to the shelf panel with glue and 6d finish nails **(photo A).** Be sure to drill $\frac{3}{32}$" pilot holes through the edge pieces so you don't split them. Keep the top surfaces of the shelf edges and shelf panel flush when fastening.

4. Position the shelf upright, and set the shelf edging on ¾"-thick spacers. Stand a side panel upright on its bottom edge, against the end of the shelf panel. Keep the edges of the side panel flush with the outside surfaces of the shelf edging. Drill $\frac{5}{64}$" pilot holes through the side panels and into the edges of the shelf panel. Counterbore the holes ¼" deep, using a ⅜" counterbore bit. Fasten the side panel to the shelf panel with glue and 1½" wood screws. Fasten the other side panel to the shelf panel.

5. Cut the stringer (C) to length.

6. Position the stringer between the side panels, flush with the top edges and centered midway across the side panels. Clamp it in place with a bar or pipe clamp. Drill pilot holes through the side panels and into the stringer. Counterbore the holes. Remove the clamps and secure the stringer with glue and 1½" wood screws **(photo B).**

MAKE THE TABLETOP FRAME.

The tabletop frame is a plywood panel framed with 1 × 4 oak. The joints in the 1 × 4 frame are mitered—you can use most manual miter boxes to cut a 1 × 4 placed on edge, but a power miter box is ideal for the job.

1. Cut the top panel (E) to size, using a circular saw and a straightedge as a cutting guide.

2. Position the top panel on the side panels. Be sure to leave an equal overhang on the ends

Tip

Ceramic tile varies greatly in size and style. This tabletop design is based on using 6 × 6" tiles with $\frac{3}{16}$" gaps between tiles. If you use tiles of a different size, you may need to resize the plywood table panel to fit your layout. Or, you can have the tiles cut to fit at the tile store.

Fill all visible screw holes with oak plugs.

Tap the tiles lightly with a rubber mallet to set them firmly in the adhesive.

and sides. Drill pilot holes through the top panel and into the side panels and stringer. Counterbore the holes. Fasten with glue and 1½" wood screws.

3. Cut the end skirts (F) and side skirts (G) to length. Although the *Cutting List* on page 79 gives exact dimensions for these parts, it's best to cut the first part slightly longer than specified. Then, custom-cut it to fit. Cut all the other skirt boards to length, using the first board as a guide **(photo C).**

4. Using a tile as a gauge, position the skirt pieces to create a lip slightly higher than the top of the tile. Drill pilot holes through the skirt boards, and fasten the boards to the edges of the top panel with glue and 6d finish nails.

FASTEN THE CORNER TRIM.

1. Cut the corner trim (H) pieces to length.

2. Fasten the corner trim to the side panel edges with glue and 3d finish nails—be sure to drill 1/16" pilot holes through the trim pieces to prevent splitting.

FINISH THE WOOD.

For clean results, perform the finishing steps on the table before installing the tile.

1. Fill all visible screw holes with oak plugs, and sand them flush with the surface **(photo D).** Finish-sand the entire coffee table, and apply sanding sealer to all exposed surfaces except the top panel. Let the sealer dry thoroughly. Then, lightly sand the sealed surfaces with 180- or 220-grit sandpaper.

2. Apply stain to the sealed oak surfaces, if desired. Then, apply two or three light coats of polyurethane.

INSTALL THE CERAMIC TOP.

1. Once the finish has dried, mask off the top edges of the skirts to protect the finished surfaces.

2. Test-fit the table tiles (I). Apply a layer of tile adhesive over the entire table surface, using a V-notch adhesive trowel. Line the borders of the table surface with plastic spacers. (We used 3/16" spacers with 6" ceramic floor tile to make a surface that fits inside the tabletop frame.)

3. Begin setting tiles into the adhesive, working in straight lines. Insert plastic spacers between tiles to maintain an even gap. Tap each tile lightly with a rubber mallet to set it into the adhesive **(photo E).** Once the tiles have been set in place, remove the spacers, and let the adhesive set overnight.

4. Use a grout float to apply a layer of grout to the tile surface so it fills the gaps between tiles **(photo F).** Wipe excess grout from the tile faces with a damp sponge. Let the grout dry for about 30 minutes (check manufacturer's directions). Wipe off the grout film from the tiles with a dry cloth, wiping diagonally across the grout joints. Let the grout set for at least a week. Then, apply silicone grout sealer to the grout joints, following manufacturer's directions.

Use a grout float to apply tile grout in the gaps between tiles in the tabletop.

PROJECT
POWER TOOLS

Picture Frame

Here's a great gift project that displays fond memories and your fine craftsmanship.

Construction Materials

Quantity	Lumber
1	¾ × ¾" × 8' birch
1	¼ × 2 × 12" birch
1	⅛ × 8 × 8" hardboard
3	⅛ × 2½ × 6½" glass

This project makes an ideal gift for grandparents, uncles, aunts, friends and neighbors. In fact, once word starts to spread that you're making these attractive tri-fold picture frames, you may become a busier woodworker, trying to keep up with all the requests. These paintable frames are designed to hold six 2¾ × 2¼" photographs, but you can make larger frames by proportionately increasing the dimensions and applying the same construction methods. The end frames have hinges mounted on opposite sides so you can open the picture frames to create a freestanding, S-curved display of your treasured memories.

OVERALL SIZE:
7¾" HIGH
11½" WIDE
¾" DEEP

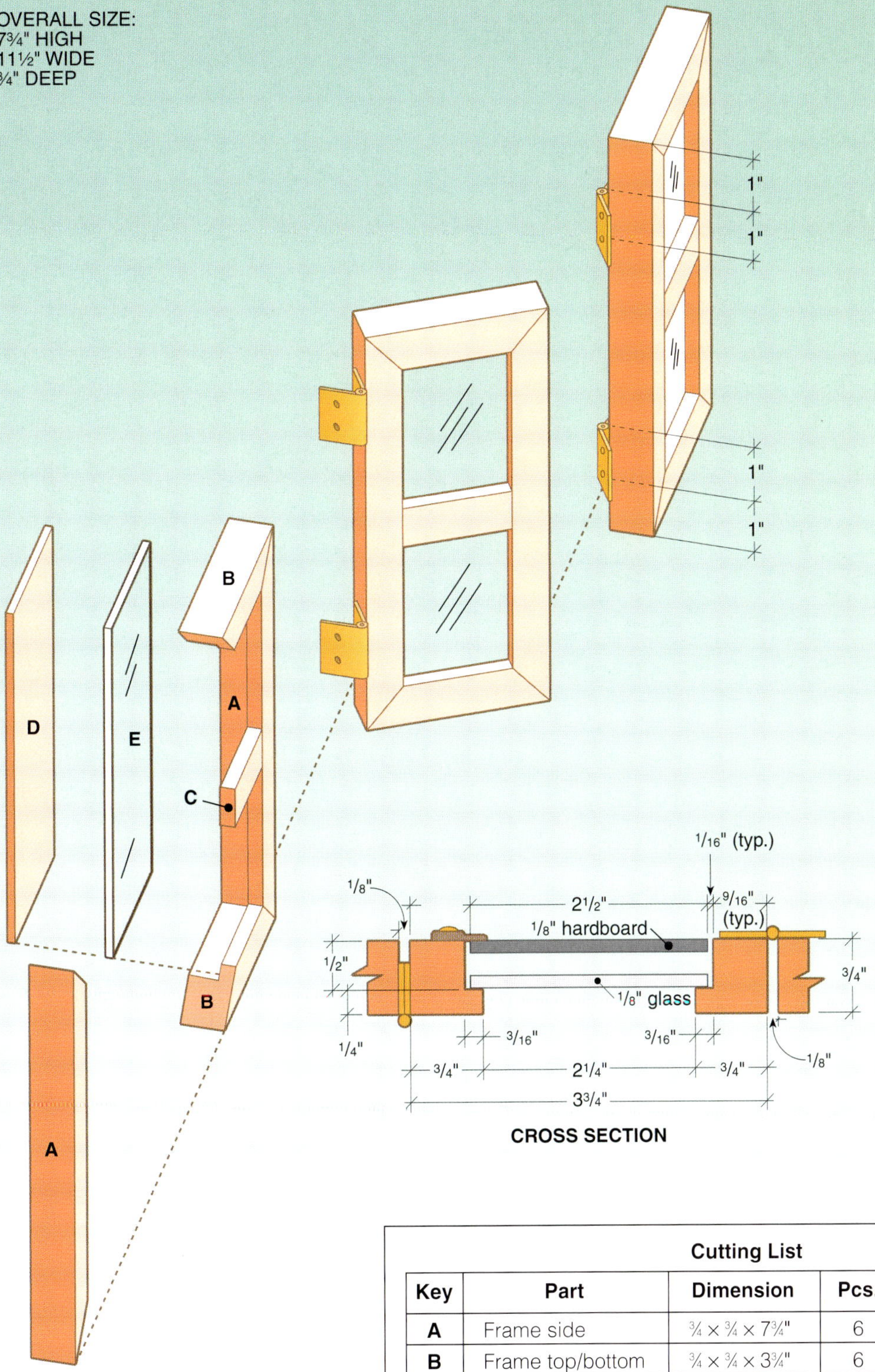

CROSS SECTION

Cutting List

Key	Part	Dimension	Pcs.	Material
A	Frame side	¾ × ¾ × 7¾"	6	Birch
B	Frame top/bottom	¾ × ¾ × 3¾"	6	Birch
C	Mullion	¼ × ¾ × 2¼"	3	Birch
D	Backer	⅛ × 2½ × 6½"	3	Hardboard
E	Glass	⅛ × 2½ × 6½"	3	Glass

Materials: Wood glue, 4 brass hinges (1 × ½"), 12 retaining clips, finishing materials.

Note: Measurements reflect the actual thickness of dimension lumber.

Use a router table and straight bit to cut the rabbets on the frame pieces.

Use a power miter box to miter-cut the frame pieces to length.

TIP

We built our frames from birch, which can be stained, painted or left unfinished, but any hardwood is suitable. Exotic woods will give your picture frame unique appeal.

Directions: Picture Frame

CUT THE PARTS.

To cut the rabbets on the inside faces of the frame pieces, we recommend using a router table and a straight router bit. Make test cuts on scrap material to ensure accurate rabbets. If you don't have a router table, use bar clamps, a straightedge, and ¾" scrap wood to hold the pieces in place while routing.

1. Set the fence of the router table to 3⁄16". Cut the rabbets on the frame pieces by making multiple passes, gradually extending the depth of the cut until you achieve the ½" depth **(photo A).** This technique creates a cleaner rabbet and reduces the risk of tearouts.

2. Using a power miter box, carefully cut the frame sides (A) and tops/bottoms (B) to length, mitering the ends at 45° **(photo B).** Clamp a stop block to the fence of the miter saw to ensure that the pieces are cut to the exact same length.

ASSEMBLE THE FRAMES.

1. Glue the frame sides, bottoms and tops together, and secure with band clamps **(photo C).** Make sure the frames are square.

2. Leave excess glue until it hardens, then gently remove the dried glue with a sharp chisel.

3. Rip-cut ¼" stock to ⅞" width, then cut the mullions (C) to length.

4. Mark a "sand-to" line on each mullion. Clamp a belt sander onto your worksurface in a horizontal position, then grind down the mullions to the marked lines **(photo D).**

5. Test-fit the mullions in the frames. Attach with glue, and clamp until dry.

ALIGN THE HINGES.

1. Measure, mark and drill pilot holes for attaching the hinges. Make sure the hinge barrels face front in one reveal and face back in the other reveal. The hinges with front-facing barrels are attached to the sides of the frames; the other hinges are mounted on the back of

Join the frame pieces with glue and secure them with band clamps until the glue dries.

Use a belt sander to grind down the mullions to the "sand-to" lines.

the frames.

2. Install the hinges, then remove them from the frames (they will be reinstalled after the finish is applied).

APPLY FINISHING TOUCHES.

1. Finish-sand the project, then finish as desired. If you want to highlight the wood grain, you can use an aniline dye to stain the wood, provided the joints are tight and clean. Otherwise, paint is always a good option.

2. After the finish dries, reinstall the hinges **(photo E).**

3. Cut the hardboard backers (D) to size.

4. Insert the glass, photographs and backers. Add a layer of cardboard as a spacer, then secure with retaining clips.

One pair of hinges is attached with the barrels facing the front; the other hinges are attached so the barrels face the back.

PROJECT
POWER TOOLS

Behind-the-sofa Bookshelf

This efficient bookshelf fits right behind your sofa or up against a wall to provide display space and a useful table surface.

Construction Materials

Quantity	Lumber
2	1 × 10" × 8' aspen
1	1 × 8" × 8' aspen
3	1 × 4" × 8' aspen
2	1 × 2" × 8' aspen
2	¾ × 2½" × 8' casing molding

The space behind your sofa may not be the first area that comes to mind when you're searching for extra storage, but it does hold many possibilities for a space-challenged home. This clever behind-the-sofa bookcase has display space below and a spacious top that combine to make a useful wood project.

The top is high enough so it can be used as an auxiliary coffee table, if you don't mind reaching up for your beverage or snack.

We used aspen to build this table, then stained it for a natural appearance. If you prefer, you can build it from pine and paint it to match or complement a sofa.

OVERALL SIZE:
34" HIGH
59" LONG
9¼" DEEP

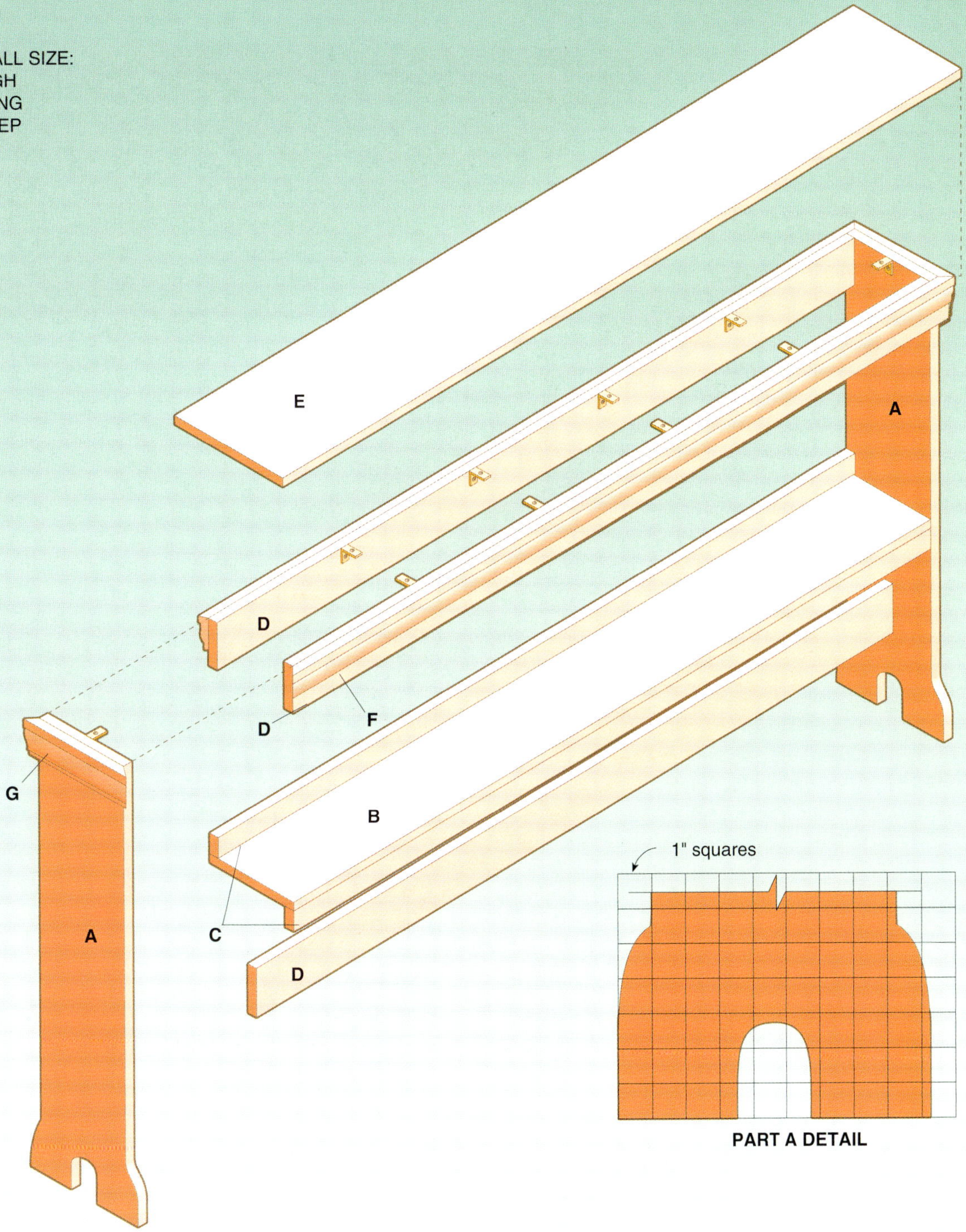

PART A DETAIL

Cutting List

Key	Part	Dimension	Pcs.	Material
A	Leg	¾ × 9¼ × 33¼"	2	Aspen
B	Shelf	¾ × 7¼ × 55½"	1	Aspen
C	Shelf rail	¾ × 1½ × 55½"	2	Aspen
D	Stretcher	¾ × 3½ × 55½"	3	Aspen

Cutting List

Key	Part	Dimension	Pcs.	Material
E	Top	¾ × 9¼ × 59"	1	Aspen
F	Face trim	¾ × 2½ × *	2	Molding
G	End trim	¾ × 2½ × *	2	Molding

Materials: #6 × 1¼" and 2" wood screws, #8 × ½" wood screws, 16-ga. × 1¼" brads, 1½" brass corner braces (10), ⅜"-dia. wood plugs, wood glue, finishing materials.

Note: Measurements reflect the actual size of dimension lumber.

***Cut to fit**

Directions: Behind-the-sofa Bookshelf

Draw the shapes for the legs onto pieces of 1 × 10, then cut out the legs with a jig saw. Make the long, straight cuts with a circular saw.

Attach the shelf by driving wood screws through counterbored pilot holes in the legs.

MAKE THE LEGS.

The decorative cutouts at the bottoms of the legs add style and create feet that add stability.

1. Cut the legs (A) to size.

2. Use the Part A Detail pattern to lay out the cutting lines for the feet at the bottoms of the legs. You may want to draw a 1"-square grid pattern at the bottom of one of the legs first. Lay out the leg shape on one leg, using a straightedge to make sure the 1" relief cuts that run all the way up the edges of the legs are straight.

3. Cut the straight section of one leg with a circular saw and a straightedge guide, and cut the patterned bottom with a jig saw. Sand the edges smooth.

4. Trace the profile onto the second leg and cut the shape to match **(photo A).**

ATTACH THE SHELF AND RAILS.

The rails attach to the front and back of the shelf to add strength and to create a lip in back so display items don't fall between the bookcase and the sofa. The front rail fits up against the bottom of the shelf, flush with the front edge. The rear rail fits on the top of the shelf, flush with the back edge.

1. Cut the shelf (B) and shelf rails (C) to length.

2. Drill rows of 3/32" pilot holes for #6 × 1¼" wood screws, 3/8" in from the front and back edges of the shelf, for attaching the rails. Locate the pilot holes at 8" intervals. Using a counterbore bit, counterbore each hole ¼" deep to accept a 3/8"-dia. wood plug. Make sure to drill the rows of counterbores on opposite faces of the shelf.

3. Apply glue to the top edge of one rail, and clamp it to the shelf, making sure the front of the rail is flush with the edge of the shelf. Drive 1¼" wood screws through the counterbored pilot holes to secure the rail. Then, attach the other rail to the opposite face of the shelf.

4. Attach the shelf and rails to the legs, use a combination square to mark reference lines across one face of each leg, 16" up from the bottom. Drill pilot holes 3/8" down from the guidelines and counterbore the holes.

5. Apply glue to the ends of the shelf and rails, and position them between the legs so the top of the shelf is flush with the reference lines. Drive 2" screws through the legs and into the shelf ends **(photo B).**

ATTACH THE STRETCHERS.

Three stretchers fit between the legs at the bottom and top to

Use 1½" corner braces and ½" wood screws to attach the top to the stretchers and the insides of the legs.

add stability. The top stretchers anchor the top.

1. Cut the stretchers (D) to length and sand them smooth.

2. Center one stretcher 6" up from the bottoms of the legs. Drill pilot holes through the legs and into the ends of the stretcher. Counterbore the holes. Attach the stretcher with glue and 2" wood screws.

3. Attach the remaining two stretchers at the tops of the legs, flush with the front, top and back edges.

ATTACH THE TOP.

Attach the top to the leg assembly with 1½" brass corner braces. Once the top is fastened, cut the molding to fit, and attach it to the top stretchers and legs to complete the bookshelf.

1. Cut the top (E) to length. Sand the top with medium-grit sandpaper to smooth out all of the edges.

2. Turn the leg assembly upside down, and position it on the underside of the top. Center the legs to create a 1" overhang on all sides. Clamp the legs to the top. Use #8 × ½" wood screws and corner braces to secure the top to the legs and stretchers **(photo C).** Use four braces per side and one on each end.

INSTALL THE TRIM.

1. Cut a piece of 2½" casing molding to about 64" in length to use for one face trim (F) piece.

2. Place the molding against a top stringer and mark the ends of the bookcase onto the molding. Make 45° miter cuts away from the marks. Tack the piece in place with a 1¼" brad. Mark and cut the other long trim piece the same way, and tack it in place.

3. Use the face trim pieces as references for cutting the end trim (G) pieces to fit.

4. Remove the trim pieces, then refasten them with glue, and drive 1¼" brads at regular intervals **(photo D).**

5. Drive two brads through each joint to lock-nail the mating trim pieces together. Set all nails with a nail set.

APPLY FINISHING TOUCHES.

1. Glue ⅜"-dia. wood plugs into all screw holes, and sand them flush with the surface.

2. Fill all nail holes with wood putty and finish-sand the bookcase with 180- or 220-grit sandpaper.

3. Apply the finish of your choice. We used mahogany-tone stain and two coats of polyurethane.

Wrap the bookcase with trim pieces made from 2½" casing molding.

PROJECT
POWER TOOLS

Mantel

Deceptively simple to build, this elegant mantel mimics the look of hardwood at a fraction of the cost.

Construction Materials

Quantity	Lumber
1	1 × 8" × 6' poplar
1	2 × 4" × 4' poplar
1	2 × 2" × 6' poplar
1	¾ × 3¾" × 5' crown molding
1	½ × ⅝" × 5' dentil molding

This mantel will receive high praise from friends and relatives. With its wide shelf and 4' length, the mantel is a great place to display family photographs or prized possessions. It is also an excellent starting point for holiday or seasonal decorating.

Though the mantel appears to be a solid piece of milled hardwood, its looks are deceiving. Stock moldings, miter cuts and lock-nailing hide a simple support framework, and an antique white paint finish disguises the mantel's use of inexpensive poplar lumber.

Don't skip this project just because you don't have a fireplace—this mantel makes a wonderful display shelf anywhere in your home.

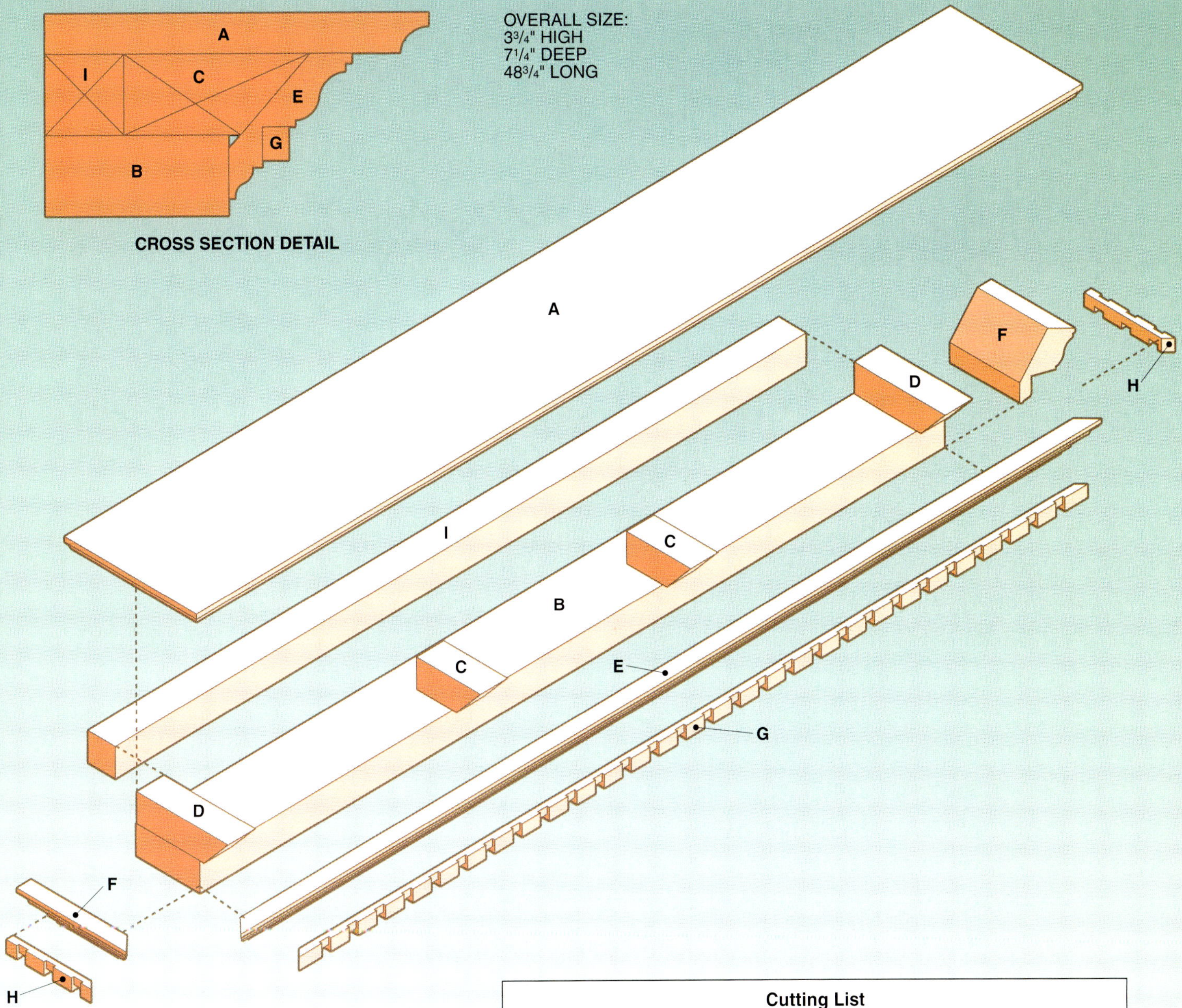

Key	Part	Dimension	Pcs.	Material
A	Top	¾ × 7¼ × 48¾"	1	Poplar
B	Bottom	1½ × 3½ × 41"	1	Poplar
C	Center support	1½ × 1½ × 3½"	2	Poplar
D	End support	1½ × 1½ × 5"	2	Poplar
E	Front crown	¾ × 3¾ × 46¼"	1	Crown molding
F	Side crown	¾ × 3¾ × 6"	2	Crown molding
G	Front dentil	½ × ⅝ × 43½"	1	Dentil molding
H	Side dentil	½ × ⅝ × 4⅝"	2	Dentil molding
I	Ledger	1½ × 1½ × 39"	1	Poplar

Materials: Wood glue, wood screws (#8 × 2¼", #6 × 1½"), 3½" wallboard screws, finish nails (2d, 4d), ⅜" wood plugs, finishing materials.

Note: Measurements reflect the actual thickness of dimension lumber.

Use a combination square to mark the location of the center supports on the ledger, then attach with glue and screws.

Attach the front crown and side crown to the bottom and supports with glue and 4d finish nails.

Directions: Mantel

CUT AND ASSEMBLE THE BOTTOM AND SUPPORTS.

1. Cut the bottom (B), center supports (C) and end supports (D) to size.

2. Miter one end of each support at 45°.

3. Mark 13" and 14½" in from each end on the bottom, and use your combination square to draw a line at each mark. Position the center supports along the reference lines, drill countersunk pilot holes, and fasten with glue and 2¼" screws **(photo A).**

4. Position the end supports (see *Diagram*), drill countersunk pilot holes, and attach with glue and 2¼" wood screws.

5. Cut the ledger (I) to length, and test-fit it between the end supports so the back edges of the ledger and bottom are flush.

TIP

We chose inexpensive poplar for our primary building material. If a more natural look is desired, you can also build the mantel from oak and finish it with stain.

ATTACH THE CROWN MOLDING.

1. Cut the front crown (E) and side crown (F) to size. Miter the ends at 45° by positioning the molding upside down in a power miter box, with one flat lip against the base of the saw, and the other lip against the saw fence.

2. Position the front crown so the top edge is flush with the top edge of the supports and the lower edge rests against the edge of the bottom. Drill pilot holes and attach the front crown to the supports and the bottom with wood glue and 4d finish nails **(photo B).**

3. Attach the side crowns in the same way, and lock-nail the crown molding joints with 2d finish nails (see *Tip*, page 150). Set all the nail heads.

ATTACH THE TOP.

1. Cut the top (A) to size and sand smooth with medium-grit sandpaper.

2. Use a router with a ⅜" roundover bit set for a ⅛" shoulder to shape the ends and front edge (first test the cut on a piece of scrap wood).

3. Place the top facedown on

For placement of drill holes, measure and mark the location of the supports on the top.

Keep the mitered joints tight when attaching the dentil molding.

your worksurface, and mark the positions of the supports on the underside **(photo C).**

4. Drill pilot holes and attach the top to the supports with glue and 4d finish nails. Set all nail heads.

ATTACH THE DENTIL MOLDING.

1. Cut the front dentil (G) and side dentil (H) to size, mitering the mating ends at 45° angles. Be sure to cut through the thicker "tooth" portion of each molding piece to ensure that the repeat pattern will match at the corners.

2. Position the front dentil molding and side dentil molding on the crown molding (see *Diagram*). Drill pilot holes and attach with glue and 4d finish nails, keeping the mitered joints tight **(photo D).** Lock-nail the joints with 2d finish nails, and set the nail heads.

MOUNT THE MANTEL.

When completed, the mantel is attached to the ledger. Anchor the ledger to the wall and test-hang the mantel before finishing it.

1. Position the ledger on the wall, checking for level. Drill pilot holes and attach the ledger to the wall with 3½" wallboard screws driven into studs.

2. Fit the mantel over the ledger and drill counterbored pilot holes through the top into the ledger.

APPLY FINISHING TOUCHES.

1. Remove the mantel from the wall and apply putty to all nail holes. Scrape off any excess glue.

2. Finish-sand the mantel, apply the finish, and allow to dry. We chose a glossy antique white paint.

3. Position the mantel over the ledger and mount it with 1½" screws driven into the counterbored holes. Insert glued plugs into the holes, sand, and touch up the finish.

TIP

The mantel can be shortened or lengthened to meet your needs. To resize, simply adjust the sizes of the top, bottom, moldings and ledger accordingly.

PROJECT
POWER TOOLS

Knickknack Shelf

Add some country charm to your home with this rustic pine knickknack shelf.

CONSTRUCTION MATERIALS

Quantity	**Lumber**
1	1 × 4" × 8' pine
2	1 × 8" × 6' pine
1	1 × 10" × 4' pine
9	¼ × 3½" × 3' beaded pine paneling
1	¾ × ¾" × 6' cove molding

Country-style furniture is becoming increasingly popular throughout the world because of its honest appearance and back-to-basics preference for function over ornate styling. In interior design catalogs, you may find many country shelving projects that are similar to this one in design and function. But our knickknack shelf can be built for a tiny fraction of the prices charged for its catalog cousins.

From the beaded pine paneling to the matching arcs on the apron and ledger, this knickknack shelf is well designed throughout. The shelf shown above has a natural wood finish, but it is also suitable for decorative painting techniques, like milkwash or farmhouse finishes.

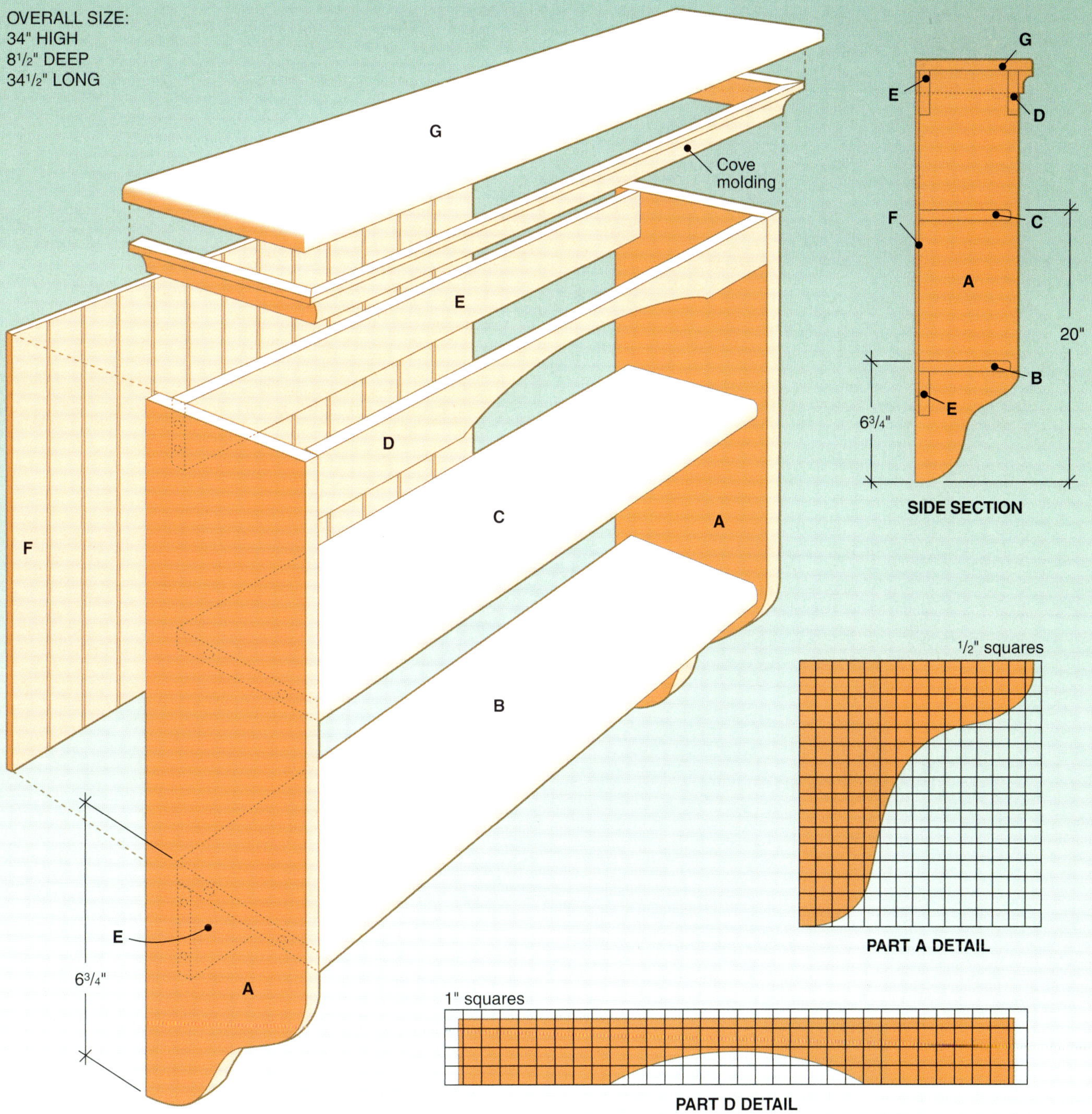

SIDE SECTION

PART A DETAIL

PART D DETAIL

Cutting List

Key	Part	Dimension	Pcs.	Material
A	Shelf side	¾ × 7¼ × 33¼"	2	Pine
B	Bottom shelf	¾ × 6¾ × 30½"	1	Pine
C	Middle shelf	¾ × 6¾ × 30½"	1	Pine
D	Apron	¾ × 3½ × 30½"	1	Pine

Cutting List

Key	Part	Dimension	Pcs.	Material
E	Ledger	¾ × 3½ × 30½"	2	Pine
F	Back panel	¼ × 3½ × 28"	9	Pine paneling
G	Cap	¾ × 8½ × 34½"	1	Pine

Materials: Wood glue, #8 × 1½" wood screws, 3d and 6d finish nails, mushroom-style button plugs, finishing materials.

Note: Measurements reflect the actual thickness of dimension lumber.

Smooth out the jig saw cuts on the apron and ledger with a drill and drum sander.

Clamp the sides and ledgers in position, then fasten with glue and screws.

Directions: Knickknack Shelf

MAKE THE FRAME COMPONENTS.

1. Cut the sides (A) to length from 1 × 8 pine.

2. Transfer the side pattern to one side (see *Diagram*). Cut out the shape and smooth the cut with a drum sander attached to your drill. Trace the finished profile onto the other side, and make the cutout.

3. Cut the apron (D) and the ledgers (E) to length from 1 × 4 pine. Transfer the apron pattern to the apron and one of the ledgers and cut with a jig saw. (see *Diagram*).

4. Smooth out any irregularities with a drum sander or belt sander **(photo A).**

ASSEMBLE THE FRAME.

1. Stand the sides on their back edges and place the upper ledger between them, with the top edges flush. Use back panel pieces as spacers under the ledger to create a recess for the back panel. Clamp the sides and ledger together with a pipe or bar clamp.

2. Insert the lower ledger with its top edge 6" up from the bottoms of the sides, also resting on spacers.

3. Clamp in place, and drill two counterbored pilot holes through the sides into the ends of the ledgers.

4. Attach the sides to the ledgers with glue and wood screws **(photo B).**

INSTALL THE BACK PANEL AND APRON.

To make the back panel (F), we used tongue-and-groove pieces of pine wainscoting paneling.

1. Attach the back panel to the backs of the ledgers, using 3d finish nails, but no glue **(photo C).** The top of the back panel

TIP

Beaded pine paneling is easy to find in a variety of styles. One of the more economical ways to purchase it is in prepackaged cartons, usually containing 10 square feet of ¼"-thick tongue-and-groove pine with face grooves that are 4" apart.

Fasten the tongue-and-groove beaded pine panel pieces to the ledgers with 3d finish nails.

should be flush with the tops of the sides.

2. Fasten the apron across the top front of the sides with wood glue and 6d finish nails. Be sure to keep the top edge of the apron flush with the tops of the sides.

BUILD AND INSTALL THE SHELVES.

1. Cut the bottom shelf (B) and middle shelf (C) to size from 1 × 8 pine.

2. Use a router with a ⅜" piloted roundover bit to round over the top and bottom edges on the fronts of the shelves **(photo D).**

3. Clamp the bottom shelf in place on top of the lower ledger, keeping the back edges flush. Drill counterbored pilot holes, and attach the shelf to the sides with glue and wood screws.

4. Install the middle shelf using the same procedure **(photo E).**

ATTACH THE CAP AND COVE.

1. Cut the cap (G) to size from 1 × 10 pine.

2. Use a router with a ⅜" roundover bit to shape the top and bottom edges of the ends and front.

3. Place a bead of glue along the top edges of the sides, apron and ledgers. Position the cap on top of the shelf assembly, overlapping 1¼" on each end and at the front.

4. Drill pilot holes to prevent splitting, and nail the cap in place with 6d finish nails.

5. Cut the pine cove molding to the appropriate lengths with mitered corners, and attach just below the bottom of the cap (see *Diagram*). Fasten in place with glue and 3d finish nails **(photo F).**

APPLY FINISHING TOUCHES.

1. Drill counterbored pilot holes in the upper ledger for mounting screws. If the mounting screws won't be going into wall studs, use hollow wall anchors.

2. Scrape off any excess glue, then finish-sand.

3. Install mushroom-style button plugs in all counterbores.

4. Apply the finish. We chose to finish our knickknack shelf with light oak stain and a satin-gloss polyurethane topcoat. You can stain the button plugs a contrasting color before inserting them into the counterbore holes.

Use a router with a ⅜" piloted roundover bit to shape the front edges of the shelves.

Drill counterbored pilot holes for the shelves, then attach with glue and 1½" wood screws.

Attach the cove molding with glue and 3d finish nails. Hold the nails with needlenose pliers when nailing in hard-to-reach areas.

PROJECT
POWER TOOLS

Folding Table

Sturdy, spacious and portable, this indoor/outdoor table folds up to be stored.

Construction Materials

Quantity	Lumber
5	2 × 4" × 8' pine
6	1 × 6" × 8' pine
3	1 × 4" × 8' pine

Bigger and better than a card table, this efficient folding table can provide additional seating at a moment's notice when company arrives. With more than 15 square feet of table surface, it is roomy enough for six adult diners. When folded up for storage, it shrinks to a diminutive 3 × 3' package that is less than 12" thick—small enough to fit into just about any closet.

If you live in a house or apartment where outdoor security is an issue, this folding table can be opened on your patio or balcony, then taken inside when you are finished. If you plan to use the table outdoors, be sure to use exterior-rated paint.

OVERALL SIZE:
29¼" HIGH
36" DEEP
63¼" LONG

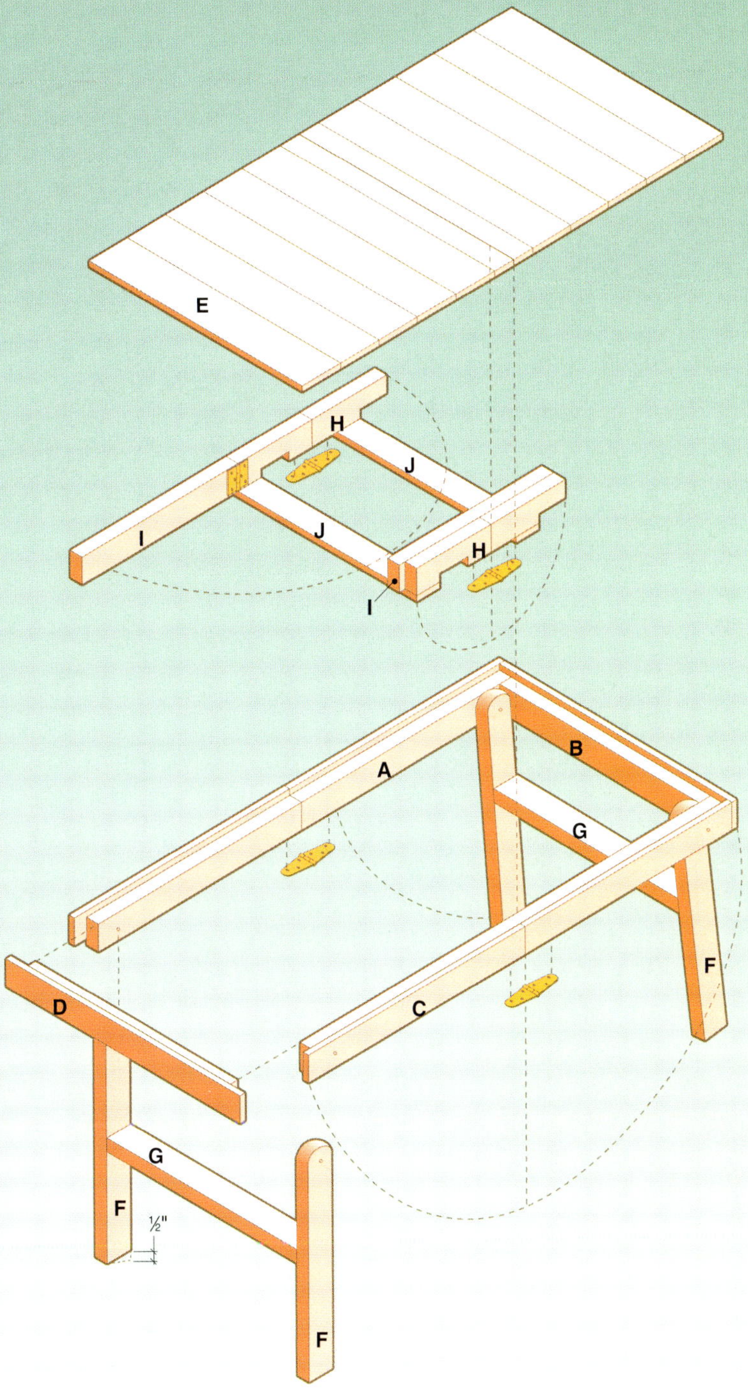

Cutting List

Key	Part	Dimension	Pcs.	Material
A	Side rail	1½ × 3½ × 62"	2	Pine
B	End rail	1½ × 3½ × 31½"	2	Pine
C	Side skirt	¾ × 3½ × 63½"	2	Pine
D	End skirt	¾ × 3½ × 34½"	2	Pine
E	Slats	¾ × 5½ × 34½"	11	Pine

Cutting List

Key	Part	Dimension	Pcs.	Material
F	Legs	1½ × 3½ × 28½"	4	Pine
G	Stretcher	1½ × 3½ × 28⅜"	2	Pine
H	Cleat	1½ × 3½ × 22"	2	Pine
I	Sweep	1½ × 3½ × 23"	2	Pine
J	Guide	¾ × 3½ × 28"	2	Pine

Materials: Wood glue, deck screws (1¼", 2", 2½"), 1½ × 6"-long strap hinges (4), 2 × 2" brass butt hinges (2), ⅜ × 4½" carriage bolts with lock nuts (4), 1"-dia. washers (8), finishing materials.

Note: Measurements reflect the actual size of dimension lumber.

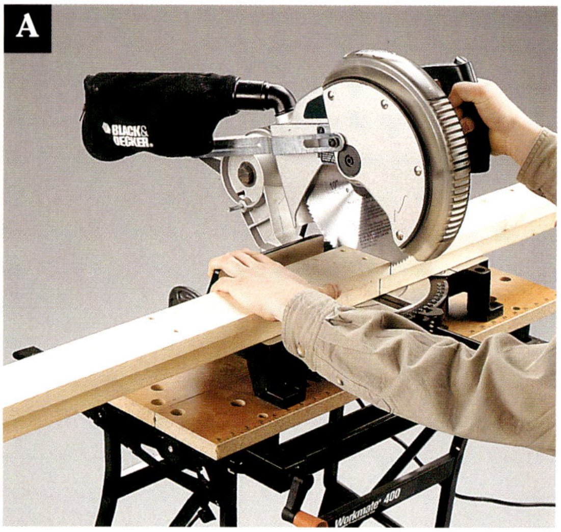

After attaching the side rails and side skirts, crosscut them in half.

The middle slat is rip-cut in half and attached on each side of the hinged joint between the sides of the tabletop frame.

Attach the guides to the cleats, flush with the edges of the notches.

Directions: Folding Table

MAKE THE SIDE SECTIONS.
Countersink all screws when assembling this table.

1. Cut the side rails (A), end rails (B), side skirts (C) and end skirts (D) to size.

2. Position a side skirt against each side rail. Make sure the side skirts overhang the side rails by ¾" on one long edge. This ¾"-wide overhang will face the top on the completed table, creating a lip for the slats (E) to sit on. Center the side skirts on the side rails so ¾" of the side skirts extends beyond the side rails at each end.

3. Clamp the side skirts to the side rails, and attach the parts with 1¼" deck screws. Leave the middles of the side skirts and side rails free of screws so they can be cut in half.

4. Draw reference lines across the center of the side skirts. Cut along the reference lines with a power miter saw, cutting the boards into two equal lengths **(photo A).** Connect the halves with 6" strap hinges, attached to the bottom edges of the side rail halves. Unscrew the parts and hinges before proceeding.

ATTACH THE END SECTIONS.

1. Cut the end rails (B) and end skirts (D) to size.

2. Position the end rails between the side rails, flush with the side rail ends. Apply glue, and drive 2½" deck screws through the side rail faces and into the end rails.

3. Position an end skirt against each end rail. Leave a ¾"-wide gap from the tops of the end skirts to the tops of the end rails to create a lip for the slats to sit on. With the ends of the end skirts flush with the side rails, drive 2½" deck screws through the end skirts and into the side rails and end rails. Reattach the side skirts with glue and wood screws, and reattach the strap hinges in their former positions.

ATTACH THE SLATS.

1. Cut the slats (E) to size.

2. Rip-cut one slat in half, using a circular saw and a straightedge guide. This divided slat will fit in the middle of the tabletop. Position one half of the ripped slat on each side of the cut at the center of the side rails. Butt the divided slat pieces together at the center so no gap is apparent. Attach each half to the side rails, using glue and 2" deck screws **(photo B).**

3. Position the other slats across the tabletop frame, spaced evenly, and attach them with 2" deck screws.

4. Drill ⅜"-dia. holes for carriage bolts through each end of the side skirts and side rails. Center the holes 4¼" in from

Drive deck screws through the slats and into the cleats below.

Fit the legs into place and attach them with carriage bolts, washers and lock nuts.

the ends of the side skirts and 1¾" up from the bottoms of the side rails. The holes will be used to attach the legs.

MAKE THE LEGS.

1. Cut the legs (F) and stretchers (G) to size.

2. Mark a point along one wide face of each leg, ½" in from the end. Draw a reference line from that point to the opposite corner on each leg. Cut along the reference lines with a circular saw. These slanted ends will be the bottoms of the legs.

3. Use a compass to draw a centered, 1¾"-radius semicircle at the other end of each leg. Mark the center of the semicircle where the point of the compass was in contact with the workpiece. Drill a ⅜"-dia. hole for a carriage bolt through the centerpoint. Use a jig saw to cut the rounded leg tops. Sand the legs smooth.

4. Use a combination square to draw a reference line across one face of each leg, 14" down from the top.

5. Position the legs in pairs on your worksurface. Slide a stretcher between each leg pair with their top faces on the reference lines. Drill pilot holes, and attach the stretchers between the legs with glue and 2½" deck screws.

MAKE THE CLEATS.

1. Cut the cleats (H) to size. The cleats are notched on one long edge to allow the table to fold in half. Each notch is 1"deep × 3½" wide.

2. Draw reference lines across one edge of each cleat, 3½", 7¼" and 18½" from one end. Use a pencil to shade from the 3½" line to the 7¼" line, and from the 18½" line to the ends of the cleats. These shaded areas mark the notches.

3. Cut the notches with a jig saw, then cut each cleat in half. Attach the cleat halves with strap hinges, positioned across the centerline.

ATTACH THE SWEEPS & GUIDES.

1. Cut the sweeps (I) and guides (J) to size.

2. Position the guides on the cleats, flush with the edges of the notches. Attach the guides to the cleats with glue and 2" deck screws **(photo C).**

3. Turn the tabletop upside down, and position the cleats and guides inside the tabletop so their hinged centers align. Center the cleats between the side rails.

4. Trace the cleat outline onto the table slats with a pencil. Remove the cleats, and drill pilot holes through the slats in the tabletop. Reposition the cleats and guides. Fasten them to the bottom of the table with glue and 2" deck screws **(photo D).**

5. Attach a 3" brass butt hinge to one end of each sweep, then attach the hinge to one end of each cleat. Make sure the sweeps are attached at opposite ends of the cleats (see *Diagram*).

APPLY FINISHING TOUCHES.

1. Fasten the legs inside the tabletop, using carriage bolts, washers and lock nuts **(photo E).**

2. Remove the hardware and fill all countersunk screw holes with wood putty. Sand the surfaces with medium sandpaper, and apply primer and paint.

3. Reattach the legs.

Corner Display Stand

This light and airy unit brings hardworking display shelving to any corner of your house.

PROJECT POWER TOOLS

The open back on this corner display stand lets you add a lot of display space to any room, without adding a lot of weight to the decor. Its roomy shelves are perfect for flower vases, fine china, souvenirs, picture frames and other knickknacks and collectibles.

Much more than a practical space-saver, the gentle arches on the front and the slatted back design of this corner display stand blend into just about any decorating style. Because it's such a simple design, it doesn't draw attention away from the items on display.

This corner display stand is also very inexpensive to build. A single sheet of plywood is more than enough to make the triangular shelves, and the shelf rails and standards are made from 1 × 4 pine. The decorative trim pieces on the edges of the shelves are cut from ordinary ¾" cove molding. These materials, together with the painted finish, give the display stand a contemporary style. You might want to try a distressed antique finish to give the stand a vintage look, or, if you're looking for furnishings with a more formal appearance, substitute oak boards and plywood, then apply a warm-toned wood stain.

Construction Materials

Quantity	Lumber
7	1 × 4" × 8' pine
1	¾" × 4' × 8' plywood
1	¾ × ¾" × 6' cove molding

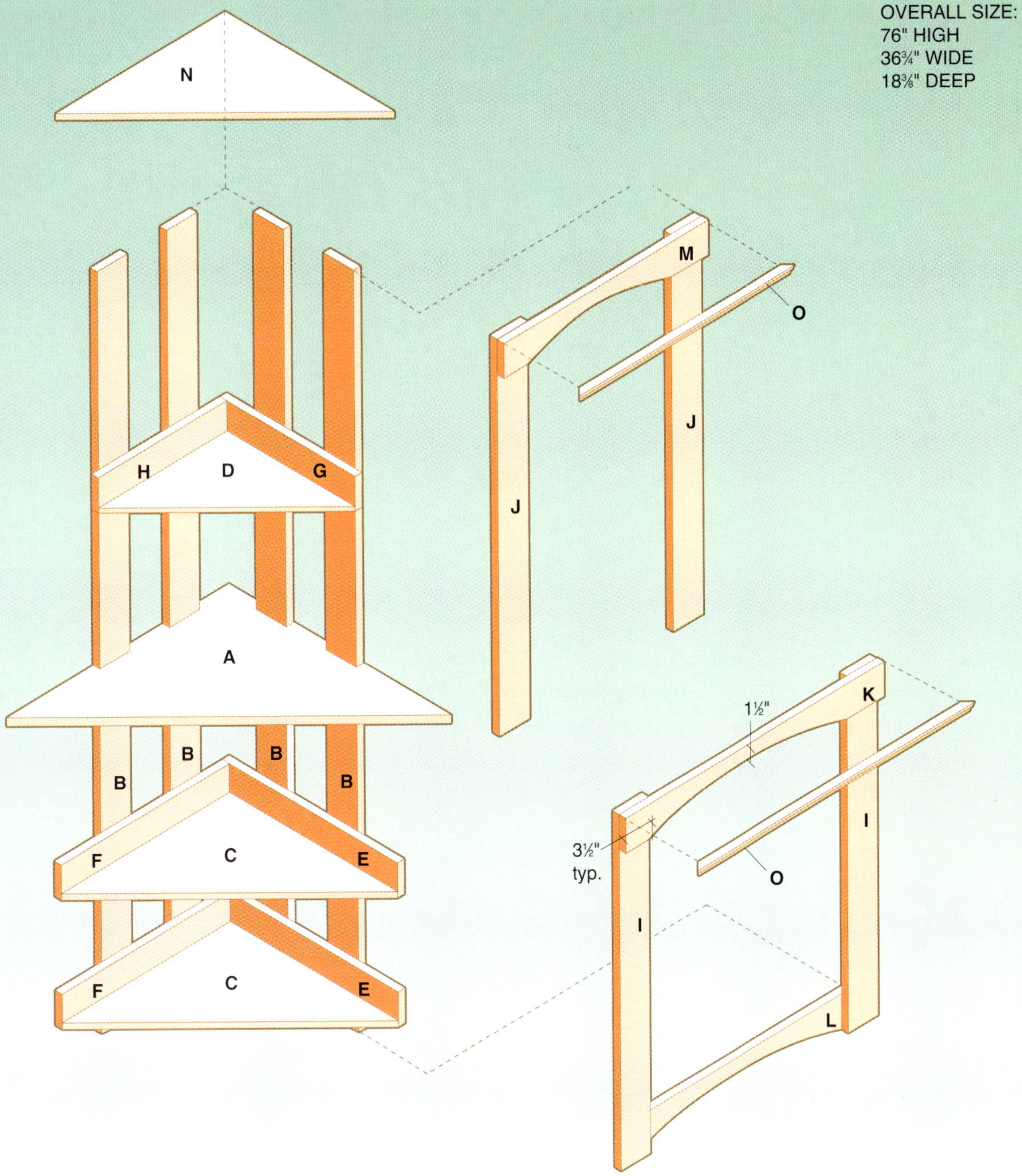

Key	Part	Dimension	Pcs.	Material
A	Center shelf	¾ × 26 × 26"	1	Plywood
B	Standard	¾ × 3½ × 75¼"	4	Pine
C	Bottom shelf	¾ × 19½ × 19½"	2	Plywood
D	Top shelf	¾ × 15 × 15"	1	Plywood
E	Bottom rail	¾ × 3½ × 20¼"	2	Pine
F	Bottom rail	¾ × 3½ × 19½"	2	Pine
G	Top rail	¾ × 3½ × 15¾"	1	Pine
H	Top rail	¾ × 3½ × 15"	1	Pine

Cutting List

Key	Part	Dimension	Pcs.	Material
I	Lower stile	¾ × 3½ × 35¼"	2	Pine
J	Upper stile	¾ × 3½ × 39¼"	2	Pine
K	Middle front rail	¾ × 3½ × 32"	1	Pine
L	Lower front rail	¾ × 3½ × 30¼"	1	Pine
M	Upper front rail	¾ × 3½ × 25¼"	1	Pine
N	Top	¾ × 21¼ × 21¼"	1	Plywood
O	Trim	¾ × ¾ × *	2	Cove molding

Materials: Wood glue, wood screws (#6 × 1½", #6 × 2"), 1¼" brads, finishing materials.

Note: Measurements reflect the actual size of dimension lumber. *Cut to fit.

Use a jig saw to cut notches for the standards in the back edges of the center shelf.

Drive screws through the standards and into the shelf rails.

Directions: Corner Display Stand

MAKE THE SHELVES.

1. Make the center shelf (A), using a circular saw and a straightedge guide to cut a 26⅛" plywood square in half diagonally.

2. Use a square to lay out ¾ × 3½"-long notches for the standards on the shelf sides, starting 4" and 12¼" in from each 90° corner, on each side. Cut the notches with a jig saw **(photo A).**

3. Cut a 19⅝"-square plywood piece in half diagonally to make the bottom shelves. Cut the top shelf (D) to size.

4. Sand the shelves to remove any rough spots.

5. Cut the bottom rails (E, F) and the top rails (G, H) to length from 1 × 4 pine.

6. Attach one longer rail (E) and one shorter rail (F) to the back edges of each bottom shelf so they make a butt joint and are flush with the ends of the shelf. Use glue and #6 × 2" wood screws. Countersink all the screw pilot holes. Attach a longer top rail (G) and shorter top rail (H) to the back edges of the top shelf, so the bottoms are flush.

Use a flexible marking guide to draw the arches in the front rails.

Assemble the arched front rails and the stiles into face frames.

ATTACH THE STANDARDS.

1. Cut the standards (B) to length.

2. Sand the standards, and clamp them together with their tops and bottoms flush. Draw reference lines across the standards 3½", 16", 35¼" and 52" from one end. Draw reference

lines on the shelf rails, 3¼" and 11½" on each side of the corner to mark the positions of the inside edges of the standards.
3. Clamp the shelves to the standards so the reference lines are aligned, then attach the standards to the shelves with glue and #6 × 2" wood screws, driven through pilot holes in the backs of the standards and into the shelves **(photo B).** Note that the center shelf should be installed so the notches fit over the standards.

BUILD THE FACE FRAMES.
1. Cut the lower stiles (I), upper stiles (J), lower front rails (K, L) and upper front rail (M) to length.
2. Mark the top and bottom arches using a thin, flexible piece of metal, plastic or wood as a marking guide. Find the center lengthwise of each rail. Mark a point 13" in from the center in both directions. Tack a 1¼" brad at these points, as close to the edge as possible. Tack a brad at the center of each workpiece, 2" up from the same edge. Hook the marking guide over the middle brad, and flex each end of the guide to the marked points. Trace the curve on each rail **(photo C),** and cut the curves with a jig saw.
3. Position the shorter of the two lower front rails (L) across the inside face of the lower stiles, with the arc pointing down. The edge of the rail containing the arc should be flush with the ends of the stiles, and the rail should be ⅞" in from the outside edges of each stile (see *Diagram*). This is the bottom of the face frame. Clamp the rail to the stiles.
4. Clamp the longer of the lower front rails (K) to the outside top face of the stiles, with the straight edge flush with the tops. The ends of the rail should be flush with the edges of the stile. Attach the rails to the lower stiles with four #6 × 1¼" screws driven at each joint **(photo D).**

ATTACH THE FACE FRAMES AND TOP.
1. Turn the stand upright, slip the lower face frame in position. The bottom rail should fit beneath the lowest shelf and the top rail should fit beneath the center shelf. Center the face frame from side to side so the overhang is equal.
2. Clamp the face frame to the stand, then attach it with #6 × 2" wood screws driven through the stiles and into the edges of the shelves, and also driven into the top of each rail through the shelf above it **(photo E).**
3. Position the upper face frame so the bottoms of the stiles rest on the center shelf, and the stiles overhang the ends of the top shelf by equal amounts. Tack the face frame in place by driving one #6 × 2" wood screw through each stile and into the front edge of the top shelf.
4. Drive screws up through the underside of the center shelf and into the bottom ends of the stiles **(photo F).**

APPLY FINISHING TOUCHES.
1. Cut the top (N) to size, and attach it to the tops of the standards and the top rail of the upper face frame with glue and screws. The back sides of the top should be flush with the outside faces of the standards.
2. Cut strips of ¾" cove molding (O) to fit along the front edges of the center shelf and top shelf, with the ends miter-cut to follow the line of each shelf. Attach the trim pieces with 1¼" brads driven into pilot holes.
3. Set all nail heads, then cover the nail and screw heads with wood putty.
4. Sand the entire piece, and paint it with primer and two coats of enamel paint.

Drive screws through the center shelf and into the face frame.

Drive wood screws up through the center shelf to secure the upper stiles.

PROJECT
POWER TOOLS

Collector's Table

Store your fine collectibles in this eye-catching conversation piece.

Construction Materials

Quantity	Lumber
1	½" × 4 × 4' oak plywood
1	½" × 4 × 8' oak plywood
1	⅜" × 2 × 2' oak plywood
2	1 × 2" × 6' oak
4	1 × 3" × 8' oak
2	1 × 4" × 6' oak
1	2 × 2" × 6' oak
3	½ × ½ × 30" scrap wood
1	¼ × 18¾ × 34¾" tempered glass

This beautiful, glass-topped collector's table is perfect for storing and displaying shells, rocks, fossils, figurines or other collectibles. It has three interchangeable drawers, so you can change the display whenever you choose—simply by rotating a different drawer into the top position under the glass. Built from oak and oak plywood, this table gives you the opportunity to demonstrate your woodworking skills and display your collections.

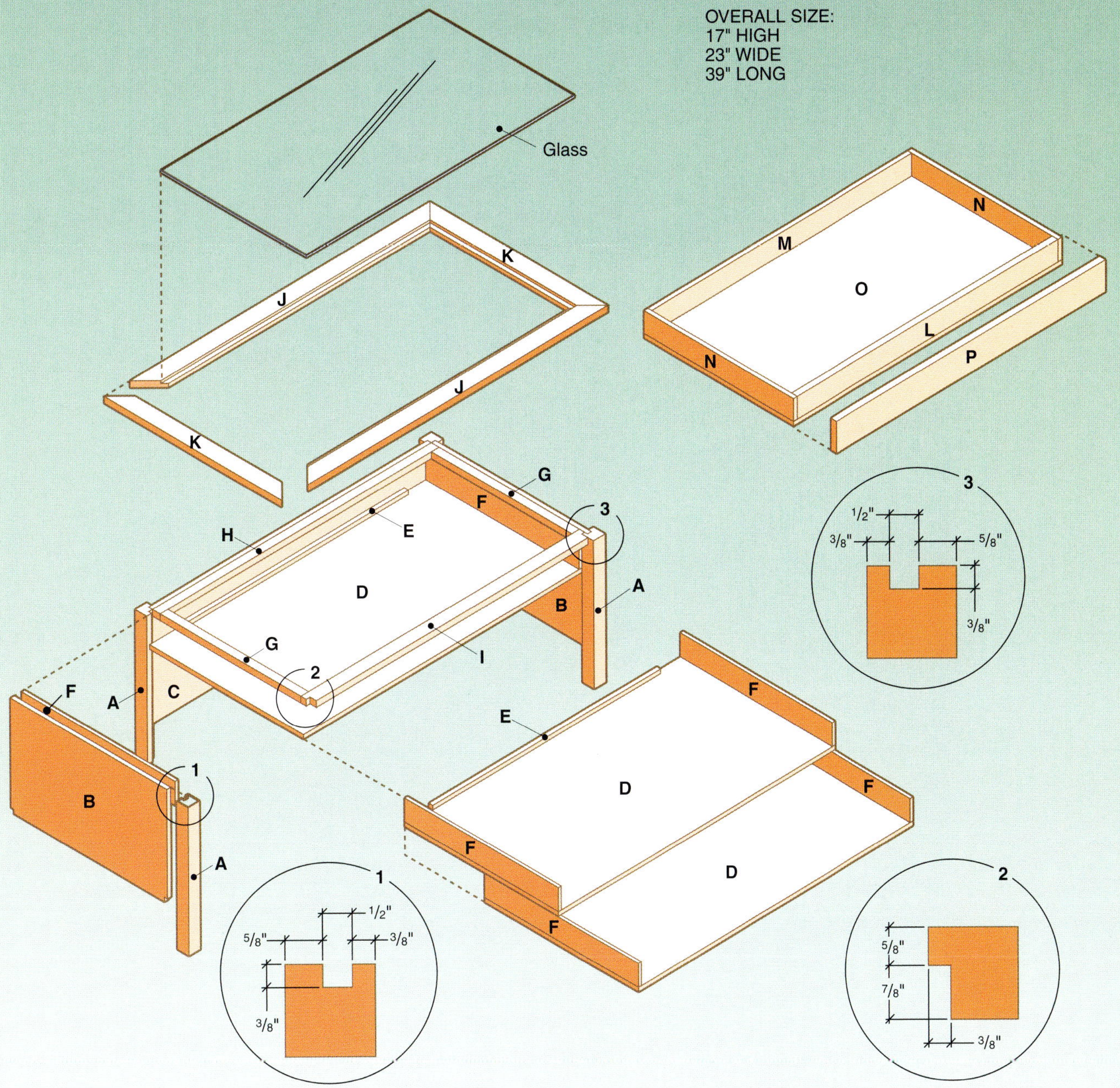

Cutting List

Key	Part	Dimension	Pcs.	Material
A	Leg	1½ × 1½ × 16¼"	4	Oak
B	End panel	½ × 20¼ × 12½"	2	Oak ply.
C	Back panel	½ × 36¼ × 12½"	1	Oak ply.
D	Shelf	½ × 19⅞ × 36¼"	3	Oak ply.
E	Drawer stop	½ × ½ × 30"	3	Scrap wood
F	Drawer guide	⅜ × 3⅛ × 19⅞"	6	Oak ply.
G	End cleat	¾ × 1 × 18¼"	2	Oak
H	Back cleat	¾ × 1 × 36¼"	1	Oak

Cutting List

Key	Part	Dimension	Pcs.	Material
I	Top rail	¾ × 1½ × 36¼"	1	Oak
J	Frame, long side	¾ × 2½ × 39"	2	Oak
K	Frame, short side	¾ × 2½ × 23"	2	Oak
L	Drawer box front	¾ × 2½ × 34¼"	3	Oak
M	Drawer box back	½ × 2½ × 34¼"	3	Oak ply.
N	Drawer box side	½ × 2½ × 19½"	6	Oak ply.
O	Drawer bottom	½ × 19½ × 35¼"	3	Plywood
P	Drawer face	¾ × 3½ × 35¼"	3	Oak

Materials: Wood glue, wood screws (1", 1¼"), ⅝" brads, 4d finish nails, finishing materials.

Note: Measurements reflect the actual thickness of dimension lumber.

Directions: Collector's Table

CUT THE LEGS.

It is important to distinguish between the left and right legs when building this table. Each pair of front and back legs has a stopped dado to hold the end panel in place. The back legs also have a second stopped dado to support the back panel (see *Detail*). We recommend that you use a router table to make these cuts.

1. Cut the legs (A) to length.

2. Measure and mark 12"-long dadoes on the legs. On the front legs, cut the dadoes on one face, using a ½" straight bit set to ⅜" depth. On the back legs, cut dadoes on two adjacent faces **(photo A).**

3. Remove the waste section between the back leg dadoes with a saw, and square off the dado ends, using a ½" chisel.

CUT THE PANELS AND ATTACH THE LEGS.

1. Cut the end panels (B) and back panel (C) to size.

2. Cut a ⅜ × ½" notch (see *Detail*) into the bottom corner of each panel, using a jig saw **(photo B).**

3. Attach a pair of legs to each end panel, using glue and brads. Set the back panel aside until later.

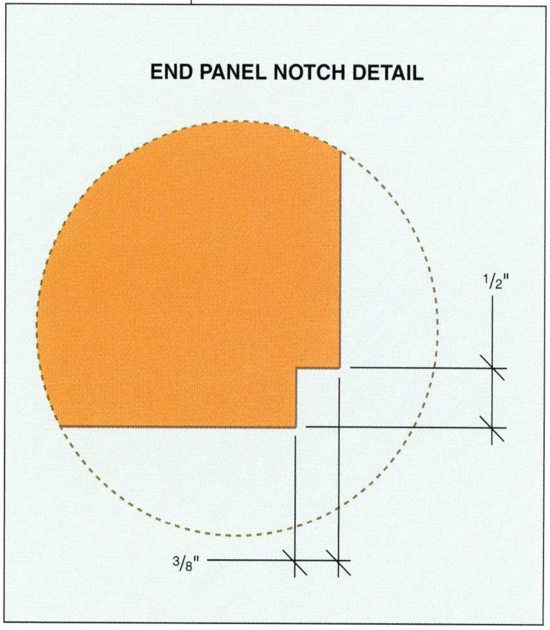

Cut ½ × ⅜"-deep stopped dadoes in the legs, using a router table. Note the waste pieces on the back legs, which you will need to remove with a handsaw and chisel.

Cut a ⅜ × ½" notch out of the bottom corners of the back and side panels where they will overhang the dadoes in the legs.

CUT THE SHELVES, DRAWER STOPS AND DRAWER GUIDES.

Because the drawer stops are hidden, they can be built from any scrap ½" lumber.

1. Cut shelves (D), drawer

Drill pilot holes and attach the bottom drawer guides to the end panel sides, using wood glue and ⅝" brads.

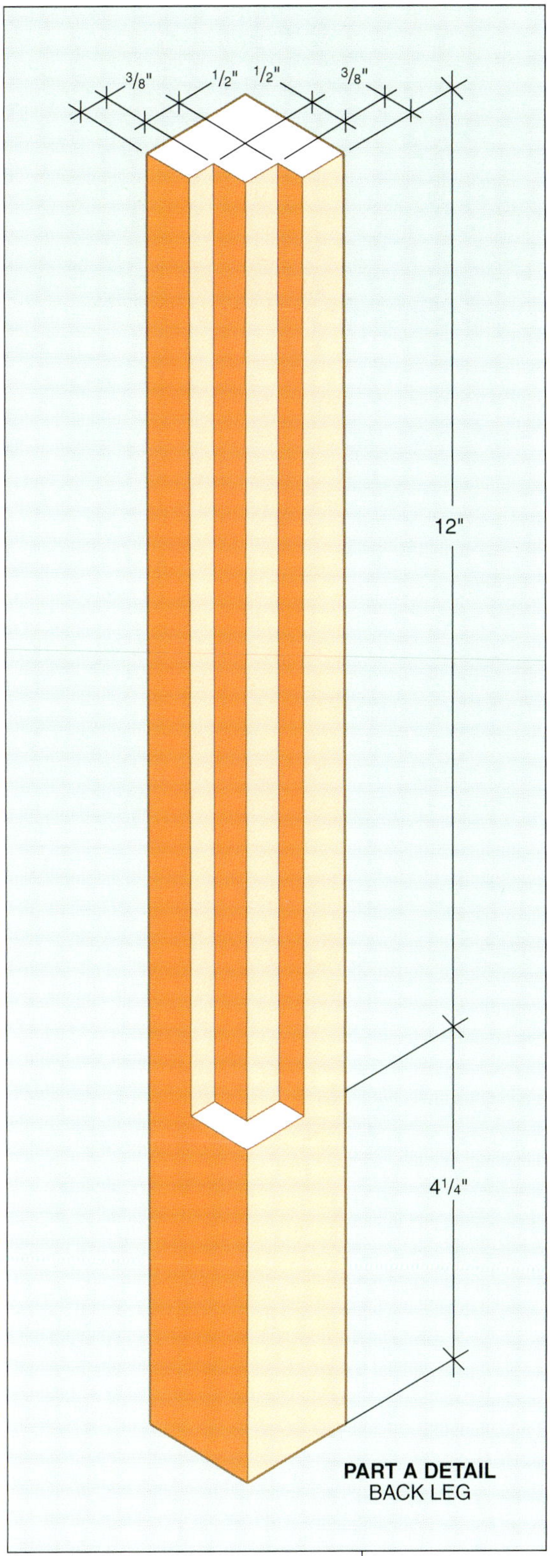

1. Cut shelves (D), drawer stops (E) and drawer guides (F) to size.
2. Attach the stops to the shelves with glue and brads (see *Diagram*).

ASSEMBLE THE CABINET.
Precision is crucial when assembling your collector's table. Sloppy construction will make it difficult to fit the drawers into the cabinet.
1. Attach the lowest drawer guides to the inside of the end panels by measuring up from the bottom edge and marking a line at 11⁄16". Position the bottom edge of the drawer guide on this line and attach with glue and brads **(photo C).**
2. Attach the back to the side assemblies by setting the back panel into the dadoes on the back legs, keeping all top edges flush. Drill pilot holes and secure the back panel with glue and brads.
3. Turn the cabinet upside down, then drill counter-sunk pilot holes and attach the bottom shelf to the edge of the drawer guides with 1" wood screws.
4. Turn the cabinet right-side-up and attach the middle shelf to the top edge of the drawer guide with 1" screws.
5. Rest the center drawer guides on the middle shelf and fasten to the end panels with glue and ¾" screws **(photo D).**
6. Install the top shelf and upper guides in similar fashion.
7. Cut the cleats (G, H) and top rail (I) to size.

TIP

Cutting stopped dadoes is a precision task. It's a good idea to practice these skills on scrap wood before you attempt this project.

Drill countersunk pilot holes and attach the center guides to the end panels, using wood screws.

Glue the miters of the top frame together, using a band clamp. Check for square by measuring diagonals.

8. Drill counterbored pilot holes and attach cleats flush with the tops of the back and side panels, using wood glue and 1¼" screws (see *Diagram*).

BUILD THE TOP FRAME.

1. Cut the long frame sides (J) and short frame sides (K) to length, mitering the ends at 45°.

2. Cut a rabbet along the inside top edge of the frame pieces, using a router with a ½" straight bit set at 5⁄16" depth.

3. Apply glue to the mitered ends and clamp the frame together, using a band clamp **(photo E).** Allow the glue to dry thoroughly.

4. Center the frame over the cabinet with a ¼" overhang on all sides, drill pilot holes and attach the frame using wood glue and 4d finish nails.

TIP

For easier access to stored collections, you can attach pull knobs to the face of each drawer.

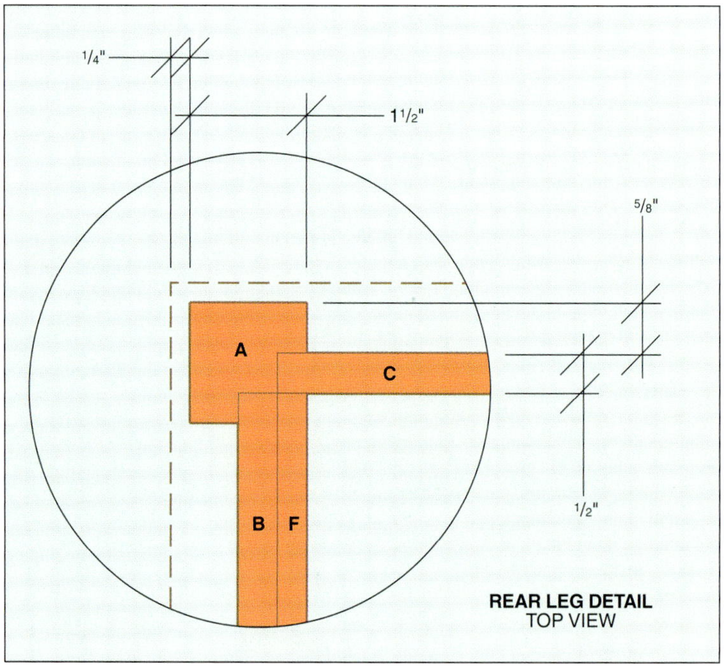

Assemble the drawer boxes and attach the bottoms with wood glue and brads. Make sure to check for square as you build each drawer.

Attach drawer faces with glue, and drive wood screws through the inside of the drawer box into the drawer face.

1. Cut the drawer box parts (L, M, N, O) to size.
2. Assemble each drawer box by positioning the front and back between the sides, drilling pilot holes, and attaching the pieces with glue and brads. Make sure drawer assemblies are square.
3. Attach the drawer bottoms, using glue and brads **(photo F).**
4. Cut the drawer faces (P) to size. Position the drawer faces on the front of the drawer boxes, so the ends are flush and there is a 5/16" overhang at the top edge and a 3/16" overhang at the bottom.
5. Drill pilot holes and attach by driving 1¼" wood screws from inside the drawer box fronts into the drawer face **(photo G).**
6. Test-fit the completed drawers in the cabinet, making sure there is ⅛" spacing between drawer faces.

FINISH THE CABINET.

1. Fill all visible nail holes with stainable putty, then sand all surfaces smooth.
2. Paint the insides and top edges of the drawer boxes (not the drawer faces) with flat black paint to highlight your collectibles. Stain the rest of the wood with a color of your choice. We used a light Danish walnut, and apply several coats of water-based polyurethane finish, sanding lightly between coats.

INSTALL THE GLASS TOP.

Wait until the project is built before ordering the glass for your collector's table. Measure the length and width of the opening, and reduce each measurement by ⅛". Tempered safety glass is a good choice, especially if you have children. Seat the glass on clear, self-adhesive cushions to quiet any potential rattles.

TIP

If you wish, the inside of the collection drawers can be lined with black velvet to provide an elegant setting for your finest collectibles.

PROJECT
POWER TOOLS

Dry Sink

This classic cabinet brings antique charm to any setting.

CONSTRUCTION MATERIALS

Quantity	**Lumber**
4	1 × 2" × 6' birch
5	1 × 3" × 8' birch
1	1 × 4" × 8' birch
2	1 × 6" × 6' birch
1	½" × 4 × 4' birch plywood
1	¾" × 4 × 8' birch plywood
3	⅜" × 4' birch dowling

Traditional dry sinks were used to hold a washbasin in the days before indoor plumbing, but today they can serve a variety of decorative and practical functions around the house. Our classic dry sink is used as a garden potting table. It's the ideal height for mixing soils, planting seeds and watering plants. The top has a handy back shelf to hold plants and accessories, while the curved front and sides are especially designed to contain messy spills. The roomy cabinet has two hinged doors for easy access and enough interior space to store pots, planters, fertilizers, insecticides and an assortment of gardening tools. This project features birch plywood panels with solid birch frames secured with strong "through-dowel" joinery.

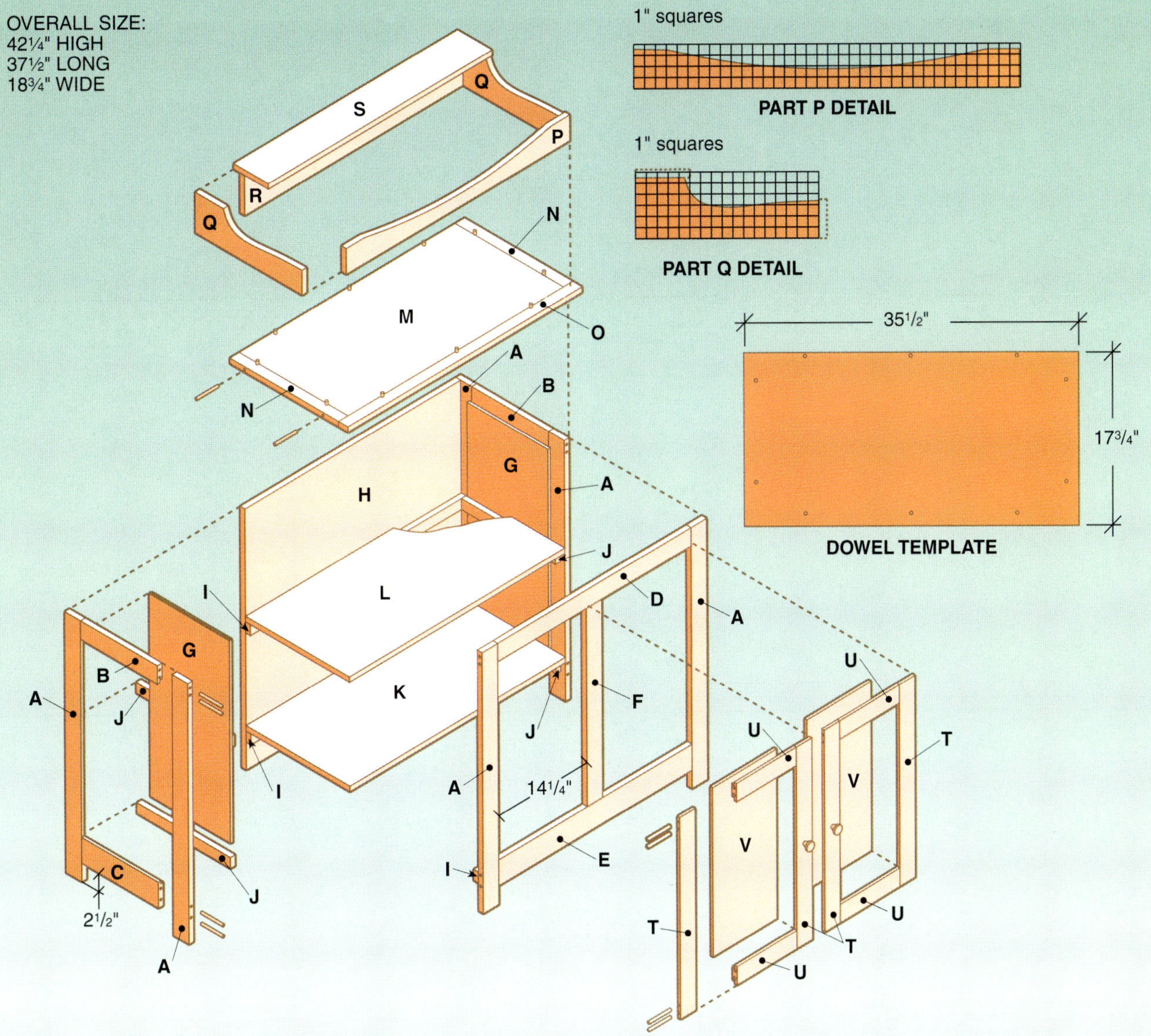

Cutting List

Key	Part	Dimension	Pcs.	Material
A	Stile	¾ × 2½ × 35¼"	6	Birch
B	Side rail, top	¾ × 2½ × 12¼"	2	Birch
C	Side rail, bottom	¾ × 3½ × 12¼"	2	Birch
D	Front rail, top	¾ × 2½ × 31"	1	Birch
E	Front rail, bottom	¾ × 3½ × 31"	1	Birch
F	Mullion	¾ × 2½ × 26¾"	1	Birch
G	Side panel	½ × 12⅞ × 27½"	2	Birch ply.
H	Back panel	¾ × 34½ × 35¼"	1	Birch ply.
I	Back, front cleat	¾ × 1½ × 34½"	3	Birch
J	Side cleat	¾ × 1½ × 15"	4	Birch
K	Bottom	¾ × 16½ × 34⅜"	1	Birch ply.

Cutting List

Key	Part	Dimension	Pcs.	Material
L	Shelf	¾ × 16⅜ × 34⅜"	1	Birch ply.
M	Top	¾ × 17¼ × 34½"	1	Birch ply.
N	Top side edge	¾ × 1½ × 17¼"	2	Birch
O	Top front edge	¾ × 1½ × 37½"	1	Birch
P	Top assem. front	¾ × 3½ × 35¾"	1	Birch
Q	Top assem. side	¾ × 5½ × 17"	2	Birch
R	Top assem. back	¾ × 5½ × 34"	1	Birch
S	Top assem. cap	¾ × 5½ × 35¾"	1	Birch
T	Door stile	¾ × 2½ × 27¼"	4	Birch
U	Door rail	¾ × 2½ × 9¾"	4	Birch
V	Door panel	½ × 10½ × 23"	2	Birch ply.

Materials: Wood glue, birch shelf nosing (⅛ × ¾ × 34½"), 16-ga. brads, #8 wood screws (1¼", 1⅝"), 4d finish nails, ⅜" inset hinges (4), ⅜ × 1" dowels (10), ⅜ × 3" dowels (40), door pulls (2), finishing materials.

Note: Measurements reflect the actual thickness of dimension lumber.

Drill holes and insert the dowels after the frame pieces have been glued together.

Carefully square the corners of the rabbets in the side panels and door panels, using a sharp chisel.

TIP

Custom-cut dowels can be difficult to fit into snug holes. To make insertion easier, score a groove along the length of each dowel. This groove allows air and excess glue to escape when driving the dowels into their holes.

Directions: Dry Sink

CUT AND ASSEMBLE THE CABINET FRAMES.

The dry sink is built with two side frames, a face frame and two door frames—all made from birch rails and stiles joined with through dowels.

1. Cut the stiles (A) and rails (B, C, D, E) and mullion (F) to length.

2. Build each side frame by gluing a top and bottom side rail between two stiles. The bottom rail should be raised $2\frac{1}{2}$" from the bottoms of the stiles. Clamp in place, check for square and let dry.

3. Drill two $\frac{3}{8}$"-dia. × 3"-deep holes through the stiles at each rail location **(photo A).**

4. Cut 3"-long dowels, and score a groove along one side. Apply glue to the dowels, then use a mallet to drive them into the holes.

5. Repeat this process to construct the front frame, using two stiles, the top and bottom front rails, and the mullion. Make sure the mullion is centered between the stiles.

6. Cut the door frame stiles (T) and rails (U) to size with a circular saw, and assemble frame parts in the same way.

Drill pilot holes, and attach cleats with wood screws to the frame but not into the ½" panel.

Clamp one side of the face frame and check for square, then clamp the other side and check for square again. Attach with finish nails and set the nailheads.

ADD THE PANELS.

The ½" plywood side panels and door panels fit into rabbets cut around the inside of the side frames and door frames.

1. Mount a ⅜" rabbet bit in your router, set to ½" depth. Cut a continuous rabbet around the inside of the side frames.

2. Square off the corners of the rabbet, using a chisel **(photo B).** On the back face of each door frame, cut a rabbet around the inside of the frame in a similar fashion.

3. Change the depth of the router bit to ⅜", and cut another rabbet around the outside edge of the door frame. This creates a lip that will overlap the face frame when the doors are attached.

4. Cut the side panels (G) and the door panels (V) to size.

5. Position each panel inside its frame, then drill pilot holes and attach the panels with 16-ga. brads.

6. Position and attach hinges and knobs on the cabinet doors.

PREPARE THE REMAINING PIECES.

1. Cut the back panel (H), bottom (K) and shelf (L) to size.

2. Cut and attach shelf nosing to the front edge of the shelf, using glue and brads.

3. Cut the front and back cleats (I) and side cleats (J) to size. On the inside faces of the face frame stiles, mark reference lines 5¼" from the bottom. On the inside faces of the back panel and side frame stiles, mark reference lines at 5¼" and 21" from the bottom.

4. Position the cleats with the top edges flush with the reference lines, with the ends of cleats set back ¾" from the front edge and 1½" from the back edge. Drill countersunk pilot holes, and attach the cleats with 1¼" wood screws **(photo C).** NOTE: Take care to screw the side cleats into the frame members only, not into the ½" panels.

5. Attach the back cleats to the back panel, and the front cleat to the inside of the face frame, using the same process.

Cut the top side edges and top front edge, and attach the pieces with wood glue. Clamp in place until the glue dries, then drill and insert dowels to strengthen the joints.

When creating the top assembly, first attach the front piece to the sides, then attach the sides to the back, using wood glue and 4d finish nails.

ASSEMBLE THE CABINET.

1. Position the back panel between the side assemblies. Drill countersunk pilot holes, and attach the sides to the back panel with 1⅝" wood screws.

2. Position the bottom over the cleats. Check to make sure the cabinet is square, then drill pilot holes and attach the bottom by driving 4d finish nails into the cleats. Position and attach the shelf in the same manner.

3. Lay the cabinet on its back and clamp the face frame in position. Check for square, then drill pilot holes and attach the face frame to the cabinet with glue and 4d finish nails driven into the side frames, bottom and shelf **(photo D).** Drive finish nails through the bottom and into the front cleat. Set all nail heads.

4. Position and mount the doors in their openings, then remove them and detach the hinges and knobs until the wood has been finished.

ASSEMBLE AND ATTACH THE TOP.

1. Cut cabinet top (M), side edges (N) and front edge (O) to size.

2. Attach the edges around the top, using glue. Clamp the pieces in place until the glue dries **(photo E).**

3. Drill holes and reinforce the joints with 3"-long dowels, following the same procedure used to construct the cabinet frames.

4. Position the top on the cabinet, leaving a ¾" overhang on both ends and the front. Drill countersunk pilot holes, and attach the top with glue and 1⅝" wood screws driven into the cabinet frames and back panel.

CREATE THE TOP ASSEMBLY.

1. Cut the top assembly parts (P, Q, R and S) to size.

2. Transfer the patterns to the pieces (see *Diagram*), then cut them out with a jig saw. Sand the cut edges smooth.

3. Position the front piece against the side pieces, so there is a ⅛" overhang on both ends. Drill pilot holes and attach the front piece to the side pieces with glue and 4d finish nails.

Use a template to ensure that the dowel holes in the top assembly will match those drilled in the top of the cabinet.

FINISH THE CABINET.

To give our dry sink a vintage look, we used a unique antiquing method that uses both stain and paint.

1. Finish-sand all surfaces and edges of the cabinet.

2. Stain the entire project and allow to dry. We used medium cherry stain.

3. Apply latex paint to the desired surfaces. We used Glidden® Centurian blue paint, applying it to all surfaces except the top.

4. Use a cloth and denatured alcohol to remove color while the paint is still damp. To mimic the look of a genuine antique, try to remove most of the paint from the corners and edges, where a cabinet typically receives the most wear.

5. Reinstall the hardware and hang the doors after the finish has dried.

4. Position the back piece between the sides, then drill pilot holes and attach the pieces with glue and 4d finish nails **(photo F).**

5. Position the cap piece so it overlaps by ⅛" on each end, then drill pilot holes, and attach with glue and 4d finish nails.

ATTACH THE TOP ASSEMBLY.

The top assembly is attached to the cabinet with dowels, positioned with the benefit of an easy-to-build template.

1. Create the template by tracing the outer outline of the top assembly on a piece of scrap plywood or hardboard. Cut the template to this size.

2. Place the template over the bottom of the top assembly, then drill ⅜"-dia. × ½"-deep dowel holes through the template and into the top assembly.

3. Place the template on the cabinet top, centered side to side with the back edges flush, and tape it in place. Drill corresponding dowel holes into the top **(photo G).**

4. Remove the template and attach the top assembly to the cabinet with glue and 1" dowels. Use weights or clamps to hold the top assembly in place until the glue dries.

TIP

Custom finishes can be tricky to create. Before attempting a unique finish, like the stain/rubbed-paint treatment used on our project, always practice on scrap materials.

Black & Decker (U.S.) Inc., Towson, MD 21286 U.S.A.
20014349

Dining Room Projects

Show off your china and your woodworking skills with these projects for your dining room. The china cabinet has a small footprint, but plenty of space to store and display dishes. The vertical display cabinet uses oak and glass to create a formal yet airy showpiece. The wine and stemware cart makes entertaining just a little bit easier. Even the functional trivet and serving tray are handsome projects that you'll be proud to show friends and family.

PROJECT
POWER TOOLS

Serving Tray

Smooth joinery and sturdy construction make serving food and beverages a snap.

Construction Materials

Quantity	Lumber
1	½ × 3¾" × 2' oak
1	½ × 2¾" × 3' oak
1	¼ × 12" × 2' birch plywood

Our serving tray is just the thing for ferrying food, drinks and dishes from kitchen to patio or dining room with a dash of style. The solid oak and warm birch tones of the tray always highlight whatever you're carrying, whether an outdoor snack of fruit and cheese or an indoor treat of coffee and cookies. The sculpted carrying handles ensure a good grip while carrying food to your guests. The serving tray is also an introduction to some advanced joinery techniques. Rabbet joints connect the frame to provide a more professional-looking appearance. The bottom panel fits into dadoes cut along the inside of each piece, and stays in place without glue. This is a great project for practicing router skills, or for showing them off if you're an accomplished woodworker.

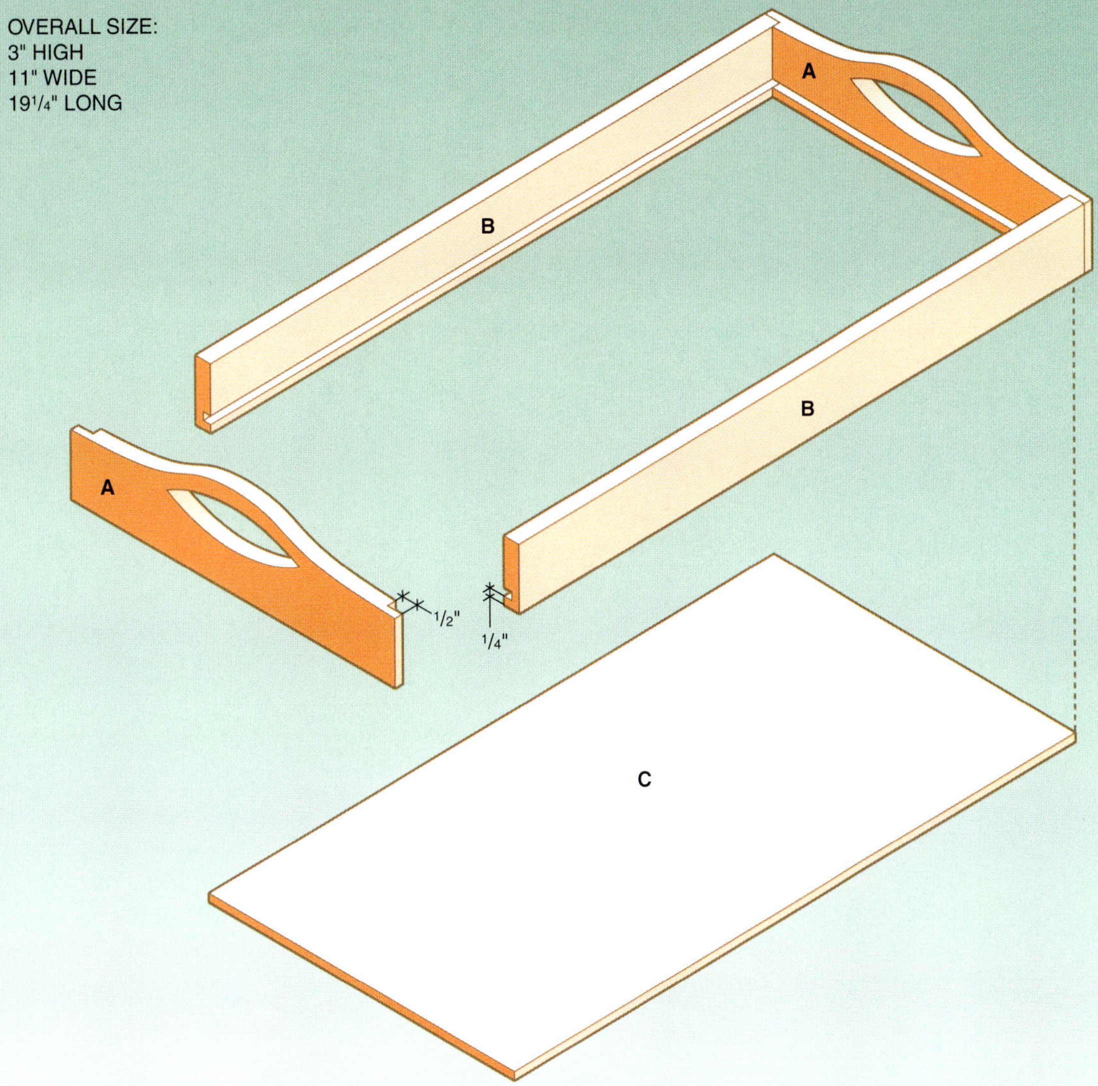

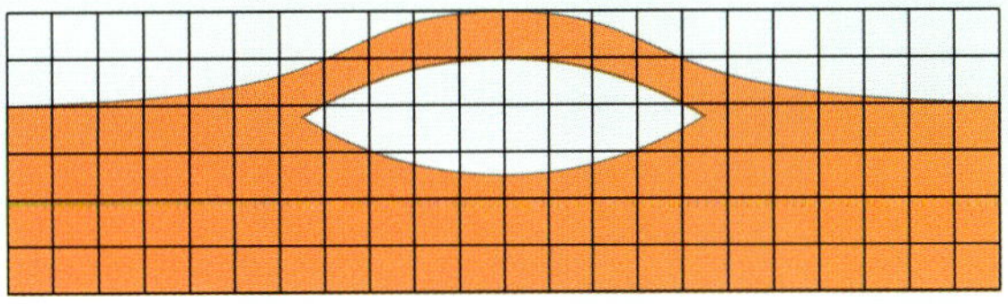

PART A DETAIL ½" squares

Cutting List

Key	Part	Dimension	Pcs.	Material
A	Frame end	½ × 3 × 11"	2	Oak
B	Frame side	½ × 2 × 18¾"	2	Oak
C	Tray bottom	¼ × 10⅜ × 18⅝"	1	Birch

Materials: Wood glue, 4d finish nails, finishing materials. Optional: ⅜" stop molding (5'), brads (½", ¾").

Note: Measurements reflect the actual thickness of dimension lumber.

Rabbet the frame ends, using a straightedge to guide the cuts.

Use bar clamps and a straightedge to hold pieces in place and ensure uniform dadoes.

Directions: Serving Tray

MAKE THE RABBETS.

The corners of the tray feature ½" rabbet joints for strength and a unified look.

1. Measure and cut the frame ends (A) to length.

2. Place the frame ends side by side on your worksurface with their ends aligned, and butt them against a scrap piece of ¾"-thick wood placed to the right of them. (Continuing each rabbet cut into the scrap wood helps prevent tearouts.) Place a straight board or straightedge over the frame ends to guide your cut, align the board and clamp in place. Use a ½" straight-cutting router bit set ¼" deep, and rabbet the two frame ends, completing the cut into the scrap board **(photo A).** Cut rabbets on both ends of the tray ends.

MAKE THE DADOES.

Dadoes in the frame sides and frame ends secure the tray bottom in place. A simple jig is used to help make uniform, straight dadoes.

1. Cut the frame sides (B) to size, and sand smooth.

2. Draw parallel lines ¼" and ½" from the bottom edges of the frame sides and frame ends to mark the dadoes. Create a cutting jig by clamping two pieces of ¾" scrap wood against the long edges of a frame side. Clamp a straightedge over the board to guide the router base while cutting the long dadoes. Make the dadoes in both frame sides with a ¼" straight-cutting router bit set ¼" deep **(photo B).** Adjust the clamps, and dado the frame ends in the same fashion.

OPTION: If you don't want to cut dadoes, you can support the tray bottom with cleats made from ⅜" stop molding. Cut the cleats to fit inside the tray, and attach them flush to the bottom edge with ¾" brads and a nail set **(photo C).** Place the bottom over the cleats, and secure with ½" brads. When using this method, you'll need to subtract ⅜" from the length and width of the tray bottom when cutting to size.

MAKE THE HANDLES.

1. Transfer the handle pattern onto each end (see *Diagram*).

TIP

Routing bits turn clockwise, making the router pull to left. When routing from left to right, place a straightedge fence between the router and you. By placing a straightedge to the left of the router's path, the router will hug the straightedge.

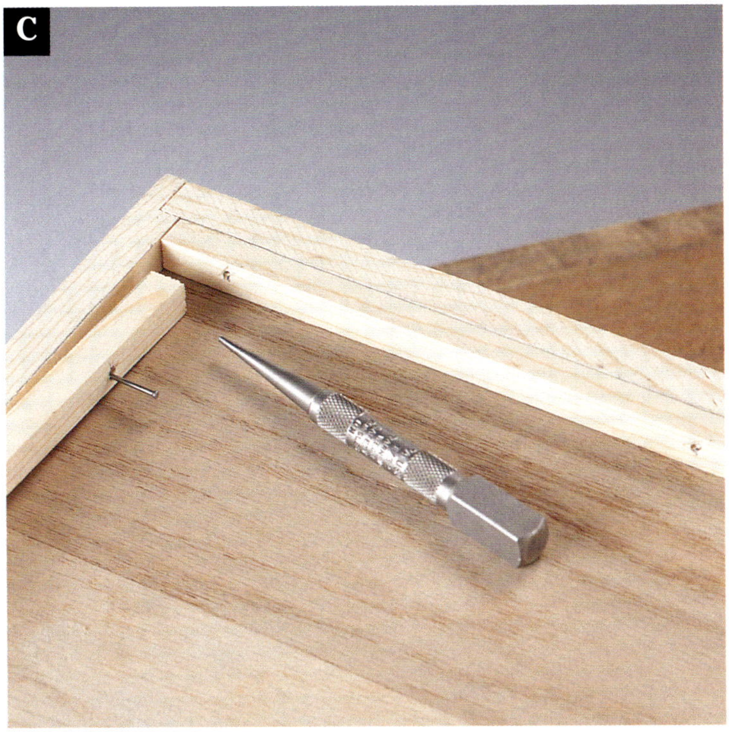

OPTION: Rather than cut dadoes, you can attach ⅜" stop molding nailed to the tray frame to support the bottom.

Drill access holes for your jig saw, and carefully cut the handles and curves.

2. Drill access holes in the handle and use a jig saw to complete each cut **(photo D).** Sand the cuts smooth.

ASSEMBLE THE TRAY.

1. Cut the tray bottom (C) to size from birch plywood and sand smooth.

2. Test-fit the tray bottom in the grooves of the frame sides and ends. Do not glue the tray bottom in the grooves. When the tray bottom is properly fitted, apply a thin film of glue to the rabbet joints. Use bar clamps to keep the unit tight from end to end and from side to side **(photo E).** Check for square by measuring diagonally from corner to corner. Realign the bar clamps until the diagonal measurements are the same.

3. Drill pilot holes through the frame ends into the frame sides, and secure the joints with 4d finish nails.

Apply glue to the rabbets, and clamp the tray together at the joints.

APPLY FINISHING TOUCHES.

1. Scrape off any excess glue at the joints. Finish-sand the tray, wipe off any sanding residue and apply a finish.

2. Mask the bottom, apply a stain on the oak sides and ends—we used rustic oak—then apply a water-resistant topcoat to the sides and ends. A natural oil applied to the birch tray bottom brings out the grain and helps resist moisture from spills. Do not wash the tray or allow it to sit on wet surfaces.

PROJECT
POWER TOOLS

Trivet

Protect your countertops, tables or furniture during teatime with our oak and ceramic trivet.

You'll love this easy-to-construct trivet with arched legs. The heavy tile stabilizes the base, making it ideal for keeping hot pots or cups off your favorite furniture or serving cart. For this project, we selected a standard colonial oak trim pattern to make the arched legs and a neutral-color tile for the base, but you can customize this trivet by using tile that matches your tea set or suits your taste. Our basic design features a single 12 × 12" tile cut down to a finished size of 6 × 9". Using one tile is a simple method that doesn't require grout, but you will find it easy to adapt this design for smaller tiles or mosaic tiles that do require grout. Simply match the size of the substrate to the finished dimensions of the tile-and-grout surface (including a grout border between the tiles and the oak frame), and cut the oak molding pieces accordingly. The construction steps remain the same.

Construction Materials

Quantity	**Lumber**
1	¾" × 2 × 2' MDF
1	⅝ × 2¼" × 4' oak molding
1	¼ × 12 × 12" tile

MDF = medium-density fiberboard

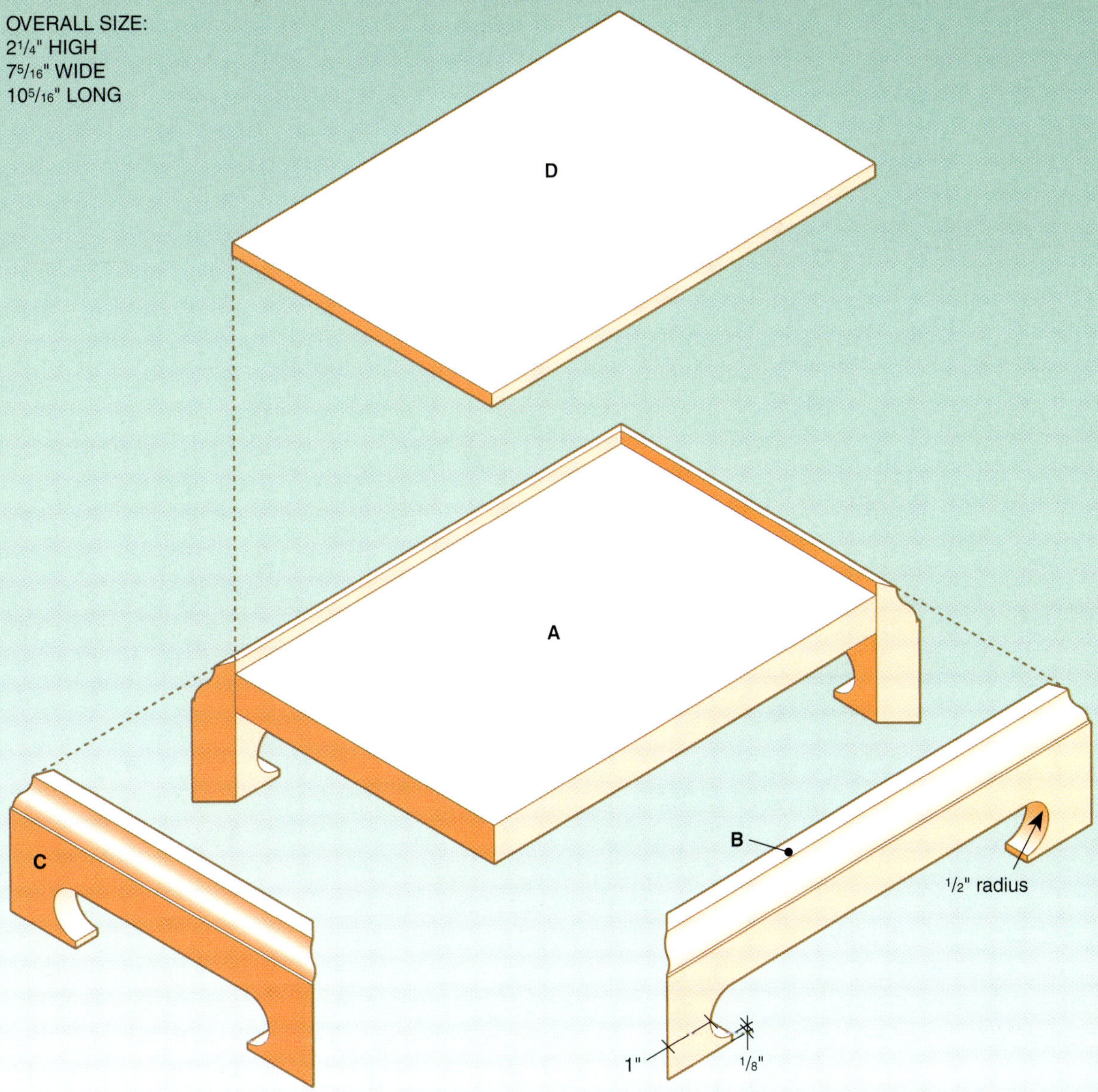

Cutting List				
Key	**Part**	**Dimension**	**Pcs.**	**Material**
A	Substrate	¾ × 6 × 9"	1	MDF
B	Side	⅝ × 2¼ × 10 5/16"	2	Oak molding
C	End	⅝ × 2¼ × 5 5/16"	2	Oak molding
D	Tile	¼ × 6 × 9"	1	Ceramic tile

Materials: Waterproof wood glue, tile adhesive, 1" brads, finishing materials. (Optional: grout, clear silicone caulk.)

Note: Measurements reflect the actual thickness of dimension lumber.

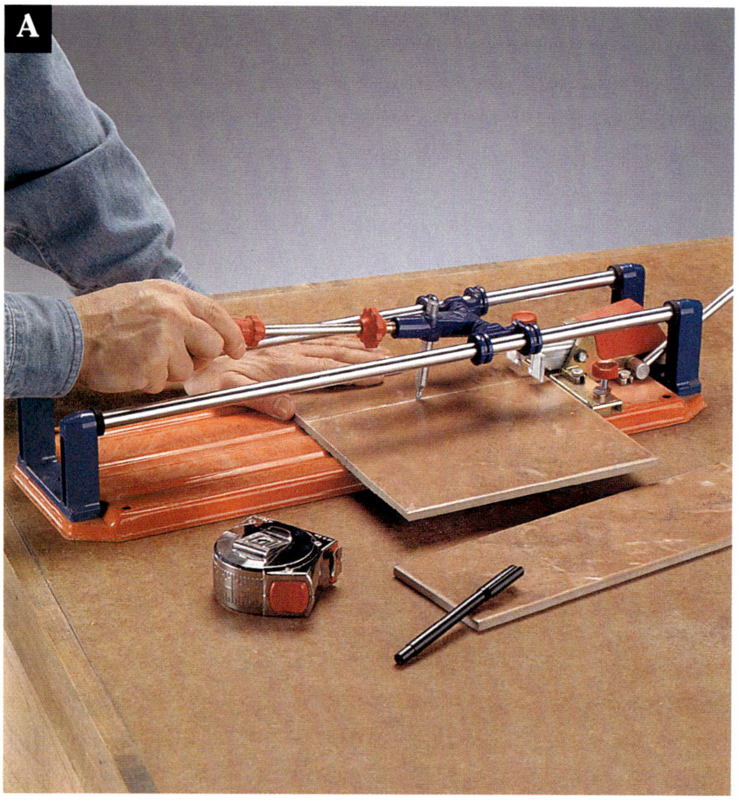

Use a tile cutter to make fast, clean cuts on ceramic tile.

Test-fit the base molding side and end pieces to the substrate and tile before applying glue.

Directions: Trivet

CUT THE TILE, SUBSTRATE, AND MOLDING.

A 12 × 12" tile cut to 6 × 9" is a convenient size for a trivet. It is large enough to hold a good-sized teapot, yet small enough to handle easily.

1. Mark and cut the tile to the correct size with a tile cutter **(photo A).** If you don't have a tile cutter, clamp the tile to your worksurface and cut it using a rod saw (like a coping saw, but with an abrasive blade designed for cutting tile).

2. Measure and cut the MDF substrate (A) to match the finished tile size.

3. Cut the sides (B) and ends (C) to length from the base molding. Make 45° miter cuts at the ends of each piece.

ATTACH THE MOLDING TO THE SUBSTRATE.

1. Place the tile face down on the worksurface and position the substrate, bottom side up, over the tile. Test-fit each side and end against the substrate.

2. Scribe a line along the edge of the substrate to mark where the substrate joins the molding **(photo B).**

3. Apply waterproof glue to the sides and ends, and attach them to the substrate so the reference marks are aligned. With the tile temporarily in place, fasten a band clamp around the perimeter at the line where the substrate edges meet the base molding **(photo C).**

4. Remove the band clamp and the tile after the glue dries.

5. Drill pilot holes through the molding into the substrate. Secure the molding with 1" brads, and recess the nail heads with a nail set.

CREATE THE LEGS.

Legs are formed by cutting holes in the molding near each corner joint.

1. Measure in 1½" inches from each corner and ⅝" up from the bottom edge. This is the centerpoint for each hole.

2. Construct a small support backer board to fit inside the skirt formed by the base molding. Attach the jig to the bench so it overhangs the edge.

3. Place the trivet on the jig, and drill holes at each centerpoint with a 1" spade bit **(photo D).** Drill only through the sides and ends, and not into the substrate.

4. Draw a connecting line

C

Use a band clamp to hold base and ends in contact with the substrate while glue dries.

D

Use scrap plywood to support trivet and prevent tearouts while drilling "leg" holes in the molding.

between the tops of each set of holes, and cut along this line with your jig saw.

5. Complete each cutout by cutting straight up from the bottom edge into the center of each hole **(photo E).**

E

Clamp the trivet to your worksurface, and carefully cut out the legs, using a jig saw.

SAND AND FINISH.

1. Sand the cutout edges, making sure to round the sharp edges on the bottom of the legs. Finish the trivet as desired.

2. Apply an even coat of tile adhesive to the top of the substrate, and set the tile into the base. Depending on the width of the gap between the molding and the tile on the finished piece, you may want to fill it with a clear silicone caulk to prevent moisture or crumbs from collecting. If you selected mosaic tiles for this project, mask the sides of the base before grouting to protect the molding and apply a silicone grout sealer when finished to prevent stains from penetrating the grout.

PROJECT
POWER TOOLS

Plate & Spoon Rack

This easy-to-build rack displays your collectibles and shows off your woodworking ability.

Construction Materials

Quantity	Lumber
1	21/32 × 24 × 47½" ponderosa pine panel

This decorative fixture, made from edge-glued ponderosa pine panels, has features you'll appreciate as your collection continues to grow. The back features three heart cutouts, and scallops along the top edge accentuate your most prized plates. The plate shelf has a groove cut into it to help stabilize up to three full-size plates, while the sides are curved to soften the edges and to better display the plates. The spoon rack sits in front of a curved background that adds interest to the unit, while the rack itself has notches that hold up to seventeen collectible teaspoons.

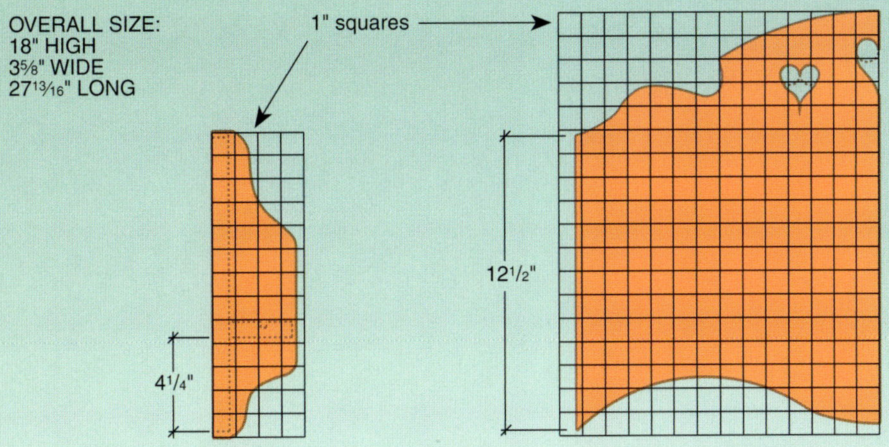

SIDE VIEW

PART A DETAIL

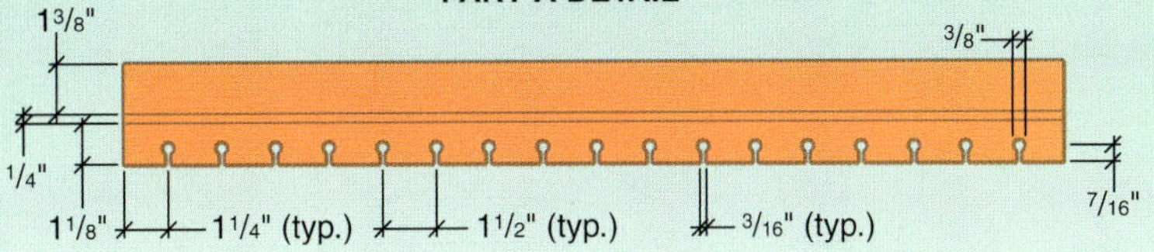

PART C DETAIL

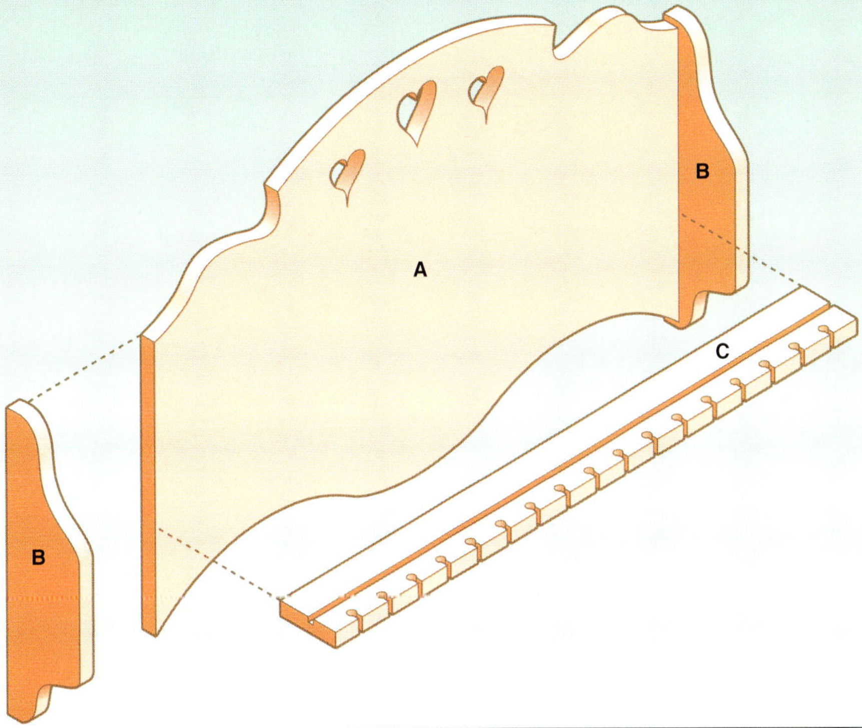

Cutting List

Key	Part	Dimension	Pcs.	Material
A	Back	21/32 × 18 × 26½"	1	Pine panel
B	Side	21/32 × 3⅝ × 13"	2	Pine panel
C	Shelf	21/32 × 2¾ × 26½"	1	Pine panel

Materials: #6 × 1½" wood screws, 4d finish nails, 2 steel keyhole hanger plates.

Note: Measurements reflect the actual thickness of dimension lumber.

Lay out the pattern on the back piece by tracing half the pattern on one side of the centerline, then flipping the pattern and tracing the other side.

Clamp the back to your worksurface, and cut the pattern, using a jig saw.

Drill out the larger heart using a 1" spade bit. Use a $\frac{7}{8}$" spade bit to create the smaller hearts. Complete the cutouts with a jig saw.

Directions: Plate & Spoon Rack

CUT AND SHAPE THE BACK.

1. Cut the back blank (A) to overall size.

2. Transfer the decorative profile onto cardboard or heavy paper (see *Diagram*). Locate the back piece centerline and work both ways, tracing the pattern on one side of the centerline, then flipping the pattern over at the centerline and tracing the other symmetrical side **(photo A).**

3. Cut the edge shapes with a jig saw, taking care that the ends, which will be attached to the sides, are finished at $12\frac{1}{2}$" **(photo B).**

CUT THE HEART DETAILS.

The back has two different-sized heart cutouts (see *Diagram*).

1. Trace the heart cutouts onto the back piece.

2. Protect your worksurface with a piece of scrap, and drill two horizontally adjacent holes, using a 1" spade bit for the larger heart and a $\frac{7}{8}$" bit for the smaller hearts **(photo C)**.

3. Complete the cutouts with a jig saw.

CUT THE SIDES.

1. Cut the side blanks (B) to overall size.Transfer the side profile to cardboard (see *Diagram*) and then trace onto one side.

2. Cut one side with a jig saw, then use it as a pattern to mark and cut the other side.

CUT AND SHAPE THE SHELF.

The shelf has a groove to hold the plates, and notches to hold the spoons.

Cut the plate groove into the shelf, using bar clamps and a straightedge to hold the shelf in place and guide the router.

Cut a 3/16"-wide notch along the front edge for each of the spoon rack holes, using a backsaw.

1. Cut the shelf (C) to size.
2. Make a simple routing jig by clamping two pieces of ¾" scrap wood against the edges of the shelf. Securely clamp a straightedge over the scrap wood to guide the router base and cut the groove at the desired location (see *Diagram*) with a ¼" straight router bit set ¼" deep **(photo D).**
3. Measure and mark the 17 spoon hole centerpoints (see *Diagram*). Drill the holes, using a ⅜" bit.
4. Complete the spoon hole cutouts, using a backsaw to make two straight cuts into the holes, leaving a 3/16" slot **(photo E).**
5. Sand all cut edges before assembling.

ASSEMBLE THE RACK.

1. Drill pilot holes into the sides and attach to the back using glue and 4d finish nails.
2. Position the shelf, then drive 4d finish nails through the sides into the shelf **(photo F).**
3. Drill countersunk pilot holes and drive wood screws through the back into the shelf.

APPLY FINISHING TOUCHES.

1. Drill or chisel out space so the keyhole hanger plates are flush with the back surface of the rack. Drive screws through the hanger plates into the back of the rack.
2. Sand smooth and apply a finish.

Attach the shelf to the sides with finish nails and to the back with wood screws.

TIP

Pine wood actually sands better with a vibrating sander than a belt sander because pitch typically builds up faster in the belt and causes burn marks or unevenness.

China Cabinet

This tall, sleek fixture displays and stores fine china and other housewares without occupying a lot of floor space.

PROJECT POWER TOOLS

This modern-looking china cabinet features a snappy, efficient design to showcase and store all types of china and dishware with equal elegance. The bottom half of the cabinet is a simple cupboard for storing everyday serving trays, napkins, silverware and miscellaneous houseware. The upper half is an open rack for displaying your favorite porcelain statues, china, vases and collectibles.

The asymmetrical design allows you to store and display a wider range of items than if the cabinet was equally weighted on the right and left. And the overall slenderness of the cabinet means you can fit it into just about any room, whether it's tucked into a corner or featured prominently along the center of a wall.

Plates and other items that are displayed in the rack area of the cabinet can be accentuated with plateholders. Or, you can do as we did and build a few custom-sized plate holders from scraps of molding. Just cut the molding into strips about the same width as the plates, and inset the strips at ¼" intervals in a plain wood frame.

Construction Materials

Quantity	Lumber
2	¾" × 4 × 8' birch plywood
2	1"-dia. × 3' dowel
1	½ × ½" × 3' quarter-round molding

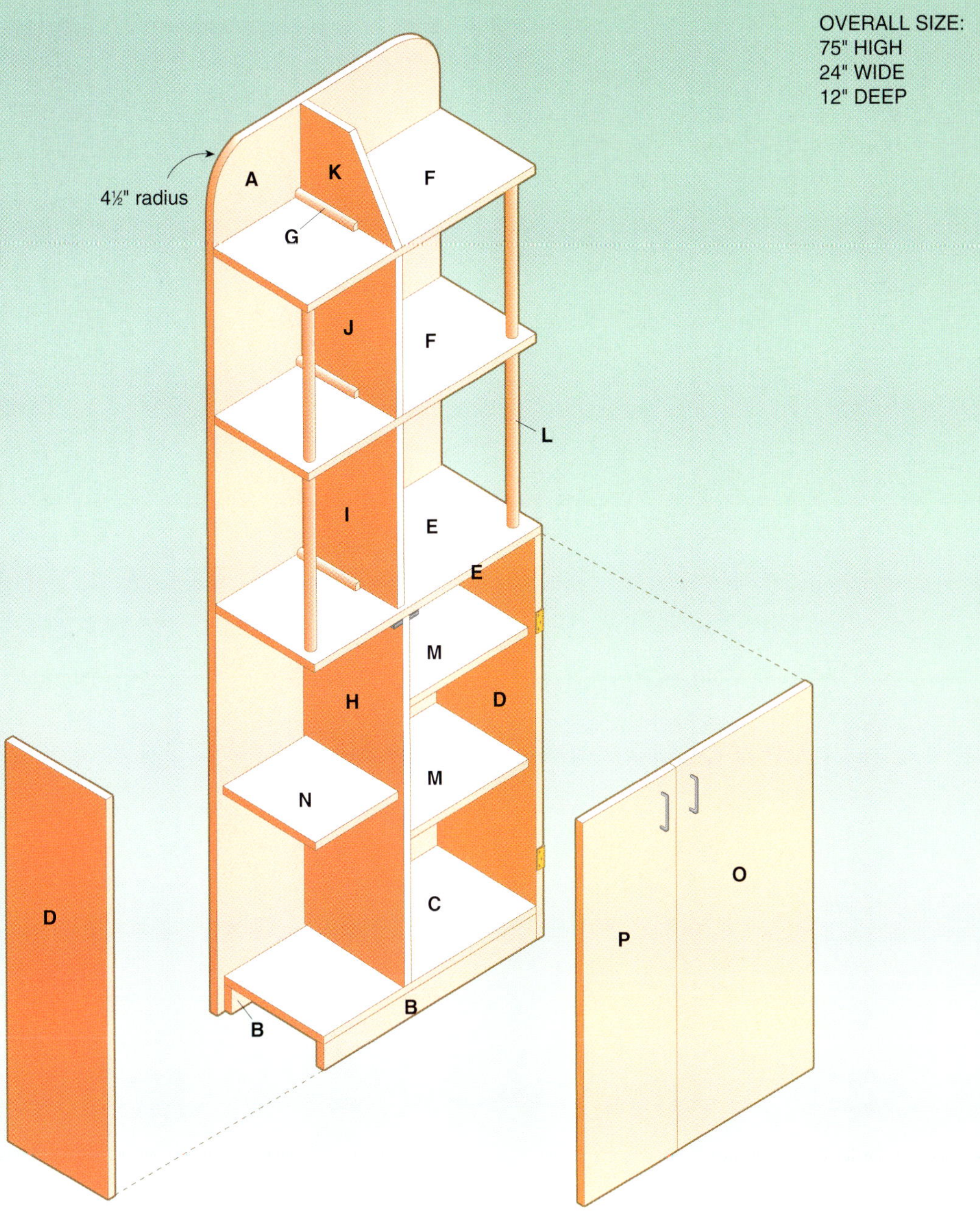

Key	Part	Dimension	Pcs.	Material
A	Back	¾ × 24 × 75"	1	Plywood
B	Bottom rail	¾ × 2¼ × 22½"	2	Plywood
C	Cupboard bottom	¾ × 10½ × 22½"	1	Plywood
D	Cupboard side	¾ × 10½ × 35¼"	2	Plywood
E	Cupboard top	¾ × 10½ × 24"	1	Plywood
F	Rack shelf	¾ × 10 × 24"	2	Plywood
G	Cleat	½ × ½ × 6"	6	Toe molding
H	Cupboard divider	¾ × 10½ × 32¼"	1	Plywood

Cutting List

Key	Part	Dimension	Pcs.	Material
I	Rack divider	¾ × 10 × 15⅛"	1	Plywood
J	Rack divider	¾ × 10 × 14¾"	1	Plywood
K	Rack divider	¾ × 10 × 7½"	1	Plywood
L	Column	1 × 30⅝"	2	Dowel
M	Cupboard shelf	¾ × 13¼ × 10"	2	Plywood
N	Cupboard shelf	¾ × 8½ × 10"	1	Plywood
O	Large door	¾ × 14⅜ × 33¾"	1	Plywood
P	Small door	¾ × 9½ × 33¾"	1	Plywood

Materials: Wood glue, wood screws (#6 × 1¼", #6 × 2"), birch veneer edge tape (50'), ⅜"-dia. birch wood plugs, 1¼" brass butt hinges (4), 1¼" brads, magnetic door catches (2), 2½" brass door pulls (2), finishing materials.

Note: Measurements reflect the actual size of dimension lumber.

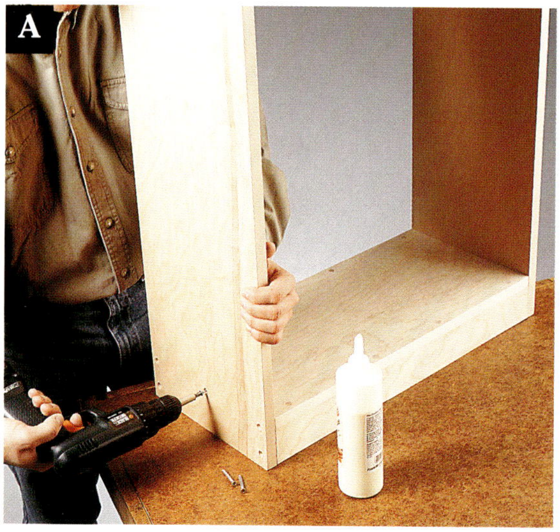

Attach the cupboard bottom by driving screws through the cupboard sides and into the edges.

Carefully sand the wood plugs to level, using a belt sander or power hand sander.

Directions: China Cabinet

MAKE THE BACK PANEL. The back panel runs the entire height of the china cabinet, anchoring both the rack and cupboard units.

1. Cut the back (A) to size.

2. Use a compass to draw a semicircle roundover with a 4½" radius at each top corner of the back panel. Cut the curves with a jig saw.

3. Use a household iron to apply birch veneer edge tape to the side and top edges of the back. Trim the excess tape with a sharp utility knife, then sand the edges smooth.

4. Mark reference points 51⅞" and 67⅜" up from the bottom edge, and 9¼" in from one side edge.

MAKE THE CUPBOARD.

1. Cut the bottom rails (B) and cupboard bottom (C) to size.

2. Apply edge tape to one long edge of the cupboard bottom.

3. Position the bottom rails beneath the cupboard bottom, flush with the edges. Drill counterbored pilot holes through the cupboard bottom and into the tops of the rails, then attach the parts with glue and #6 × 2" wood screws.

4. Cut the cupboard sides (D) to size, and apply edge tape to the front edges.

5. Position the cupboard bottom between the cupboard sides. Drill counterbored pilot holes, then apply glue and drive wood screws through the sides and into the edges of the cupboard bottom **(photo A).**

6. Cut the cupboard top (E) to size, and apply edge tape to the front and side edges. Attach it to the tops of the cupboard sides with glue and screws driven down through the cupboard top and into the tops of the sides.

ATTACH CUPBOARD SHELVES AND DIVIDER.

1. Cut the cupboard divider (H) and cupboard shelves (M, N) to size. Apply veneer tape to the front edges of all shelves.

Check the columns for square before attaching them to the cabinet top.

2. Draw reference lines on the cupboard bottom and cupboard top, 9¼" in from the left cupboard side, for positioning the divider between them.

3. Set the divider between the cupboard top and bottom, so the left face is aligned with the reference lines. Attach the divider with glue and wood screws, driven through the top and bottom and into the divider.

4. Draw reference lines on the right side and right face of the divider, 12" and 24" up from the bottoms, for positioning the larger cupboard shelves (M). Draw reference lines for the smaller cupboard shelf (N) 16" up from the bottoms on the left side and left face of the divider.

5. Apply glue to the side edges of all three shelves and position them between the cupboard sides and the divider, with their bottoms on the reference lines. Make sure the back edges of the shelves are flush with the back edges of the sides. Fasten the shelves with #6 × 2" wood screws, driven through the sides and the divider, and into the edges of the shelves.

6. Glue ⅜"-dia. birch wood plugs into all the exposed counterbores in the cupboard. When the glue has dried, carefully sand down the plugs. **(photo B).**

7. Attach the back panel to the cupboard with glue and #6 × 2" wood screws.

MAKE AND MARK THE RACK PARTS.

1. Cut the rack dividers (I, J, K) to full size. The upper divider (K) is trimmed off at an angle on the front edge by marking a point on one long edge, 5¼" from one end. Draw a straight line from that point to the bottom corner on the opposite end and cut along the line.

2. Cut the two rack shelves (F) to size, sand smooth, then attach veneer edge tape to the front edges of the rack dividers, and to the front and side edges of the rack shelves. With the taped edges facing you, draw reference lines on the shelves, 9¼" in from the left sides.

3. Drill two 1"-dia. holes for the columns (L) all the way through one shelf. The center of each hole should be 1¾" in from the front edge and 1¼" in from the side edge of the shelf. This shelf will become the lower rack shelf.

4. Cut the columns (L) to length.

INSTALL THE RACK.

1. Use glue and #6 × 2" wood screws, driven through counterbored pilot holes in the back panel, to fasten the lower rack divider (I) in position at the marks on the shelf and back panel. Use a square to make sure the divider is perpendicular to the back panel.

2. Cut cleats from quarter-round molding (G) to size, and use glue and 1¼" brads to attach the cleats on each side of the divider, flush against the back.

3. Apply glue to the top edge of the lower divider, and position the shelf with the 1"-dia. holes on top of the divider, so the holes are in front. Attach the shelf to the divider with wood screws, driven through the back and into the shelf, and through the shelf and into the lower divider.

4. Apply glue to the bottom of each column, and slide them through the holes in the shelf. Use a square to make sure they are straight **(photo C),** then drive a #6 × 1¼" wood screw up through the cabinet top and into the bottom of each column.

5. Position the middle rack divider (J) on the shelf. Fasten it with glue, screws and cleats.

6. Attach the upper shelf to the middle divider and back panel with glue and wood screws.

7. Drive #6 × 1¼" wood screws through the shelf and into the tops of the columns.

8. Apply glue to the back and bottom edges of the upper divider, and attach it with wood screws and cleats.

INSTALL THE DOORS.

1. Cut the doors (O, P) to size. Apply edge tape to all edges of each door.

2. Attach 1¼" brass butt hinges to the doors, 3½" down from the top edges, and ½" up from the bottom edges. Fasten the doors to the cupboard sides, flush with the cabinet top **(photo D).**

3. Install magnetic door catches on the cupboard divider and doors. Attach door pulls to the outside faces of the doors, 1½" down from the top edges of the doors, and 1½" in from the inside edges.

4. Finish-sand, wipe clean with a tack cloth, then apply your finish of choice. We applied two coats of polyurethane over unstained wood.

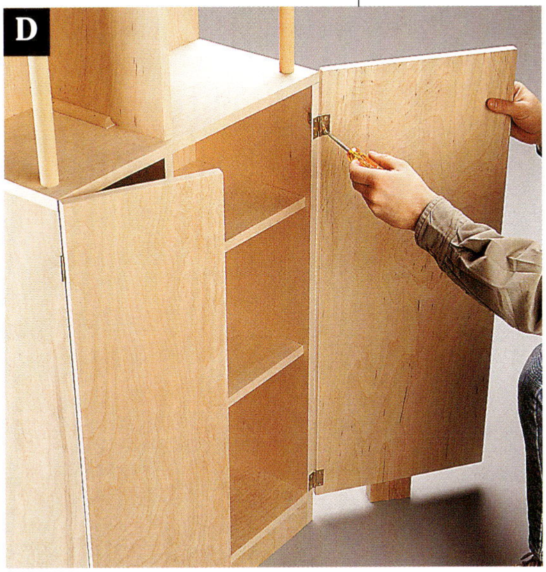

Hang the doors with brass butt hinges.

PROJECT
POWER TOOLS

Sideboard

This elegant sideboard has plenty of room to hold everything from a meal with all the trimmings to stacks of important files.

The sideboard is an attractive, multipurpose fixture that can be used as a food serving counter, file holder—anything that requires shelf or counter space. The sideboard is a traditional home fixture, adding low-profile storage to just about any area of the home. Positioned against a wall or behind a desk, the sideboard is out of the way, yet is perfect for storing games, photo albums and other items you want to keep close at hand.

We made the sideboard out of oak and oak plywood. The construction is simple and sturdy. Two long interior shelves span the length of the project, giving you a surprising amount of storage space for such a small unit. The top shelf is concealed by two plywood doors, while the bottom shelf is left open for easy access to stored items. Cove molding fastened around the edges of the top and the curved profiles of the legs add a touch of style to this simple project.

Construction Materials

Quantity	Lumber
1	¾" × 4 × 8' oak plywood
2	1 × 4" × 8' oak
2	¾ × ¾" × 8' oak cove molding

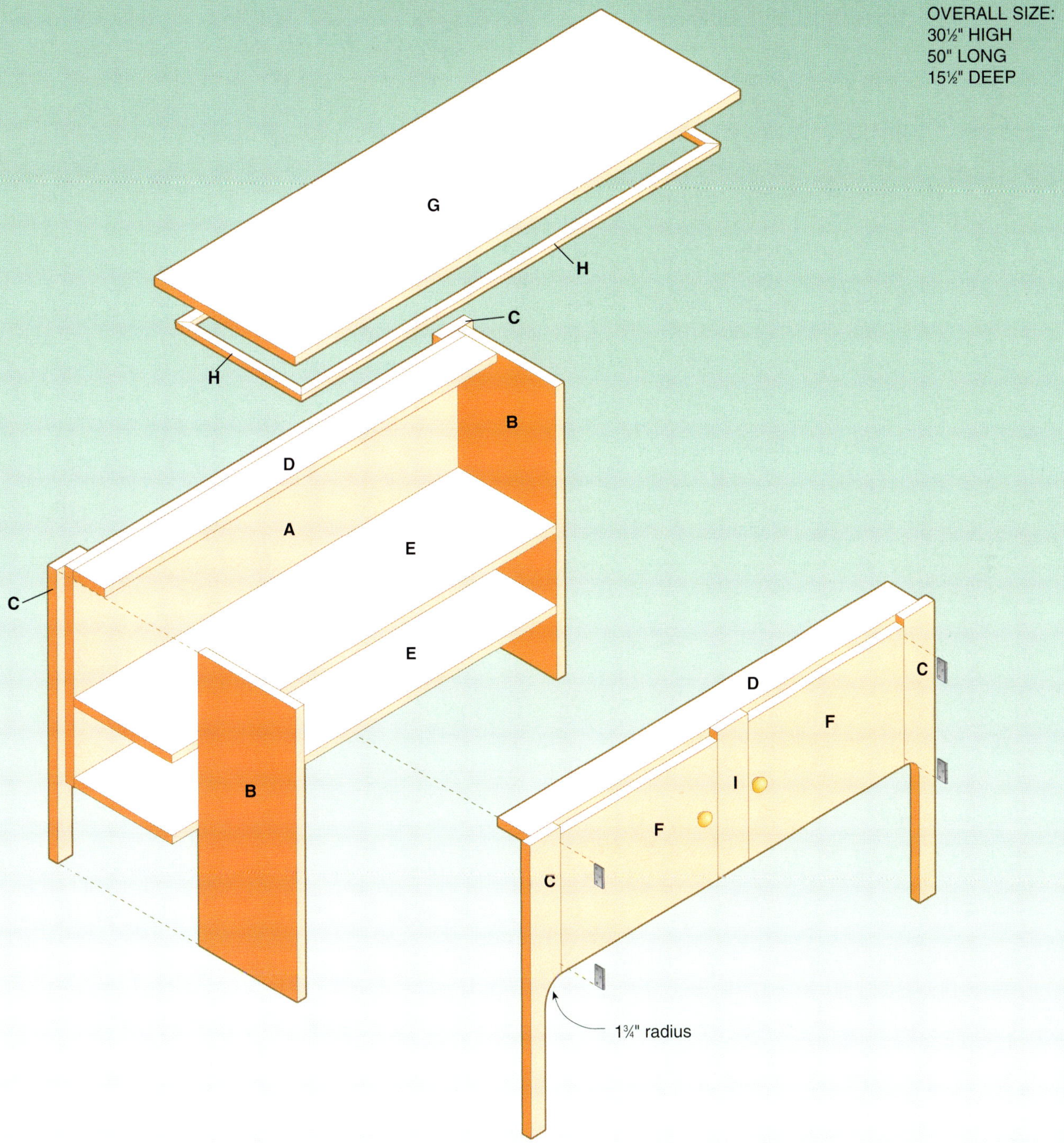

Cutting List

Key	Part	Dimension	Pcs.	Material
A	Back panel	¾ × 20 × 44"	1	Plywood
B	End panel	¾ × 11 × 29¾"	2	Plywood
C	Leg	¾ × 3½ × 29¾"	4	Oak
D	Cleat	¾ × 2½ × 44"	2	Plywood
E	Shelf	¾ × 10¼ × 44"	2	Plywood

Cutting List

Key	Part	Dimension	Pcs.	Material
F	Door	¾ × 13⅛ × 17⅞"	2	Plywood
G	Top panel	¾ × 15½ × 50"	1	Plywood
H	Top trim	¾ × ¾ × *	4	Cove molding
I	Stile	¾ × 3½ × 14"	1	Oak

Materials: #6 × 1" and 2" wood screws, 16-ga. × 1¼" brads, 1½ × 3" brass butt hinges (4), ⅞"-dia. tack-on furniture glides (4), 1"-dia. brass knobs (2), roller catches (2), ¾" oak veneer edge tape (35'), ⅜"-dia. oak plugs, wood glue, finishing materials.

Note: Measurements reflect the actual size of dimension lumber.
*Cut to fit.

Directions: Sideboard

MAKE THE CARCASE.

For all screws used in this project, drill 3/32" pilot holes. Counterbore the holes 1/4" deep, using a 3/8" counterbore bit.

1. Cut the back panel (A), end panels (B) and shelves (E) to size. Sand the shelf edges.

2. Use a household iron to apply self-adhesive edge tape to one long edge of each shelf. Trim the edges with a utility knife. Sand all parts smooth.

3. Set the back flat on your worksurface. Position one face of an end panel against each short edge of the back panel, making sure the top edges are flush. Attach the panels with glue and drive 2" wood screws through the end panels and into the back. Be sure to keep the outside face of the back panel flush with the back edges of the end panels.

4. Position the bottom shelf between the end panels, making sure the edge with the veneer tape faces away from the back panel. The bottom face of the shelf should be flush with the bottom edge of the back. Attach the bottom shelf with glue and drive 2" wood screws through the end panels and back panels and into the shelf.

5. Set the carcase (or cabinet frame) upright. Position 5 1/4"-wide spacer blocks on the bottom shelf. Set the top shelf on the spacer blocks. Attach the top shelf with glue and 2" wood screws **(photo A).**

6. Cut the cleats (D) to size, and sand them smooth.

7. Use glue and 2" wood screws to fasten one cleat between the end panels so one long edge is flush with the front edges of the end panels.

8. Attach the remaining cleat to the end and back panels so one long edge is butted against the back panel. Both cleats should be flush with the tops of the carcase.

MAKE THE LEGS.

The sideboard legs have curves that taper them to 1 3/4" in width.

1. Cut the legs (C) to length.

2. Designate a top and bottom of each leg. Draw a centerline from top to bottom on each leg. Then, draw reference lines across the legs, 14" and 15 3/4" up from the bottom. Set a compass to draw a 1 3/4"-radius semicircle. Set the point of the compass on the lower reference line, as close as possible to one long edge. Draw the semicircle to complete the curved portion of the cutting line.

3. Clamp the legs to your worksurface, and use a jig saw to cut them to shape, starting at the bottom and following the centerline and semicircle all the way to the end of the top reference line **(photo B).** Sand the cutouts smooth.

A

Use 5 1/4" spacer blocks set on the bottom shelf to position the top shelf for fastening.

B

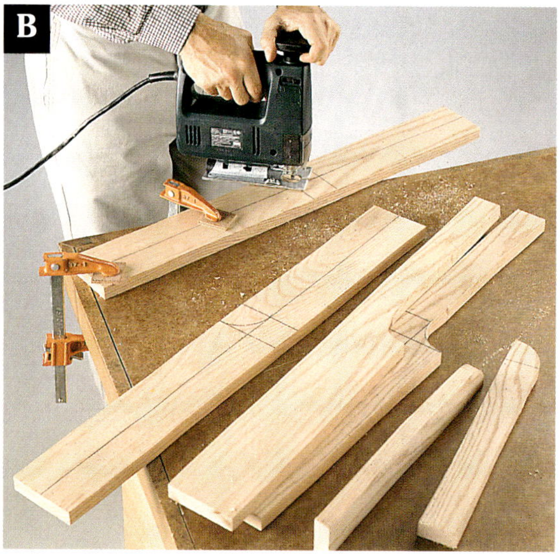

Cut the curved tapers in the legs with a jig saw.

C

Fasten the legs to the front edges of the end panels. Make sure the outside edges of the legs overhang the end panels by 1/4".

Measure the front and back overhang to make sure the carcase is centered on the top panel.

Miter-cut cove molding to cover the joint between the top panel and the carcase.

ATTACH THE LEGS AND STILE.

1. Position two legs against the front edges of the end panels, with the cutout edges facing in. Make sure the legs are flush with the end panels at the top and bottom edges, and that they overhang the outside faces of the end panels by ¼". Attach the legs to the edges of the end panels with glue and 2" wood screws **(photo C).**

2. Cut the stile (I) to length.

3. Center the stile between the legs so it spans the gap between the cleat and top shelf. Make sure the bottom edge of the stile is flush with the bottom of the top shelf. Attach it with glue and 2" wood screws.

4. Turn the project over. Fasten the remaining legs to the back and ends. Maintain the ¼" overhang of the end panels, and keep the top edges flush.

INSTALL THE TOP PANEL.

1. Cut the top panel (G) to size.

2. Apply edge tape to all four edges of the top. Sand the surfaces smooth.

3. Lay the top on your worksurface with its better face down. Center the carcase over the top. The top should extend 1½" beyond the front and back of the legs, and 2¼" beyond the outside faces of the end panels **(photo D).** Drive 1" wood screws through the cleats and into the top.

4. Cut the top trim (H) to fit around the underside of the top, miter-cutting the ends at 45° angles so they fit together at the corners.

5. Drill 1⁄16" pilot holes through the trim pieces to prevent splitting. Apply glue and drive 1¼" brads through the top trim and into the top panel. Set the brads with a nail set **(photo E).**

ATTACH THE DOORS.

1. Cut the doors (F) to size.

2. Apply edge tape to all four edges of each door.

3. Attach 1½ × 3" brass butt hinges to one short edge of each door, starting 2" in from the top and bottom. Mount the doors on the carcase by attaching the hinges to the legs **(photo F).** Make sure the bottom edges of the doors are flush with the bottom of the top shelf.

Attach each door to a leg, using 1½ × 3" butt hinges.

APPLY FINISHING TOUCHES.

1. Fill all nail holes with stainable wood putty. Glue oak plugs into all screw holes. Finish-sand all of the surfaces. Remove the door hinges and apply the finish of your choice.

2. Reattach the doors after the finish has dried. Fasten 1"-dia. brass knobs to the door fronts, and mount roller catches on the doors and stile, 5" down from the top of the stile. Tack furniture glides to the bottom ends of the legs.

Wine & Stemware Cart

This solid oak cart with a lift-off tray allows you to transport and serve your wine safely and provides an elegant place to display your vintage selections.

PROJECT POWER TOOLS

Construction Materials

Quantity	**Lumber**
2	1 × 12" × 6' oak
1	1 × 4" × 8' oak
1	1 × 4" × 6' oak
1	1 × 3" × 2' oak
1	1 × 2" × 4' oak
1	½ × 2¾" × 2' oak*
1	½ × 3¾" × 4' oak*

*Available at woodworker's supply stores.

With our versatile oak wine and stemware cart, you can display, move and serve wine and other cordials from one convenient station. This cart can store up to 15 bottles of wine, liquor, soda or mix, and it holds the bottles in the correct downward position to prevent wine corks from drying out.

The upper stemware rack holds more than a dozen long-stemmed wine or champagne glasses, and a removable serving tray with easy-to-grip handles works well for cutting cheese and for serving drinks and snacks. Beneath the tray is a handy storage area for napkins, corkscrews and other items. Sturdy swivel casters make this wine rack fully mobile over tile, vinyl or carpeting.

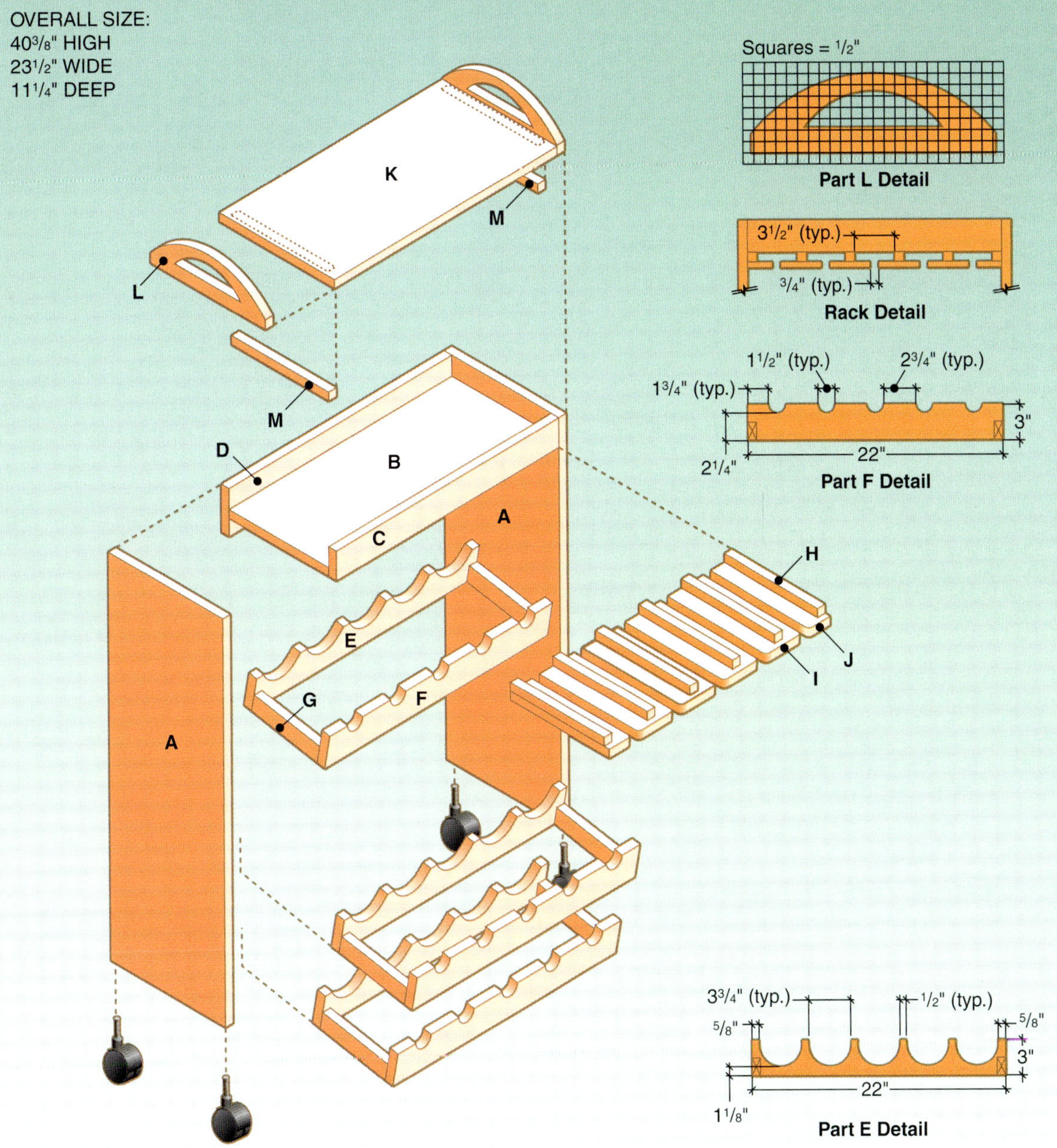

Key	Part	Dimension	Pcs.	Material
A	Side	¾ × 11¼ × 34"	2	Oak
B	Top	¾ × 9¾ × 22"	1	Oak
C	Front stretcher	¾ × 2½ × 22"	1	Oak
D	Back stretcher	¾ × 4 × 22"	1	Oak
E	Wine rack, back	¾ × 3 × 22"	3	Oak
F	Wine rack, front	¾ × 3 × 22"	3	Oak
G	Wine rack, cleat	¾ × 1½ × 6½"	6	Oak

Cutting List

Key	Part	Dimension	Pcs.	Material
H	Stemware slat	¾ × ¾ × 9¼"	6	Oak
I	Stemware plate	½ × 3½ × 9¾"	4	Oak
J	End plate	½ × 2⅛ × 9¾"	2	Oak
K	Tray	¾ × 11¼ × 22"	1	Oak
L	Tray handle	¾ × 3½ × 11¼"	2	Oak
M	Tray feet	¾ × ¾ × 9½"	2	Oak

Materials: #6 × 1", 1¼" and 1½" wood screws, ⅜"-dia. oak plugs, casters (4), wood glue, finishing materials.

Note: Measurements reflect the actual size of dimension lumber.

Use a spacer to keep the slats aligned properly, and attach them with glue and screws.

Use a drum sander attached to your portable drill to smooth the jig saw cuts on the wine racks.

Directions: Wine & Stemware Cart

CONSTRUCT THE SIDES AND STEMWARE RACK.

Before fastening frame parts together, make sure the assembly is square (see *Tip*).

1. Cut the cart sides (A), top (B) and back stretcher (D) from 1 × 12 oak. Cut the front stretcher (C) from 1 × 3 oak and the stemware slats (H) from 1 × 4 oak. Cut the plates (I) and end plates (J) from ½"-thick oak.

2. Clamp a belt sander to your worksurface, and use it as a grinder to round over the front corners of the stemware plates, and one front corner of each end plate.

3. Sand all of the pieces smooth.

4. Place the top flat on your worksurface. Arrange the slats on its bottom face, flush with the back edge. Space the slats 3½" apart, using a piece of scrap wood as a spacer **(photo A).** Keep the outer slats flush with the ends of the top. Drill ³⁄₃₂" pilot holes through the slats, and counterbore the holes ⅛" deep, using a ⅜" counterbore bit. Attach the slats with glue and 1¼" wood screws.

TIP

To check for square, measure your project from one corner diagonally to its opposite corner. Repeat the procedure for the other two corners. If the two diagonal lines are equal, your assembly is square.

BUILD THE WINE RACKS.

First assemble the wine racks as individual units. Then, attach them to the sides of the cart.

1. Cut the wine rack backs (E) and fronts (F) from 1 × 4 oak, and cut the cleats (G) from 1 × 2 oak.

2. Measuring from one end, mark points at 2½", 6¾", 11", 15¼" and 19½" on the long edges of the wine rack backs and fronts.

3. Use a compass set at 1⅞" for the rack back. Set the point of the compass on each reference mark, as close as possible to the edge, and draw the five semicircles. Set the compass for ¾" and draw the semicircles for the rack front. Carefully make the cutouts with a jig saw.

4. Position the cleats between the rack fronts and backs, and drill two pilot holes through the faces of the fronts and backs and into the ends of the cleats. Counterbore the holes ¼" deep. Join the pieces with glue and 1½" wood screws.

Measure ½" along the front and 2½" along the back of each side, and connect the marks for the bottom rack alignment.

Clamp a 4 × 10" spacer between the bottom and middle racks for proper positioning.

Drive screws through the slats to secure the top to the sides.

5. Fill the counterbores with glued oak plugs. Sand the plugs flush with the surface, and smooth any rough edges. Clamp each completed rack to your worksurface, and sand the cutouts smooth with a drum sander **(photo B).**

ATTACH THE WINE RACKS.

1. Measure up ½" from the bottom on the inside face of each side piece, and make a mark at the front edge. Measure up 2½" from the bottom, and make a mark at the back edge. Draw an angled reference line between the marks **(photo C).**

2. With one of the side pieces lying flat on your worksurface, position a wine rack so the bottom edge is on the reference line and the front edge is set back ¾" from the front edge of the side piece. Drill pilot holes through the rack cleats, and counterbore the holes ⅛" deep. Attach the rack to the side with glue and 1¼" wood screws.

3. Attach the middle and top racks in the same manner, using a 4 × 10" spacer to position them correctly **(photo D).**

4. Use bar or pipe clamps to hold the remaining side piece in position. Make sure the bottom rack is on the reference line, and use the spacer to set the positions of the middle and top racks. Fasten the racks to the side piece.

5. Arrange the stretchers

between the sides so their top and outside edges are flush with the tops and outside edges of the sides. Drill pilot holes through the sides and into the ends of the stretchers. Counterbore the holes ¼" deep. Attach the stretchers with glue and 1½" wood screws.

ATTACH THE TOP ASSEMBLY.

1. Lay the cart on its side, and clamp the top between the side pieces. The bottom face of the top should be flush with the bottom edge of the front stretcher.

2. Measure the distance between the top and the top ends of the sides to make sure the top is level. Drill pilot holes through the outer slats and into the sides, and counterbore the holes ⅛" deep. Apply glue to the edges of the top and to the outside edges of the outer slats. Position the top, and drive 1¼" wood screws through the outer slats and into the sides **(photo E).**

3. Drill three evenly spaced pilot holes, counterbored ¼" deep, through both stretchers and into the edges of the top, and secure the pieces with 1½" wood screws.

Use a ¾"-thick spacer to guide the placement of the stemware plates.

> **TIP**
>
> *Jig saw blades cut on the upward stroke, so the top side of the workpiece may splinter. To protect the finished or exposed side of a piece, make the cut with the piece's face side down. This way, if the edge splinters, it will remain hidden on the unexposed side. Remember to maintain a fast blade speed if you are cutting with a coarse-tooth blade. When cutting curves, use a narrow blade, and move the saw slowly to avoid bending the blade. Some jig saws have a scrolling knob that allows you to turn the blade without turning the saw.*

COMPLETE THE RACK AND FIT THE CASTERS.

Attach the stemware plates to the slats to complete the stemware rack.

1. Set the cart upside down on your worksurface. Position an end plate onto an outside slat, with its square side flush against the side panel and its square end flush against the back stretcher. Drill two pilot holes down through the end plate, taking care to avoid the screws in the slat beneath. Counterbore the holes ⅛" deep, and fasten the plate with glue and 1" wood screws.

2. Repeat these steps to position and attach the remaining plates. Use a ¾"-thick spacer between the plates to ensure uniform spacing **(photo F).**

3. Drill holes into the bottom edges of the cart sides, and test-fit the casters **(photo G).** Position the holes so they are centered on the edge from side to side and are no less than 1" from the front and back side edges. For the casters to work properly, the holes must be perpendicular to the bottom edges of the sides.

Drill holes for the casters in the bottom edges of the sides.

Drill a pilot hole, and cut the inside handle profile with a jig saw. Use scrap wood as a backer board to prevent splintering.

MAKE THE TRAY.

The wine cart tray is an oak board with handles and narrow feet.

1. Cut the tray (K) from 1 × 12 oak, and cut the tray handle (L) blanks from 1 × 4 oak. Cut the ¾ × ¾" feet (M) from leftover 1 × 12.

2. Transfer the pattern for the handles onto one of the blanks (see *Diagram*).

3. Drill a starter hole on the inside portion of the handle, using a backer board to prevent splintering. Use a jig saw to cut along the pattern lines **(photo H).**

4. Trace the outline of the shaped handle onto the remaining handle blank. Cut the pattern on the second handle. Clamp the two handles together, and gang-sand them so their shapes are identical.

5. Position the tray between the handles, and drill three evenly spaced pilot holes through the side of each handle. Counterbore the holes ¼" deep. Attach the handles to the ends of the tray with glue and 1½" wood screws.

6. Position the tray feet on the bottom edge of the tray, ⅛" in from the side edges and ⅞" from the front and back edges. Drill pilot holes through the feet, and counterbore the holes ⅛" deep. Attach the feet with glue and 1" wood screws.

APPLY FINISHING TOUCHES.

1. Glue oak plugs into all visible counterbore holes, and sand flush with the surface. Finish-sand the entire cart.

2. Apply your choice of stain and a polyurethane topcoat and allow the finish to dry. We used a rustic oak stain and two coats of polyurethane.

NOTE: If you will be using the tray as a cutting board, be sure to apply a nontoxic finish.

3. Install the casters on the bottom of the cart. You may want to use at least one locking caster so your cart stays put.

TIP

Applying a thin coat of sanding sealer before staining helps the wood absorb stain evenly and can eliminate blotchy finishes. Sanding sealer is a clear liquid, usually applied with a brush. Read the package labels of the different products you plan to use to make sure the finishes are compatible.

Vertical Display Cabinet

Sturdy but airy, this open display unit combines the warmth of oak with the glimmer of glass.

PROJECT POWER TOOLS

CONSTRUCTION MATERIALS

Quantity	Lumber
1	1 × 1" × 8' oak
12	1 × 2" × 8' oak
2	1 × 4" × 8' oak
1	1 × 4" × 4' oak
1	1 × 6" × 8' oak
1	¾" × 4 × 4' oak plywood
1	3½" × 8' oak crown
1	8' oak base shoe
3	⅜ × 16¾ × 39¼" tempered glass

Compare the design and price of our vertical display cabinet to those available in stores, and you'll be impressed. Though the materials are not expensive, this project is by no means cheaply constructed. The slender stiles are made from oak for strength. The oak back braces perform double duty by adding an unusual visual element as well as reinforcing the cabinet. Transparent glass shelves give the cabinet a modern appeal, while oak crown and base trim pieces lend classic elegance.

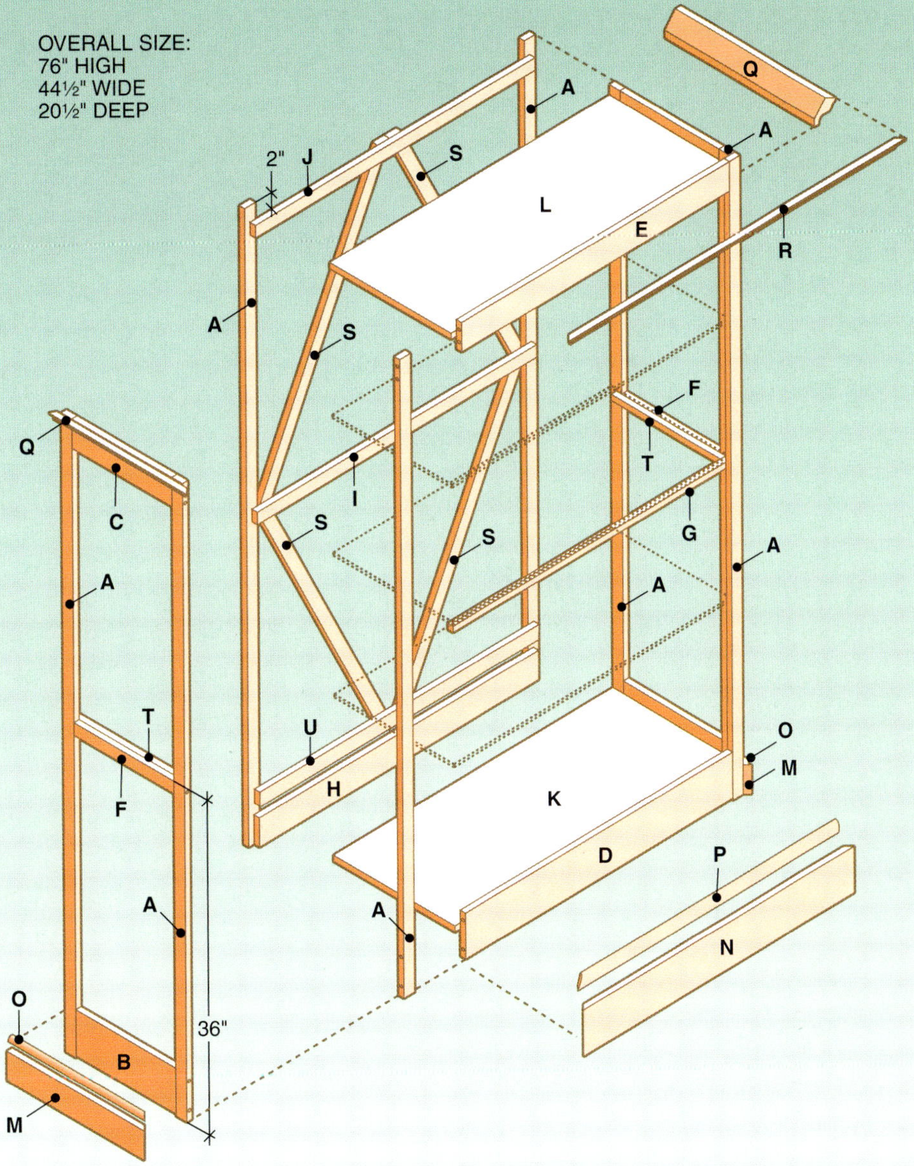

Cutting List

Key	Part	Dimension	Pcs.	Material
A	Stile	¾ × 1½ × 76"	8	Oak
B	Short bottom rail	¾ × 5½ × 14"	2	Oak
C	Short top rail	¾ × 3½ × 14"	2	Oak
D	Long bottom rail	¾ × 5½ × 38"	1	Oak
E	Long top rail	¾ × 3½ × 38"	1	Oak
F	Center rail	¾ × 1½ × 14"	2	Oak
G	Front shelf rail	¾ × ¾ × 39½"	1	Oak
H	Back bottom cleat	¾ × 3½ × 39½"	1	Oak
I	Back shelf rail	¾ × 1½ × 39½"	1	Oak
J	Back top cleat	¾ × 1½ × 39½"	1	Oak
K	Bottom	¾ × 17 × 39½"	1	Oak ply.

Cutting List

Key	Part	Dimension	Pcs.	Material
L	Top	¾ × 17 × 39½"	1	Oak ply.
M	Side base	¾ × 3½ × 19¼"	2	Oak
N	Front base	¾ × 3½ × 42½"	1	Oak
O	Side base cap	⅜ × ¾ × 19¼"	2	Oak base shoe
P	Front base cap	⅜ × ¾ × 42½"	1	Oak base shoe
Q	Side crown mldg.	¾ × 3½ × 21"	2	Oak crown
R	Front crown mldg.	¾ × 3½ × 44½"	1	Oak crown
S	Back brace	¾ × 1½ × 39¾"	4	Oak
T	Center shelf cleat	¾ × ¾ × 15⅜"	2	Oak
U	Bottom stretcher	¾ × 1½ × 39½"	1	Oak

Materials: Wood glue, #6 wood screws (1¼", 1½"), 4d finish nails, 1" brads, ⅜" × 4' oak doweling (2), ⅜" oak plugs, plastic pin-style shelf supports (12), self-adhesive shelf cushions, finishing materials.

Note: Measurements reflect the actual thickness of dimension lumber.

Use a wood mallet to pound ⅜" glued oak dowels into the end frame.

Measure the diagonals to check for square. If the measurements are equal, the frame is square.

Directions: Vertical Display Cabinet

MAKE THE END FRAMES. Dowel joints make the end frames sturdy and rigid. Through-dowel joints are the easiest dowel joints to make—all you need is a good bar or pipe clamp and the ability to drill a reasonably straight guide hole.

1. Cut the stiles (A), short bottom rails (B), short top rails (C) and center rails (F) to size, and sand smooth.

2. Make a reference mark on each stile 36" down from the top edge. Position a top short rail between two stiles with the top edges flush. Position a bottom rail ¼" up from the bottom of the stiles, and place the center rail so the top edge lies on the 36" mark.

3. Cut 20 lengths of ⅜" dowling, 2½" long. Score the edges of the dowels to make them easier to insert (see *Tip*).

4. Drill ⅜ × 2½"-deep holes through the stiles into the rails (see *Diagram*).

5. Apply glue to the joints and drive dowels into the holes **(photo A).**

6. Check to make sure the end frames are square, then clamp the pieces together until the glue dries.

MAKE THE FRONT FRAME. You'll want to choose wood with matching or similar grain patterns for the front frame, base and crown molding to further enhance the beauty of your project.

1. Cut the long bottom rail (D) and long top rail (E) to size, and sand smooth.

2. Position the rails between the two stiles (the top rail should be flush, the bottom rail should be ¼" up from the ends of the stiles).

3. Drill holes and attach the

TIP

Custom-cut dowels can be difficult to fit into snug holes. To make insertion easier, score a groove along the length of each dowel. This groove allows air and excess glue to escape when driving the dowels into their holes.

Position the back over the end frames at the ¾" space, and join with glue and screws.

rails and stiles with glued ⅜" dowels.
4. Cut the front shelf rail (G) to size, and sand smooth.
5. Lay the front frame face-down, then position the front shelf rail so the top edge is flush with the 36" reference lines on the stiles and the ends are set back ¾" from the edges of the stiles.
6. Drill countersunk pilot holes and fasten the shelf rail with glue and 1¼" screws.

MAKE THE BACK FRAME.
1. Cut the back bottom cleat (H), the back shelf rail (I) and the back top cleat (J) to size, and sand smooth.
2. Lay two stiles on your work-surface, and position the bottom cleat over the stiles so the bottom edges are flush and the ends of the cleat are set in ¾" from the edges of the stiles.
3. Drill countersunk pilot holes and attach the cleat with glue and 1¼" screws.
4. Position the back top cleat over the stiles so the top edge is 2" down from the top of the stiles and the ends are set in ¾" from the edges. Attach the top cleat with glue and counter-sunk screws.
5. Measure the diagonals of the frame to check for square **(photo B).**

ASSEMBLE THE CABINET.
1. Position the end frames up-right on their back edges, then lay the front frame over them (the stiles on the end frames should fit tightly against the in-set cleats on the front frame).
2. Check for square by measur-ing diagonals, then drill coun-terbored pilot holes and join the front frame to the end frames with glue and 1½" screws.
3. Turn the assembly over so the front frame faces down, then position and attach the back frame with glue and coun-terbored 1½" screws **(photo C).**

ATTACH THE BOTTOM, TOP AND STRETCHER.
1. Cut the bottom (K) and top (L) to size, and sand the edges smooth.
2. Position the bottom piece in the cabinet so its bottom sur-face is set 3½" up from the lower ends of the stiles (at the rear, the bottom piece will rest on the back cleat).
3. Drill countersunk pilot holes through the bottom rails and into the bottom, then attach with glue and 1½" screws.
4. Fasten the top in similar fash-ion. Position the top piece in the cabinet so the top surface is 1¼" below the top ends of the stiles (at the back, the top piece will rest on the back cleat). Drill countersunk pilot holes and attach the top with glue and 1½" screws.
5. Cut the bottom stretcher (U) to size, and sand smooth. Posi-tion it over the rear edge of the bottom piece, then attach it to the stiles with glue and coun-tersunk 1¼" screws.

ATTACH THE BACK BRACES.
The easiest way to cut the an-gled back braces is to position the 1½" stock for the first brace across the back of the cabinet, mark and cut the proper

Secure the back braces at the centerpoints to create a diamond.

Miter the crown molding by positioning the molding upside down in the miter box. Cut the moldings about ½" too long, then test-fit the pieces and trim as needed for a tight fit at the mitered corners.

angles, then use this piece as a template for cutting the remaining braces.

1. Cut blanks for the back braces (S) to length.

2. Mark the horizontal centerpoints of the back stretcher and back top cleat. On each end of the back shelf rail, mark vertical centerpoints ¾" inch from the bottom edge.

3. Position a back brace diagonally from the back top cleat to the back shelf rail, with the ends touching the reference marks. Use a T-bevel to mark horizontal cutting lines across the ends of the brace, parallel to the edges of the top cleat and shelf cleat.

4. Cut the angles on the ends of the brace, then use this brace as a template to cut the other three.

5. Drill countersunk pilot holes, and attach the back braces with glue and 1¼" screws **(photo D).**

ATTACH THE TRIM.

Cut the trim pieces slightly longer than needed so you can test fit and trim to the exact length for a precise fit.

1. Cut all base pieces (M, N), cap pieces (O, P) and crowns (Q, R) to length, mitering the appropriate ends at 45° **(photo E).**

2. Position the base pieces around the front and sides of the cabinet, flush with the bottom ends of the stiles, then drill pilot holes and attach with 4d finish nails.

3. Position the caps on the base pieces, drill pilot holes and secure with glue and brads.

4. Position the crown moldings so the bottom edges are 1½" from the bottom of the top rails, drill pilot holes and attach with 4d finish nails. Lock-nail the mitered joints (see *Tip*).

TIP

Lock-nailing is a technique used to reinforce mitered joints. The idea is to drive finish nails through both mating surfaces at the joint. Start by drilling pilot holes all the way through one board (to avoid splitting the wood) and partway into the other mating surface. Drive a small finish nail (2d or 4d) or a brad through each pilot hole to complete the lock-nailing operation.

Attach the center shelf cleats to the center rails with glue, and clamp the pieces together.

Use a pegboard template to align the shelf support holes in the stiles and back braces.

ADD THE SHELF SUPPORTS.

The shelves are spaced for an airy, open feeling, but more shelves could be added if you wish. Simply determine the shelf placement and repeat steps 3 and 4.

1. Cut the center shelf cleats (T) to size, and sand smooth.

2. Apply glue, then position the cleats against the center rails so the top edges are flush, and clamp in place until the glue dries **(photo F).**

3. Cut an 8 × 20" pegboard template to position the shelf support holes. Outline a horizontal row of holes 16" up from the bottom.

4. Rest the template on the top edge of the bottom rails and bottom stretcher, and drill holes in the back braces and stiles **(photo G).**

5. Drill holes for the upper shelf in similar fashion, resting the template on the center rails and back shelf rail.

APPLY FINISHING TOUCHES.

It's a good idea to order the glass shelves after you have completed the project. Measure the length and width for each shelf opening and reduce each measurement by 1/8". Let the glass shop know that you are providing the finish cut dimensions, so the cutter doesn't add an additional reduction.

Order tempered safety glass because it is stronger than ordinary glass and does not form sharp shards if broken.

1. Insert 3/8" glued oak plugs into counterbores, and apply stainable putty to all visible nail holes.

2. Finish-sand, then apply the finish of your choice. We used a walnut stain and a polyurethane finish. Because oak is an open grained wood, you may want to apply grain filler to create a smoother finish.

3. Attach self-adhesive plastic cushions to the shelf supports to prevent rattling, then install the glass shelves.

BLACK&DECKER
Plywood
Saw Blade
7¼"
Cat. No. 73-004 or 63-004
BLACK & DECKER
For Plywood
For smooth cuts in plywood, paneling, veneers and pl
STAEDTLER
ADDRESSES
STAEDTLER
MARS 964
TAIWAN

Home Office Projects

Make your home office space work harder with these projects that increase storage options or work surfaces. The library table is a perfect place for the kids to spread out their homework and the card table comes in handy when a bit of extra work space is needed. The secretary topper is sized to fit on the writing desk, but it doesn't need to stay in the office—these useful cubbyholes can be equally helpful in the kitchen or bedroom. You're sure to enjoy getting down to business using furniture you have made yourself.

PROJECT
POWER TOOLS

Secretary Topper

Transform a plain table, desk or cabinet top into a fully equipped secretary with this box-style topper.

In the furniture world, a secretary is a free-standing, upright cabinet with a drop-down worksurface that conceals numerous storage cubbies when raised. The traditional secretary also has two or three large drawers at the bottom. With this secretary topper, we zeroed in on the cubbyhole feature, creating a simple storage unit that will convert just about any flat surface into a functioning secretary.

The fixed shelves are designed to accommodate papers up to legal size, while the adjustable shelf can be positioned to hold address and reference books. The vertical slats with the cutout dividers are good for storing incoming or outgoing mail, and the handy drawer is an ideal spot to keep small desktop items.

We made this simple wood project from oak and oak plywood. If you are building a secretary topper to complement an existing piece of furniture, try to match the wood type and finish of the piece.

NOTE: This secretary topper is sized to fit on top of the Writing Desk featured on pages 174 through 179.

Construction Materials

Quantity	Lumber
1	¼" × 2 × 3' oak plywood
2	1 × 10" × 8' oak
1	½ × 8" × 6' oak
1	¼ × 2" × 7' oak mull casing

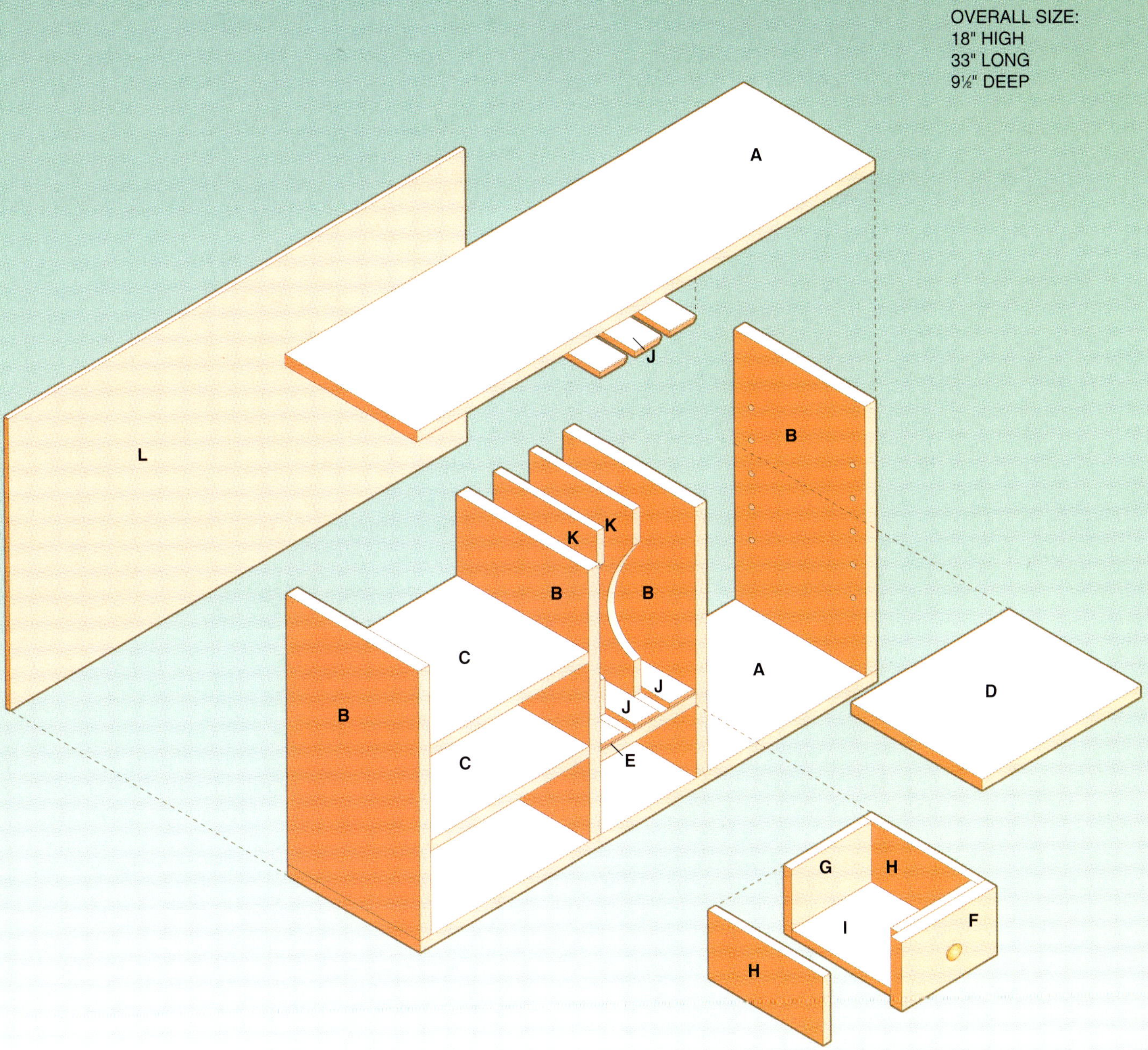

Cutting List				
Key	**Part**	**Dimension**	**Pcs.**	**Material**
A	Top/bottom	¾ × 9¼ × 33"	2	Oak
B	Partition	¾ × 9¼ × 16½"	4	Oak
C	Fixed shelf	¾ × 9¼ × 11½"	2	Oak
D	Adjustable shelf	¾ × 9¼ × 11¼"	1	Oak
E	Bin top	¾ × 9¼ × 7"	1	Oak
F	Drawer front	¾ × 4⅛ × 6¾"	1	Oak

Cutting List				
Key	**Part**	**Dimension**	**Pcs.**	**Material**
G	Drawer end	½ × 4⅛ × 5¾"	2	Oak
H	Drawer side	½ × 4⅛ × 8¼"	2	Oak
I	Drawer bottom	½ × 5¾ × 7¼"	1	Oak
J	Bin spacer	¼ × 2 × 9"	6	Mull casing
K	Divider	½ × 7¼ × 11½"	2	Oak
L	Back panel	¼ × 17⅞ × 32¾"	1	Plywood

Materials: #6 × 1⅝" wood screws, 16-ga. × ¾" and 1" brads, ¼"-dia. shelf pins (4), ¾"-dia. brass knob (1), ⅜"-dia. oak plugs, adhesive felt pads (6), wood glue, finishing materials.

Note: Measurements reflect the actual size of dimension lumber.

Use pegboard as a drilling template to align the shelf pin holes in the partitions.

Fasten the back panel to the cabinet with brads, keeping the framework square.

Directions: Secretary Topper

For all screws used in this project, drill 3/32" pilot holes. Counterbore the holes 1/4" deep, using a 3/8" counterbore bit.

MAKE THE SHELF FRAMEWORK.

1. Cut the partitions (B), fixed shelves (C) and bin top (E) to length. Sand the parts smooth.

2. Draw reference lines across the faces of two partitions, 5" up from the bottom edge and 5 3/4" down from the top edge. Use glue to fasten the shelves between the two partitions, keeping their bottom edges flush with the reference lines. Drive 1 5/8" wood screws through the partitions and into the ends of the shelves.

3. Draw reference lines on the outside face of the left partition, 4 1/4" up from the bottom edge. Use glue and 1 5/8" wood screws to fasten the bin top to the partition, with its bottom edge on the reference line. Make sure the front and rear edges are flush.

4. Fasten an unattached partition to the free end of the bin top with glue and 1 5/8" wood screws, keeping the front and back edges flush.

5. Drill holes in the partitions for the adjustible shelf in the left section. Clamp a piece of pegboard to one face, and use it as a drilling template **(photo A).** Drill 1/4"-dia. × 3/8"-deep holes into the partition. Wrap masking tape around your drill bit as a depth marker to keep you from drilling through the pieces. After you drill holes in one partition, use tape to mark the locations of the pegboard holes you used. Repeat the drilling with the opposing partition. Keep the same end up and the same edge in front. Sand the pieces smooth.

COMPLETE THE CABINET.

1. Cut the top/bottom panels (A) to length.

2. Attach a panel to the ends of the partitions at the top and at the bottom of the framework. Apply glue, and drive 1 5/8" wood screws through the outside faces of the panels and into the ends of the partitions.

3. Fasten the remaining partition between the top and bottom panels, making sure the outside face is flush with the ends of the panels.

4. Cut the back (L) to size, and sand it smooth.

5. Fasten the back to the cabinet with 3/4" brads **(photo B).** Fasten one end of the back and check for square. Adjust it as needed, and fasten the remaining sides. The panel should be centered on the framework, with a slight reveal at all of the edges.

MAKE THE DRAWER.

Cut the drawer parts from 1/2"-thick × 8"-wide oak stock.

1. Cut the drawer ends (G), drawer sides (H) and drawer bottom (I) to size. Sand the parts smooth.

2. Fasten the drawer ends between the drawer sides with glue, and drive 3/4" brads through the drawer sides and into the drawer ends. Make sure the outside faces of the drawer ends are flush with the ends of the drawer sides.

3. Position the drawer bottom

Drill pilot holes and fasten the drawer bottom with ¾" brads.

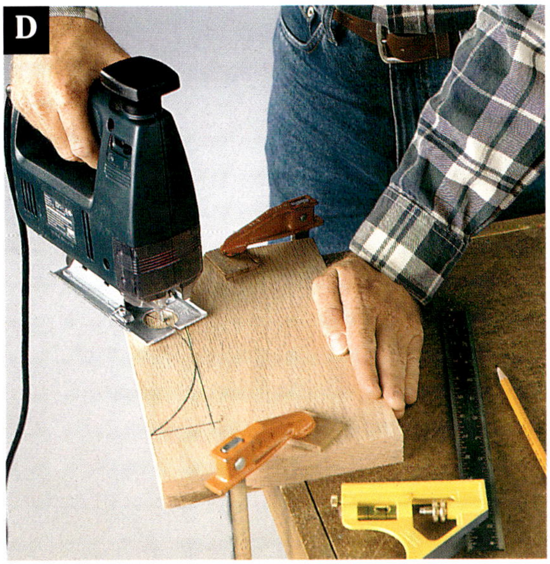

Gang-cut curves into the dividers, using a jig saw.

inside the drawer ends and sides. Drill 1⁄16" pilot holes through the sides and ends, and fasten the bottom with ¾" brads **(photo C).** Do not use glue to fasten the bottom.

4. Cut the drawer front (F) to size from 1 × 10 stock, and sand it smooth.

5. Center the drawer front on one drawer end. With the edges flush, attach the drawer front with glue, and drive 1" brads through the end and into the front.

INSTALL THE VERTICAL DIVIDERS.

1. Cut the bin spacers (J) and dividers (K) to length.

2. Draw a curve on the front edge of one divider, starting 2¼" in from the top and bottom edges, and making it 2" deep at the center. Clamp the dividers together with their edges flush. Gang-cut them along the cutting line with a jig saw **(photo D)**. Gang-sand the pieces, using a drum sander attachment on an electric drill.

3. Bevel the front edges of the bin spacers by mounting a belt sander to your workbench, and clamp a scrap guide to the worksurface to stabilize the parts as you sand the ends of the dividers **(photo E).**

4. Use ¾" brads to fasten two of the bin spacers to the bin top, flush against the partitions and butted against the back panel. Fasten two more bin spacers to the top panel.

5. Insert the dividers. Fasten the last bin spacers between them.

APPLY FINISHING TOUCHES.

1. Cut the adjustable shelf (D) to length.

2. Fill all screw holes with glued oak plugs. Set all nails with a nail set, and fill the holes with wood putty. Remove the dividers, and finish-sand all the parts. Apply a finish.

3. Attach a ¾" brass knob to the drawer front. Insert the shelf pins and adjustable shelf. Attach self-adhesive felt pads to the bottom of the topper.

Clamp a belt sander to your workbench to make the divider bevels.

Bookcase

A simple, functional bookcase on which to set your picture frames, books and decorations, this project is as useful as it is attractive.

PROJECT POWER TOOLS

An attractive bookcase adds just the right decorative and functional touch to a family room or den. And you don't need to shell out large amounts of cash for a high-end bookcase or settle for a cheap, throw-together particleboard unit—this sturdy bookcase looks great and will last for many years.

Four roomy shelf areas let you display and store everything from framed pictures to reference manuals. The decorative trim on the outside of the bookcase spices up the overall appearance of the project, while panel molding along the front edges of the shelves softens the corners and adds structural stability. With a few coats of enamel paint, this bookcase takes on a smooth, polished look.

Although the project is constructed mostly of plywood, the molding that fits around the top, bottom and shelves allows the bookcase to fit in almost anywhere in the house. This bookcase is a great-looking, useful addition to just about any room.

Construction Materials

Quantity	Lumber
1	¾" × 4 × 8' birch plywood
1	¼" × 4 × 8' birch plywood
2	¾ × 1⅝" × 8' panel molding
1	¾ × ¾" × 6' cove molding
2	¾ × ¾" × 8' quarter-round molding
1	¾ × 2⅝" × 6' chair-rail molding

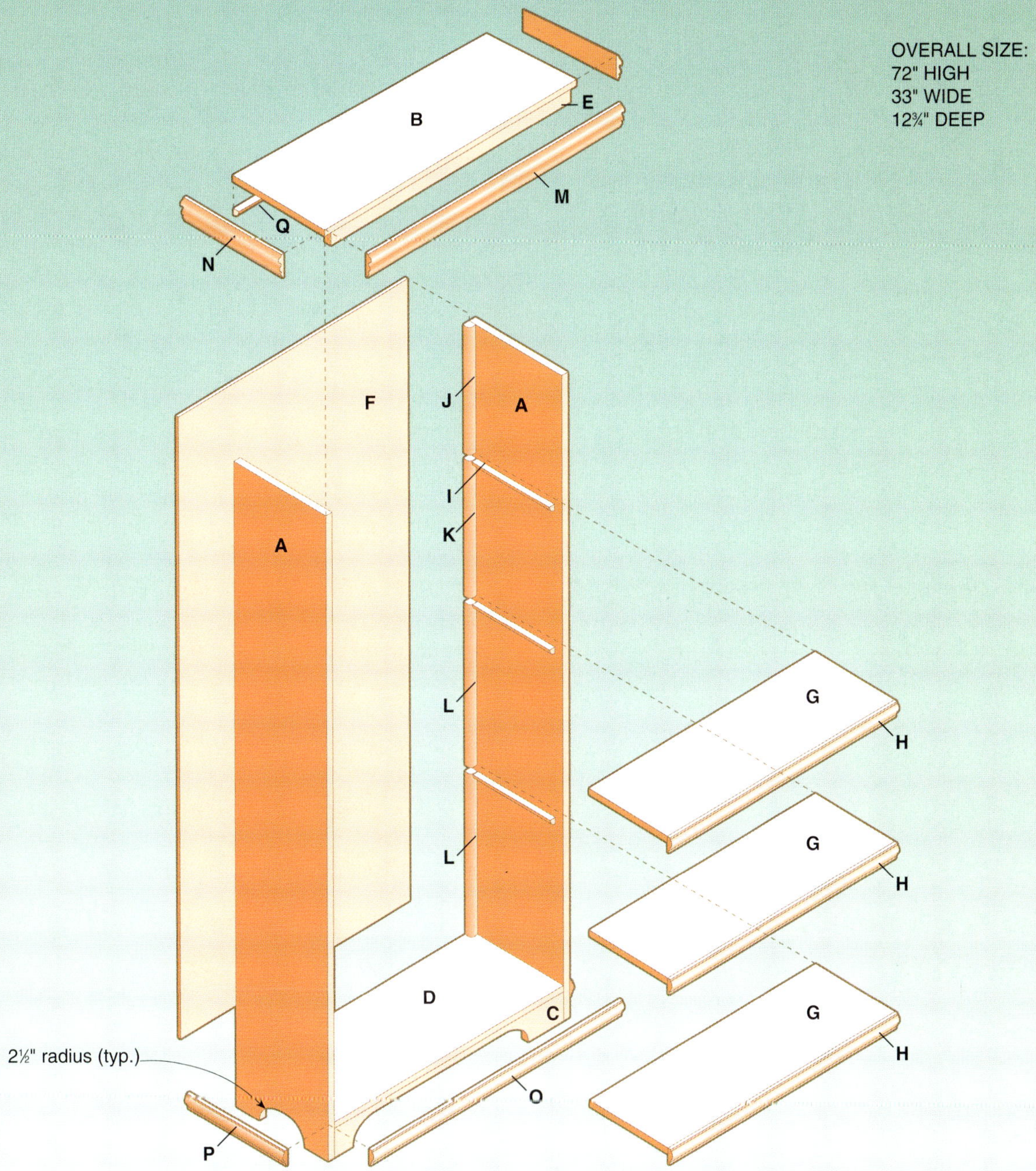

Cutting List

Key	Part	Dimension	Pcs.	Material
A	Side	¾ × 12 × 71¼"	2	Plywood
B	Top	¾ × 11¾ × 31½"	1	Plywood
C	Front rail	¾ × 3¼ × 30"	1	Plywood
D	Bottom	¾ × 11¾ × 30"	1	Plywood
E	Top rail	¾ × 1½ × 30"	1	Plywood
F	Back	¼ × 30 × 68¾"	1	Plywood
G	Shelf	¾ × 10½ × 30"	3	Plywood
H	Shelf nosing	¾ × 1⅝ × 30"	3	Panel molding
I	Shelf cleat	¾ × ¾ × 9¾"	6	Cove molding

Cutting List

Key	Part	Dimension	Pcs.	Material
J	Back brace	¾ × ¾ × 14"	2	Quarter-round
K	Back brace	¾ × ¾ × 15"	2	Quarter-round
L	Back brace	¾ × ¾ × 18"	4	Quarter-round
M	Top facing	¾ × 2⅝ × 33"	1	Chair-rail molding
N	Top side molding	¾ × 2⅝ × 12¾"	2	Chair-rail molding
O	Bottom facing	¾ × 1⅝ × 33"	1	Panel molding
P	Bottom side molding	¾ × 1⅝ × 12¾"	2	Panel molding
Q	Back brace	¾ × ¾ × 28½"	1	Quarter-round

Materials: #6 × 2" wood screws, 4d and 6d finish nails, 16-ga. × 1" and 1¼" brads, 16-ga. × ¾" wire nails, ¾" birch veneer edge tape (25'), wood glue, finishing materials.

Note: Measurements reflect the actual size of dimension lumber.

Directions: Bookcase

MAKE THE SIDES AND FRONT RAIL.

1. Cut the sides (A) and front rail (C) to size from ¾"-thick plywood. Sand the parts smooth and clean the edges thoroughly.

2. Cut two strips of self-adhesive edge tape slightly longer than the long edge of the side piece. Attach the tape to one long edge of each side piece by pressing it onto the wood with a household iron set at a medium-low setting. The heat will activate the adhesive. Trim and sand the edges of the tape.

3. Designate a top and bottom to each side. Draw a cutting line across each side, 2½" up from the bottom edge. Draw marks on the bottom edges of the sides, 5½" in from the front and rear edges. Set a compass to draw a 2½"-radius arc, using the marks on the bottom edges as centerpoints. Set the point of the compass as close as possible to the bottom edges of the sides, and draw the arcs. Use a jig saw to cut the arch.

4. Repeat these steps to make the arch in the front rail, but place the point of the compass 4¾" in from each end of the front rail. Cut the front rail to shape with a jig saw **(photo A).**

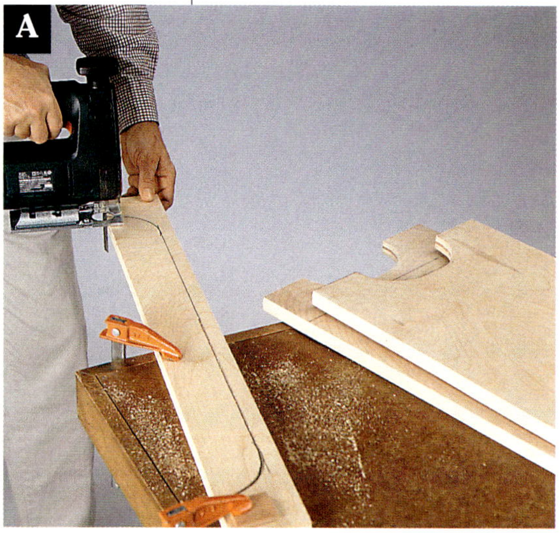
Cut arches along the bottoms of the side panels and front rail to create the bookcase "feet."

BUILD THE CARCASE.

The top, bottom and sides of the bookcase form the basic cabinet—called the carcase.

1. Cut the top (B), bottom (D) and top rail (E) to size. Sand the parts smooth.

2. Draw reference lines across the faces of the sides, 3¼" up from the bottom edges. Set the sides on edge, and position the bottom between them, just above the reference lines. Attach the bottom to the sides with glue and 2" wood screws, keeping the front edges flush. Drill 5/64" pilot holes for the screws. Counterbore the holes ⅛" deep, using a ⅜" counterbore bit.

3. Set the sides upright, and position the front rail between the sides, flush with the side and bottom edges. Glue the rail edges. Then, clamp it to the bottom board. Drill 1/16" pilot holes, and secure the front rail with 6d finish nails driven through the sides, and 1¼" brads driven through the bottom **(photo B).** Set all nails with a nail set.

4. Use glue and 6d finish nails to attach the top to the top ends of the sides, keeping the side and front edges flush.

5. Fasten the top rail between the sides, flush with the front edges of the sides and top. Use glue and 6d finish nails to secure the top rail in place.

MAKE THE BACK.

1. Cut the back braces (J, K, L, Q) to length.

2. Set the carcase on its side. Starting at the bottom, use glue and 1¼" brads to fasten the back braces to the sides and top, ¼" in from the back edges **(photo C).** Use a ¾"-thick spacer to create gaps

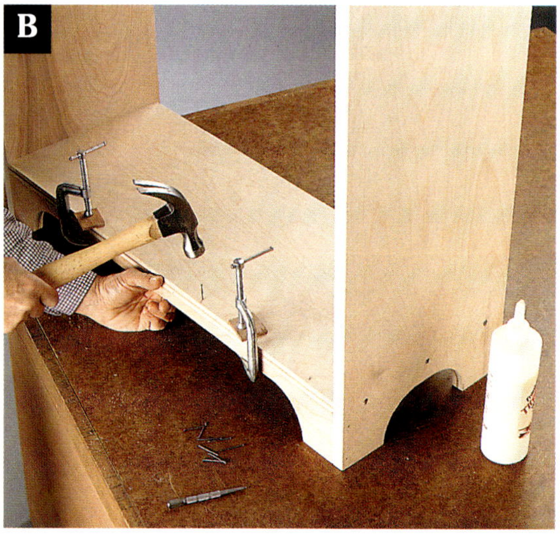
Clamp the front rail to the bottom, and fasten it with glue, finish nails and brads.

Attach the back braces to the sides, creating a ¼" recess for the back panel.

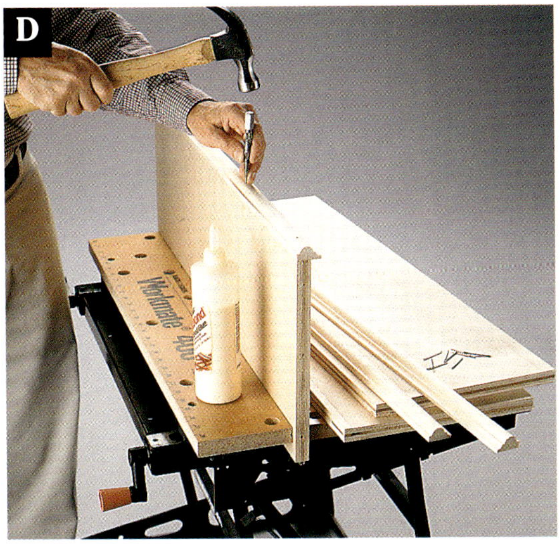

Attach strips of panel molding to the front edges of the shelves.

Attach the shelf cleats with glue and brads.

for the shelves between the strips. Install the top back brace (Q) flush with the back edge of the top. Place the carcase on its front edges.

3. Cut the back (F) to size.

4. Set the back in place so it rests on the back braces. Check for square by measuring diagonally from corner to corner across the back. When the measurements are the same, the carcase is square. Drive ¾" wire nails through the back and into the back braces. Do not glue the back in place.

MAKE THE SHELVES.

1. Cut the shelves (G) and shelf nosing (H) to size.

2. Drill 1/16" pilot holes through the nosing pieces. Use glue and 4d finish nails to attach the nosing to the shelves, keeping the top edges flush **(photo D).** Set the nails with a nail set.

3. Cut the shelf cleats (I) to length.

4. Use a combination square to draw reference lines perpendicular to the front edges of each side to help you position the shelf cleats. Start the lines at the top of the lower back braces (K, L), and extend them to within 1" of the front edges of the sides. Apply glue to the cleats, and position them on the reference lines. Attach the shelf cleats to the inside faces of the sides with 1" brads **(photo E).**

5. Apply glue to the top edges of the shelf cleats. Then, set the shelves onto the cleats. Drive 6d finish nails through the sides and into the ends of the shelves.

6. Drive ¾" wire nails through the back panel and into the rear edges of the shelves.

APPLY FINISHING TOUCHES.

1. Cut the top facing (M), top side molding (N), bottom facing (O) and bottom side molding (P) to length. Miter-cut both ends of the top facing and bottom facing and the front ends of the side moldings at a 45° angle so the molding pieces will fit together at the corners.

2. Fasten the top molding with glue and 4d finish nails, keeping the top edges flush with the top face of the top piece.

3. Attach the bottom facing, keeping the top edges flush with the top face of the bottom.

4. Draw reference lines on the sides to help you align the bottom side molding. The reference lines should be flush with the top of the bottom facing **(photo F).** Attach the bottom side molding.

5. Set all nails with a nail set, and fill the nail holes with wood putty. Finish-sand the project and apply the finish of your choice—we used primer and two coats of enamel paint.

Using a combination square, draw lines on the sides, aligned with the top of the bottom facing.

PROJECT
POWER TOOLS

Library Table

This oak library table features a clean, sophisticated appearance that suits any family room or study.

CONSTRUCTION MATERIALS

Quantity	Lumber
1	¾" × 4 × 8' oak plywood
1	½" × 2 × 4' oak plywood
2	1 × 2" × 8' oak
3	1 × 4" × 8' oak
2	1 × 6" × 6' oak
2	2 × 2" × 8' oak

High-quality, stylish furniture doesn't need to be overly expensive or difficult to make, and this library table is the proof. We used a traditional design for this old favorite. The simple drawer construction, beautiful oak materials and slender framework add up to one great-looking table.

Consider the possibilities for this table in your family room or study. These areas of the home call out for a simple yet elegant table to support a lamp or books, or just to add a decorative accent. We applied a two-tone finish. But no matter how you finish it, this library table serves many needs—and it looks great in the process.

OVERALL SIZE:
30" HIGH
52" LONG
26" DEEP

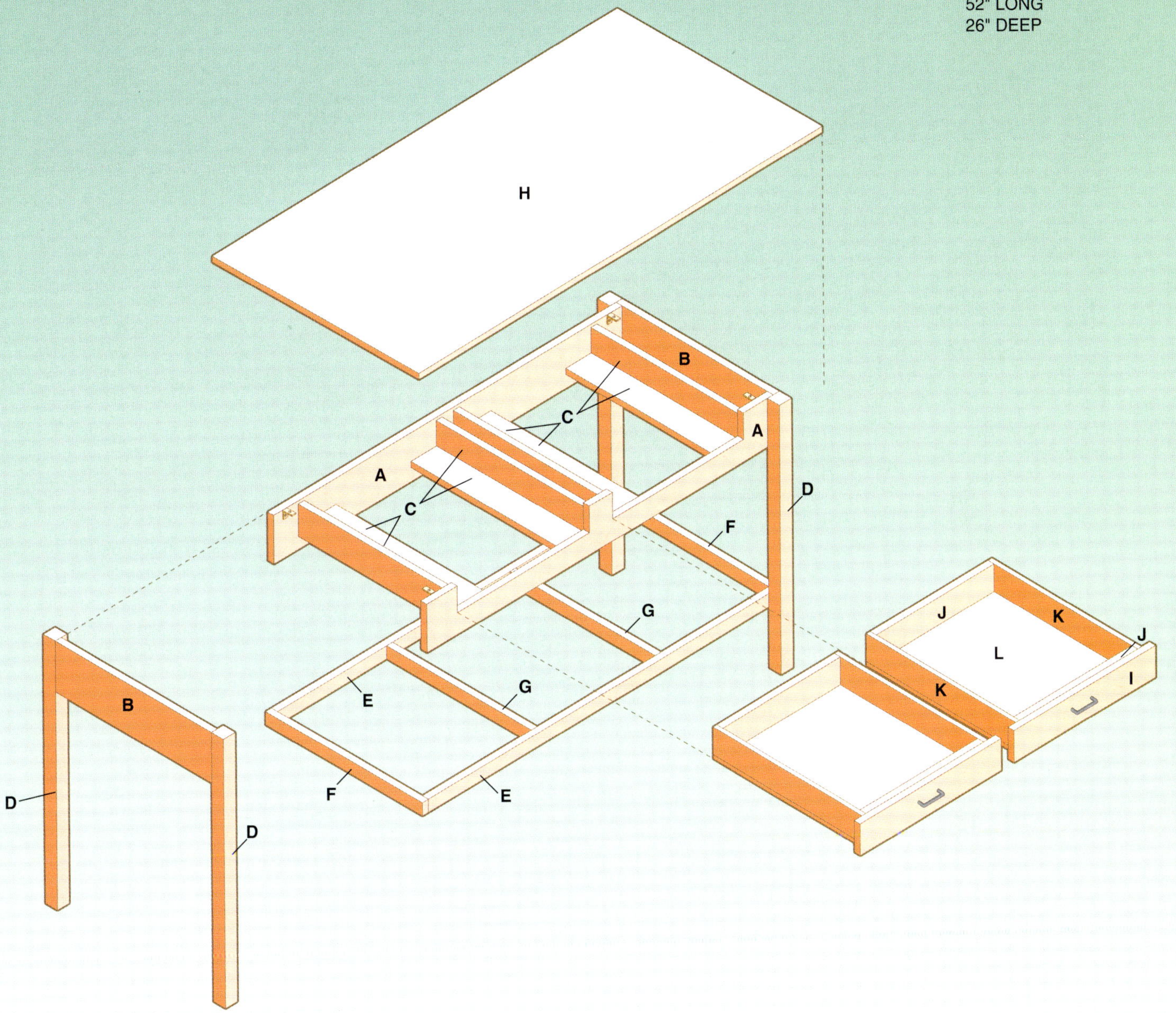

Key	Part	Dimension	Pcs.	Material
A	Side	¾ × 5½ × 44½"	2	Oak
B	End	¾ × 5½ × 20"	2	Oak
C	Guide	¾ × 3½ × 18½"	8	Oak
D	Leg	1½ × 1½ × 29¼"	4	Oak
E	Side rail	¾ × 1½ × 44½"	2	Oak
F	End rail	¾ × 1½ × 20"	2	Oak

Cutting List

Key	Part	Dimension	Pcs.	Material
G	Cross rail	¾ × 1½ × 18½"	2	Oak
H	Top	¾ × 26 × 52"	1	Plywood
I	Drawer front	¾ × 3½ × 18"	2	Oak
J	Drawer end	¾ × 2⅜ × 15⅞"	4	Oak
K	Drawer side	½ × 2⅜ × 19"	4	Plywood
L	Drawer bottom	½ × 16⅞ × 19"	2	Plywood

Materials: #6 × 1", 1⅝" and 2" wood screws, 4d and 6d finish nails, 2" corner braces with ⅝" screws (4), 4" drawer pulls (2), ⅞"-dia. rubber feet (4), tack-on furniture glides (4), ¾" oak veneer edge tape (15'), ⅜"-dia. oak plugs, wood glue, finishing materials.

Note: Measurements reflect the actual size of dimension lumber.

Measure the diagonals and adjust the apron frame as needed until it is square.

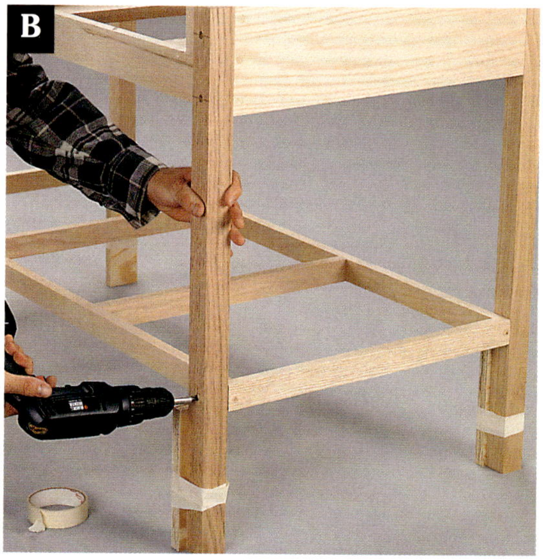

Tape 8"-long blocks of scrap wood to the legs to hold the rail assembly for installation.

Directions: Library Table

For all screws used in this project, drill 3/32" pilot holes. Counterbore the holes 1/4" deep, using a 3/8" counterbore bit.

MAKE THE APRON ASSEMBLY.

1. Cut the sides (A) and ends (B) to length and sand the pieces smooth.

2. Draw two 3"-deep × 17"-long rectangular outlines for the drawer cutouts on the front side. The outlines should start 3¾" in from each end of the front. Make cutouts with a jig saw, using a straightedge as a guide.

3. Attach the sides between the ends with glue, and drive 1⅝" wood screws through the ends and into the sides. The outside faces of the sides should be flush with the ends of the end pieces.

4. Cut the guides (C) to length.

5. Fasten the guides together in right-angle pairs by butting one guide's long edge against the face of another guide, while keeping the ends flush. Attach the guides with glue and 1⅝" wood screws.

6. Position the guide pairs between the sides so the inside faces are flush with the bottom and sides of the rectangular cutouts. Make sure the vertical halves of the guides do not extend above the top edges of the sides. (Set the guide pairs on spacers to keep them aligned with the cutouts as you work.) Before fastening the guides, check the apron frame for square by measuring from corner to corner **(photo A).** If the measurements are not the same, adjust as needed. Drill 1/16" pilot holes and drive 6d finish nails through the sides and into the guides to fasten them in place. Set the nails with a nail set.

MAKE THE RAIL ASSEMBLY.

1. Cut the side rails (E), end rails (F) and cross rails (G) to length.

2. Position the side rails on edge. Attach the side rails between the end rails with glue and 1⅝" wood screws. The

Support the drawer with ½"-thick scrap wood. Then, center the drawer front by measuring the overhang on both sides.

resulting frame should sit flat on your worksurface.

3. Attach the cross rails between the side rails, 14" in from the inside faces of the end rails.

4. Fill all screw holes with oak plugs, and sand them flush with the surface. Sand the rail assembly smooth.

ASSEMBLE THE TABLE.

1. Cut the legs (D) to length, and sand them smooth.

2. Use glue and 2" wood screws to fasten the legs to the apron so the top edges and outside end faces are flush. Position the screws so they do not strike the screws joining the apron parts.

3. Stand the table up. Clamp or tape 8"-long scrap blocks to the inside edges of the legs, flush with the bottom leg ends. These blocks hold the rail assembly in place as you attach it. Fasten the rail assembly to the legs with glue and 2" wood screws. Make sure the end rails are flush with the outside edges of the legs **(photo B).**

4. Cut the top (H) to size. Clean the edges thoroughly.

5. Cut strips of self-adhesive edge tape slightly longer than all four edges of the top. Attach the tape by pressing it onto the edges with a household iron set at a medium-low setting. The heat will activate the adhesive. Trim the excess tape and sand the edges smooth.

6. Sand the top. Choose the smoothest, most attractive side to face up. Draw reference lines on the underside of the top, 3¾" in from the long edges. Fasten two 2" corner braces on each line, 5¼" in from the ends, using ⅝" screws. Center the apron assembly on the top and attach it to the braces.

MAKE THE DRAWERS.

1. Cut the drawer ends (J) and drawer sides (K) to size. Sand the pieces smooth.

2. Fasten the drawer ends between the drawer sides, using glue and 4d finish nails. Drill ¹⁄₁₆" pilot holes through the sides to prevent splitting. Make sure the outside faces of the drawer ends are flush with the ends of the drawer sides.

3. Cut the drawer bottoms (L) to size, and sand them smooth.

4. Center the bottoms over the drawer assemblies, and drill pilot holes for 4d finish nails. Attach the bottom to the drawer ends and sides, driving the nails through the bottom and into the edges. Do not use glue to attach the drawer bottoms.

5. Cut the drawer fronts (I) to length.

6. Attach the drawer fronts by first setting the drawers on a ½"-thick piece of scrap wood. This will ensure that the top-to-bottom spacing is correct when you attach the drawer fronts. Position the drawer fronts against the drawer ends, centering them from side to side **(photo C).** Clamp the drawer fronts in place. Drive 1" wood screws through the drawer ends and into the drawer fronts. Test-fit the drawers and adjust the fronts if they are uneven on the front of the apron.

APPLY FINISHING TOUCHES.

1. Set all nails with a nail set, and fill the nail holes with wood putty. Fill all screw holes with oak plugs. Finish-sand the entire project. Apply the finish of your choice and allow to dry.

2. Install the drawer pulls on the drawer fronts. Wax the tops of the guides with paraffin. Insert the drawers, and set the table on its back edges. Attach ⅞"-dia. rubber feet to the bottoms of the drawers to prevent them from being pulled out of the table **(photo D).** Tack furniture glides to the leg bottoms.

Slide the drawers into place. Then, install rubber feet at the back corners to serve as drawer stops and keep the drawers centered.

PROJECT
POWER TOOLS

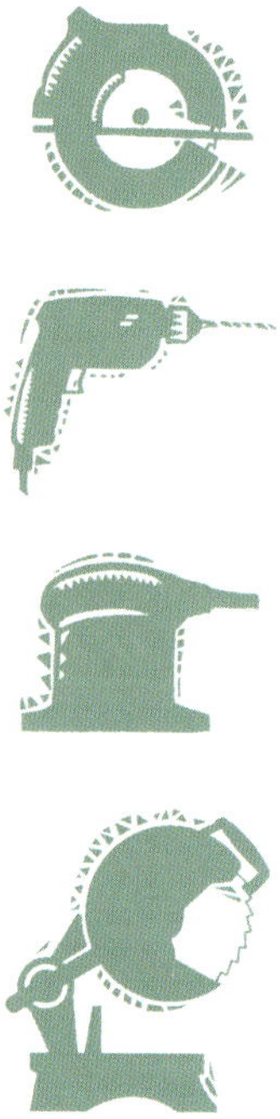

Card Table

This stylish table proves that card tables don't always have to be flimsy and unappealing.

Construction Materials

Quantity	Lumber
1	½" × 4 × 4' oak plywood
2	2 × 2" × 8' pine
2	1 × 3" × 8' pine
4	¾ × ¾" × 8' oak edge molding

The card table has always been thought of as overflow seating for those houseguests who are most lacking in seniority. But the diners assigned to this contemporary wood card table will feel more like they have favored status. The warm tones of the oak tabletop contrast vividly with the painted legs and apron for a lovely effect that will blend into just about any setting—from formal dining to a Friday night poker game.

The fold-up legs on this card table are attached with fasteners designed especially for card tables. You can find these fasteners and the oak apron trim at most hardware and woodworking supply stores.

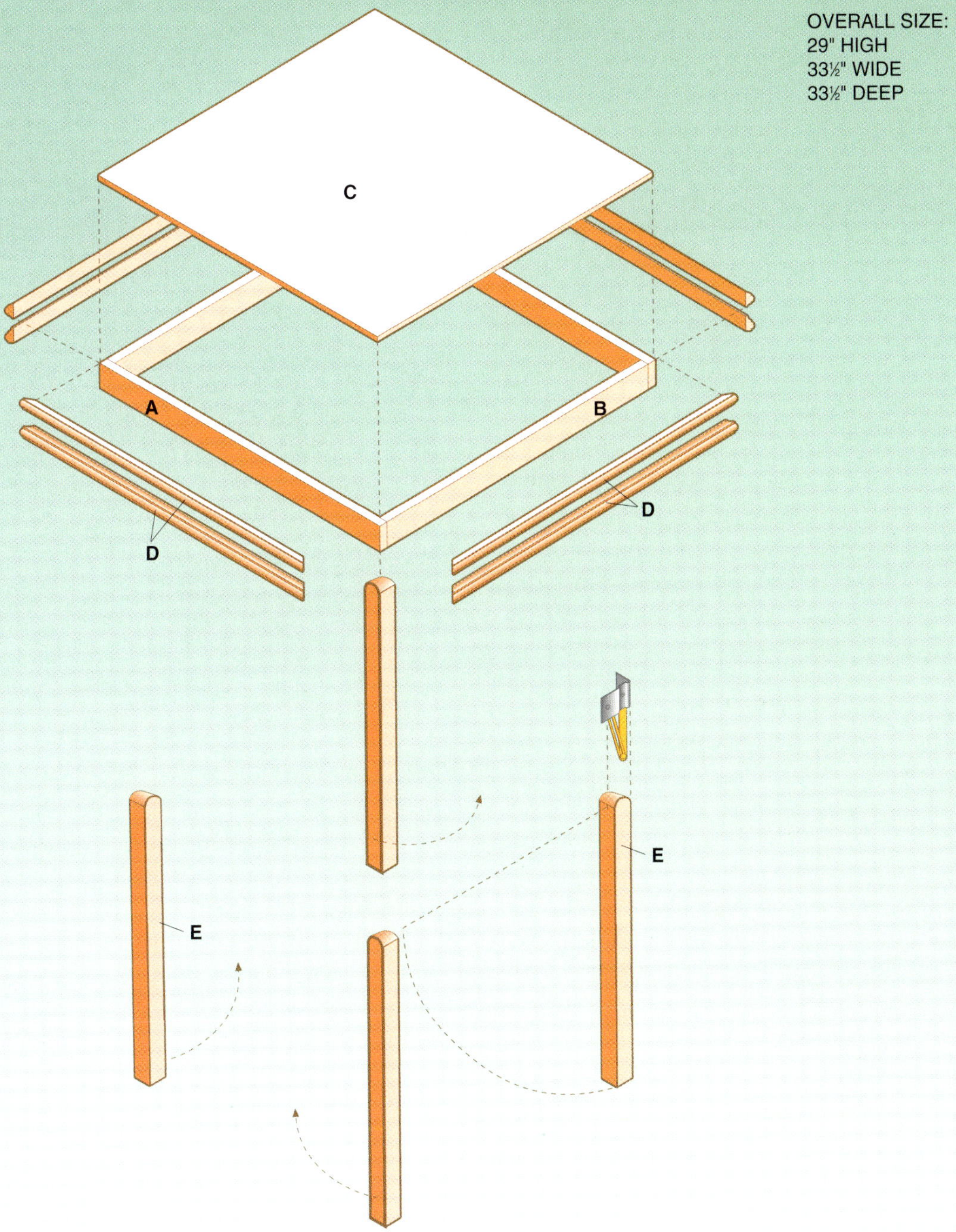

Cutting List

Key	Part	Dimension	Pcs.	Material
A	Side apron	¾ × 2½ × 32"	2	Pine
B	End apron	¾ × 2½ × 30½"	2	Pine
C	Tabletop	½ × 32 × 32"	1	Plywood

Cutting List

Key	Part	Dimension	Pcs.	Material
D	Edge trim	¾ × ¾ × *	8	Edge molding
E	Leg	1½ × 1½ × 28"	4	Pine

Materials: #6 × 1½" wood screws, 3d finish nails, ¼ × 2" machine bolts with locking nuts (4), card-table leg fasteners (4), oak-tinted wood putty, wood glue, finishing materials.

Note: Measurements reflect the actual size of dimension lumber.

***** Cut to fit.

Directions: Card Table

BUILD THE TABLETOP.

The tabletop for this card table is a sheet of oak plywood framed with an apron made from 1 × 3 pine. Strips of oak molding attached around the top and bottom of the apron protect the edges of the table when it is being stored.

1. Cut the side aprons (A) and end aprons (B) to length.

2. Fasten the end aprons between the side aprons with glue and 1½" wood screws to form a square **(photo A).** Drill 5⁄64" pilot holes for the screws. Counterbore the holes ⅛", using a ⅜" counterbore bit. Keep the outside edges and faces of the aprons flush.

3. Cut the tabletop (C) to size, using a circular saw and a straightedge as a cutting guide.

4. Position the tabletop on the frame, keeping the edges flush with the outer faces of the aprons. Fasten the tabletop to the top of the frame with glue and 3d finish nails **(photo B).**

SHAPE THE LEGS.

1. Cut the legs (E) to length.

2. Round over one end of each leg so it will pivot smoothly inside the card-table leg fastener: Center the point of a compass ¾" in from the end of the leg, and draw a ¾"-radius curve. Cut the curves with a jig saw.

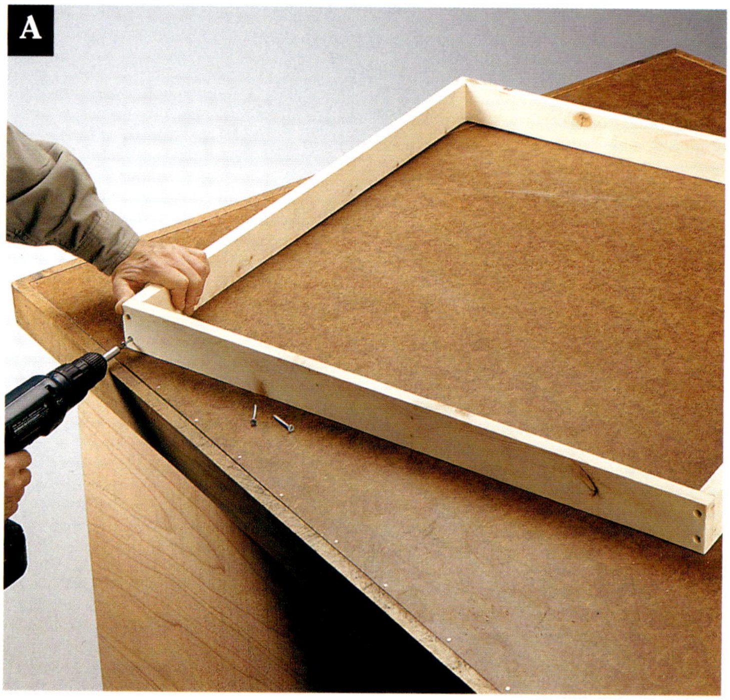

Fasten the end aprons between the side aprons with glue and wood screws to construct the apron frame.

PAINT THE FRAME AND LEGS.

If you plan to apply a combination finish, paint the legs and frame before you assemble the table and attach the edge trim.

1. Finish-sand the pine surfaces and wipe them clean. Apply primer to the aprons and legs.

2. Apply several coats of enamel paint in the color of your choice.

ATTACH THE EDGE TRIM.

When the paint has dried, attach the edge trim to the tabletop edges and the aprons. Use a plain or decorative molding, but be sure to use oak to match the tabletop.

1. Miter-cut the edge trim pieces (D) to length, using a power miter saw or hand miter box. The best method is to cut the 45° miter on one end of the first piece, and position the trim against the apron or tabletop edges. Mark the appropriate length, and miter-cut the other end.

2. Fasten the edge trim to the aprons or the tabletop edge using wood glue and 3d finish nails. To prevent splitting, drill 1⁄16" pilot holes through the trim pieces before driving the nails. Continue this process, keeping the mitered ends tight when marking for length **(photo C).** Be sure to keep the tops of the upper trim pieces flush with the surface of the tabletop. Keep the bottoms of the lower trim pieces flush with the bottoms of the aprons.

FASTEN THE LEGS AND HARDWARE.

The legs attach to the table with locking card-table leg fasteners.

1. Attach a leg fastener to the rounded end of each leg. Fastening methods may vary, so read and follow the manufacturer's directions that come with the hardware.

TIP

Use sanding sealer before you apply wood stain to create more even absorption that helps eliminate blotchy finishes. Sanding sealer is a clear product, usually applied with a brush. Check the product labels on all of the finishing products you plan to apply to make sure they are compatible. To be safe, choose either water-based or oil-based products for the whole project.

Fasten the oak plywood tabletop to the top of the apron frame with glue and finish nails.

Glue and nail oak trim around the tabletop and apron, making mitered joints at the corners.

Attach the card-table leg fasteners to the rounded ends of the legs. Then, attach them at the inside corners of the tabletop frame.

2. Lay the tabletop upside down on a flat worksurface. Attach the leg fasteners to the insides of the aprons at each corner of the tabletop frame **(photo D).** Test the legs to make sure they fit properly when folded up and that the fasteners operate smoothly. Also, check to make sure the table is level and stable when resting on a flat surface. Make any needed adjustments to the positioning or length of the legs. Then, fully tighten all hardware screws.

APPLY FINISHING TOUCHES.

1. Set all nails with a nail set, and fill the nail holes with oak-tinted wood putty. Finish-sand the unfinished surfaces and wipe them clean.

2. Apply sanding sealer for an even finish (see *Tip*). If desired, apply a wood stain to color the wood. If you are using medium to dark stain, mask the painted surfaces first. Apply two or three light coats of a protective topcoat to the entire table.

Drafting Stool

Simple and sturdy, this oak beauty keeps your posture perfect as you work at your drafting table or writing desk.

PROJECT POWER TOOLS

Proper seating is the key to comfort and productivity at a writing desk, drafting table or any workstation. An ultra-soft reclining or swiveling chair can sometimes make you drowsy, resulting in poor seated posture and sore muscles. On the other hand, an unsupportive, rigid chair with a low backrest can make working at your desk uncomfortable and unpleasant. This drafting stool offers firm support without lulling you to sleep.

We designed this solid oak stool for use with the writing desk (page 174). The style and scale of the stool match those of the writing table, but you'll find there are many additional uses for this versatile project. You may want to use it as a bar stool in your den, or place it in the kitchen to provide seating at your breakfast counter.

We used oak lumber, but you can select building materials to match your desk or room decor. For a finished look, we filled the screw holes in our chair with oak plugs, but contrasting plugs would provide an interesting design element. There certainly are many options for building and using this drafting stool. Best of all, this piece is much easier to build than its appearance suggests.

Construction Materials

Quantity	Lumber
3	1 × 2" × 8' oak
2	1 × 4" × 6' oak
2	2 × 2" × 8' oak

OVERALL SIZE:
34¼" HIGH
18½" WIDE
17½" DEEP

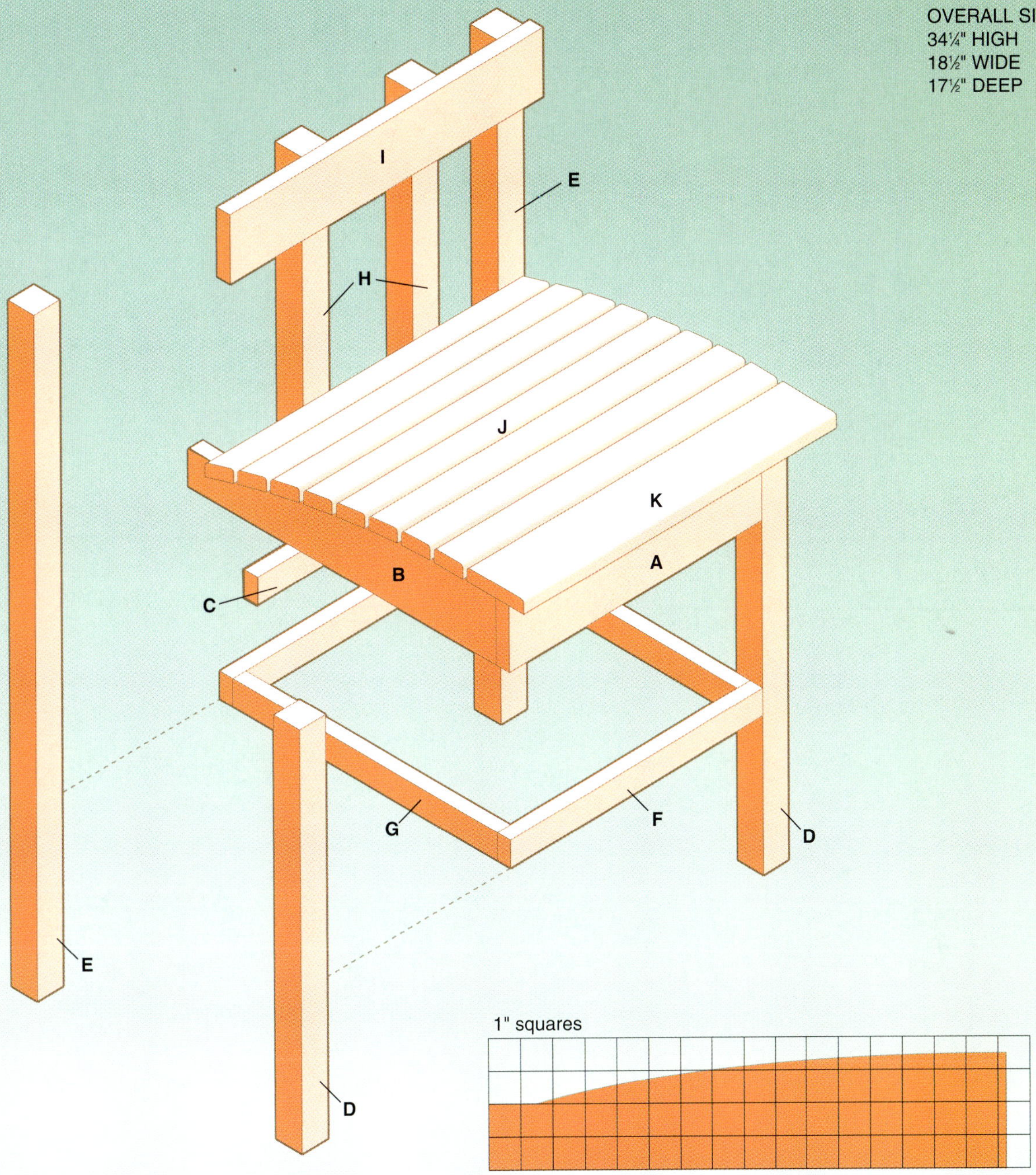

PART B DETAIL

Cutting List

Key	Part	Dimension	Pcs.	Material
A	Front	¾ × 3½ × 15"	1	Oak
B	Side	¾ × 3½ × 16¼"	2	Oak
C	Back	¾ × 2 × 13½"	1	Oak
D	Front leg	1½ × 1½ × 21¼"	2	Oak
E	Rear leg	1½ × 1½ × 34¼"	2	Oak
F	End rail	¾ × 1½ × 15"	2	Oak

Cutting List

Key	Part	Dimension	Pcs.	Material
G	Side rail	¾ × 1½ × 15½"	2	Oak
H	Back brace	1½ × 1½ × 16½"	2	Oak
I	Backrest	¾ × 3½ × 18½"	1	Oak
J	Slat	¾ × 1½ × 18½"	8	Oak
K	Front slat	¾ × 3½ × 18½"	1	Oak

Materials: #6 × 1⅝" wood screws, 10d finish nails, ⅜"-dia. oak plugs, wood glue, finishing materials.

Note: Measurements reflect the actual size of dimension lumber.

Gang-sand the sides with a belt sander, making sure their profiles are identical.

Align the seat frame on the top reference lines, and fasten it to the legs.

Directions: Drafting Stool

MAKE THE SEAT FRAME.
For all screws used in this project, drill 3/32" pilot holes. Counterbore the holes 1/4" deep, using a 3/8" counterbore bit. The seat frame is sloped from front to back, forming the seat shape. Make this slope by cutting the side pieces, following the pattern on page 171.

1. Cut the front (A), sides (B) and back (C) to length.

2. Draw a grid with 1" squares onto a face of a side piece (use *Part B Detail)*. Cut the side to shape with a jig saw, and sand the cut edges.

3. Trace the outline of the finished side onto the other side piece, and cut it to shape. Clamp the sides together, and gang-sand them with a belt sander to make sure their profiles are identical **(photo A).**

4. Position the front against the front ends of the sides. Fasten the front to the sides with glue, and drive 1 5/8" wood screws through the front piece and into the ends of the sides.

5. Position the back (C) between the sides so the rear face is 1 1/2" in from the ends of the sides. Make sure the bottom edges of the parts are flush. Fasten the back with glue, and drive 1 5/8" wood screws through the sides and into the back.

ATTACH THE LEGS.
Before attaching the frame and legs, draw reference lines to mark the positions for the legs.

1. Cut the front legs (D) and

Clamp the backrest in place at the tops of the rear legs. Then, fasten it with glue and wood screws.

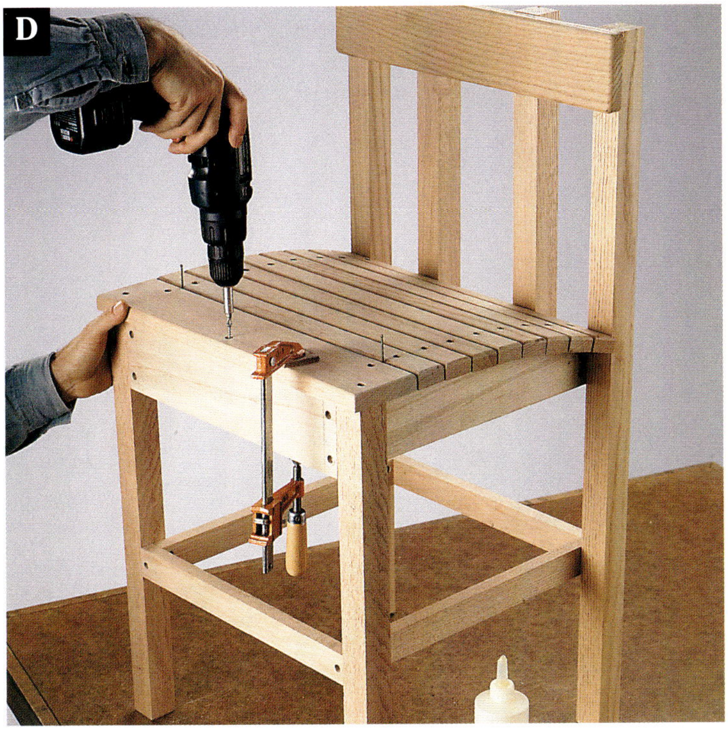

Using 10d nails as spacers, fasten the seat slats to the top of the seat frame, finishing with the front slat.

rear legs (E) to length. Sand the parts smooth. Draw reference lines on the inside face of each leg, 8" and 17¾" up from the bottom end.
2. Position one front leg and one rear leg on your worksurface. Set the seat frame on the legs so the bottom edge is flush with the top reference lines. Apply glue and fasten the seat frame to the rear leg, keeping the ends flush and the frame square to the leg. Drive 1⅝" wood screws through the seat side and into the leg.
3. Fasten the frame to the front leg with glue and 1⅝" wood screws **(photo B).** Make sure the seat frame is flush with the front edge of the front leg and with the top reference line.
4. Turn the assembly over. Attach the remaining front leg and rear leg, using the same methods.

ATTACH THE RAILS.
1. Cut the end rails (F) and side rails (G) to length.
2. Position the side rails between the end rails so their top edges are flush and the outside faces of the side rails are flush with the ends of the end rails. Fasten the pieces with glue and 1⅝" wood screws.
3. Position the rail assembly between the legs so its bottom edges are flush with the bottom reference lines. Attach the assembly with glue, and drive 1⅝" wood screws through the side rails and into the legs. To avoid hitting the screws in the rail assembly, these screws must be slightly off center. The front and rear edges of the rail assembly should be flush with the front and rear leg edges.

ATTACH THE BACK BRACES AND BACKREST.
1. Cut the back braces (H) and backrest (I) to length.
2. Clamp the backrest to the fronts of the rear legs so the top edges are flush. The backrest should extend ¼" past the rear legs on both sides. Check the back legs for square, and drill staggered pilot holes with ⅜"-deep counterbores through the legs. Apply glue and fasten the backrest to the rear legs with 1⅝" wood screws **(photo C).**
3. Drill ⅜"-deep counterbores into the braces. Attach the back braces to the back and backrest with glue and 1⅝" wood screws. Use a piece of 1 × 4 scrap as a spacer to maintain an equal distance between the rear legs and back braces.

ATTACH THE SLATS.
1. Cut the slats (J) and the front slat (K) to length. Sand the slats, slightly rounding over the top edges.
2. Attach the slats with glue and 1⅝" wood screws, starting at the rear of the seat, with the first slat flush against the legs and back braces. Maintain a ⅛"-wide gap between slats—10d finish nails make good spacers. The slats should overhang both sides of the seat frame by ¼".
3. Test-fit the front slat, and trim it, if necessary, so it overhangs the front piece by ½". Clamp the front slat to the seat frame, and attach it with glue and 1⅝" wood screws **(photo D).**

APPLY FINISHING TOUCHES.
1. Insert glued oak plugs into all screw holes, and sand the plugs flush with the surface.
2. Finish-sand all surfaces with 180-grit sandpaper.
3. Apply the finish of your choice. We used three coats of tung oil.

PROJECT
POWER TOOLS

Writing Desk

Build this practical, attractive writing desk for a fraction of the cost of manufactured models.

CONSTRUCTION MATERIALS

Quantity	Lumber
1	¾" × 4 × 8' oak plywood
2	1 × 2" × 6' oak
2	1 × 4" × 6' oak
1	1 × 6" × 8' oak
1	1 × 10" × 6' oak
2	2 × 2" × 8' oak
1	¼" × 2 × 4' acrylic sheet
2	¾ × 1⁵⁄₁₆" × 6' oak panel molding
2	⅜ × 1¹⁄₁₆" × 6' oak stop molding

A beautiful piece of furniture, this writing desk is based loosely on popular Shaker styling. With its hinged top, you have access to a storage area for keeping important papers organized and out of the way. We built the writing desk out of red oak, an attractive and durable hardwood, so the project will look great for a long time. Designed to match the drafting stool and secretary topper (pages 154, 170), the writing desk also works well as a stand-alone piece. And, it can be built for a fraction of the cost of similar furnishings, even those sold by catalog. The worksurface is covered with a sheet of clear acrylic, giving you a hard, smooth surface for writing. When the acrylic gets scratched or worn, just slip it out of the top frame and turn it over.

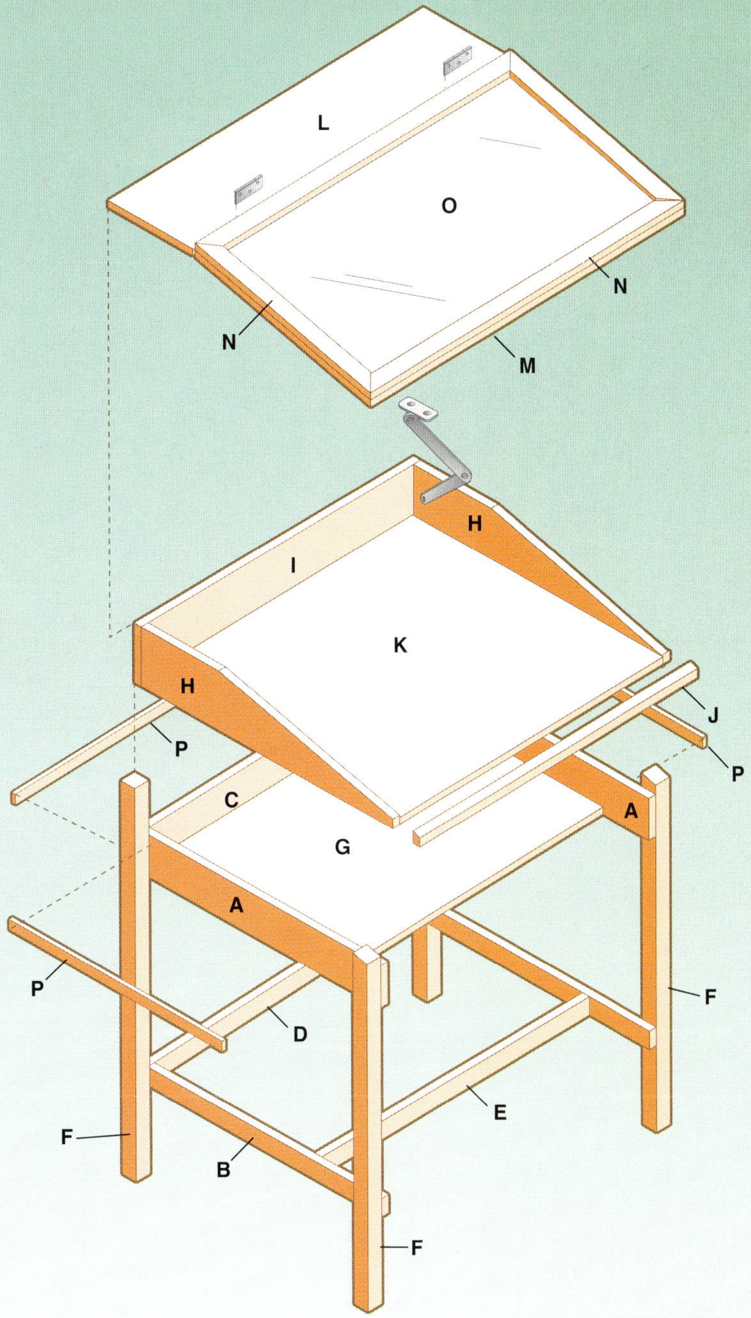

OVERALL SIZE:
37¼" HIGH
34" WIDE
30½" DEEP

Cutting List

Key	Part	Dimension	Pcs.	Material
A	Apron side	¾ × 3½ × 24¾"	2	Oak
B	Side rail	¾ × 1½ × 24¾"	2	Oak
C	Apron back	¾ × 3½ × 30"	1	Oak
D	Back rail	¾ × 1½ × 30"	1	Oak
E	Kick rail	¾ × 1½ × 28½"	1	Oak
F	Leg	1½ × 1½ × 35¾"	4	Oak
G	Shelf	¾ × 20 × 28½"	1	Plywood
H	Desk side	¾ × 5½ × 26½"	2	Oak

Cutting List

Key	Part	Dimension	Pcs.	Material
I	Desk back	¾ × 5½ × 30"	1	Oak
J	Desk front	¾ × 1 × 30"	1	Oak
K	Desk bottom	¾ × 26½ × 28½"	1	Plywood
L	Desk top	¾ × 9¼ × 34"	1	Oak
M	Worksurface	¾ × 21 × 34"	1	Plywood
N	Top molding	¾ × 1 5/16 × *	4	Panel molding
O	Top protector	¼ × 19⅛ × 32⅛"	1	Acrylic
P	Side trim	⅜ × 1 1/16 × *	3	Stop molding

Materials: #6 × 1⅝" and 2" wood screws, #6 × 1" brass wood screws, 16-ga. × ¾" and 1" brass brads, 1½ × 3" brass butt hinges, 6" heavy-duty lid-support hardware, ¾" oak veneer edge tape (25'), ⅜"-dia. oak plugs, wood glue, finishing materials.

Specialty tools: Block plane, plastic cutter.

Note: Measurements reflect the actual size of dimension lumber. * Cut to fit.

Fasten the apron assembly between the back legs with glue and wood screws.

Attach the front legs to the free ends of the apron sides and side rails.

Directions: Writing Desk

JOIN THE LEGS AND THE APRON.

For all screws used in this project, drill 3/32" pilot holes. Counterbore the holes 1/4" deep, using a 3/8" counterbore bit.

1. Cut the legs (F) to length. Sand the parts smooth.

2. Set the legs together, edge to edge, with their ends flush. Draw reference lines across the legs, 8" and 30 1/4" up from one end. These lines mark the positions of the apron and rail assemblies.

3. Cut the apron sides (A) and apron back (C) to length.

4. Butt the ends of the apron sides against the face of the apron back. Attach the pieces with glue, and drive 2" wood screws through the apron back and into the sides. Make sure the outside faces of the sides are flush with the ends of the apron back.

5. Set a pair of legs on your worksurface, about 30" apart, with the reference lines facing each other. Position the apron assembly between the legs so the top edges of the assembly are flush with the top reference lines. The back face of the apron should be flush with the back edges of the legs. Drive 1 5/8" wood screws through the apron sides and into the legs **(photo A).** Position the screws so they do not strike the screws in the apron assembly.

Use a block plane to trim the desk front to match the slanted profiles of the desk sides.

INSTALL THE FRAME RAILS.

1. Cut the side rails (B), back rail (D) and kick rail (E) to length.

2. Attach the side rails to the

TIP

When planing hardwood, always follow the grain. If your planing strokes are resulting in ragged cuts rather than smooth shavings, switch the direction of your planing strokes.

D

Use a circular saw and a straightedge as a guide to make a slight bevel on the front edge of the desk top.

E

Trace the angles of the desk sides onto the front legs. Then, trim the legs to follow the sides.

back rail with glue. Drive 2" wood screws through the back rail and into the ends of the side rail. Make sure the outside faces of the side rails are flush with the ends of the back rail.

3. Position the kick rail between the side rails so its front face is 7" in from the front ends of the side rails. Make sure the top and bottom edges are flush. Attach the kick rail with glue, and drive 2" wood screws through the side rails and into the ends of the kick rail.

4. Position the rail assembly between the legs with the bottom edges on the lower reference lines. Keep the back face of the back rail flush with the back edges of the legs, and attach the assembly with glue. Drive 1⅝" wood screws through the side rails and into the legs.

5. Position the front legs on the apron sides and side rails, keeping the edges flush with the reference lines **(photo B).** The front edges of the legs should be flush with the ends of the apron sides and side rails. Make sure the parts are square, and fasten the legs with glue. Drive 1⅝" wood screws through the apron sides and side rails and into the legs.

MAKE THE SHELF.

1. Cut the shelf (G) to size.

2. Apply self-adhesive edge tape to one long edge of the shelf, using a household iron. Trim and sand the taped edges.

3. Position the shelf between the apron sides so it butts against the face of the apron back. The shelf should be flush with the bottom edges of the apron assembly, and the taped edge of the shelf should face forward. Attach the shelf to the apron with glue, and drive 1⅝" wood screws through the apron sides and back and into the edges of the shelf.

BUILD THE DESK BOX.

1. Cut the desk sides (H) to length.

2. Make the slanted cuts on the top edges by marking points on one long edge of each desk side, 8¼" in from one end.

Draw reference lines on the opposite end of each side, 1" up from the bottom edge. Draw straight cutting lines connecting the marks. Cut along the lines with a circular saw, using a straightedge as a cutting guide.
3. Cut the desk back (I) and desk bottom (K) to size.
4. Cut the desk front (J), using a circular saw and a straightedge as a cutting guide to rip-cut a 1"-wide strip from a 1 × 4 or 1 × 6.
5. Attach the desk sides to the desk back, flush with the ends of the desk back. Apply glue and drive 2" wood screws through the back and into the edges of the sides.
6. Position the desk bottom between the desk sides, keeping the front and bottom edges flush. Attach the bottom with glue, and drive 1⅝" wood screws through the desk sides and back and into the bottom.
7. Fasten the desk front to the front edge of the desk bottom with glue and 1⅝" wood screws. The ¾"-thick edge should be flush with the bottom face of the desk bottom.
8. Trim the desk front to match the slanted profiles of the desk sides. Draw reference lines on each end of the desk front, extending the slanted profiles of the desk sides. Use a combination square to draw a reference line across the front face of the desk front, connecting the ends of the reference lines. Use a block plane to trim the profile of the desk front to match the angles of the desk sides **(photo C).** To avoid damaging the desk sides, start the trimming with the plane and finish with a sander.

Permanently fasten the top and side pieces of the frame around the worksurface.

MAKE THE DESK TOP.

1. Cut the desk top (L) to length.
2. Bevel the desk top along one long edge where it meets the worksurface (M). To make the cut, adjust the blade angle on a circular saw to cut a ⅛" bevel on the front edge of the desk top. First make test cuts on scrap pieces. Clamp a straightedge guide to the desk top, and make the bevel cut on one long edge of the workpiece **(photo D).**

INSTALL THE DESK BOX.

1. Stand the leg assembly up. Set the desk assembly on top of the side aprons, making sure the back edges are flush.
2. To cut the front legs to match the slanted profiles of the desk sides, first trace the angles of the desk sides onto the front legs **(photo E).** Remove the desk assembly, and use a circular saw to cut the front legs along the cutting lines.
3. Replace the desk, and make sure the front legs are cut at, or slightly below, the desk side profiles. Fasten the desk assembly with glue, and drive 1⅝" wood screws through the desk sides and into the legs.
4. Position the desk top on the flat section of the desk sides so the back edge of the desk top overhangs the back of the legs by ⅛". The top should overhang the outside faces of the back legs by ½" on each side. Make sure the beveled edge faces forward and slants in from top to bottom. Attach the desk top with glue, and drive 1⅝" wood screws through the top and into the edges of the desk sides and back.
5. Cut the side trim (P) pieces to fit between the legs on the sides and back, covering the joint where the desk assembly meets the aprons. Tack the side trim over the joint, using ¾" brass brads.

MAKE THE WORK-SURFACE.

The molding nailed to the top of the plywood worksurface holds

Score the acrylic sheet repeatedly, using a plastic cutter and a straightedge as a guide.

the acrylic protector in place. One piece of the molding is removable, allowing you to replace the acrylic if it gets worn.

1. Cut the worksurface (M) to size. Apply edge tape to all four edges of the board.

2. Cut the top molding (N) to fit around the edges of the worksurface. Miter-cut the corners of the molding pieces to make miter joints.

3. Use glue and ¾" brads to attach the top molding to the sides and top of the worksurface **(photo F).**

4. Drive 1" brads through one molding piece and into the other at each joint, lock-nailing the pieces. To secure the bottom piece of molding, clamp it in place on the worksurface. From underneath the worksurface, drill 1¼"-deep pilot holes, 9/16" in from the front edge. Place a piece of tape on your drill bit as a depth guide to avoid drilling through the face of the molding. Counterbore the holes. Drive 1" brass wood screws through the pilot holes and into the molding.

ADD THE TOP PROTECTOR.

Cut the top protector (O) to size, using a plastic cutter and a straightedge as a cutting guide. Make repeated cuts to score the material deeply **(photo G).** Then, holding the straightedge next to the score line, bend the sheet to break it at the line.

APPLY FINISHING TOUCHES.

1. Fill all screw holes with oak plugs. Set the nails with a nail set, and fill the nail holes with wood putty. Finish-sand all of the surfaces, and apply a finish to the project. We used three coats of clear tung oil.

2. Attach 1½ × 3" brass butt hinges to the top edge of the worksurface, and fasten it to the desk top **(photo H).** Because the worksurface is fairly heavy, you may need to support it from behind as you fasten the hinges.

3. Install a 6" heavy-duty lid support on one desk side inside the storage compartment. Fasten the arm of the support to the worksurface, near the top edge of the bottom face.

4. Remove the screws holding the removable top molding piece, and insert the top protector into the frame. Attach the molding.

Attach the worksurface to the beveled edge of the desk top with evenly spaced hinges.

PROJECT
POWER TOOLS

Nesting Office

The basic building blocks of a home office, designed to fit together in one small space.

Construction Materials

Quantity	Lumber
3	2 × 2" × 8' oak
4	1 × 4" × 8' oak
2	1 × 2" × 8' oak
4	¾" × 2 × 4' oak plywood
1	⅜ × 1$\frac{1}{16}$" × 6' oak stop molding
2	¾ × ¾" × 8' oak cove molding

The desk and credenza are the two principal furnishings needed in any home office. This nesting office pair features both components at full size. But because they fit together, they can be stored in about the same amount of space as a standard medium-size desk. Made of oak and oak plywood, both pieces are well constructed and pleasing to the eye. The desk has a large writing surface, and the credenza is a versatile rolling storage cabinet with a hanging file box and shelves for storage of books, paper and other materials. Flip-up tops let you use the credenza as an auxiliary writing or computer surface while storing office supplies below.

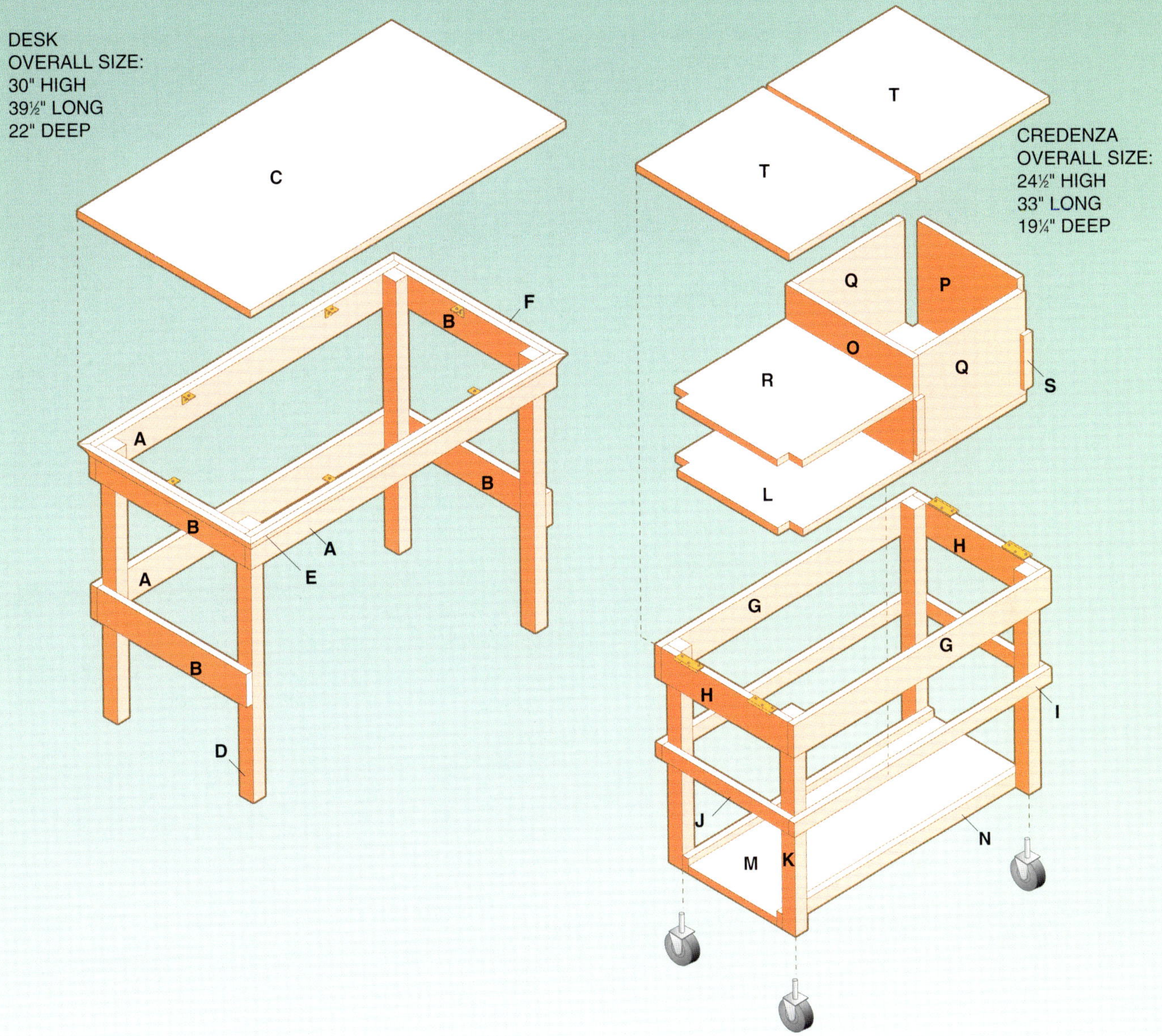

Key	Part	Dimension	Pcs.	Material
A	Desk side	¾ × 3½ × 38"	3	Oak
B	Desk end	¾ × 3½ × 19"	4	Oak
C	Desktop	¾ × 22 × 39½"	1	Plywood
D	Desk leg	1½ × 1½ × 29¼"	4	Oak
E	Side molding	¾ × ¾ × *	2	Cove molding
F	End molding	¾ × ¾ × *	2	Cove molding
G	Credenza side	¾ × 3½ × 33"	2	Oak
H	Credenza end	¾ × 3½ × 16"	2	Oak
I	Middle rail	¾ × 1½ × 33"	2	Oak
J	End rail	¾ × 1½ × 16"	2	Oak

Cutting List

Key	Part	Dimension	Pcs.	Material
K	Credenza leg	1½ × 1½ × 21¼"	4	Oak
L	Middle shelf	¾ × 16 × 31½"	1	Plywood
M	Bottom shelf	¾ × 11½ × 31½"	1	Plywood
N	Bottom rail	¾ × 1½ × 31½"	2	Oak
O	Divider	¾ × 11¼ × 16"	1	Plywood
P	End panel	¾ × 11¼ × 13"	1	Plywood
Q	Side panel	¾ × 11¼ × 13⅞"	2	Plywood
R	Bin bottom	¾ × 15⅜ × 16"	1	Plywood
S	Stop	⅜ × 1 1/16 × 7"	6	Stop molding
T	Bin lid	¾ × 16⅜ × 19¼"	2	Plywood

Materials: #6 × 1" and 1⅝" wood screws, 16-ga. × 1" brads, 1½ × 3" brass butt hinges (4), 2½" swivel casters (4), 1¼" brass corner braces with ⅝" brass wood screws (6), brass lid supports (4), ¾" oak veneer edge tape (50'), ⅜"-dia. oak plugs, wood glue, finishing materials.

Note: Measurements reflect the actual size of dimension lumber.

* Cut to fit.

Check with a combination square to make sure the desk legs are square to the ends.

Glue oak plugs into the screw holes to cover the screws.

Directions: Nesting Office

For all screws used in this project, drill 3/32" pilot holes. Counterbore the holes 1/4" deep, using a 3/8" counterbore bit.

Fasten the desktop to the desk base with brass corner braces.

MAKE THE DESK-LEG PAIRS.

1. Cut the desk ends (B) and desk legs (D) to length. Sand the pieces smooth.

2. Lay the legs on a flat surface, arranged in pairs. Lay the desk ends across the legs to form the leg pair assemblies. One desk end in each leg pair should be flush with the tops of the legs, and the bottom of the other desk end should be 10½" up from the bottoms of the legs. Apply glue to the mating surfaces, then clamp the leg pair assemblies together. Check the assemblies with a square to make sure the legs are square to the end boards **(photo A).** Fasten the pieces together by driving 1⅝" wood screws through the desk ends and into the legs.

ASSEMBLE THE DESK BASE.

1. Cut the desk sides (A) to length and sand them smooth.

2. Drill a pair of pilot holes about 1½" in from each end of each desk side board. Before drilling the pilot holes, check the leg pairs to make sure the pilot holes will not run into the screws joining the end boards and the legs.

3. Apply glue to the mating ends of one side board, and clamp it in place so it spans between the leg pairs, flush with the tops of the legs and the outside faces of the desk ends. Check to make sure the leg pairs are square to the desk side. Drive 1⅝" wood screws through the pilot holes. Install the other top desk side, using the same method.

4. Use glue and 1⅝" wood screws to attach the lower side board to the legs so the top is flush with the tops of the end boards in the leg pairs. After the glue has set, insert glued oak plugs into all screw holes **(photo B).** Sand the plugs flush with the surface.

5. Sand the entire desk base with medium-grit sandpaper to smooth the surfaces and dull any sharp edges.

Install strips of oak cove molding along the underside of the desktop.

TIP

Plain file boxes can be easily converted to hanging file boxes by installing a self-standing metal hanger system. Sold at office supply stores, the thin metal standards and support rods are custom-cut to fit the box, then assembled and set in place. The metal tabs on the hanging folders fit over the metal support rods.

ATTACH THE DESKTOP.

Fasten the plywood desktop to the base with corner braces. These allow the desktop to expand and contract without splitting the wood.

1. Cut the desktop (C) to size.
2. Sand the edges smooth, and wipe them clean.
3. Cut strips of self-adhesive edge tape to fit the edges. Use a household iron set at low to medium heat to press the veneer onto the edges. After the adhesive cools, trim any excess tape with a utility knife. Sand the edges of the tape smooth with fine-grit sandpaper.
4. Place the desktop on your worksurface with the top facedown, and center the desk base on the desktop. The desktop should overhang the base by ¾" on all sides. Clamp the base in place, and arrange 1¼" brass corner braces along the inside edges of the desk side and end boards. Use two braces on each side and one at each end. Drill pilot holes, and drive ⅝" brass wood screws to attach the desktop **(photo C).**

ATTACH THE DESK MOLDING.

Fit the side and end molding pieces underneath the desktop, and fasten them to the desk sides and ends.

1. Cut the side molding (E) and end molding (F) pieces to fit the desk dimensions, miter-cutting the ends at a 45° angle.
2. Drill 1/16" pilot holes through the molding pieces, and position them against the bottom of the desktop. Apply glue to the molding, including the mitered ends, and attach the pieces with 1" brads **(photo D).**

MAKE THE CREDENZA BASE.

The credenza base is similar to the desk base. Build the leg pairs first, then join them together with long side boards. Remember to check the frame parts for square before you fasten them.

1. Cut the credenza sides (G), credenza ends (H), middle rails (I), end rails (J) and credenza legs (K) to length.
2. Arrange the legs in pairs with the end rails and credenza ends positioned across them. The credenza

Attach the credenza ends and end rails to the legs with glue and wood screws.

Fasten the bottom shelf by driving wood screws through the bottom rails and into the legs.

Cut notches at each corner of the middle shelf so it will fit between the credenza legs.

ends should be flush with the outside edges and tops of the legs. The end rails should be flush with the outside edges of the legs, with the bottom edges of the rails 12" down from the tops of the legs. Apply glue to the mating surfaces, and clamp the parts together. Make sure the assemblies are square, then drive 1⅝" wood screws through the ends and rails and into the legs **(photo E).**

3. Set the leg pairs on one side edge, spacing them about 30" apart. Position a credenza side so its top edge is flush with the tops of the credenza ends. The ends of the side board should be flush with the outside faces of the credenza ends. Fasten the side piece with glue, and drive 1⅝" wood screws through the side and into the legs.

4. Attach the middle rail, flush with the end rails in the leg assemblies, using the same methods. Attach the other credenza side and middle rail to complete the base.

MAKE THE CREDENZA SHELVES.

1. Cut the middle shelf (L), bottom shelf (M) and bottom rails (N) to size. Apply self-adhesive edge tape to both short edges of the bottom shelf.

2. Position a bottom rail against each long edge of the bottom shelf. Make sure the ends are flush and the bottom edges of the rails are flush with the bottom face of the shelf. Fasten the parts with glue, and drive 1⅝" wood screws through the bottom rails and into the edges of the bottom shelf.

3. Position the bottom shelf between the credenza legs so the bottom edges are flush. Drive 1⅝" wood screws through the

Glue the bin bottom between the credenza sides, flush with their bottom edges, and secure it with screws.

Attach strips of oak stop molding to cover the exposed plywood edges of the bins on the outside of the credenza.

bottom rails and into the credenza legs **(photo F).**

4. Use a jig saw to cut a 1½ × 1½" notch in each corner of the middle shelf so it will fit between the credenza legs **(photo G).**

5. To attach the middle shelf between the middle rails and end rails, apply glue to the inside edges of the rails, and slide the shelf into position. The shelf should be flush with the bottom edges of the rails. Drive 1⅝" wood screws through the middle and end rails and into the middle shelf.

MAKE THE CREDENZA BINS.

The credenza bins include a file box for hanging file folders and a supply storage box. Both bins have a flip-up lid.

1. Cut the divider (O), end panel (P), side panels (Q) and bin bottom (R) to size.

2. Cut 1½ × 1½" notches in both corners at one end of the bin bottom so it will fit between the credenza legs.

3. Position the side panels on top of the middle shelf so their outside edges are flush against the legs. Apply glue and drive 1" wood screws through the side panels and into the credenza sides and middle rails.

4. Position the end panel between the legs, with its bottom edge flush against the middle shelf. Apply glue and drive 1" wood screws through the end panel and into the credenza end and end rail.

5. Slide the divider into place so it butts against the inside edges of the side panels and is flush with the tops of the side panels. Fasten the divider with glue, and drive 1⅝" wood screws through the divider and into the edges of the side panels.

6. From the outside of the credenza, drill evenly spaced pilot holes for the bin bottom in the credenza sides and end, ⅜" up from the bottom edges of the boards. Apply glue to the edges of the bin bottom and slip it into place, flush with the bottom edges of the credenza sides and ends **(photo H).** Drive 1⅝" wood screws through the sides and ends and into the edges of the bin bottom.

7. Cut the stops (S) to length.

8. Drill 1/16" pilot holes through the stop pieces. Position the stops to conceal the joints and the edges of the panels that make up the large credenza bin. Use glue and 1" brads to attach the stops **(photo I).**

9. Cut the lids (T) to size from a single plywood panel. Apply edge tape to all of the edges. Do not attach the lids until after the finish has been applied.

APPLY FINISHING TOUCHES.

1. Insert glued oak plugs into all visible screw holes in the desk and credenza. Sand the plugs flush with the surface. Set all nails with a nail set, and fill the nail holes with wood putty.

2. Finish-sand both furnishings with 180- or 220-grit sandpaper. Then, apply the finish of your choice. You may find it easier to finish the desk if you remove the desktop first. It is important that you finish the underside as well as the top. We used only a clear topcoat for a light, contemporary look. You may prefer to use a light or medium wood stain first.

3. When the finish has dried, reattach the desktop. Fasten 1½ × 3" brass butt hinges to the bottom faces of the credenza lids, 2¼" in from the side edges. The backs of the hinge barrels should be flush with the back edges of the lids when closed. Attach the bin lids to the credenza by fastening the hinges to the credenza ends. Attach sliding lid supports to the lids and inside faces of the credenza sides to hold the lids open for access to the bins.

4. Attach a 2½" swivel caster to the bottom end of each credenza leg.

Bedroom Projects

A beautiful mission lamp and a practical night stand to put it on; a spacious armoire and a delightful jewelry box. These projects and more are here for you to create. Sleep tight and dream of creating more attractive and practical projects.

Mission Lamp Base

The beauty and texture of oak combine with a simple style and charm in this traditional table lamp.

PROJECT POWER TOOLS

This decorative lamp base provides just the right accent for a family room tabletop or bedside stand. It's made of red oak, and the design is simple and stylish. The clean, vertical lines of the oak slats are rooted in the popular Mission style.

The oak parts are joined with glue and nails, so the lamp base goes together with a minimum of time and fuss.

Once the base is assembled, just insert the lamp hardware, which you can buy at any hardware store. Lamp hardware kits include all of the components you need—harp, socket, cord and tubing. Make sure to follow manufacturer's directions when installing the hardware.

When you're finished, buy an attractive shade, either contemporary or classic, and set the lamp on a nightstand or table.

Construction Materials

Quantity	Lumber
1	1 × 8" × 2' oak
2	1 × 2" × 10' oak
1	1 × 3 × 12" oak

OVERALL SIZE:
19¼" HIGH
8" WIDE
8" DEEP

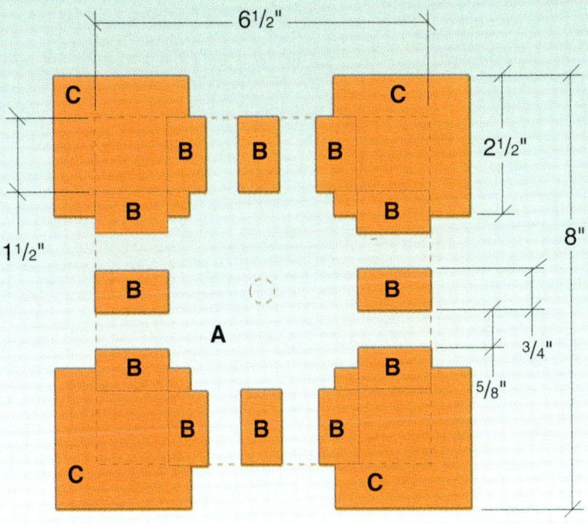

PLAN VIEW

Cutting List

Key	Part	Dimension	Pcs.	Material
A	Plate	¾ × 6½ × 6½"	2	Oak
B	Slat	¾ × 1½ × 17"	12	Oak
C	Foot	¾ × 2½ × 2½"	4	Oak

Materials: 3d and 6d finish nails, lamp hardware kit, felt pads, wood glue, finishing materials.

Note: Measurements reflect the actual size of dimension lumber.

Tape the plates edge to edge, and use a square to lay out the slat positions.

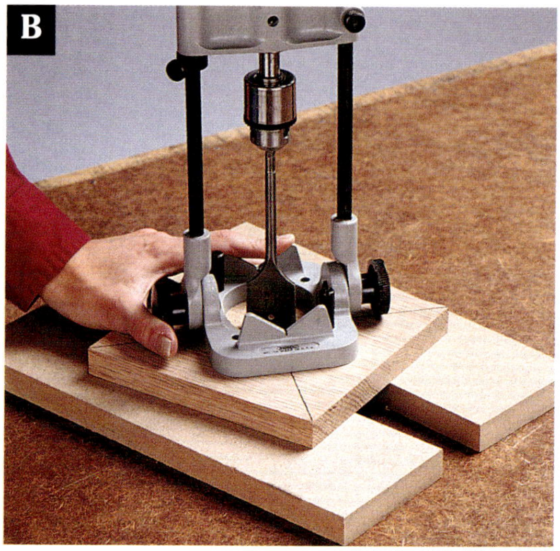

Use a portable drill guide to make accurate center holes in the plates.

Drill pilot holes through the plates for finish nails.

Directions: Mission Lamp Base

PREPARE THE PLATES.

1. Cut the plates (A) to size, and sand the pieces smooth with medium-grit sandpaper.

2. Set the plates flat on your worksurface, edge to edge, with their ends flush, and tape them together. Following the *Diagram*, lay out the slat placement, using a combination square to ensure the lines are square and identical on both plates **(photo A).**

3. Draw diagonal lines from corner to corner, on the opposite sides of each plate, to locate the centers of the pieces. Drill a 1"-dia. × ¼"-deep counterbore hole on the bottom center of the lower plate, using a spade bit **(photo B).** Use a portable drill stand to hold the drill straight. This hole will receive a washer when you assemble the lamp.

4. Use the same technique to drill a ⅜"-dia. hole through the center of the counterbore and the center of the other plate for the lamp rod. To prevent splintering when the drill bit exits the other side, use a backer board when drilling holes through your workpiece.

5. Drill 1/16" pilot holes for finish nails through the plates to secure the slats **(photo C).** Each slat should have two finish nails attaching it to each plate.

CUT AND ATTACH THE SLATS.

1. Cut the slats (B) to length. Only a portion of each slat will be fully visible on the completed lamp, so choose the best sides and edges of the slats to be exposed.

2. Finish-sand the slats. Be careful not to round the edges.

3. Attach the slats to the top plate, one at a time. First, apply glue to the top end of the slat. Then, drive 6d finish nails through the pilot holes in the top plate and into the end of the slat **(photo D).** For best results, fasten each slat with one nail, and check the positioning.

TIP

Traditionally, Mission-style furnishings have a dark finish. If your goal is to create a true reproduction of the Mission style, use a dark walnut stain to finish your lamp base.

Then, make any necessary adjustments, and drive the second nail.

4. Fasten the bottom ends of the slats to the lower plate, using glue and 6d finish nails. Make sure the counterbore for the lamp hardware is on the bottom.

CUT AND ATTACH THE FEET.

1. Cut the feet (C) to size from the leftover 1 × 8 stock.

2. Gang-sand the pieces to a uniform shape, and finish-sand them with fine-grit sandpaper.

3. Draw reference lines on each foot to mark its position on the base plate. Measure ¾" from the outside edge of two adjacent sides, and draw lines across the face of the foot, parallel to the side edges. These lines show where the four feet meet the plate corners (see *Diagram*).

4. Drill two ⅟₁₆" pilot holes for finish nails through each foot. Apply glue, and follow the reference lines to position the feet on the bottom face of the bottom plate. The two outside edges of the feet should overhang the corner edges of the plate by ¾".

5. Secure the feet by driving 3d finish nails through the feet and into the bottom plate.

Attach the slats to the top plate with glue and 6d finish nails.

Install the threaded lamp rod, and secure it to the bottom plate with a washer and nut.

APPLY FINISHING TOUCHES.

1. Set all nails in the lamp base with a nail set. Fill the nail holes with tinted wood putty, and sand the putty flush with the surface. Then, finish-sand the entire project.

2. Finish the lamp as desired (see *Tip*). We used a light oak stain and added two coats of wipe-on tung oil for a protective topcoat.

3. When the finish has dried, attach self-adhesive felt pads to the bottom of the feet to prevent scratching on tabletop surfaces.

INSTALL THE HARDWARE.

With the wood parts assembled, install the lamp kit components to complete the project. Always follow manufacturer's instructions when installing hardware.

1. Cut the lamp rod to length so that it extends from plate to plate. Insert the rod through the holes in the plates.

2. Attach the harp to the top plate. Then, secure the tube to the bottom plate with a washer and nut **(photo E).**

3. Thread the cord through the rod, and wire the ends to the socket according to the manufacturer's directions.

PROJECT
POWER TOOLS

Room Divider

Crafted from cedar boards and lauan plywood, this portable room divider makes it easy to create a new living space.

CONSTRUCTION MATERIALS

Quantity	**Lumber***
3	1 × 4" × 8' cedar
3	¾ × ¾" × 8' mahogany cove molding
1	¼" × 4 × 4' lauan plywood

*Materials for a single room divider section.

Strips of lauan plywood are woven together and set in rustic cedar frames to make this room divider. Held together with brass hinges, the sections of the divider can be arranged to fit almost any room. Use it as a partition to make a romantic dining nook in a large living area. Or, position the room divider near a sunny window to establish a tranquil garden retreat without adding permanent walls. There are many creative uses for this versatile decorative barrier.

The instructions for building the room divider show you how to make one section. Add as many additional sections as required.

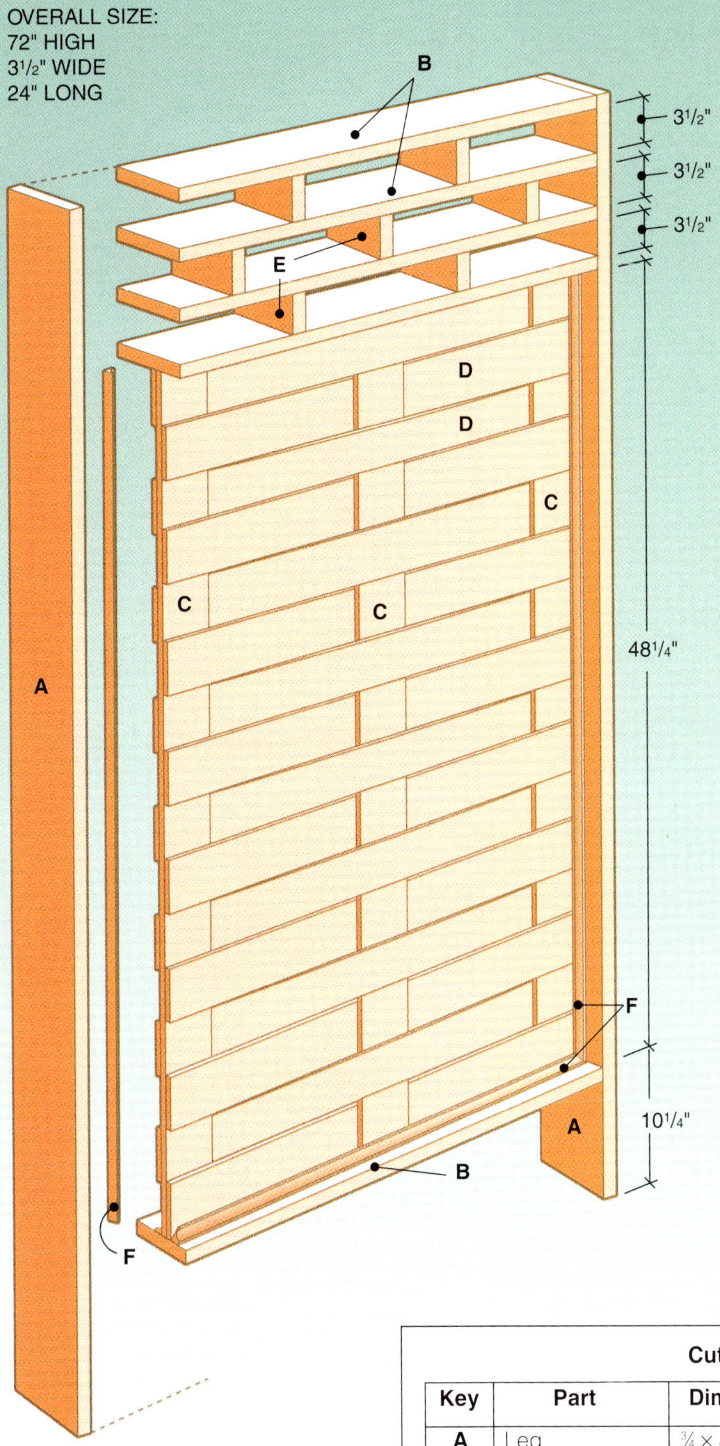

Cutting List

Key	Part	Dimension	Pcs.	Material
A	Leg	¾ × 3½ × 72"	2	Cedar
B	Stretcher	¾ × 3½ × 22½"	5	Cedar
C	Vertical slat	¼ × 3 × 48"	3	Plywood
D	Horizontal slat	¼ × 3 × 22½"	16	Plywood
E	Divider	¾ × 3½ × 3½"	7	Cedar
F	Retaining strip	¾ × ¾" × *	8	Cove molding

Materials: 2" deck screws, 2d finish nails, 2" brass butt hinges, wood glue, finishing materials.

Note: Measurements reflect the actual size of dimension lumber.

*Cut to fit.

Directions: Room Divider

MAKE THE FRAME.

The frame consists of two legs and five stretchers. Starting from the bottom, the first and second stretchers form the top and bottom borders of the woven panel.

1. Cut the legs (A) and stretchers (B) to length.

2. Measure and mark the positions for the stretchers on the inside faces of the legs. To make sure the measurements are exactly the same on both legs, tape the pieces together, edge to edge. Make sure the top and bottom edges are flush. Measure and mark a reference line 10¼" from the bottom ends of both legs. These lines mark the top edge of the bottom stretcher. Next, measure and mark lines 48¼" up the legs from the first reference lines **(photo A).** These lines mark the bottom edge of the second stretcher. The top stretcher should be positioned between the legs, flush with the top ends. Mark the remaining stretcher positions as desired. We arranged them equally between the top and second stretchers, about 3½" apart.

3. Drill two 3/32" pilot holes through the outside faces of the legs at the center position of each stretcher. Counterbore the holes ⅛" deep, using a ⅜" counterbore bit. Glue the ends of the stretchers and position them between the legs. Clamp the frame together and measure diagonally from corner to corner to make sure the frame is square. Fasten the stretchers to the legs with 2" deck screws.

Tape the legs together with their edges flush, and gang-mark the stretcher positions on the inside faces.

Weave the 16 horizontal slats through the three vertical slats to make the divider panel.

MAKE THE DIVIDER PANEL.

The divider panel consists of 19 strips of ¼"-thick lauan plywood woven together without fasteners or glue. This step is easy to complete if you work on a flat surface.

1. Cut the vertical slats (C) and horizontal slats (D) to size. Sand the edges smooth.

2. Lay the vertical slats on your worksurface. Weave the horizontal slats between the vertical slats in an alternating pattern to form the panel **(photo B).**

INSTALL THE DIVIDER PANEL.

To hold the divider panel in the frame, fasten retaining strips along the inside faces of the legs and stretchers on both sides of the panel.

1. Use a miter box or a power miter saw to cut the retaining strips (F) to length from ¾"-thick mahogany cove molding. Miter-cut the retaining strips to fit the inside of the frame.

2. Mark reference lines along

Attach the retaining strips with 2d finish nails.

Connect the divider sections with brass butt hinges.

the inside faces of the legs, and on the faces of the stretchers at either end of the divider panels, $1\frac{3}{8}$" in from one edge. Position the molding on the outside of the reference lines, so one flat face is flush with the line. Attach the retaining strips to the frame with 2d finish nails **(photo C).** Set the nails with a nail set.

3. Place the woven panel against the retaining strip frame, and secure the panel by attaching the other retaining strips so they are snug against the opposite face of the panel.

APPLY FINISHING TOUCHES. Inserting the dividers is the final construction step for the room divider section. These pieces are purely decorative and can be spaced apart in any pattern. Cut them to fit snug between the top stretchers so they won't need fasteners.

1. Measure the distance between the top stretchers, and cut the dividers (E) to length. Sand the dividers smooth.

2. Set the dividers between the stretchers, positioning them in a way that is visually pleasing.

3. Fill all visible screw holes with tinted wood putty, and sand the legs smooth.

4. Join individual dividers with evenly spaced 2" butt hinges **(photo D).** To attach the hinges, clamp the sections together with scrap wood spacers in between. The spacers should have the same thickness as the barrels of the hinges. Use cardboard pads to prevent the clamps from damaging the soft wood of the frames.

5. Cedar lumber, mahogany trim and lauan plywood do not require a protective finish, so we left them unfinished. If you prefer a glossier look, apply a coat of tung oil to the parts before assembly.

TIP

There is significant color variation in lauan plywood, ranging from soft yellow to deep purple—sometimes within the same panel. Keep this in mind when you are selecting your lumber.

PROJECT
POWER TOOLS

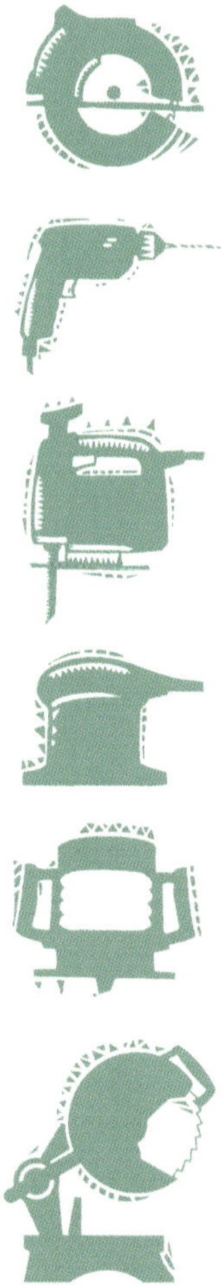

Jewelry Box

This piece of fine furniture will be a worthy home for your family treasures.

Construction Materials

Quantity	**Lumber**
1	¾ × 24 × 48" MDF*
1	½ × 12 × 30" birch plywood
1	½ × 24 × 30" birch plywood
1	¼ × 12 × 24" hardboard

*Medium-density fiberboard

Without a suitable home, jewelry has a way of getting jumbled, tangled or misplaced. This elegant and roomy jewelry box solves that problem with pizzazz.

Our classically proportioned chest—like all fine furniture—is as functional as it is beautiful. Three spacious drawers accommodate everything from fun and funky costume jewelry to the finest family heirlooms. A simple system of dadoes and rabbets achieves the close tolerances and tight joints that characterize true quality woodwork.

The timeless design of this piece allows for many options in materials and finish, providing great flexibility for customizing your box to suit a special person or unique situation.

Building this project as a gift will showcase your thoughtfulness as well as your woodworking skills.

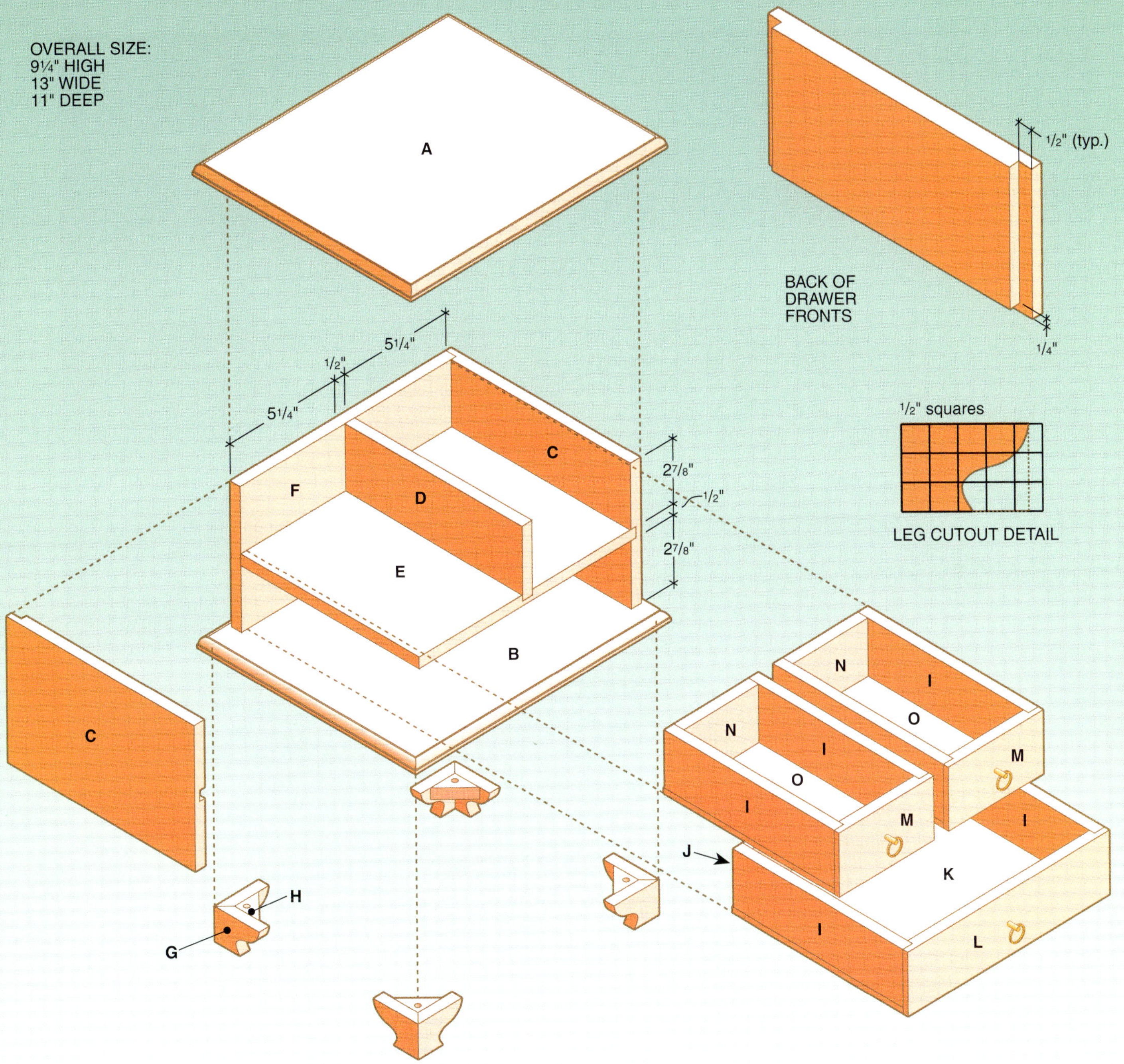

Cutting List

Key	Part	Dimension	Pcs.	Material
A	Top	¾ × 11 × 13"	1	MDF
B	Bottom	¾ × 11 × 13"	1	MDF
C	Side	½ × 6¼ × 9½"	2	Birch ply.
D	Divider	½ × 3⅛ × 9"	1	Birch ply.
E	Shelf	½ × 9 × 11"	1	Birch ply.
F	Back	½ × 6¼ × 11"	1	Birch ply.
G	Leg	½ × 1½ × 2¼"	8	Birch ply.
H	Glueblock	½ × 1¼ × 1¼"	4	Birch ply.

Cutting List

Key	Part	Dimension	Pcs.	Material
I	Drawer side	½ × 2½ × 8¹¹⁄₁₆"	6	Birch ply.
J	Long drwr. back	½ × 2½ × 9⅜"	1	Birch ply.
K	Long drwr. bottom	¼ × 8¾ × 10⅜"	1	Hardboard
L	Long drwr. front	½ × 2¾ × 10⅜"	1	Birch ply.
M	Short drwr. front	½ × 2¾ × 4⅞"	2	Birch ply.
N	Short drwr. back	½ × 2½ × 3⅞"	2	Birch ply.
O	Short drwr. bottom	¼ × 4⅞ × 8¾"	2	Hardboard

Materials: Wood glue, brads, 4d finish nails, #6 × 1" screws, drawer pulls (3), finishing materials.

Note: Measurements reflect the actual thickness of dimension lumber.

To cut the shelf dadoes, rout both sides in one pass, using a clamped straightedge as a guide for the router base.

Apply glue to the shelf, the divider and the shoulders of the rabbets before attaching the back.

Directions: Jewelry Box

CUT AND SHAPE THE CABINET PARTS.

1. Cut the top (A) and bottom (B) from ¾" MDF.

2. Rout the top edges of both pieces using a ⅜" roundover bit set for a ⅛" shoulder.

3. Measure and cut the sides (C), divider (D), shelf (E) and back (F).

4. Mark the sides and the shelf for location of dadoes (see *Diagram*), and mark the back edges of the sides for rabbets.

5. Cut the dadoes. Clamp the side blanks with back edges butted. Clamp a straightedge in place to guide the router base **(photo A),** and use a ½" straight router bit set ¼" deep.

6. Cut the divider dado in the shelf and the back rabbets in the sides.

7. Drill pilot holes in the dadoes and rabbets.

ASSEMBLE THE CABINET.

1. Attach the divider to the shelf with glue and brads. Stand the shelf/divider assembly on end and attach one side with glue and brads; flip the assembly and attach the other side.

2. Stand the partially assembled cabinet on its front and attach the back with glue and brads **(photo B).**

3. Center the top on the assembly, drill pilot holes, and fasten with glue and 4d finish nails.

4. Flip the cabinet over and attach the bottom the same way.

MAKE AND ATTACH THE LEGS.

1. Cut four blanks, 6" or longer, from ½ × 1½" stock.

2. Transfer the leg profile (see *Diagram*) to the ends of the blanks and cut the profiles with a jig saw.

3. Clamp the blanks together and gang-sand the cut edges with a drum sander mounted in your drill.

4. Cut four pairs of legs (G) to length, mitering the ends at 45° **(photo C).** Cut four *pairs* rather than eight identical pieces. Cut the glueblocks (H) to size from ½" scrap.

5. Assemble the legs by gluing them in pairs to the glueblocks. Use masking tape to hold the pieces together. Allow the glue to dry.

6. Position the legs on the cabinet bottom, drill pilot holes and attach with glue and 1" screws **(photo D).**

After the leg blanks have been profiled and sanded, cut the leg pieces to length with a power miter box.

Attach the legs with screws and glue, leaving a 3/8" overhang along both sides.

BUILD THE DRAWERS.

1. Cut the drawer faces (L, M) to size.

2. Rabbet the drawer faces to accept the 1/2" drawer sides and 1/4" bottoms (see *Diagram*).

3. Cut the drawer sides (I) and drawer backs (J, N) to size.

4. Drill pilot holes and assemble the drawer boxes with glue and brads.

5. Cut the drawer bottoms (K) and (O) to size from 1/4" hardboard and fasten with glue and brads (**photo E).**

6. Measure and drill holes for the drawer pulls.

APPLY FINISHING TOUCHES.

Set all nail heads, and fill voids with putty. Finish-sand the project, finish as desired and install drawer pulls.

Attach the drawer bottoms with glue and brads. The bottoms hold the drawers square so they fit within their compartments.

Nightstand

A back rail adds style to our nightstand and keeps you from knocking bedside items to the floor. Put our nightstand at your bedside for a classic touch of bedroom beauty.

PROJECT POWER TOOLS

The nightstand is a classic piece of furniture that will never go out of fashion. Our nightstand has a simple design with a solid, traditional look. The arched back rail and base pieces add style and grace to the nightstand, while the handy drawer gives you a great place to store bedside items.

Assembling this little beauty is easy. The box frame is made by attaching the sides, back and shelves. It is topped with a decorative back rail and wings. These pieces do more than dress up the nightstand—they reduce the risk of knocking over that insistent alarm clock when you lurch to shut it off in the morning.

Once the top sections are complete, you can make and attach the arched base. The drawer comes next. We avoided expensive metal track glides and instead used friction-reducing plastic bumpers and tack-on glides for easy installation and convenience.

Our nightstand is built from edge-glued pine panels that you can purchase at most building centers.

CONSTRUCTION MATERIALS

Quantity	Lumber
2	1 × 16" × 8' edge-glued pine
1	1 × 4" × 4' pine

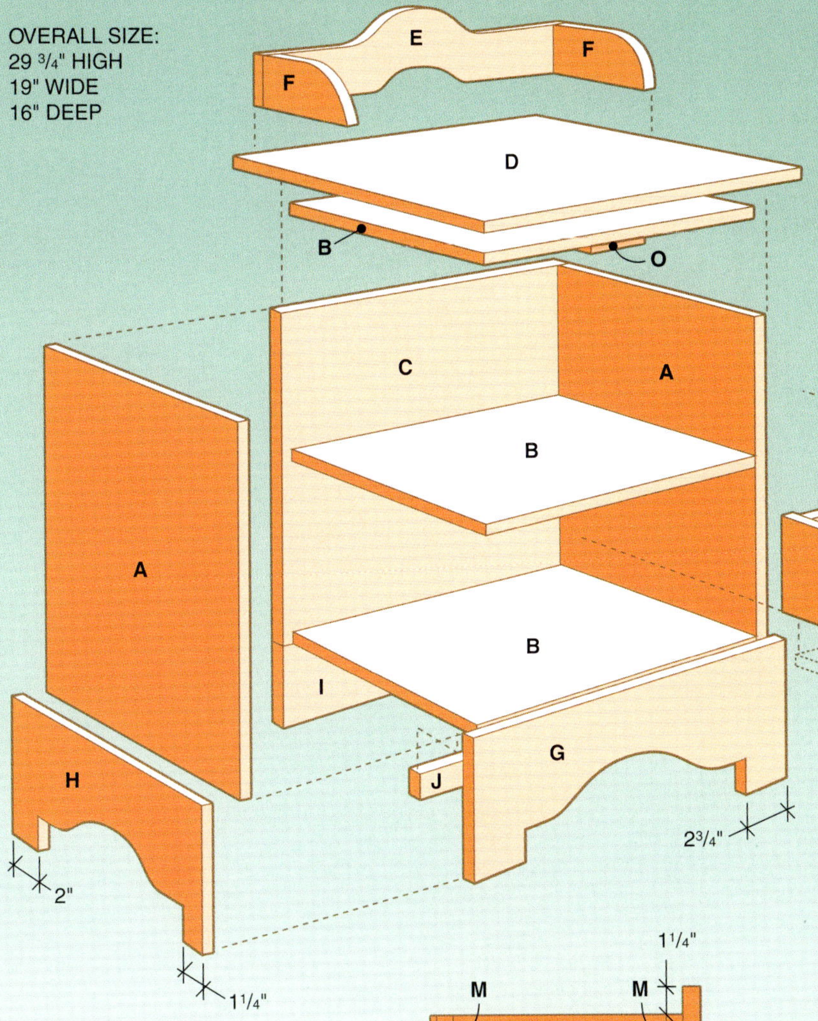

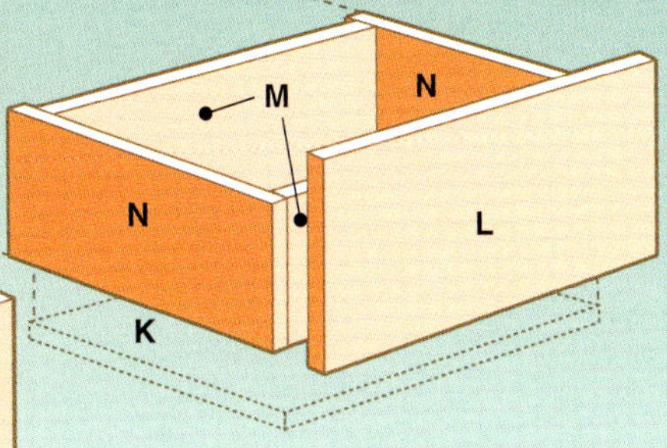

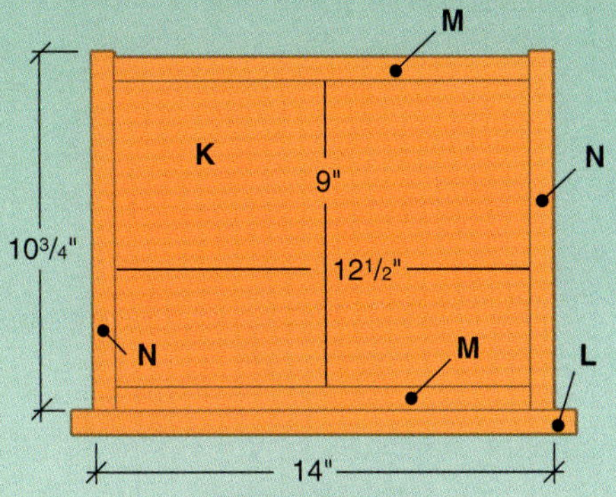

DRAWER DETAIL

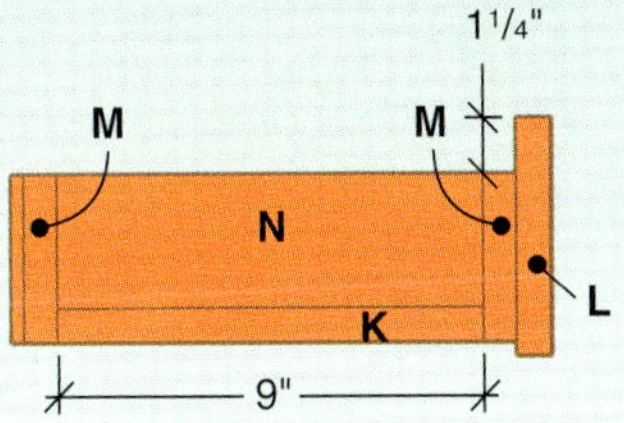

DRAWER SIDE

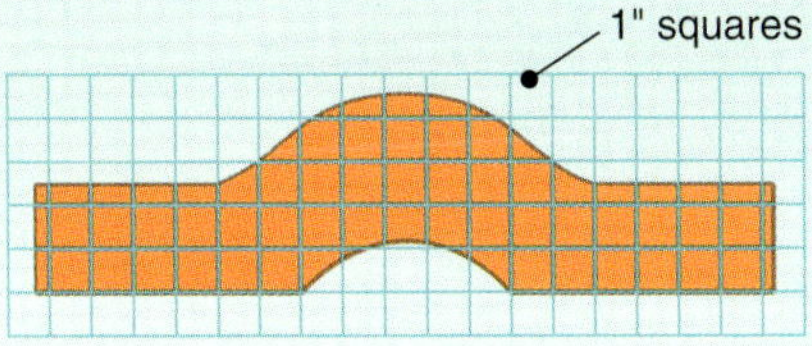

PART E DETAIL

Cutting List

Key	Part	Dimension	Pcs.	Material
A	Side	¾ × 13¼ × 17"	2	Pine
B	Shelf	¾ × 13¼ × 14½"	3	Pine
C	Back	¾ × 16 × 17"	1	Pine
D	Top	¾ × 16 × 19"	1	Pine
E	Back rail	¾ × 4½ × 17½"	1	Pine
F	Wing	¾ × 2½ × 5½"	2	Pine
G	Base front	¾ × 8 × 17½"	1	Pine
H	Base side	¾ × 8 × 14"	2	Pine

Cutting List

Key	Part	Dimension	Pcs.	Material
I	Base back	¾ × 4 × 16"	1	Pine
J	Base cleat	¾ × 2 × 16"	1	Pine
K	Drawer bottom	¾ × 9 × 12½"	1	Pine
L	Drawer front	¾ × 5 × 15¾"	1	Pine
M	Drawer end	¾ × 3½ × 12½"	2	Pine
N	Drawer side	¾ × 3½ × 10¾"	2	Pine
O	Stop cleat	¾ × 1½ × 3"	1	Pine

Materials: 1¼", 1½", and 2" deck screws, 6d finish nails, wooden knobs (2), plastic drawer stop, tack-on drawer glides, stem bumpers, wood glue, finishing materials.

Note: Measurements reflect the actual size of dimension lumber.

Attach the back to one side. Then, check for square.

Trace the back rail pattern and cut the piece to shape with a jig saw.

Directions: Nightstand

For all screws used in this project, drill 3/32" pilot holes. Counterbore the holes 1/8" deep, using a 3/8" counterbore bit.

BUILD THE BOX FRAME.

1. Cut the sides (A) and shelves (B) to size, and finish-sand the pieces.

2. Use glue and 2" deck screws to fasten the top and bottom shelves between the sides. Attach one shelf flush with the top ends of the sides and the other shelf flush with the bottom ends. Make sure the screws are centered and the front and back shelf edges are flush with the side edges.

3. Cut the back (C) to size, and sand it smooth. Attach it along the back edge of one side with glue and 2" deck screws **(photo A).**

4. Use a framing square to check the outside of the box to be sure the sides are square with the shelves. If they are not, apply pressure to one side to draw the pieces square. This can be done by hand or by attaching a bar or pipe clamp diagonally from one side to the other. When the pieces are square, clamp them in place, and finish attaching the back to the remaining sides and shelves.

MAKE THE BACK RAIL AND WINGS.

1. Cut the back rail (E) and wings (F) to size.

2. Transfer the pattern (see *Part E Detail*) for the back rail (see *Tip*). Cut the piece to the finished shape, using a jig saw

Fasten the wings to the back rail with glue and screws.

TIP

When transferring a grid diagram, you can enlarge the diagram on a photocopier and trace it onto a piece of cardboard to form a tracing template.

Draw reference lines on the top. Then, drill pilot holes and attach the back rail and wings.

Attach the top assembly to the top shelf with glue and screws.

(photo B). Sand the back rail smooth.

3. Shape the wings by using a compass to draw a 2½" radius arc. Place the compass point as close as possible to the bottom edge, 2½" back from the front and trace the arc. Cut the curve with a jig saw. Cut the second wing, and gang-sand the wings smooth.

4. Drill pilot holes in the back rail ⅜" in from the ends. Fasten the wings to the back rail with glue and 1½" deck screws **(photo C).**

COMPLETE THE TOP SECTION.

1. Cut the top (D) to size, and sand it smooth.

2. Center the back rail and wings onto the top with the back rail flush with the top's back edge. Draw a 5½"-long line marking the outside edge of each wing. The lines should be ¾" in from the side edges of the top.

3. Drill pilot holes through the top, ⅜" inside each line for attaching the wings **(photo D).** Attach the back rail and wings to the top with glue, and drive 1½" deck screws through the bottom face of the top and into the back rail and wings.

4. Center the top assembly over the top shelf, with the back edges flush. Attach the top assembly by driving 1¼" deck screws through the top shelf and into the top **(photo E).**

ATTACH THE MIDDLE SHELF.

1. Draw reference lines across the inside faces of the sides, 5½" down from the top edges of the sides.

2. Position the top of the middle shelf below the reference lines with its front edge flush with the front edges of the sides. Fasten the shelf with glue, and drive 2" deck screws through the sides and into the edges of the shelf. This shelf supports the drawer, so make sure it is square to the sides.

MAKE THE BASE CUTOUTS.

1. Cut the base front (G), base sides (H), base back (I) and base cleat (J) to size.

2. Make the decorative cutout on the base front, by draw verti-

Use a combination square to mark the finish nail position on the base front and sides.

cal lines 2¾" in from each end. Using the template you made for the back rail, center the top of the arc 3" down from the top edge of the base front. Trace the curved line along the top of the template until it intersects the two vertical lines (see *Diagram*). Cut out the detail with a jig saw, and sand the piece smooth.

3. Make the cutout on one of the base sides, using the template. Draw a vertical line on the base side piece, 1¼" in from the front end and 2" in from the rear end. Center the arc of the template 3" from the top of the base side, and trace the curve to meet the vertical lines. Cut the piece with a jig saw and sand it smooth.

4. Use the finished base side to trace an identical pattern onto the other base side. Make the cutout with a jig saw, and sand the piece smooth.

ASSEMBLE THE BASE.

1. Butt the front ends of the base sides against the base front so the top edges are flush and the outside faces of the base sides are flush with the ends of the base front. Drill 1/16" pilot holes through the base front and into the sides. Attach the pieces with glue and 6d finish nails.

2. Position the base back between the base sides so that its top edge is ½" below the top edges of the base sides and the back edges are flush. Attach the base back with glue, and drive 6d finish nails through the sides and into the ends of the base back.

3. Attach the base cleat to the inside face of the base front with glue, and drive 1¼" deck screws through the cleat and into the base front. Leave a ½" space between the top edge of the cleat and the top edge of the base front.

ATTACH THE FRAME.

1. Draw a reference line for finish nails, ¼" below the top edge of the base front and sides **(photo F).**

2. Set the nightstand box frame into the base so it rests on the base back and base cleat.

3. Drill evenly spaced 1/16" pilot holes along the reference lines. Fasten the base by driving 6d finish nails through the base front and sides and into the sides and bottom shelf.

BUILD THE DRAWER.

1. Cut the drawer bottom (K), drawer front (L), drawer ends (M) and drawer sides (N) to size. Sand the parts smooth.

2. Position the drawer bottom between the drawer ends, keeping the bottom edges and the ends flush. Attach the pieces with glue, and drive 1½" deck screws through the drawer ends and into the drawer bottom.

3. Align the drawer sides so their front edges are flush with the front face of the front drawer end. Fasten the sides to the bottom and ends with glue and 1½" deck screws **(photo G).** The rear ends of the drawer sides should overhang the rear end of the drawer by ¼".

4. Draw a reference line along the inside face of the drawer front ¼" above the bottom edge. Lay the drawer front flat on your worksurface. Center the drawer from side to side on the drawer front with its bottom edge on the reference line. Apply glue, and drive 1¼" deck screws through the drawer end and into the drawer front **(photo H).**

INSTALL THE STOP CLEAT AND DRAWER KNOBS.
Used in conjunction with a purchased drawer stop, the stop cleat prevents the drawer from pulling completely out of the nightstand. A drawer stop is a small plastic bracket with an adjustable stem that catches the stop cleat when the drawer is opened.

1. Cut the stop cleat (O) to size.
2. Center the cleat on the bottom face of the top shelf so its front edge is ¾" in from the front edge of the top shelf. The length of the cleat should run parallel to the front edge of the shelf, and its 1½" face should contact the shelf face.
3. Attach the stop cleat with glue, and drive 1¼" deck screws through the cleat and into the top shelf.
4. Fasten the drawer knobs to the drawer front. Be sure to space the knobs evenly, and center them from top to bottom on the drawer front.

APPLY FINISHING TOUCHES.
1. Set all nails with a nail set, and fill the nail and screw holes with wood putty. Finish-sand the entire project.
2. Paint the nightstand inside and out, including the drawer. Apply a polyurethane topcoat to protect the painted finish.

INSTALL THE HARDWARE.
You have a number of glide options for the drawer. We used inexpensive plastic glides and stem bumpers. You can buy these glides and bumpers at any building center. Always follow manufacturer's directions when installing hardware.
1. Align the glides along the path of the drawer, and tack them in place.The glides we used have metal points, and they are installed like thumbtacks.
2. Drill holes for the stem bumpers into the drawer bottom. Apply glue to the bumpers, and insert them into the holes.
3. Install the drawer stop by drilling a 3⁄16"-dia. hole on the rear drawer end, ½" below the top edge. Apply glue to the drawer stop and attach it to the drawer end.
4. Insert the drawer. With the drawer open slightly, reach in and rotate the drawer stop until it is in position to catch the stop cleat.

Fasten the drawer sides to the drawer ends and drawer bottom with glue and screws.

Align the drawer front, and attach the pieces by driving screws through the drawer end.

PROJECT POWER TOOLS

Cedar Chest

This compact cedar chest has the potential to become a cherished family heirloom.

CONSTRUCTION MATERIALS

Quantity	Lumber
3	1 × 2" × 8' cedar
1	1 × 3" × 10' cedar
1	1 × 6" × 8' cedar
3	1 × 8" × 8' cedar
1	2 × 2" × 8' cedar
1	¾" × 2 × 4' plywood

The cedar chest has a long history as a much-appreciated graduation gift. The appreciation will be even greater for a cedar chest you have built yourself. And short of a packing crate, you won't find a simpler chest to build anywhere.

Despite its simplicity, this cedar chest has all the features of a commercially produced chest costing hundreds of dollars. The framed lid is hinged in back and can be locked open with an optional locking lid support. A removable tray fits inside the chest for storing delicate items. The main compartment is fitted with aromatic cedar panels to keep sweaters or your favorite linen treasures safe from moth damage and musty odors.

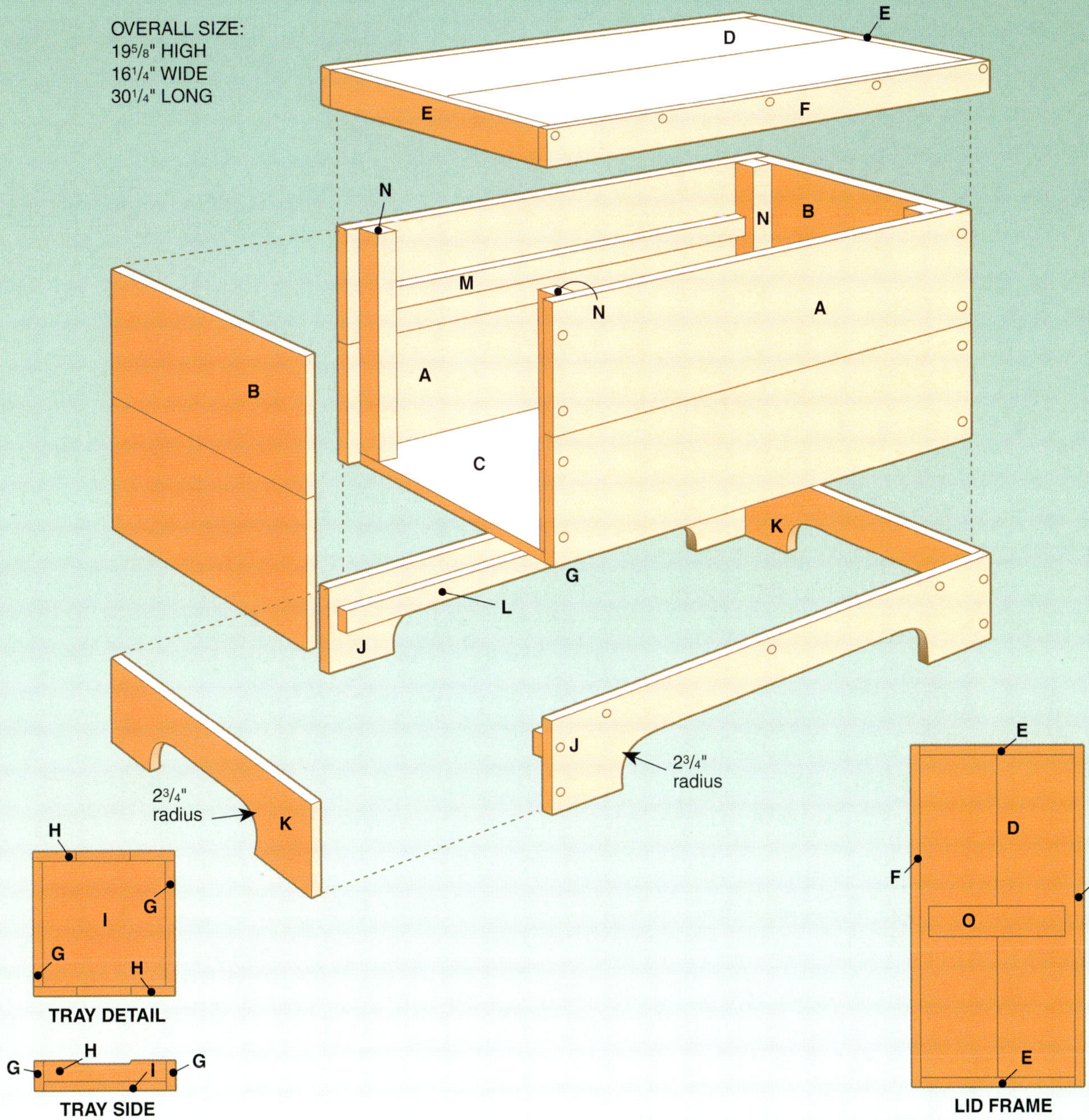

Key	Part	Dimension	Pcs.	Material
A	Side	⅞ × 7¼ × 28"	4	Cedar
B	End	⅞ × 7¼ × 12½"	4	Cedar
C	Bottom	¾ × 12½ × 26¼"	1	Plywood
D	Top	⅞ × 7¼ × 28½"	2	Cedar
E	End lip	⅞ × 1½ × 14½"	2	Cedar
F	Side lip	⅞ × 1½ × 30¼"	2	Cedar
G	Tray side	⅞ × 2½ × 12¾"	2	Cedar
H	Tray end	⅞ × 2½ × 11¾"	2	Cedar

Cutting List

Key	Part	Dimension	Pcs.	Material
I	Tray bottom	⅞ × 2½ × 12¾"	4	Cedar
J	Side plate	⅞ × 5½ × 29¾"	2	Cedar
K	End plate	⅞ × 5½ × 14¼"	2	Cedar
L	Base cleat	⅞ × 1½ × 28"	2	Cedar
M	Chest cleat	⅞ × 1½ × 23¼"	2	Cedar
N	Corner post	1½ × 1½ × 13¾"	4	Cedar
O	Top cleat	⅞ × 2½ × 12"	1	Cedar

Materials: 1¼" and 2" deck screws, 2d finish nails, 1½ × 2" brass butt hinges (2), lid support, optional hardware accessories, aromatic cedar panels, panel adhesive, ⅜"-dia. cedar plugs, wood glue, finishing materials.

Note: Measurements reflect the actual size of dimension lumber.

Drive screws through the posts and into the ends.

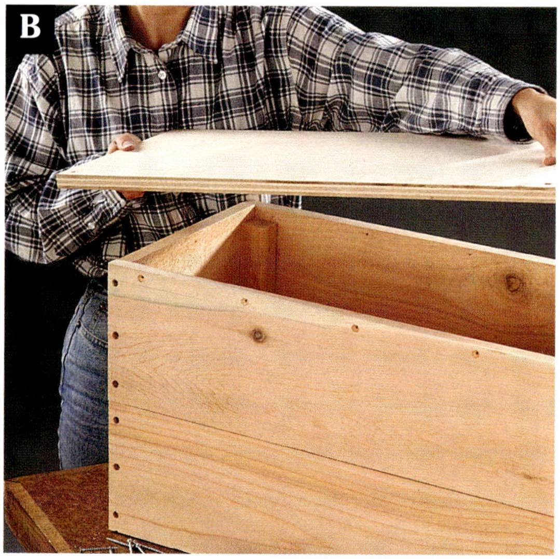

Install the bottom onto the corner posts and fasten it to the sides and ends of the chest.

Directions: Cedar Chest

For all screws used in this project, drill 3/32" pilot holes. Counterbore the holes 1/4" deep, using a 3/8" counterbore bit.

BUILD THE BOX FRAME.

1. Cut the chest sides (A), chest ends (B) and corner posts (N) to length. Sand the pieces smooth with medium-grit sandpaper.

2. Use glue and 2" deck screws to fasten two chest ends to each pair of corner posts, with their tops and side edges flush **(photo A).** When using cedar that is rough on one side, be sure that exposed surfaces are consistent in texture. For this project, make sure all rough surfaces are facing inside.

Attach the top cleat to the undersides of the tops, making sure it is centered between the ends and the sides.

3. Apply glue to the outside edges of the corner posts, and fasten the chest sides to the chest ends by driving 2" deck screws through the chest sides and into the edges of the chest ends. Make sure the top and side edges are flush. If the box frame is assembled correctly, there will be a 3/4"-wide space between the bottom of the corner posts and the bottom edges of the box frame.

4. Cut the bottom (C) to size.

5. Turn the box frame upside down. Fasten the bottom to the corner posts, ends and sides with glue and 2" deck screws **(photo B).**

6. Seal the inside surfaces with an oil finish or sealer to prevent warping and splitting.

BUILD THE TOP ASSEMBLY.

1. Cut the top pieces (D) and the top cleat (O) to length. Cut the end lips (E) and side lips (F) to length. Sand the pieces smooth.

2. Use bar or pipe clamps to

TIP

Cedar is a good wood type for the beginner because it is very forgiving of mistakes. It is also a traditional wood for building chests and trunks. But if you want to create a more elegant chest that is better able to take a fine finish, substitute clear redwood.

Smooth the jig saw cuts on the radius cutouts using a drum sander attachment and drill.

Set the box frame into the base, and fasten it with evenly spaced screws.

hold the tops together, edge to edge, with their ends flush. Use a combination square to measure and mark the top cleat position on the inside faces of the tops. Make sure the top cleat is centered, with its side edges 13" from the ends of the tops and with its ends centered between the side edges of the tops. Attach the cleat to the tops with glue and 1¼" deck screws **(photo C).**

3. Attach the side lips and end lips to the edges of the tops with glue and 2" deck screws. Make sure the top edges of the lips and tops are flush.

BUILD THE BASE.

1. Cut the side plates (J) and end plates (K) to length.

2. Use a compass and a straightedge to draw the curved cutouts on the side and end plates. Make marks along the bottom edge of the side plates, 6¾" in from each end. Set a compass to draw a 2¾" radius curve. Hold the compass point on the mark, as close as possible to the bottom edge, and draw the curve onto the face of the side plate. Then, using a straightedge, draw a straight line 2¾" from the bottom edge of the side plate, intersecting the tops of the curves. Repeat these steps to draw the cutouts on the end plates, but hold the compass point 5⅞" from the ends. Make the cutouts with a jig saw.

3. Use a drill and a drum sander attachment to smooth the curves of the cutouts **(photo D).** Finish-sand the side plates and end plates.

4. Fasten the end plates between the side plates with glue. Drive 2" deck screws through the faces of the side plates and into the ends of the end plates.

5. Cut the two base cleats (L) to length.

6. Use glue to fasten the base cleats to the inside faces of the side plates, 2¾" from the bottom edges, flush with the top of the cutouts. Drive 1¼" deck screws through the cleats and into the side plates.

ATTACH THE BOX FRAME AND BASE.

1. Test-fit the box frame in the base, making sure it sits squarely on top of the cleats.

2. Apply glue to the mating surfaces, and attach the base by driving evenly spaced 1¼" deck screws through the end plates and side plates and into the box frame **(photo E).**

TIP

When constructing pieces that fit inside other pieces (as the chest fits inside the base), build the inside piece first. The outer parts can always be cut larger or smaller to fit the inner ones.

Tape the tray ends together. Then, draw a slot across the joint to mark identical handle cutouts.

Attach the tray bottoms to the tray ends and sides with glue and screws.

MAKE THE TRAY.

1. Cut the tray sides (G), tray ends (H) and tray bottom (I) pieces to length.

2. Lay out the tray handles by placing the tray ends side by side, with the ends flush. Tape the pieces together. Mark a 1½"-wide × 5"-long slot with ¾"-radius curves centered on each end of the slot where the two pieces meet **(photo F).** Make the cuts with a jig saw. Use a drum sander attachment on a drill to smooth out the radius cuts.

3. Attach the tray sides between the tray ends with glue and 2" deck screws.

4. Fasten the tray bottoms between the tray sides and ends with glue and 2" deck screws **(photo G).** Finish-sand the entire tray, and smooth out any sharp edges.

INSTALL AROMATIC CEDAR PANELS.

1. Cut aromatic cedar liner panels to fit the inside of the chest. Use panels that are no thicker than ¼".

2. Attach the liner panels to the sides, ends and bottom with panel adhesive and 2d finish nails **(photo H).** Set the nails with a nail set.

TIP

Aromatic cedar paneling, often described as "closet liner," has a strong cedar scent that keeps away insects that can damage stored items. The paneling is sold in board packages (usually covering 14 square feet) or in thin sheets that resemble particleboard.

MAKE AND INSTALL THE CHEST CLEATS.

1. Cut the chest cleats (M) to length. Finish-sand the cleats.

2. Install the chest cleats so their top edges are 3½" from the tops of the chest sides. They should fit snugly between the corner posts. Attach the cleats with glue, and drive 1¼" deck screws through the cleats and into the sides.

INSTALL THE TOP ASSEMBLY.

1. Place the top assembly over the chest box, and use masking tape to mark where the lower edge of the lip contacts the back side. Install two 1½ × 2" brass butt hinges on the back of the chest box, 6" in from each end. Mount the hinges so the leaves are above the contact line and the barrels are below the contact line.

2. Place the chest and top assembly on a flat worksurface. Prop the chest box against the top so the unfastened leaves of the hinges rest on the inside of the lip of the top assembly. Insert spacers equal to the thickness of the hinge barrel between the chest and lip. (Ordinary wood shims work well for this.) Fasten the hinges to the lip using the screws provided with the hinge hardware **(photo I).** Test the lid assembly and hinges for proper operation and fit.

3. Install a locking lid support between the lid assembly and

Install aromatic cedar panels to the sides, ends and bottom, using panel adhesive and 2d finish nails.

TIP

Use the right tools and techniques when applying stencils. A special brush is recommended for stencils (they resemble old-style shaving brushes). Use special stenciling paint, which is very dry so it does not leak under the stencil. Attach the stencil securely, and dab the dry paint onto the surface with the brush. Do not remove the stencil until the paint has dried.

the chest box to hold the lid in an open position during use. For just a little more money, you can purchase hardware accessories called soft-down supports, which let the lid close gently instead of slamming down.

4. Install chest handles and brass corner protectors, if desired.

APPLY FINISHING TOUCHES.

1. Fill all exposed counterbore holes with cedar plugs. Apply glue to the edges of the plugs and tap them in place with a hammer. Sand the plugs flush with the surrounding surface. Finish-sand all of the outside surfaces of the chest.

2. Set the tray on the chest cleats and slide it back and forth to test the fit. Adjust the fit, if necessary, using a belt or palm sander and medium-grit sandpaper. Finish-sand the tray to remove any sanding scratches and roughness.

3. Finish the chest and tray as desired. We chose a traditional clear finish to provide a rustic, natural appearance. To apply this type of finish, first brush on a coat of sanding sealer to ensure even absorption (a good idea with soft wood like cedar). Then, apply two light coats of tung-oil finish, and buff the surface to a medium gloss with a buffing pad. Apply finish to the chest cleat pieces but leave the cedar panels bare. After the finish is applied, dried and buffed, you may want to stencil a design or monograms onto the chest. If you choose to monogram the chest, look for plain stencils that are 1" to 2" tall, to keep in scale with the size of the chest. Very ornate typestyles are hard to stencil, and generally are not in tune with the rustic look of a cedar chest (see *Tip*, above). If you are interested in stenciling a design or emblem onto the chest, consider a simple pattern. Almost any nature motif (like pinecones) is a good choice.

Install brass butt hinges on the chest box and lid assembly. Use wood shims as spacers to help align the hinges.

PROJECT POWER TOOLS

Armoire

With a simple, rustic appearance, this movable closet can blend into almost any bedroom.

Construction Materials

Quantity	Lumber
3	¾" × 4 × 8' birch plywood
1	¼" × 4 × 8' birch plywood
1	1 × 2" × 8' pine
6	1 × 3" × 8' pine
1	1 × 6" × 8' pine
1	1½"-dia. × 2' fir dowel

Long before massive walk-in closets became the norm in residential building design, homeowners and apartment-dwellers compensated for cramped bedroom closets by making or buying armoires. The trim armoire design shown here reflects the basic styling developed during the heyday of the armoire, but at a scale that makes it usable in just about any living situation. At 60" high and only 36" in width, this compact armoire still boasts plenty of interior space. Five shelves on the left side are sized to store folded sweaters and shirts. And you can hang several suit jackets or dresses in the closet section to the right.

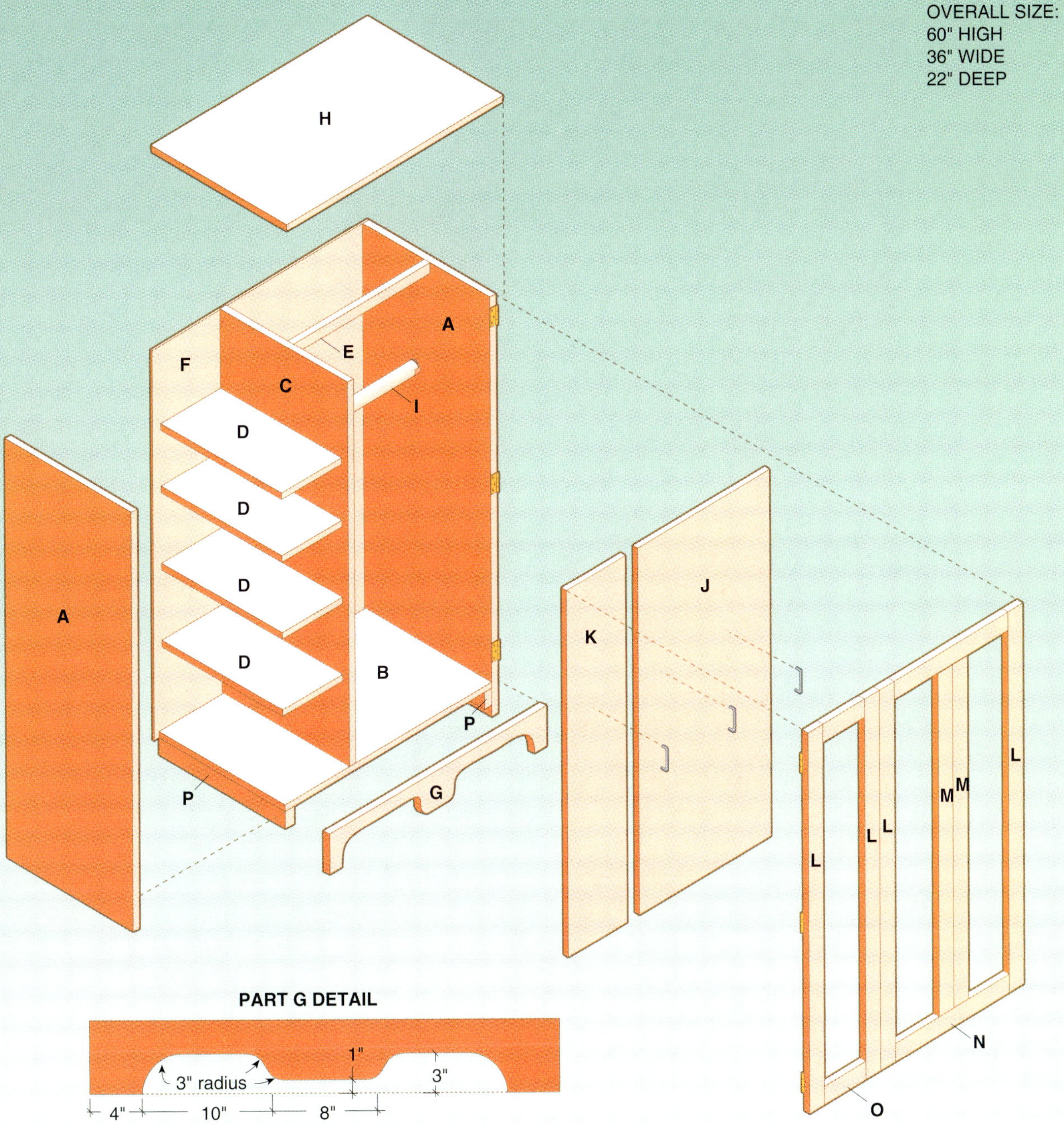

Cutting List

Key	Part	Dimension	Pcs.	Material
A	Side panel	¾ × 21 × 59¼"	2	Plywood
B	Bottom panel	¾ × 21 × 34½"	1	Plywood
C	Center panel	¾ × 21 × 53¾"	1	Plywood
D	Shelf	¾ × 10⅞ × 20¼"	4	Plywood
E	Stringer	¾ × 1½ × 22⅞"	1	Pine
F	Back	¼ × 36 × 54½"	1	Plywood
G	Front skirt	¾ × 5½ × 36"	1	Pine
H	Top panel	¾ × 22 × 36"	1	Plywood

Cutting List

Key	Part	Dimension	Pcs.	Material
I	Closet rod	1½ × 22⅞"	1	Fir
J	Closet door panel	¾ × 22 7/16 × 52⅛"	1	Plywood
K	Shelf door panel	¾ × 10 7/16 × 52⅛"	1	Plywood
L	Door stile	¾ × 2½ × 53⅝"	4	Pine
M	False stile	¾ × 2½ × 48⅝"	2	Pine
N	Closet door rail	¾ × 2½ × 18 15/16"	2	Pine
O	Shelf door rail	¾ × 2½ × 6 15/16"	2	Pine
P	Cleat	¾ × 1½ × 21"	2	Pine

Materials: #6 × 1¼" wood screws, 3d and 6d finish nails, closet rod hangers (2), wrought-iron hinges and pulls, magnetic door catches, ¾" birch veneer edge tape (50'), wood glue, finishing materials.
Note: Measurements reflect the actual size of dimension lumber.

Apply veneer edge tape to the exposed plywood edges. Trim off excess tape with a sharp utility knife.

Directions: Armoire

PREPARE THE PLYWOOD PANELS.

Careful preparation of the plywood panels that become the sides, bottom, top and shelves is key to creating an armoire with a clean, professional look. Take the time to make sure all the parts are perfectly square. Then, apply self-adhesive veneer edge tape to all plywood edges that will be visible. If you plan to paint the armoire, you can simply fill the edges with wood putty and sand them smooth before you apply the paint.

1. Cut the side panels (A), bottom panel (B), center panel (C) and shelves (D) to size, using a circular saw and a straightedge as a cutting guide. We used birch plywood because it is easy to work with and takes wood stain well. Smooth the surfaces of the panels with medium-grit sandpaper.

2. Apply self-adhesive veneer edge tape to the front edges of the center panel, side panels and shelves. Cut the strips of edge tape to length and position them over the plywood edges. Then, press the strips with a household iron set on a low-to-medium heat setting. The heat from the iron activates the adhesive.

3. Trim the excess tape with a sharp utility knife **(photo A).** Sand the trimmed edges and surfaces of the edge tape with medium-grit sandpaper.

ASSEMBLE THE CARCASE.

The *carcase* for the armoire (or any type of cabinet) is the main cabinet box. For this project, the carcase includes the

Clamp the bottom panel between the sides and fasten it to the cleats with glue and finish nails.

Fasten the shelves between the side panel and center panel with glue and finish nails.

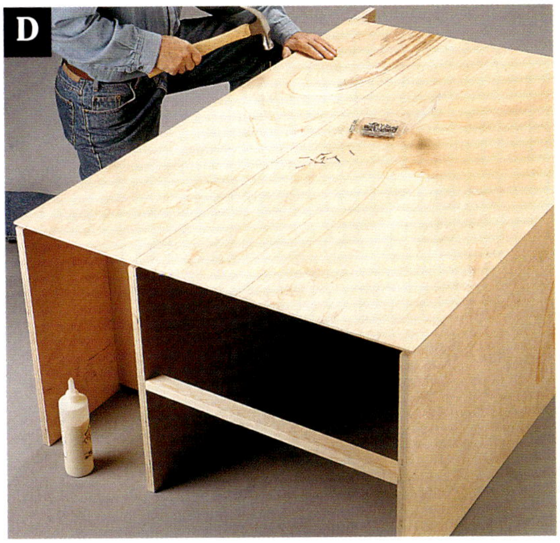

Nail the ¼"-thick back panel to the back edges of the carcase to help keep it square.

Lay out the decorative cutout at the bottom of the front skirt board, using a compass to make the curves. Then, cut with a jig saw.

side, bottom and center panels. Fasten the panels together with wood glue and finish nails. Make sure all of the joints are square and the edges are flush.

1. Lay out the cleat positions on the lower sections of the side panels. Measure up 4¾" from the bottom edges of the side panels, and draw a reference line across the inside face of each side panel.

2. Cut the cleats (P) to length.

3. Position the cleats just below the reference lines. Secure them with glue, and drive 3d finish nails through the cleats and into the side panels.

4. Stand the side panels upright on their bottom edges. Apply a bead of wood glue to the top of each cleat. Place the bottom panel between the side panels on top of the cleats, and clamp it in place. Make sure the taped front edges of the side panels and bottom panel are flush. Drive 6d finish nails through the bottom panel and into each cleat. Then, drive nails through the side panels and into the edges of the bottom panel **(photo B).**

5. Lay the assembly on its back edges. Use a pair of shelves as spacers to set the correct distance between the center panel and the left side panel (as seen from the front of the carcase). Make sure the taped panel edges are at the front of the carcase. Fasten the center panel to the bottom panel with glue, and drive 6d finish nails through the bottom panel and into the edge of the center panel.

INSTALL THE SHELVES.

1. Draw reference lines for the shelves on the inside face of the left side panel and on the left face of the center panel. Measure up from the top of the bottom panel, and draw lines at 13", 23⅞", 33¾" and 44⅛". Use a framing square to make sure the lines are perpendicular to the front and back edges of the panels.

2. Arrange the shelves so the tops are just below the reference lines, flush with the back edges of the carcase (creating a ¾" recess in front of each shelf). Attach the shelves with glue, and drive 6d finish nails through the side panel and center panel, and into the edges of the shelves **(photo C).** Brace each panel from behind as you drive the nails.

ATTACH THE STRINGER AND BACK PANEL.

1. Cut the stringer (E) to length.

2. Fasten the stringer between the center panel and side panel with glue and 6d finish nails. The stringer should be centered between the fronts and backs of the panels and flush with the tops.

3. Cut the back panel (F) to size from ¼"-thick plywood.

4. Measure the distances between opposite corners of the carcase to make sure it is square (the distances between corners should be equal). Adjust the carcase as needed. Then, position the back panel over the back edges of the carcase so the edges of the back panel are flush with the outside faces and top edges of the side panels. Fasten the back panel by driving 3d finish nails through the back and into the edges of the side, center and bottom panels **(photo D).**

Mount the top panel so it covers the top edge of the back panel and overhangs the front edges of the side panels by ¾".

Attach strips of 1 × 3 to the fronts of the door panels to create a frame.

MAKE AND ATTACH THE FRONT SKIRT.

1. Cut the front skirt (G) to length.

2. Lay out the curves that form the ends of the decorative cutouts on the skirt board (see *Diagram*), by making a mark 7" in from each end. Use a compass to draw a 3"-radius curve to make the outside end of each cutout, holding the point of the compass on the 7" mark, as close as possible to the bottom edge of the board. Then, make a mark 11¾" in from each end of the skirt board. Holding the compass point at the bottom edge, draw a 3"-radius curve to mark the top, inside end of each cutout. Measure 16⅞" in from each end of the skirt board, and mark points that are 1¾" down from the top edge of the board. Set the point of your compass at each of these points and draw 3"-radius curves that mark the bottom, inside ends of the cutouts. Then, at the middle of the bottom edge of the board, measure up 1" and draw a line parallel to the bottom edge, intersecting the inside ends of the cutout lines. Finally, draw lines parallel to the bottom edge of the board, 3" up, to create the top of each cutout. Make the cutout on the skirt board with a jig saw **(photo E).** Sand the saw cuts smooth with medium-grit sandpaper.

3. Position the skirt board against the front of the armoire carcase to make sure the ends of the skirt are flush with the outside faces of the side panels and the top of the skirt is flush with the top of the bottom panel. Fasten the front skirt to the front edges of the side panels and bottom panel with glue and 6d finish nails.

MAKE AND ATTACH THE TOP PANEL.

1. Stand the armoire upright, and measure the distance between the outside faces of the side panels—it should be 36".

2. Cut the top panel (H) to size.

3. Test-fit the top panel to make sure the edges are flush with the outside faces of the side panels. The back edge should be flush with the outside face of the back panel, and the front edge of the top should overhang the front of the carcase panels by ¾". Apply veneer edge tape to all four edges of the top panel.

4. Fasten the top panel to the center panel, side panels and stringer with glue and 6d finish nails, making sure it is in the same position as it was when you test-fit the piece **(photo F).**

BUILD THE DOORS.

1. Cut the closet door panel (J) and shelf door panel (K) to size. Sand the edges and surfaces of the door panels to smooth out the saw blade marks and any rough spots. Apply edge tape to the edges of each door panel. Trim off the excess tape, and sand the edges smooth.

2. Cut the door stiles (L), false stiles (M), closet door rails (N) and shelf door rails (O) to

Hang the armoire doors with pairs of hinges attached to the door stiles and the front edges of the side panels.

length. (*Rails* are the horizontal frame pieces; *stiles* are the vertical frame pieces.)

3. Position the rails and stiles on the front faces of the door panels so they overhang all edges of the panels by 3/4". Make sure the rails and stiles meet at right angles to make perfectly square frames. Attach the rails and stiles to both door panels with glue, and drive 3d finish nails through the frame pieces and into the panels.

4. Turn the door panels over on your worksurface. To reinforce the joints between the stiles and rails and the door panels, drill 5/64" pilot holes through the panels and into the stiles and rails. Counterbore the holes 1/8" deep, using a 3/8" counterbore bit. Fasten the pieces together with 1 1/4" wood screws **(photo G).**

5. Mark points along the outside edge of each outer door stile, 8" down from the top and 8" up from the bottom. Mount door hinges to the edges of the stiles at these points. Then, position the doors in place, and fasten the hinges to the side panels **(photo H).** Be sure to adjust the hinges to allow for a 1/8"-wide gap between the doors. Also leave a slight gap between the top end of the doors and the top panel and between the bottom of the doors and the front skirt.

APPLY THE FINISH.

It is easiest to finish the parts of the armoire before you attach the rest of the hardware.

1. Set all nails with a nail set. Fill all nail and screw holes with wood putty, and sand the dried putty flush with the surface. Sand all of the wood surfaces with medium (150-grit) sandpaper. Finish-sand the surfaces with fine sandpaper (180-or 220-grit).

2. Wipe the wood clean. Then, brush on a coat of sanding sealer so the wood will accept the wood stain evenly. Be sure to read the manufacturer's directions before applying any finishing products. Apply a wood stain and let it dry completely. Apply several coats of topcoating product. We used two thin coats of water-based, satin polyurethane. If you prefer, you can leave the wood unstained and simply apply a protective topcoat.

INSTALL THE HARDWARE.

1. Install door pulls on the door panels, 25" up from each bottom rail and centered between the stiles. We used hammered wrought-iron pulls for a rustic appearance.

2. Mount closet rod hangers to the sides of the closet compartment, 11" down from the top panel. Cut the closet rod (I) to length, and set it into the closet rod hangers. Applying finishing materials to the closet rod is optional.

3. To keep the doors closed tight when not in use, install magnetic door catches and catch plates on the upper inside corners of the doors and at the corresponding locations on the bottom of the top panel. For extra holding power, also install catches at the bottoms of the doors.

TIP

An armoire is basically a freestanding closet. But with a few modifications, it can become a custom furnishing that meets a variety of specific needs. To improve its usefulness as a dressing cabinet, attach a full-length dressing mirror to the inside of one of the doors. Rearrange the shelf positions, drill a few holes in the back, and you have a beautiful entertainment center. Or, add more shelves and tuck the armoire in your kitchen to be used as a portable pantry.

DYSPEPSIA BREA
(from page 97, Ladies' Indi
Companion)
1 cup warm water (110
2 teaspoons sugar
2 cups warm milk (1
¼ cup plus 2 tablesp
margarine, melted
¼ cup molasses
1 tablespoon plus
7 cups whole wh
RIC
(from
and

Kitchen Projects

There's something for everyone in this chapter. You can add storage space or organize it more efficiently with a pantry cabinet or a pine pantry. Roll out more work space with the utility cart or create a permanent addition with the kitchen island. Simplify outdoor dining with a silverware caddy and display your favorite colorful mugs with the mug rack. Any project you choose will make your kitchen more efficient and user-friendly.

PROJECT
POWER TOOLS

Cookbook Easel

The acrylic shield on this easel protects your cookbooks and lets you concentrate on the cooking.

Construction Materials

Quantity	Lumber
1	¾" × 2' × 2' basswood panel
1	¼" × 1' × 2' acrylic

Cookbooks are hard to read when they're covered with flour, batter or tomato sauce. And they tend to take up precious counterspace when open. Our cookbook easel has a removable acrylic shield to protect your favorite cookbooks from messy spatters. The slanted vertical design keeps cookbooks conveniently open and upright, so you can quickly refer to cooking instructions at a glance. The adjustable shield easily accommodates everything from hefty cooking encyclopedias to small church cookbooks. Rounded corners add a pleasant touch and soften the overall appearance. To keep the easel from sliding around on the countertop, we added self-adhesive rubber feet to the bottom.

OVERALL SIZE:
11½" HIGH
21" WIDE
5½" LONG

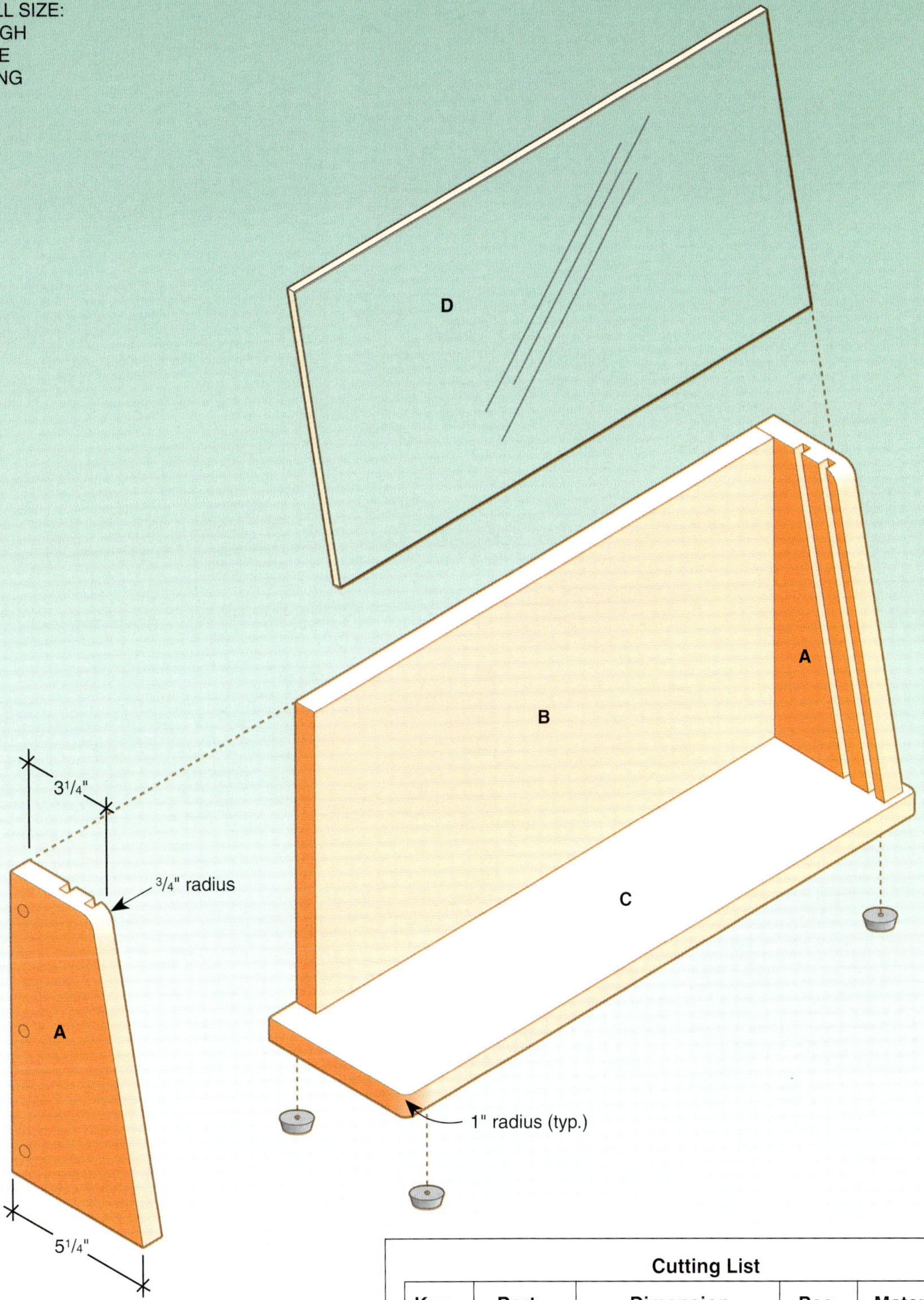

Cutting List

Key	Part	Dimension	Pcs.	Material
A	Side	¾ × 5¼ × 10¼"	2	Basswood
B	Back	¾ × 18¾ × 10¼"	1	Basswood
C	Base	¾ × 5½ × 21"	1	Basswood
D	Shield	¼ × 19¼ × 10¼"	1	Acrylic

Materials: Wood glue, wood screws (#6 × 1½"), self-adhesive rubber feet (4), ⅜"-dia. birch plugs, finishing materials.

Note: Measurements reflect the actual thickness of dimension lumber.

To make the jig, trace an outline of a side on a piece of plywood and cut with a jig saw.

Draw lines to mark the placement and width of the dadoes.

Directions: Cookbook Easel

MAKE THE SIDES.

1. Cut the sides (A) from ¾" basswood panel, using a circular saw. Each side is 5¼" wide at the bottom and 3¼" wide at the top.

2. Sand the cuts smooth with medium-grit sandpaper.

CUT THE DADOES.

Use a plywood jig to keep the small sides stationary.

1. Place a side on the center of a piece of ¾" scrap plywood and trace its outline.

2. Drill an access hole in the plywood and use a jig saw to make the cut **(photo A).**

3. Draw parallel lines ⅝", ⅞", 1¾" and 2" from the angled edge on the inside face of each side to mark the dado locations **(photo B).**

Using a shooting board as a guide, begin and end the dadoes in the plywood jig to avoid any tearouts.

4. Position one side in the plywood jig. Align a shooting board on the plywood so the edge of the shooting board aligns with the marked lines on the side, and temporarily screw it in place.

5. Cut the dadoes using a ¼" bit set ⅝" deep (to allow for a ⅜"-deep dado and the ¼" shooting

TIP

A shooting board is nothing more than a piece of hardboard with a straightedge guide attached. The distance between the straightedge and the edge of the hardboard exactly equals the distance between the edge of the router base and the bit.

Round the edges on the sides and base with a belt sander.

Find the center of the assembly and mark on the base and back to properly place the screw holes.

board). Begin the router cut in the plywood, proceed smoothly across the side piece and continue into the plywood **(photo C).** Reposition the shooting board to make the second cut.

6. Turn the jig over, insert the other side piece, and repeat the cutting process.

ROUND THE CORNERS.

1. Cut the back (B) and base (C) to size, and sand smooth.

2. Draw ¾"-rad. roundovers on the top front corners of the sides and 1"-rad. roundovers on the two front corners of the base, using a compass.

3. Clamp a belt sander to your worksurface at a 90° angle and round the corners on each part **(photo D).**

ASSEMBLE THE EASEL.

1. Position the back between the sides so the edges are flush, and drill three counterbored pilot holes evenly spaced in the sides.

2. Apply glue to the edges and drive 1½" wood screws through pilot holes into the back. Mark centerpoints on the base and back to help you align the parts correctly **(photo E).**

3. Drill pilot holes in the base and counterbore from the underside. Position the base and back so the centerpoints are aligned and join the base to the assembly with glue and wood screws. Make sure the screws don't interfere with the dadoes.

4. Cut the acrylic shield (D) to size with a circular saw, sand the short edges, and insert. Leave the protective covering on the acrylic while sawing.

APPLY FINISHING TOUCHES.

1. Pound glued ⅜" birch plugs into the counterbored holes **(photo F).**

2. Sand the plugs flush with a power sander, and finish-sand the easel.

Use a wood mallet to drive in glued ⅜" birch plugs without damaging the surface of the wood.

3. Apply the finish of your choice.

4. Attach self-adhesive feet to the base after the finish dries.

Spice Holder

A light, open design keeps all your spices in plain sight and within easy reach.

PROJECT
POWER TOOLS

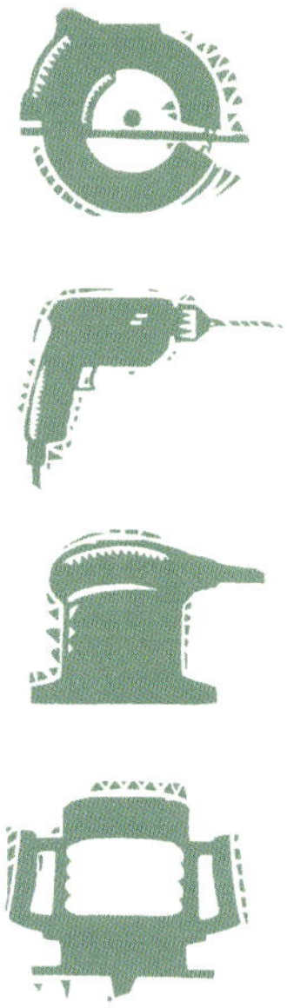

So often, spices for your favorite dishes are hidden away in the back corners of kitchen cabinets—used, and then stuffed behind other cooking supplies without a moment's thought. Until, that is, the next time you are fumbling in a dark cabinet for the oregano while a sauce burns on the stove. Experienced chefs always have a spice holder within reach. Ours has four shelves, with room for a variety of ingredients. You can take an instant inventory of your supplies and have favorite herbs handy for sudden culinary inspirations.

The series of arcs cut into the spice holder form gentle waves that gives the pine construction a soft, flowing appeal, and a small scallop in the back echoes this pattern. The front of the shelves are rounded, so you can reach for spices without worrying about sharp edges. Though it's designed to rest on a countertop, this spice holder can also be fitted with another shelf and mounted on the wall.

Construction Materials

Quantity	Lumber
1	1 × 6" × 8' pine
1	1 × 10" × 8' pine

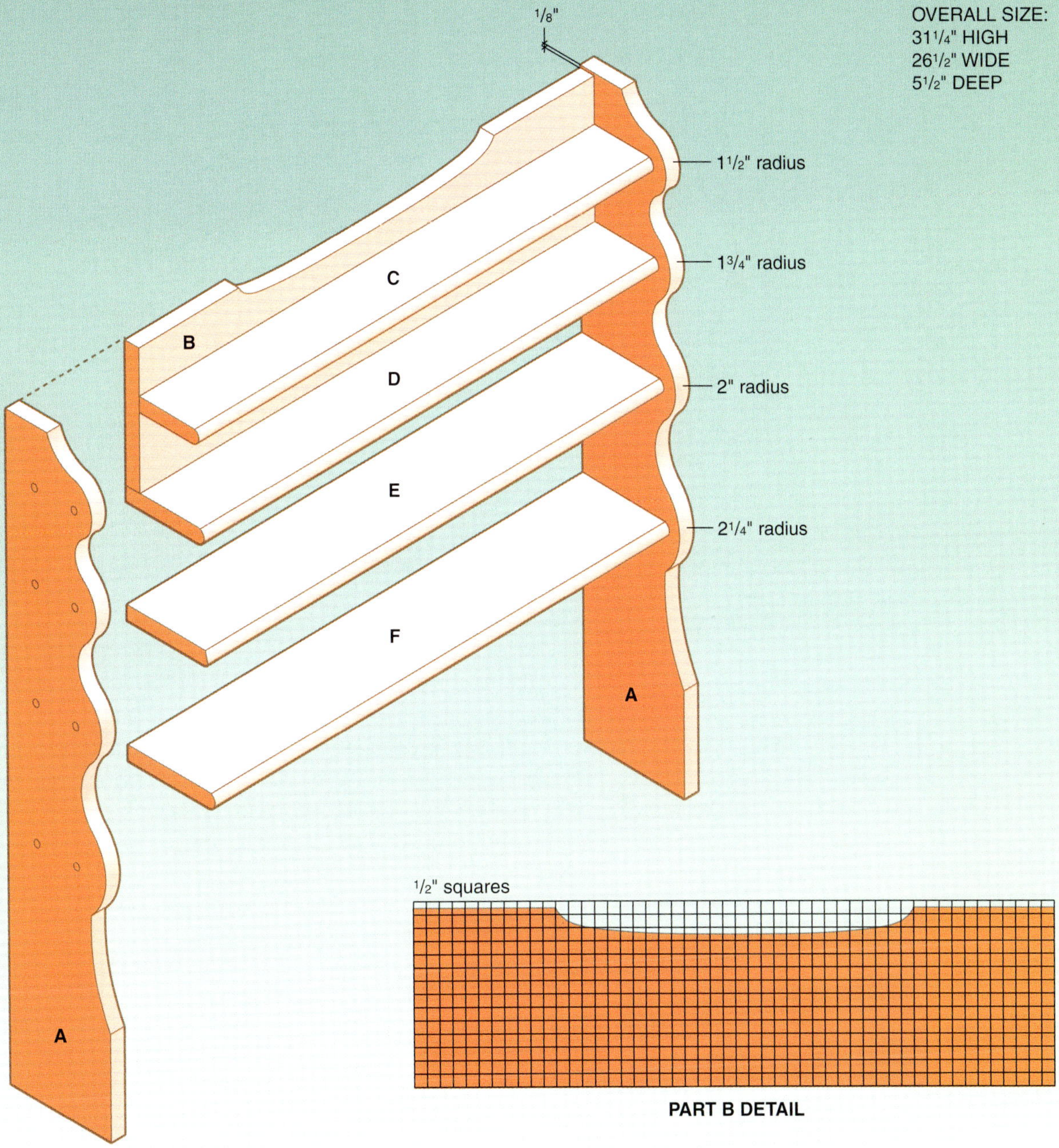

OVERALL SIZE:
31 1/4" HIGH
26 1/2" WIDE
5 1/2" DEEP

1/2" squares

PART B DETAIL

Cutting List

Key	Part	Dimension	Pcs.	Material
A	Side	¾ × 5½ × 31¼"	2	Pine
B	Back	¾ × 6¾ × 25"	1	Pine
C	Shelf	¾ × 3¼ × 25"	1	Pine
D	Shelf	¾ × 4¼ × 25"	1	Pine
E	Shelf	¾ × 4½ × 25"	1	Pine
F	Shelf	¾ × 4¾ × 25"	1	Pine

Materials: Wood glue, #8 screws (1⅝"), ⅜" birch plugs, finishing materials.

Note: Measurements reflect the actual thickness of dimension lumber.

Clamp each shelf to your worksurface for smooth, even router cuts. Flip the shelves to complete each roundover.

Make the side curves with a jig saw. Use clamps to keep parts steady while cutting.

Directions: Spice Holder

MAKE THE SHELVES.

The shelves all differ in depth and are cut from dimension lumber.

1. Measure and rip shelves C, D, and E from 1 × 10 pine, and shelf F from 1 × 6 pine, using your circular saw.

2. Clamp each shelf to your worksurface, and round the front using a router with a ⅜" roundover bit and bearing guide **(photo A).** Sand all edges smooth.

MAKE THE SIDES.

A series of arcs and reference lines indicate cutting lines and shelf positions.

1. Cut the sides (A) to size from 1 × 6 pine, and sand all cuts smooth.

2. Draw reference lines across the sides for the curves and shelves, starting from the bottom of each side, at points 12", 18½", 24", and 28½" along a long edge. The arcs you draw from the template (see *Part A Detail*) will be centered on these lines.

3. Transfer the template arcs to each side, and blend all of the arcs together with graceful curves.

4. Clamp each side to your worksurface, and use a jig saw to cut along the arcs **(photo B).**

MAKE THE BACK ASSEMBLY.

1. Cut the back (B) to size from 1 × 10 stock.

2. Draw a curve 1" deep and 14" long, centered on one long

Sand the curves with a drum sanding attachment and a drill.

TIPS

If you do not own a router, you can complete the roundovers on the front edges of each shelf by planing down the edges with a block plane. Planing goes more smoothly if you plane so the wood grain runs "uphill" ahead of the plane. Don't try to remove too much wood at one time; smooth, easy strokes will achieve the best results. Sand to smooth the plane cuts.

Attach the top shelf to the back assembly from behind with glue and countersunk screws.

Be sure to counterbore all the pilot holes on the sides before driving screws.

edge of the back, and cut with a jig saw (see *Part B Detail*).

3. Attach a 1"-dia. drum sander to your drill, and sand the curves of each piece smooth **(photo C).**

4. Clamp the bottom edge of the back against shelf D, keeping the back flush with the square edge of the shelf. Attach with glue and countersunk 1⅝" screws driven through the bottom of the shelf and into the edge of the back.

5. Align the top shelf (C) on the back so the top edge is 2¼" down from the top edge of the back. Glue and clamp in place, and secure with countersunk screws driven through the back and into the shelf **(photo D).**

ATTACH THE REMAINING PARTS.

1. Place the back assembly and remaining shelves in position between the sides. Center the shelves on the reference lines and keep the back edges flush.

2. Use pipe clamps to hold the spice rack together, and counterbore ⅜" pilot holes through the sides and into the ends of each shelf. Keep the counterbores lined up horizontally for an even look.

3. Remove the clamps, apply glue, and then reclamp, continually checking to make sure the assembly is square. Secure the shelves with 1⅝" screws driven through the counterbored pilot holes **(photo E).**

APPLY FINISHING TOUCHES.

1. Insert glued birch button plugs into each counterbored hole and let dry.

2. Finish-sand the entire project, and apply a light oil or stain and a polyurethane topcoat.

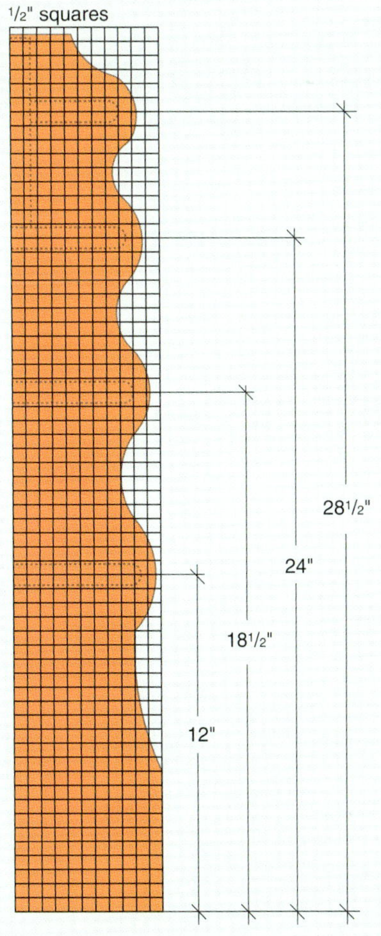

PART A DETAIL

PROJECT
POWER TOOLS

Mug Rack

Your everyday coffee mugs become decorative kitchen items when displayed on this original mug rack.

A mug rack gives you a great way to combine storage and decoration. Just put your mugs in this simple, convenient frame to display them on your kitchen countertop or hang them on a wall. The mugs are always there when you need them, and instead of taking up valuable shelf space, they become decorative kitchen items for all to see. Colorful mug designs look great against the beaded siding board backing on the rack. Paint the project to match your kitchen, or cover it with a clear finish to preserve the natural look of the wood. You can hang your mugs on Shaker pegs, which are easy to install. Fit the bottom and back of the mug rack with rubber bumpers for increased stability. With a minimum investment of work and expense, you can create this mug rack as a decorative home accent.

Construction Materials

Quantity	Lumber
1	1 × 4" × 10' pine
1	1 × 8" × 8' beaded siding board

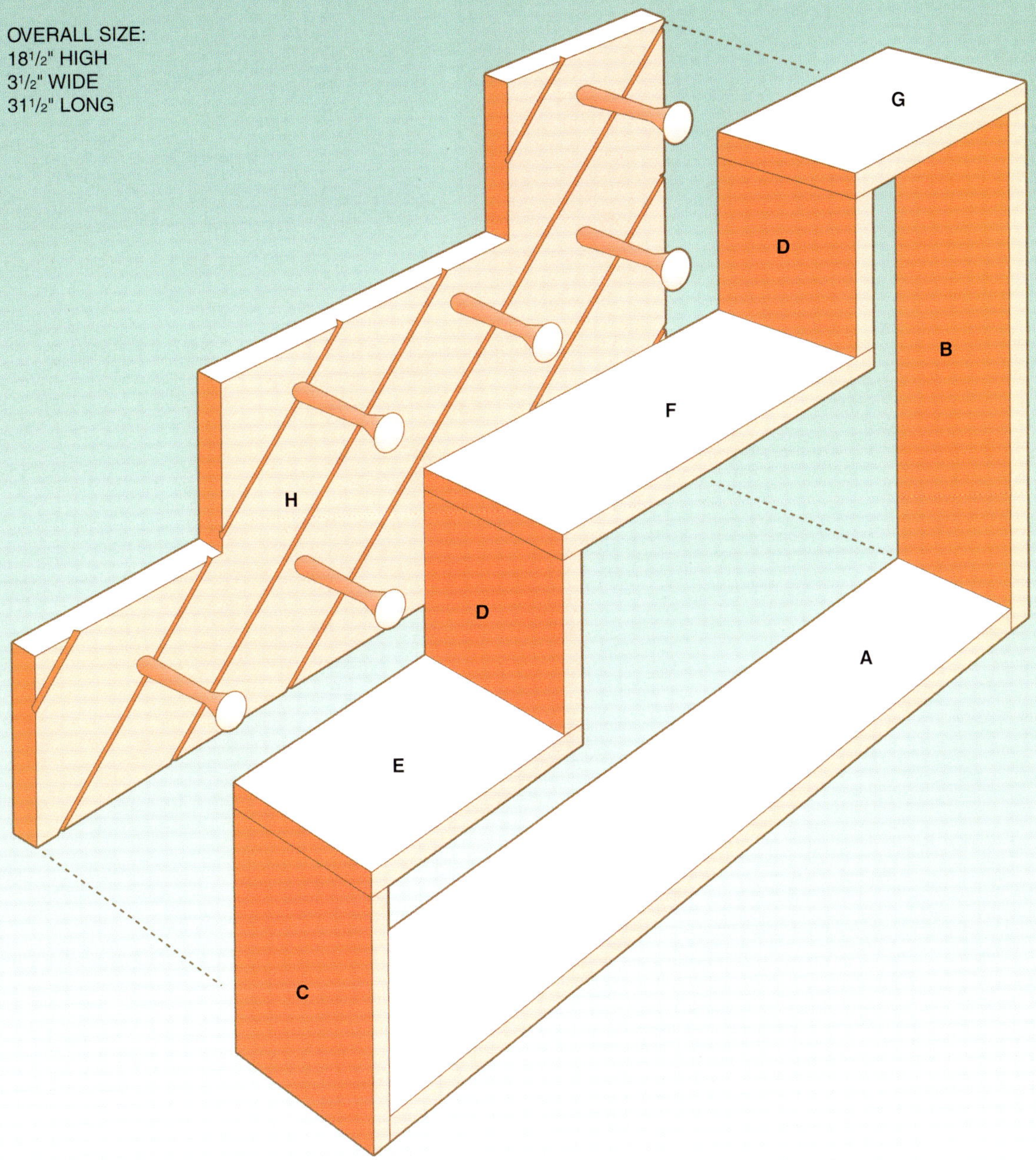

Cutting List

Key	Part	Dimension	Pcs.	Material
A	Frame bottom	¾ × 3½ × 29½"	1	Pine
B	Tall end	¾ × 3½ × 17¾"	1	Pine
C	Short end	¾ × 3½ × 9¾"	1	Pine
D	Divider	¾ × 3½ × 3¼"	2	Pine

Cutting List

Key	Part	Dimension	Pcs.	Material
E	Lower shelf	¾ × 3½ × 7½"	1	Pine
F	Middle shelf	1½ × 3½ × 15"	1	Pine
G	Top shelf	¾ × 3½ × 10½"	1	Pine
H	Backing	18½ × 31½"*	1	Siding

Materials: Wood glue, 4d finish nails, Shaker pegs (8), rubber feet (4), finishing materials.

Note: Measurements reflect the actual thickness of dimension lumber.

*Cut to fit

Attach the dividers to the tops of the lower and middle shelves using glue and finish nails.

Fasten the top shelf to the middle shelf divider.

Directions: Mug Rack

ASSEMBLE THE FRAME.

1. Cut the frame bottom (A), tall end (B), short end (C), lower shelf (E), middle shelf (F), top shelf (G) and dividers (D) to size from 1 × 4 pine.

2. Sand out any rough edges with medium (100- or 120-grit) sandpaper, then finish-sand with fine (150- or 180-grit) sandpaper.

3. Fasten the ends to the bottom with glue and 4d finish nails driven through the ends into the frame bottom edges. Make sure the edges are flush.

4. Attach the dividers to the tops of the lower and middle shelves with glue and finish nails **(photo A).** Make sure the end of each shelf is flush with the end of each divider. Use support blocks to help you keep the pieces stationary on the worksurface.

5. Glue and nail the middle shelf to the top of the lower shelf divider. Make sure the divider edges and middle shelf edges are flush. Fasten the top shelf to the middle shelf divider, once again keeping the edges flush **(photo B).**

6. Glue and finish nail the shelves flush with the tall and short ends to complete the mug rack frame.

> TIP
>
> *Siding is available in many different patterns, such as tongue-and-groove, shiplap or channel groove. Each pattern has a different joint pattern and appearance. These siding styles all cut easily with a circular saw or jig saw, but be careful of kickback, which can cause the material to jump off the table with dangerous force.*

BUILD AND ATTACH THE BACKING.

The backing (H) fits into the frame and holds the Shaker pegs. Make the backing from pieces of beaded siding.

1. Cut and join backing pieces as necessary to create an 18½ × 31½" panel.

2. Place the mug rack frame on the backing pieces so their grooves run diagonally at about a 60° angle. The backing should completely fill the space inside the frame.

3. Remove the frame, then glue the backing pieces together and let them dry.

4. Place the frame on the backing pieces and trace the cutting lines onto the back panel, following the inside of the frames **(photo C).** Remove the frame and use a straightedge or square to retrace or straighten the lines.

Trace the shape of the frame onto beaded siding and cut it to fit.

Fasten the backing into the frame with finish nails, then set the nails.

5. Cut the backing to shape with a straightedge guide and a jig saw. Test-fit the backing in the mug rack frame. If necessary, trim it to fit the frame.

6. Fasten the backing with glue and 4d finish nails driven through the frame and into the edges of the backing panel **(photo D).**

7. Set the nails and fill all the nail holes.

ATTACH THE MUG PEGS.

1. Measure and mark a vertical line 4½" from the tall end. Then draw three more vertical lines spaced 7¼" apart, marking the peg centerpoints along these lines at 5½", 11" and 16½" from the bottom shelf.

2. Drill ½ × ⅝"-deep holes for the mug pegs at these centerpoints **(photo E).**

3. Glue and insert pegs into the holes. Remove any excess glue.

APPLY THE FINISHING TOUCHES.

1. Sand all the surfaces smooth.

2. Apply paint or finish. We used a linseed oil finish on our mug rack. Use a finish that will withstand kitchen moisture levels.

3. Hang the mug rack on the wall, or install rubber bumpers on the bottom for stable countertop placement after the finish has dried.

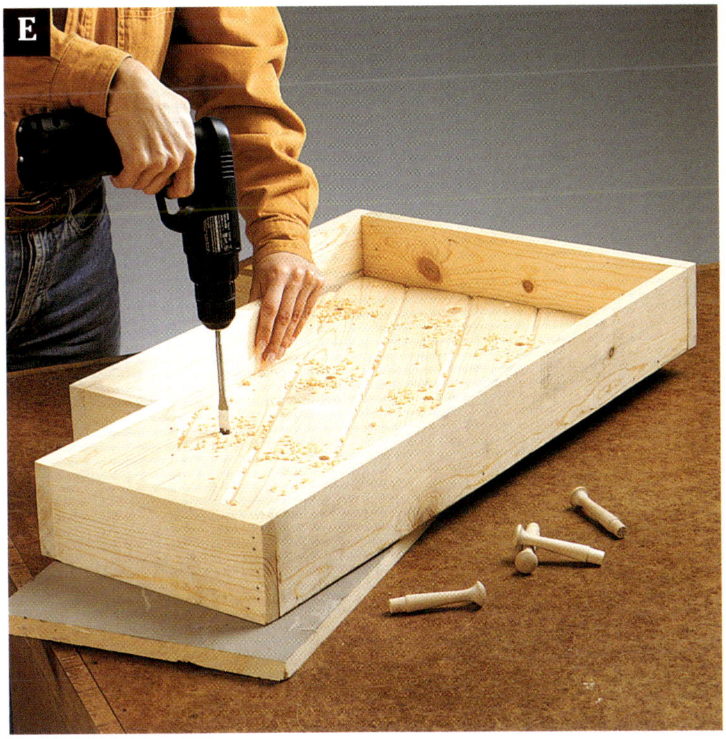

Measure and mark peg locations on the backing, then drill peg holes with a spade bit. Do not drill all the way through the backing.

PROJECT
POWER TOOLS

Stepstool

Make every step a step in the right direction with our oak stepstool.

Construction Materials

Quantity	Lumber
1	1 × 10" × 3' oak
1	¾" × 2 × 4' oak plywood

The next time you need to retrieve an out-of-reach item in your kitchen, don't stand on a dining-room chair. Instead, make use of our handy stepstool—it's wide, stable, and reinforced with stretchers underneath each step. The stepstool brings you to the right height for dusting hard-to-reach areas, like valances and windowtops, and for reaching what you need from that topmost shelf. You'll find the stepstool is also a great place for small children to sit safely out of your way and still feel part of the kitchen action. The steps are cut from solid oak to guarantee a flat, stable surface. We cut shallow arcs into the bottom of each side panel to create four "feet," and repeated the curves on the front stretchers. A roundover router bit softens the front edge of each step.

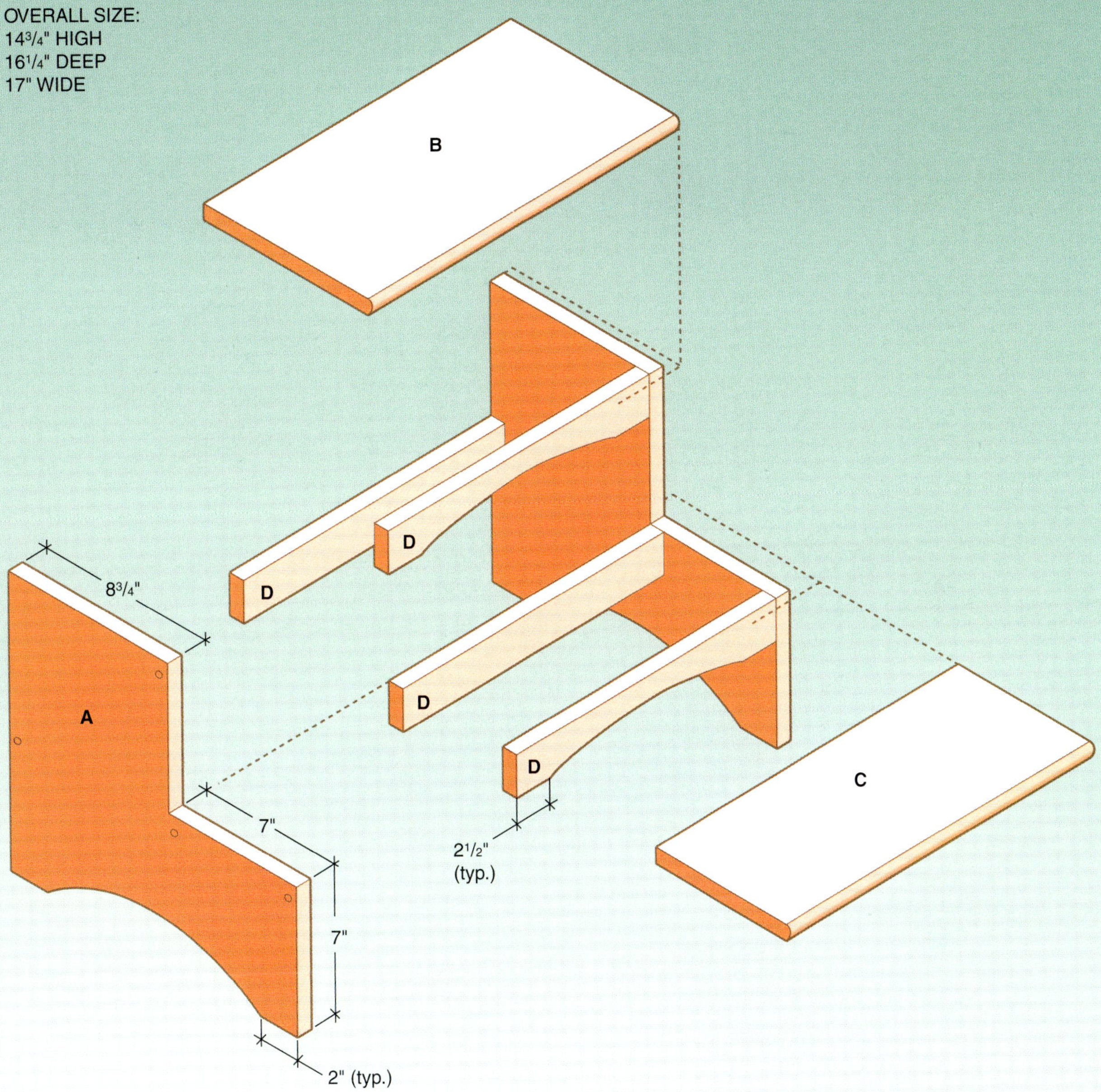

Cutting List

Key	Part	Dimension	Pcs.	Material
A	Side	¾ × 15¾ × 14"	2	Plywood
B	Top step	¾ × 9¼ × 17"	1	Oak
C	Bottom step	¾ × 7½ × 17"	1	Oak
D	Stretcher	¾ × 2 × 14"	4	Plywood

Materials: Wood glue, wood screws (#8 × 1⅝"), ⅜"-dia. oak wood plugs, oak-veneer edge tape (5'), finishing materials.

Note: Measurements reflect the actual thickness of dimension lumber.

Use a makeshift bar compass to achieve smooth, uniform arcs on the front stretchers.

Shorten the compass to draw the arcs on each side piece.

Directions: Stepstool

CUT THE SIDES AND STRETCHERS.

1. Cut the side pieces (A) and stretchers (D) to size from oak plywood.

2. Cut a 7 × 7" notch out of one corner on each side piece using a jig saw.

3. Sand the cut smooth.

4. Clamp a stretcher and a ¾"-thick piece of scrap wood at least 2 ft. long to your worksurface. Mark the center of the stretcher, and extend the line down the scrap. Mark 2½" in from each end along the bottom edge of the stretcher to indicate the ends of the arc.

5. Cut a narrow strip of wood 21½" long for the arm of the bar compass. Drill a small hole ½" in from both ends, one for the pencil tip, one for the brad. With the pencil on one of the reference marks, nail the brad to the centerline. Then draw arcs on two of the stretchers **(photo A).**

6. Cut the compass to 10½", and drill a new pencil hole ½" from the end. Clamp the side pieces to your worksurface and make reference marks 2" in from each corner on the bottom edge of the sides. Position the compass as for the stretchers, nail in place, and draw arcs on each side piece **(photo B).**

7. Cut all arcs with a jig saw. Clamp the stretchers together and gang-sand the cuts smooth with a drum sander attached to your drill **(photo C).** Do the same for the arcs on the side pieces.

8. Cut iron-on veneer tape to length, and apply it to the exposed front and back edges of the side pieces with an iron **(photo D).** To ensure a strong adhesive bond, press a clean block of scrap wood against the strip to flatten the tape as you go. Let the tape cool, and trim the edges with a utility knife.

ASSEMBLE THE FRAME.

1. Position the arched stretchers between the side pieces so the edges and corners are flush (see *Diagram*), and drill counterbored pilot holes. Attach the side pieces to the stretchers with glue and screws.

2. Position the non-arched stretchers at the same height as the lower arched stretcher. Drill counterbored pilot holes for the remaining stretchers, and attach with wood glue and screws.

Clamp the stretchers together and sand the arcs smooth, using a drum sander attached to a drill.

Apply veneer tape to the front and back edges of the side pieces to give them a solid wood appearance.

CUT AND ATTACH THE STEPS.

1. Cut the top step (B) and bottom step (C) to length from 1 × 10 oak. Rip the bottom step to width.

2. Clamp each step to your worksurface, and round the front edges with a router and a 3/8" roundover bit. Sand the edges smooth.

3. Position the top step on the assembly so the rear edges are flush and the front overhangs the stretcher by 1/2". Center the top step from side to side.

4. Drill counterbored pilot holes to connect the step to the side pieces and the arched stretcher. Apply glue, and drive screws through the holes.

5. Repeat this process for the bottom step.

APPLY FINISHING TOUCHES.

1. Fill all counterbored holes with glued oak plugs.

2. Finish-sand the project. We used two stains for a two-tone look, applying a light cherry stain for the steps and a dark mahogany stain for the side pieces and stretchers. When staining, mask off the edges of the steps where they contact the side pieces and stretchers **(photo E).** If you wish, you can stencil a decorative design on the sides of the stool. Complete the finish with several coats of water-based polyurethane.

Use masking tape to mask off borders where different stains meet.

PROJECT POWER TOOLS

Silverware Caddy

This decorative display rack brings convenience to dinnertime chores.

CONSTRUCTION MATERIALS

Quantity	Lumber
1	½ × 8" × 4' oak

Silverware caddies used to be common accessories when large family gatherings were regular occurrences. A caddy eliminated lugging handfuls of silverware to and from the table, made setting the table a speedy chore and kept utensils ready at attention for the next meal. Our silverware caddy is crafted from traditional, sturdy oak and features a decorative cloverleaf carrying grip. The rounded handle and divider interlock, creating four sections to keep knives, spoons and dinner and salad forks separate and upright for easy access. This is an easy afternoon project that will give long-lasting "service" to any dinner table. If you will be painting the caddy, choose ½" birch plywood rather than oak.

OVERALL SIZE:
12½" HIGH
7" WIDE
7" LONG

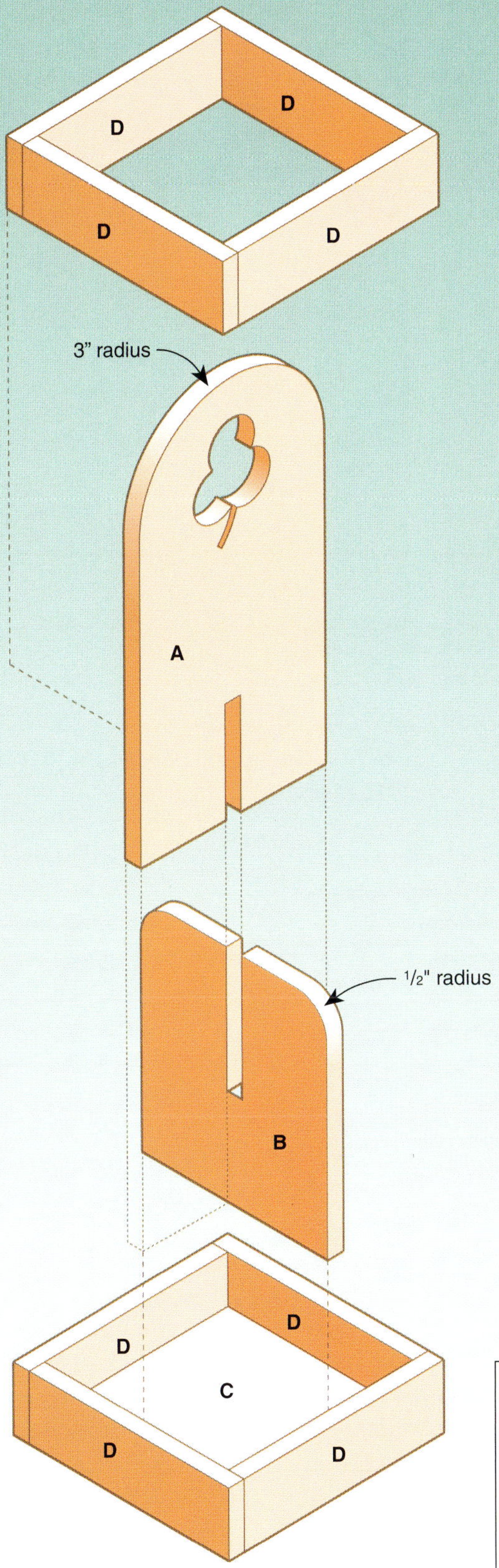

PART A DETAIL

Cutting List

Key	Part	Dimension	Pcs.	Material
A	Handle	½ × 6 × 12"	1	Oak
B	Divider	½ × 6 × 6"	1	Oak
C	Base	½ × 6 × 6"	1	Oak
D	Side	½ × 2 × 6½"	8	Oak

Materials: Wood glue, 16-ga. 1" finish nails, finishing materials.

Note: Measurements reflect the actual thickness of dimension lumber.

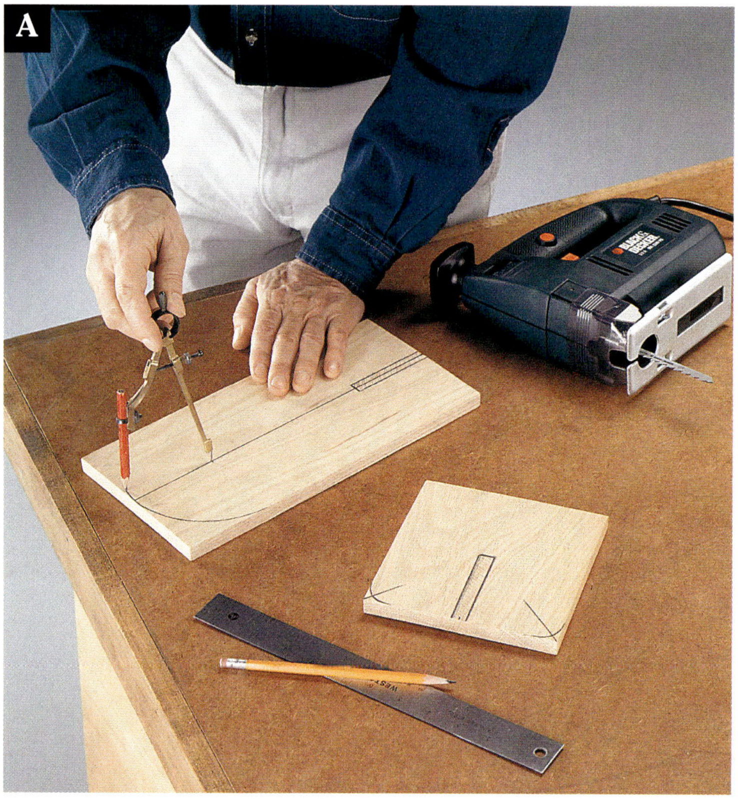

Mark curves and notch locations on reference lines using a compass.

Clamp pieces to your worksurface to ensure steady cuts.

Directions: Silverware Caddy

MAKE THE HANDLE AND DIVIDER.

Corners on the handle and divider are curved, and the pieces are notched to fit together.

1. Cut the handle (A) and divider (B) to size.

2. Mark a centerline down the length of each piece, and draw a $\frac{1}{2} \times 3$" notch at one end centered along each line. At the other end of the handle, place a compass point on the centerline, 3" from the edge, and draw a 3"-rad. curve. At the notched end of the divider, bisect each corner with a 45° line. Place a compass point on the 45° line $1\frac{1}{16}$" from the corner, and draw $\frac{1}{2}$"-rad. curves on each corner **(photo A).**

3. Clamp each piece to your worksurface, and cut the curves and notches with a jig saw **(photo B).**

4. Slide the notched ends together to test-fit, then use a chisel to clean out the notches and make adjustments.

CUT THE HANDHOLD.

1. Transfer the clover template to paper, and trace the pattern onto the handle surface, using the centerline for correct alignment (see *Diagram*).

2. Cut out each leaf of the clover with a $1\frac{1}{2}$"-dia. hole saw **(photo C).** Keep a scrap piece of wood underneath to prevent the hole saw tearing through the other side of the handle.

3. Cut out the clover stem with a jig saw and chisel.

4. Sand all cuts to remove splinters, and sand the inside of the clover leaf with a 1"-dia. or smaller drum sander attached to your drill **(photo D).**

ASSEMBLE THE BASE AND SIDES.

1. Cut the sides (D) and base (C) to size, and sand smooth.

2. Butt each side end against the face of another side to make the side frames square (see *Diagram*). Drill pilot holes at the side joints to ease assembly. Glue and nail four sides together with finish nails and repeat to make two square frames. Check for square when nailing, then recess all nail heads with a nail set.

3. Place the base inside one of the frames, drill pilot holes and attach the base with glue and nails.

4. Set the handle and divider inside to test-fit, then apply

Use a hole saw to cut quickly and cleanly. Place a backer board underneath to prevent tearouts on the other side of handle.

Use a drum sander or sandpaper wrapped around a dowel to smooth the inside of the cutout.

glue to the joint. Attach the handle and divider to the base assembly with glue and finish nails.

5. Slide the remaining frame over the handle and divider. Keep a 1¼" gap between frames, and attach the frame to the handle and divider with glue and finish nails **(photo E).**

APPLY FINISHING TOUCHES.

1. Fill all nail holes with wood putty.

2. Sand smooth, and apply the finish of your choice. We used a light cherry stain. If you choose paint, use a nontoxic interior-rated latex enamel.

Maintain a 1¼" gap between frames when assembling.

PROJECT
POWER TOOLS

Plate Rack

This compact plate rack is a handsome display case for your favorite dinnerware.

Construction Materials

Quantity	Lumber
1	1 × 2" × 4' oak
1	1 × 6" × 2' oak
1	1 × 10" × 3' oak
3	¾ × ¾" × 2' oak stop molding
7	⅜"-dia. × 3' oak dowels

The holding capacity and clean vertical lines of this plate rack could easily make it a beloved fixture in your kitchen. An open design lets air circulate to dry mugs, bowls and plates efficiently. The rack is handsome enough to double as a display rack to showcase your dinnerware. Even though it has a small 9¼ × 21½" footprint, the rack lets you dry or store up to 20 full-size dinner plates plus cups or glasses. The tall dowels in the back of the rack are removable so you can rearrange them to accommodate large or unusually shaped dishes.

OVERALL SIZE:
17" HIGH
9¼" WIDE
21½" LONG

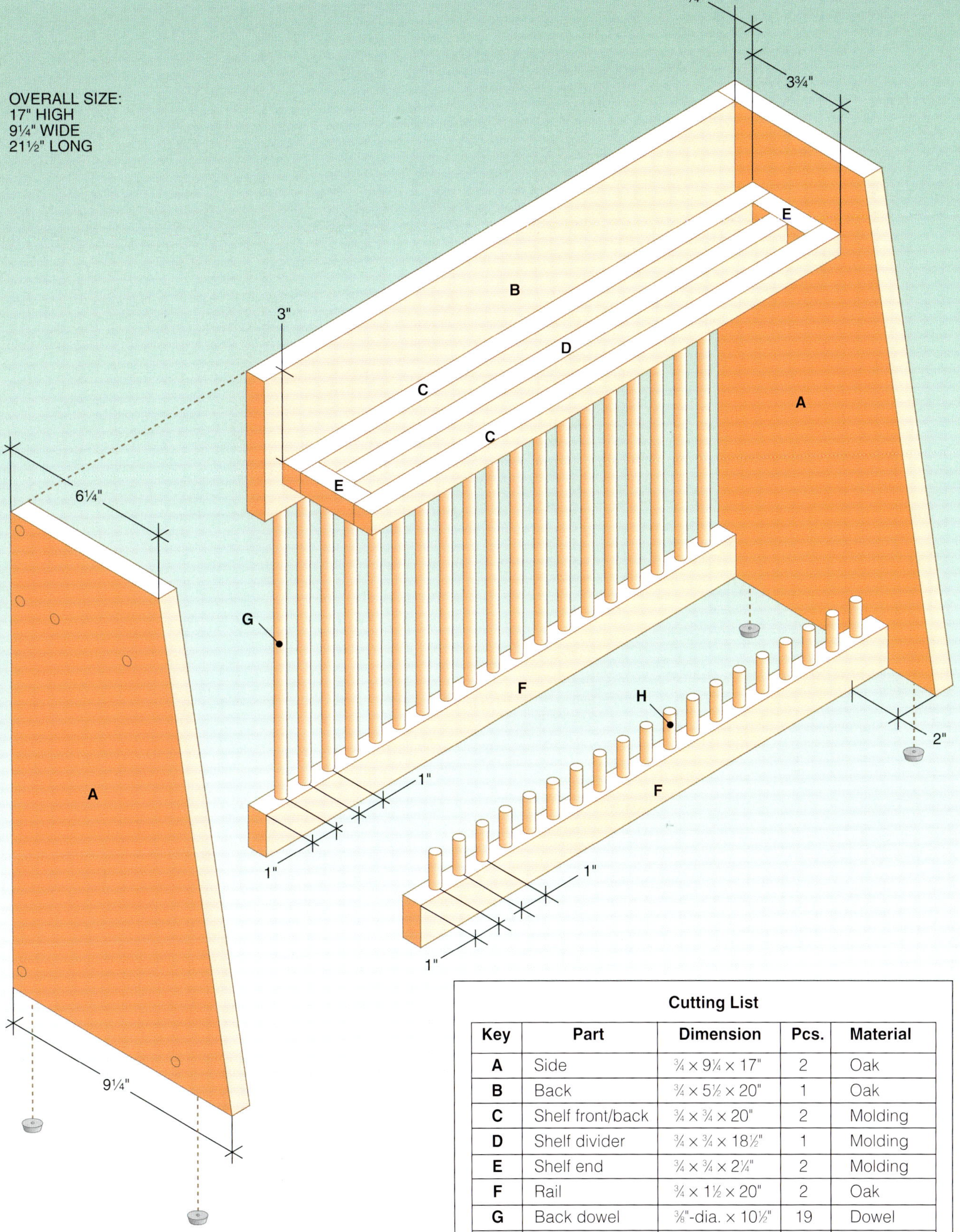

Cutting List

Key	Part	Dimension	Pcs.	Material
A	Side	¾ × 9¼ × 17"	2	Oak
B	Back	¾ × 5½ × 20"	1	Oak
C	Shelf front/back	¾ × ¾ × 20"	2	Molding
D	Shelf divider	¾ × ¾ × 18½"	1	Molding
E	Shelf end	¾ × ¾ × 2¼"	2	Molding
F	Rail	¾ × 1½ × 20"	2	Oak
G	Back dowel	⅜"-dia. × 10½"	19	Dowel
H	Front dowel	⅜"-dia. × 1⅝"	19	Dowel

Materials: Waterproof glue, #8 x 1⅝" screws, 4d finish nails, ⅜"-dia. flat oak plugs, rubber feet (4), finishing materials.

Note: Measurements reflect the actual thickness of dimension lumber.

Lay out the sides so they are 9¼" long at the bottom and 6¼" wide at the top.

Clamp the rails and back together and mark the dowel holes.

Directions:
Plate Rack

CUT THE SIDES.

1. Lay out and mark the sides (A) so they are 9¼" long at the bottom and 6¼" wide at the top.
2. Connect these marks, and cut along the diagonal line with a circular saw **(photo A).**

CUT AND DRILL BACK AND RAILS.

1. Cut the back (B) and rails (F) to length, and clamp them together.
2. Measure and mark the dowel holes (see *Diagram*) on the edge of each part **(photo B).** Mark the bit with tape, and drill the ¼"-deep dowel holes in the two rails. Move the tape to ½" and drill the deeper dowel holes in the back.

ASSEMBLE SIDES, BACK AND RAILS.

1. Drill ⅜"-dia. counterbored pilot holes through the sides where the back and back rail will be attached.
2. Apply waterproof glue, and attach the pieces with wood screws.

BUILD THE SHELF.

1. Cut the shelf front and back pieces (C), divider (D) and ends (E) to length.
2. Position the shelf front, back and ends together, and drill pilot holes for 4d finish nails.

Glue and nail divider in place.

Apply glue, and nail together.
3. Glue and nail the divider in place **(photo C).**

TIP

To make installing the longer 10½" back dowels easier, drill the dowel holes in the back a full ½" deep. When assembling, slide the dowels into the ½" holes in the back piece and let them drop down into the ¼" holes in the back rail. This lets you easily remove specific dowels to accommodate larger dishes or bowls. Dowel sizes tend to vary so test your dowel sizes by drilling a hole in scrap wood first, using a brad-point bit slightly larger than the ⅜" dowel.

Use a ¾" spacer to position shelf while you drill counterbored pilot holes.

Insert dowels into the holes under the back first, then drop them down into the holes in the rail.

4. Carefully drill counterbored pilot holes through the sides where the shelf attaches. To properly position the shelf, lay the entire unit on its back. Position the shelf 3" down from the top of the rack, using a ¾"- thick piece of scrap material as a spacer between the shelf and the back **(photo D).** Drill the pilot holes into the long shelf pieces and not through the dividers. Apply glue, and secure the shelf with wood screws.

CUT AND INSERT DOWELS.

1. Cut the back dowels (G) to length. Position these longer dowels by inserting them into the holes in the back, then dropping them down into the back rail **(photo E).**

2. Cut the front dowels (H) to length. Sand the edges of one end of each dowel. Using waterproof glue, secure the unsanded ends of the front dowels into the front rail holes.

ATTACH THE FRONT RAIL.

1. Position the front rail 2" back from the front edge of the rack, and drill counterbored pilot holes through the sides.

2. Apply waterproof glue, and screw the front rail in place **(photo F).**

APPLY FINISHING TOUCHES.

1. Fill all counterbored screw holes with oak plugs. Sand the entire rack and all dowels with 150-grit sandpaper.

2. Apply a water-based polyurethane finish.

3. Attach rubber feet to the bottom of the rack.

Clamp the front rail, predrill the sides, counterbore, glue and screw in place.

TIP

If you plan on consistently using dishes of unusual size, you may choose to change the location of the front rail. The location specified will work well for plates as small as 7" and as large as 11".

PROJECT
POWER TOOLS

Bread Box

This easy-to-build bread box creates a safe, crush-proof haven for a loaf of bread or other tasty bakery goods.

The old guessing game "20 Questions" would often start with the query, "Is it bigger than a bread box?" Though bread boxes aren't as common as they once were, they're still useful items that add a decorative touch to any kitchen. Our classic design emphasizes simplicity, featuring a compact footprint so it easily fits between other appliances or on a countertop, kitchen table or pantry shelf. The sturdy, oak construction has rounded edges and an angled lid that shows off the rich oak grain and warm color. The solid oak lid is mounted with a 12"-wide piano hinge. We stained our bread box and then applied a stenciled label to add a personal touch. Choose a stain or style that matches your kitchen decor, or try adding decorative painting effects like borders, antique letters or rosemaling to add the finishing touch to your own bread box.

CONSTRUCTION MATERIALS

Quantity	**Lumber**
2	½ × 7¼ × 36" oak
1	¾ × 7¼ × 24" oak

We found ½ × 7¼"-wide oak available in 24", 36" and 48" lengths.

OVERALL SIZE:
8" HIGH
13⅝" WIDE
6" DEEP

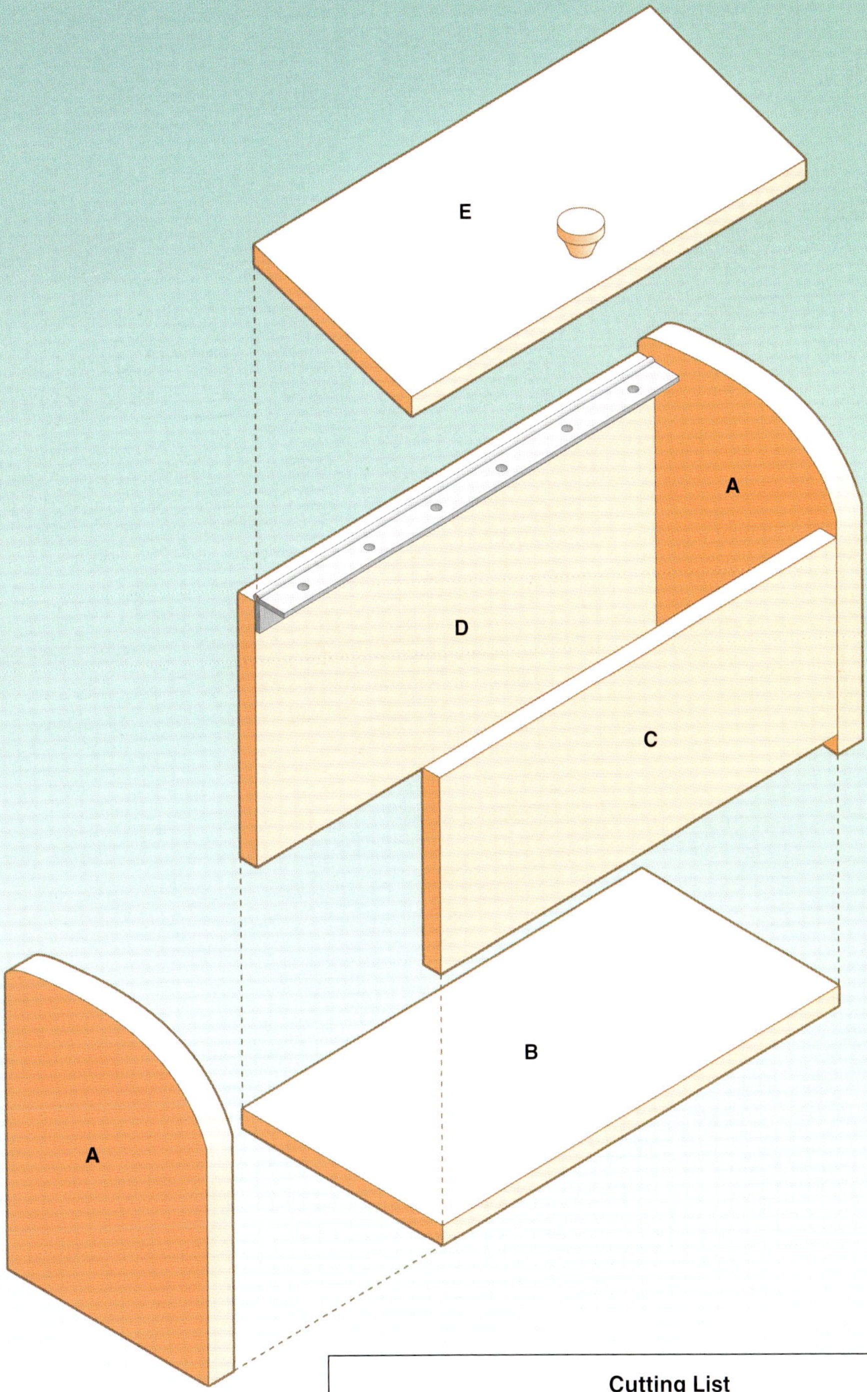

Cutting List

Key	Part	Dimension	Pcs.	Material
A	Side	¾ × 6 × 8"	2	Oak
B	Bottom	½ × 6 × 12⅛"	1	Oak
C	Front	½ × 5 × 12⅛"	1	Oak
D	Back	½ × 6¾ × 12⅛"	1	Oak
E	Lid	½ × 5⅝ × 12"	1	Oak

Materials: Wood glue, 12" piano hinge, porcelain knob (1"-dia. × ¾" length), 4d finish nails, finishing materials.

Note: Measurements reflect the actual thickness of dimension lumber.

Rip the sides from one piece of wood then cut them to length.

Tape sides together and sand the corners to create identical profiles.

Directions: Bread Box

RIP-CUT THE SIDES.

The sides are narrower than common lumber width, so it is necessary to rip the lumber lengthwise.

1. Rip the sides (A) to width from ¾" oak lumber. Rip both sides at the same time, using a straightedge to guide your jig saw or circular saw **(photo A).**

2. Cut the sides to length.

PROFILE THE SIDES.

The sides are curved to soften the overall profile of the bread box.

1. Transfer the curve outline (see *Part A Detail*) onto each side, and cut the rough profile with a jig saw.

2. Tape the sides together, and use a belt sander clamped to your worksurface to sand matching profiles on each side **(photo B).** Take care when sanding not to remove too much material from the sides.

> **TIP**
>
> *When ripping lumber to obtain the correct width, use a straightedge to guide your saw. Make sure you use a new, sharp blade to minimize rip marks and rough edges. Then belt-sand or block-plane the pieces smooth.*

CUT THE REMAINING PIECES.

1. Cut the bottom (B), front (C), back (D) and lid (E) to length from ½" stock.

2. Cut each piece to its appropriate width, then sand all the pieces smooth. The bottom, front and back pieces are ⅛" longer than the lid to allow it to swing freely up and down on the piano hinge.

ASSEMBLE THE BREAD BOX.

1. Drill 1⁄16"-dia. pilot holes through the bottom. Glue the front and back pieces to the bottom, clamp them in place, and nail with 4d finish nails.

2. Position the sides against the

Lay the assembly on its back, position the lid and install the piano hinge.

Use a stencil to transfer a pattern onto the bread box lid.

assembly, and drill pilot holes through the sides. Apply glue, clamp and nail.

ATTACH THE HINGE.

1. Center the hinge on the lid, drill pilot holes, and fasten with hinge screws. Be careful not to drill too far into the ½" wood.
2. Lay the box on its back with the lid in the open position. Open the hinge and fasten the hinge to the back **(photo C).**

APPLY FINISHING TOUCHES.

1. Sand all surfaces smooth.
2. Finish the bread box. We used a classic walnut stain and a non-toxic, water-based polyurethane topcoat. Finish the inside as well as the outside of the box and lid to prevent warping from moisture and to make cleaning the entire box easier. If you decide to add your own graphic element to the lid or to other areas of the box, do so before applying a topcoat. You can personalize your bread box by stenciling words, distressing surfaces to create special antiquing effects, transferring unique designs, or rosemaling. We created a stencil out of a sheet of acetate and painted a simple graphic on the lid **(photo D).**
3. Locate and drill a pilot hole and attach a knob to the lid after the finish cures.

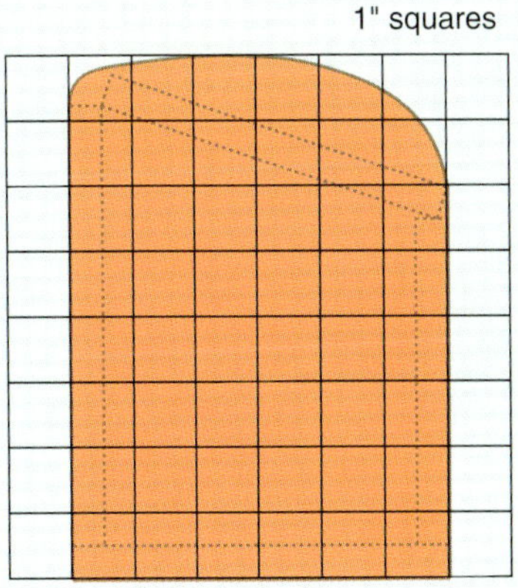

PART A DETAIL

Vegetable Bin

Whether your vegetables come from the garden or the grocer, our oak bin keeps them organized and out of the way.

PROJECT POWER TOOLS

Not all foods require immediate refrigeration. Onions, potatoes, garlic, shallots and avocados are just some of the foods that don't need to take up precious refrigerator space. But when countertop real estate is at a premium, veggies clutter up needed table space or remain in paper bags. Our vegetable bin provides an attractive, spacious alternative for storing fresh vegetables and fruits. Three separate sections, with hinged bin faces on the sides and top, keep vegetables apart and in place and make access easy. The sturdy oak construction also provides protection for more fragile items, so your prize tomatoes can stay safely in the shade. The bin's compact vertical design takes up just over a square foot, and the rich oak finish trim makes it a handsome addition to any kitchen.

Construction Materials

Quantity	Lumber
1	¾" × 4 × 4' oak plywood
1	¾ × 1½" × 4' oak
1	¾ × 11¼" × 6' oak
1	½ × ½" × 4' quarter-round molding

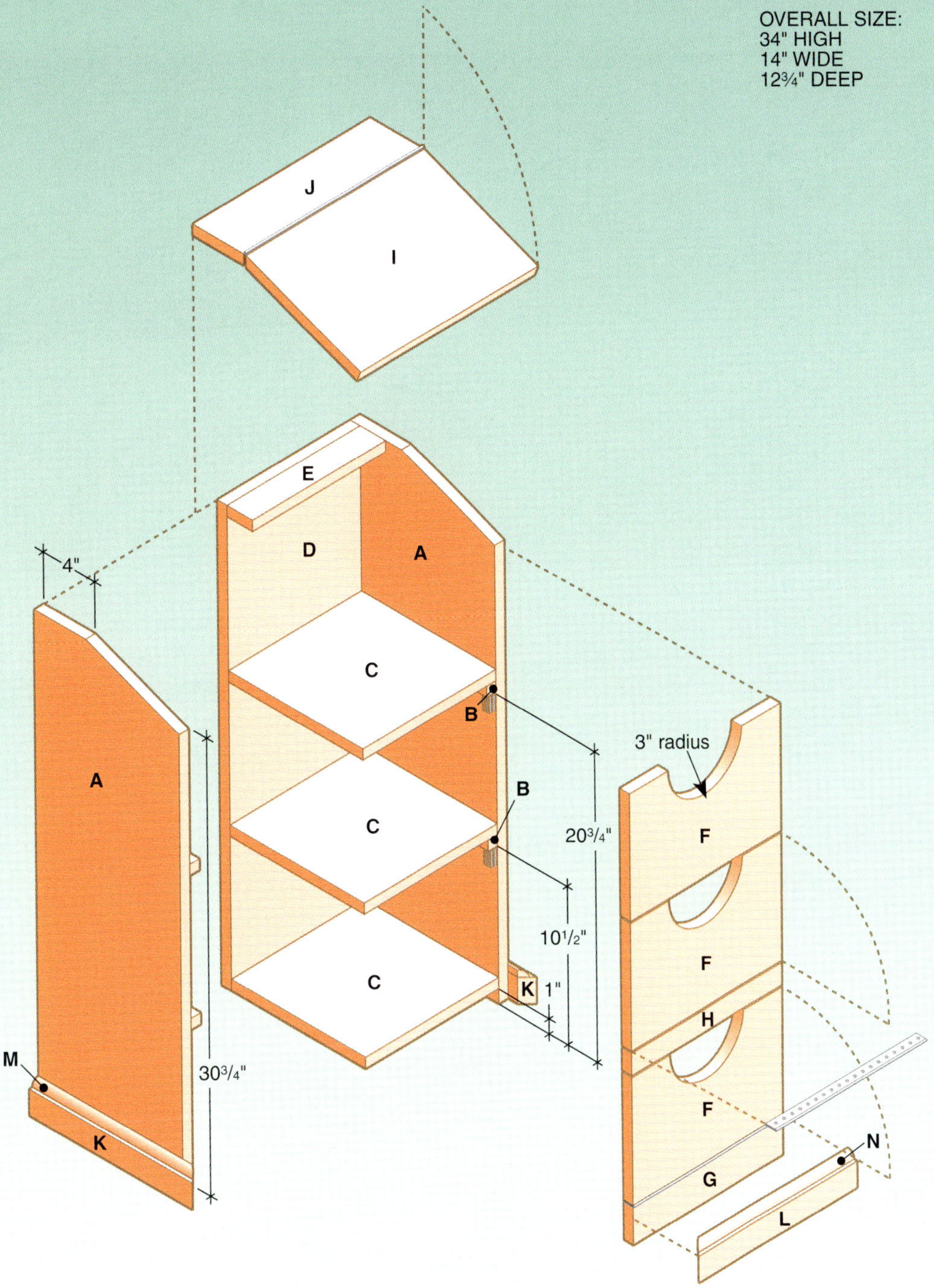

Key	Part	Dimension	Pcs.	Material
A	Side panel	¾ × 11¼ × 33¼"	2	Plywood
B	Shelf cleat	¾ × ¾ × 10½"	4	Oak
C	Shelf	¾ × 10½ × 10½"	3	Plywood
D	Back	¾ × 10½ × 32¼"	1	Plywood
E	Top cleat	¾ × 2 × 10½"	1	Plywood
F	Bin face	¾ × 8½ × 12"	3	Oak
G	Lower rail	¾ × 2½ × 12"	1	Oak

Cutting List

Key	Part	Dimension	Pcs.	Material
H	Upper rail	¾ × 1½ × 12"	1	Oak
I	Lid	¾ × 9½ × 14"	1	Oak
J	Fixed top	¾ × 4 × 14"	1	Oak
K	Base trim side	¾ × 1½ × 12¾"	2	Oak
L	Base trim front	¾ × 1½ × 13½"	1	Oak
M	Quarter-round side	½ × ½ × 12½"	2	Molding
N	Quarter-round front	½ × ½ × 13"	1	Molding

Materials: Wood glue, oak-veneer edge tape (20'), #6 × 1¼" wood screws, wire brads (1¼", 1½"), 1½" × 36" piano hinge, magnetic door catches (2), chain stops (2), finishing materials.

Note: Measurements reflect the actual thickness of dimension lumber.

Apply oak-veneer edge tape with a household iron, and trim with a utility knife when cool.

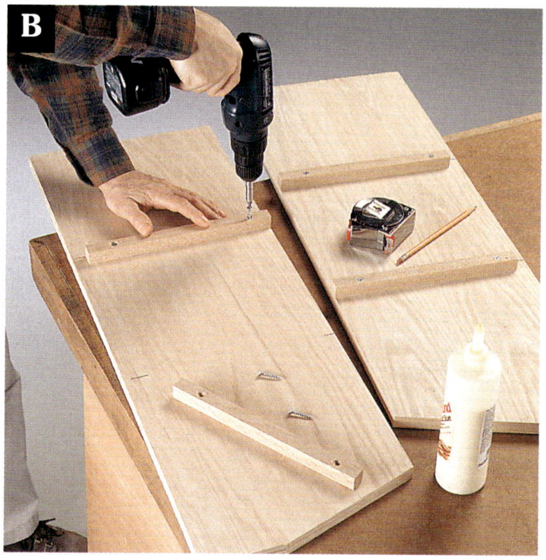

Align cleats on the reference lines, and fasten with glue and screws.

Directions: Vegetable Bin

MAKE THE SIDES.

1. Cut the side panels (A), shelves (C), back (D) and top cleat (E) to size from plywood, and rip the shelf cleats (B) to size from 1 × 12 oak. Sand all edges smooth.

2. Draw a cutting line for the front corners on each side panel (see *Diagram*), and cut along the line with a jig saw to shape the side panels.

3. Clamp each side panel in an upright position, and apply oak-veneer edge tape to all edges, using a household iron **(photo A).** Let cool, and trim the edges with a utility knife.

4. Measure and mark cleat and shelf locations across the inner face of each panel 1", 10½" and 20¾" from the bottom. Drill countersunk pilot holes, then use glue and screws to attach the cleats to the side panels **(photo B).** The bottom of the cleats should be flush with the marked lines, and the front of the cleats should be flush with the front edges of the side panels.

Use a nail set to recess nail heads flush with the shelves.

ATTACH THE SIDES AND BACK.

1. Position the bottom shelf between the side panels so the bottom edge of the shelf rests on the 1" reference line. Keep the front edge flush with the side panels, and fasten with glue and screws. Attach the remaining shelves to the cleats with glue and 1¼" brads, using a nail set to recess the nail heads **(photo C).**

2. Use glue and screws to attach the back to the shelves. Place the top cleat flush against the top of the assembly, and fasten with screws driven through the back and into the cleat **(photo D).**

3. Drive 1½" brads through each side panel into the ends of the top cleat and the edges of the back piece.

MAKE THE BIN FACES AND LID.

The lower bin faces are hinged for easy access. The upper bin face is permanently fixed, and

Attach the top cleat from behind with glue and screws, and set in place with two brads at each end.

Attach the rails, and then adjust and fasten the bin lids to the hinges.

access is gained through a hinged lid.

1. Rip-cut the bin faces (F) lower rail (G), upper rail (H), lid (I) and fixed top (J) to size.

2. Use a circular saw to cut a 10° bevel into the back edge of the lid.

3. Mark the lengthwise centerpoint of each bin face. Draw a 3"-rad. arc centered on each point. Cut each arc with a jig saw and sand smooth.

4. Cut the piano hinge into two 11" sections and one 13" section, using a hacksaw. Center the 11" piano hinges on the lower and upper rails. Drill pilot holes and attach the hinges with the enclosed screws.

5. Position the hinged rails on the bin. The lower rail should be flush with the bottom of the bin. The bottom edge of the upper rail should be flush with the middle shelf, 11¼" from the bottom of the bin. Drill pilot holes and attach the rails to the front of the bin with glue and 1½" brads. Secure the bin faces to the hinges using the enclosed mounting hardware **(photo E).**

6. Lay the upper bin face in position, flush with the bottom of the top shelf. Drill pilot holes and attach the upper bin face with glue and 1½" brads.

7. Center and attach the 13" piano hinge onto the fixed top, drill pilot holes, and fasten with screws.

8. Center the fixed top (hinge up) on top of the assembly, flush with the back edge, then drill pilot holes. Fasten with glue and 1¼" screws driven up through the top cleat into the fixed top. Attach the beveled edge of the lid to the hinge so it folds down correctly over the side panels.

MAKE THE BASE TRIM.

1. Cut base trim sides (K) and base trim front (L) from 1 × 2 oak, and cut the quarter-round sides (M) and quarter-round front (N) to length, mitering the butting ends at 45° angles.

2. Drill pilot holes and attach the base trim pieces with glue and 1¼" brads, and add the quarter-round pieces above the base trim.

APPLY FINISHING TOUCHES.

1. Fill any exposed nail holes, and finish-sand the entire project, using caution around veneered edges. Use a nontoxic finish, such as water-based polyurethane, and let dry.

2. Install magnetic catches in the two lower bins, and fasten stop-chains to support the lids when open **(photo F).**

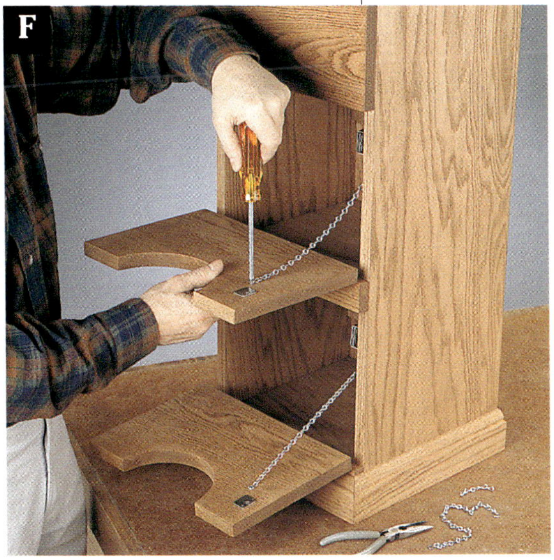

Attach stop-chains to hold bin lids in place when open and magnetic catches to secure the lids when closed.

Pantry Cabinet

This adjustable cabinet provides the versatility needed to organize your pantry.

PROJECT POWER TOOLS

Most pantries are great for storing kitchen supplies or appliances that you don't use every day but like to have nearby. However, if your pantry itself is poorly organized and inconvenient to use, it winds up as wasted space in your home. To get the most from your pantry, we devised our cabinet for maximum vertical storage capacity. Standing 84" high, the cabinet features three solid shelves for storing heavy goods and two adjustable shelves to fit large or awkward items. You can use this pantry cabinet as a freestanding unit against a wall or as a divider in a larger pantry. The open construction also means you can identify what you have on hand at a glance. Included in the instructions is a simple option for converting an adjustable shelf into a rack that is perfect for stable storage of wine, soda or other bottled liquids.

Construction Materials

Quantity	Lumber
14	1 × 4" × 8' pine
2	¾ × ¾" × 6' pine stop molding

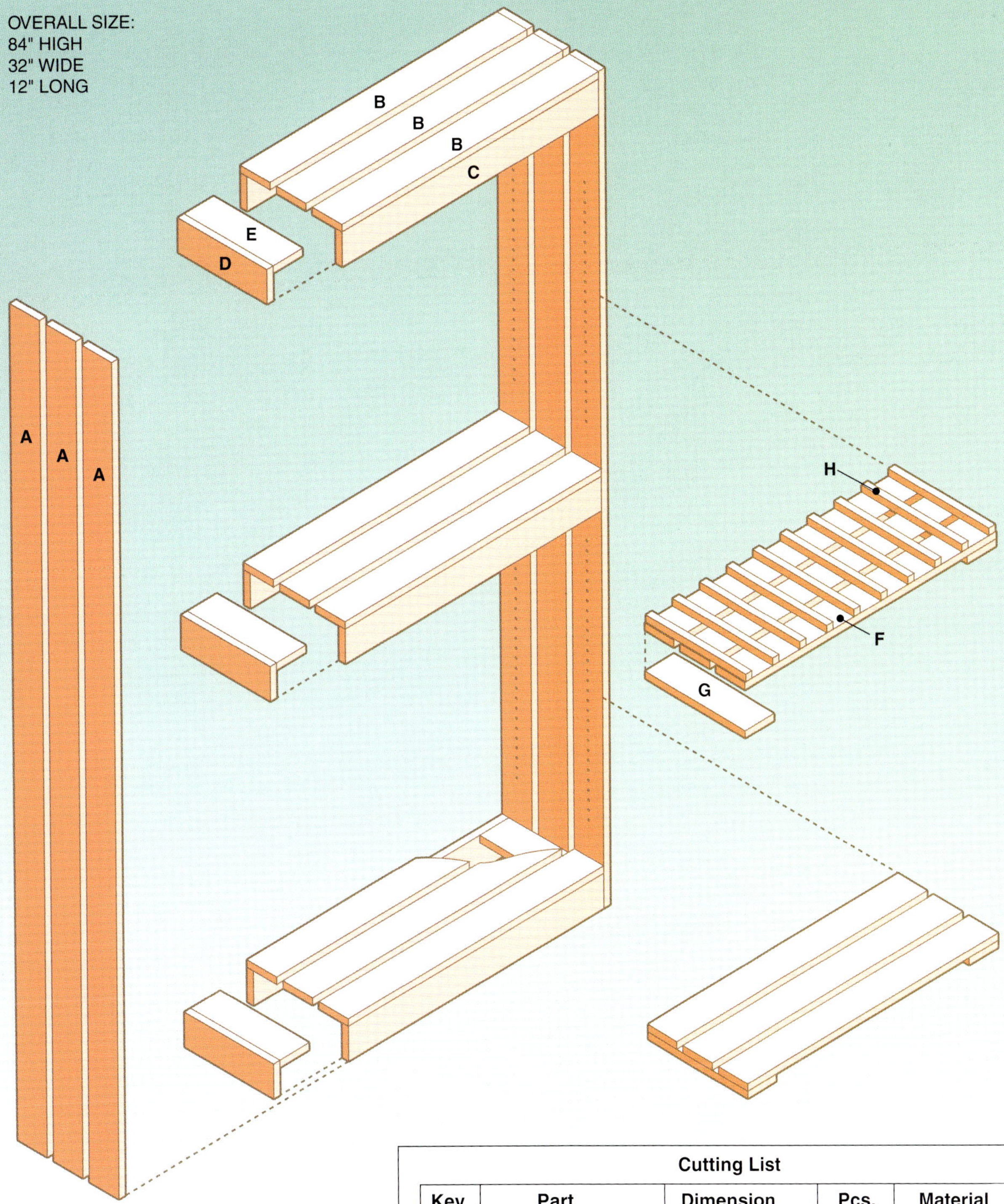

Cutting List

Key	Part	Dimension	Pcs.	Material
A	Side slats	¾ × 3½ × 84"	6	Pine
B	Fixed-shelf slat	¾ × 3½ × 30½"	9	Pine
C	Fixed-shelf face	¾ × 3½ × 30½"	6	Pine
D	Fixed-shelf end	¾ × 3½ × 10½"	6	Pine
E	Fixed-shelf stretcher	¾ × 3½ × 10½"	6	Pine
F	Adjust.-shelf slat	¾ × 3½ × 30⅜"	6	Pine
G	Adjust.-shelf stretcher	¾ × 3½ × 12"	4	Pine
H	Wine-shelf slat	¾ × ¾ × 12"	10	Pine

Materials: Wood glue, wood screws (#6 × 1¼", #8 × 1⅝"), ¼" shelf pins (8), birch plugs (⅜"), finishing materials.

Note: Measurements reflect the actual thickness of dimension lumber.

Join the shelf faces to the ends by driving 1⅝" screws through counterbored pilot holes.

Apply glue and drive counterbored screws into the shelf faces and shelf ends to connect the stretchers.

Directions: Pantry Cabinet

MAKE THE FIXED SHELVES. The fixed shelves comprise the bottom, middle and top of the pantry cabinet.

1. Cut the shelf faces (C), shelf ends (D), and shelf stretchers (E) to size from 1 × 4" pine. Sand the cuts smooth with medium-grit sandpaper.

2. Position the shelf ends between the shelf faces so the corners are flush.

3. Drill ⅜" counterbored pilot holes through the shelf faces into each shelf end. (Keep all counterbores aligned throughout the project to ensure a professional look.) Join the shelf faces and the shelf ends together with wood glue and 1⅝" wood screws driven through the pilot holes **(photo A).** Repeat for the other two fixed-shelf frames.

4. Place a stretcher inside the corner of a shelf frame so the stretcher face is flush with the top edges of the frame. Counterbore pilot holes on the shelf faces and ends, and attach the stretcher with glue and 1⅝" screws driven through the pilot holes. Repeat for the other side of the shelf frame and for the other two shelves **(photo B).**

5. Cut the shelf slats (B) to size and sand the edges smooth.

6. Place three slats on your worksurface. Turn one shelf frame over so the stretchers are on the bottom, and place the shelf frame on top of the slats. Move the slats so the corners and edges are flush with the shelf frame. Space the slats ¾" apart and then attach the slats with glue and 1¼" screws countersunk through the bottom of the stretchers into each of the shelf slats **(photo C).** Repeat for the remaining two fixed shelves.

ASSEMBLE THE CABINET. The fixed shelves are connected directly to the side slats

TIP

Buy or make wood plugs to fill counterbored screw holes. Building centers and woodworker's stores usually carry a variety of plug types in several sizes and styles. To cut your own wood plugs, you can use a special-purpose plug cutting tool (sold at woodworker's stores), or a small hole saw that mounts to your power drill (sold at building centers). The diameter of the plug must match the counterbore drilled into the wood.

Join the fixed-shelf slats to the stretchers with glue and 1¼" screws driven through the undersides of the stretchers.

When attaching the side slats, position the outer side slats so the edge is flush with the edges of the fixed shelves.

to provide stability. The base of the pantry cabinet is wide enough to allow the cabinet to stand alone so long as the cabinet is square. Make sure all joints are square and the edges are flush during this final assembly.

1. Cut the side slats (A) to size, and sand to smooth out rough edges.

2. On each side slat, draw a reference line 40" from the bottom end. These lines mark the location of the bottom edge of the middle fixed shelf. To attach the side slats, align all three shelves on end roughly 40" apart, and lay a side slat over them. Adjust the top and bottom shelves so they are flush with the side slat ends and corners. Adjust the lower edge of the middle shelf so it rests on the reference line.

3. Make sure the fixed shelves are correctly aligned and that the corners are square. Counterbore pilot holes through the side slats into the fixed-shelf ends and attach with glue and 1¼" screws. Position the next side slat flush with the other edge of the fixed shelves, and attach with glue and screws driven through counterbored pilot holes. Center the middle side slat by spacing the slat ¾" between the outer slats and attach with glue and screws.

4. With a helper, carefully turn the assembly over so it rests on the attached side slats. Position a side slat over the fixed-shelf ends as before, check to make sure the corners and edges are flush, and attach the side slat to the fixed shelves **(photo D).** Attach the remaining side slats to the fixed shelves, checking for square as you go.

DRILL THE PEG HOLES.

The rows of holes on the inner faces of the side slats are used to hold the pegs for adjustable shelving. Using a drilling template ensures that the holes are

TIP

You may find it helpful to clamp workpiece parts during the assembly process. Clamping will hold glued and squared parts securely in place until you permanently fasten them with screws. Large, awkward assemblies are more manageable with the help of a few clamps.

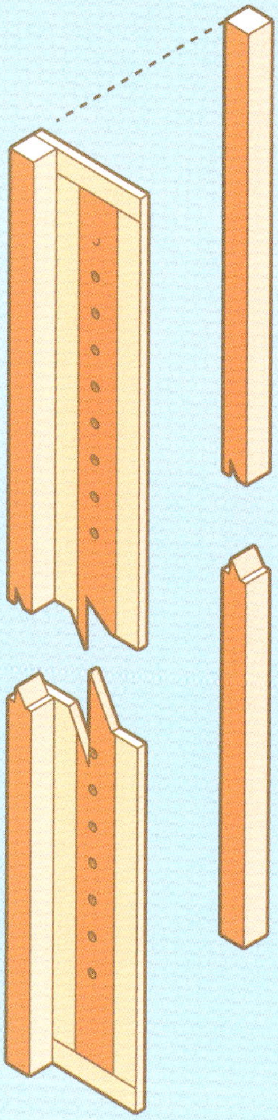

Tip

MAKE A DRILLING TEMPLATE.

Drilling the holes for shelf pegs is simplified by using a template made from a 4 × 34" strip of ⅛ or ¼" pegboard and two 34"-long strips of ¾ × ¾" scrap wood (you can also use stop molding).

First, use masking tape to outline a row of holes on the pegboard. Position one of the ¾" strips against the pegboard so the edge is about 1¾" from the outlined holes. Fasten this guide strip with glue. When the glue dries, turn the template over and attach the second ¾" guide strip, aligning it with the first strip.

Use a pegboard template for uniform placement of peg holes.

perfectly aligned, and the shelves are level when installed (see *Tip*).

1. Wrap masking tape around the tip of a ¼" drill bit at a depth of ½" to mark drilling depth.

2. Position the drilling template against the inside face of a side slat with the ¾" guide strip resting against the edge of the slat. Drill a row of peg holes along the inner face of the side slat, using the pegboard holes as a guide. Make sure not to drill beyond the masking tape depth guide attached to your bit.

3. Rotate the template and position it against the other side slat so the other guide strip is resting against the edge of the slat and the opposite face of the template is facing out. Drill another row of holes exactly parallel to the first **(photo E).**

After drilling all the holes, sand the slats to remove any roughness.

MAKE THE ADJUSTABLE SHELVES.

Our project includes two adjustable shelves, but you can choose to build more. The adjustable shelves are similar in design to the fixed shelves, but without shelf faces or ends.

1. Cut two stretchers (G) and three slats (F) for each shelf, and sand smooth.

2. Lay three slats on your worksurface. Arrange the stretchers over the ends of the slats so the edges and corners are flush, and the slats are spaced ¾" apart.

3. Drill pilot holes through the stretchers into the slats, and fasten with glue and countersunk 1¼" wood screws.

4. Cut the wine shelving slats (H) to size from ¾" pine, using a circular saw and straightedge guide. (Or, you can use pine stop molding.) Sand the cuts smooth.

5. Place the first slat on the adjustable shelf, ⅛" from one end. Keep the ends of the wine slats even with the edges of the shelf slats, and attach with glue and 4d finish nails. Use a 2½"-wide spacer to guide placement for the rest of the slats, and nail in place. Recess all the nail heads on the wine slats with a nail set as you go **(photo F).**

APPLY FINISHING TOUCHES.

1. Pound glued ⅜"-dia. birch plugs into all counterbored holes using a wood or rubber mallet **(photo G).**

2. Carefully sand the plugs flush with a belt sander, then finish-sand the pantry with fine-grit sandpaper.

3. Apply your choice of finish. We brushed a light coat of linseed oil onto the pantry to preserve the natural appearance. If you prefer paint, use a primer and a good-quality enamel.

4. Insert ¼" shelf pins at the desired heights and rest the adjustable shelves on top of the pins after the finish dries.

Use a 2½"-wide spacer to ensure uniform placement of the wine shelf cleats.

Pound glued ⅜" birch plugs into counterbored screw holes.

PROJECT
POWER TOOLS

Kitchen Island

Our stand-alone cabinet and countertop island expands the versatility of any kitchen.

Construction Materials

Quantity	Lumber
7	⅝" × 2' × 4' pine panel
4	1 × 2" × 8' pine
1	1 × 4" × 4' pine
1	2 × 8" × 2' pine
4	¾ × ¾" × 8' pine stop molding
1	¾" × 4' × 4' particleboard
1	¼" × 4' × 4' tileboard

This project is a great looking alternative to more expensive custom cabinetry. The kitchen island gives you additional space for preparing food, as well as a convenient spot to enjoy a light snack or a quick meal. The ends, back panels and shelves are constructed from edge-glued pine, a convenient building material with an appealing pattern. The front of the island has a finished face frame and adjustable shelving for storage. The countertop has an 8" overhang and provides room for two to sit comfortably. We used tileboard as the countertop, but laminate or ceramic tile are also good choices.

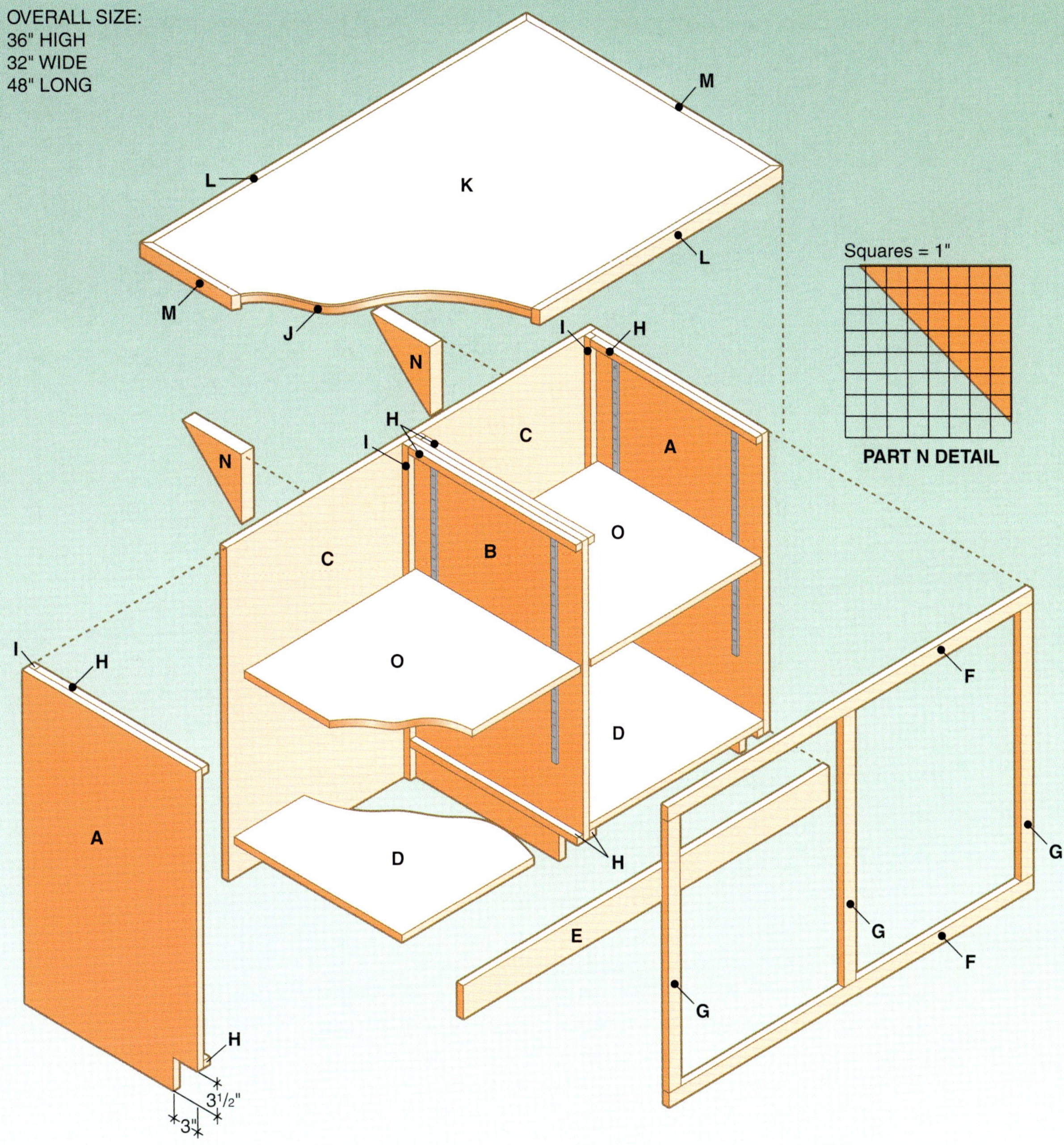

Cutting List

Key	Part	Dimension	Pcs.	Material
A	End	⅝ × 21½ × 35"	2	Pine panel
B	Divider	⅝ × 21½ × 35"	1	Pine panel
C	Back	⅝ × 22⅛ × 35"	2	Pine panel
D	Bottom	⅝ × 21⅛ × 21½"	2	Pine panel
E	Toe board	¾ × 3½ × 44¼"	1	Pine
F	Rail	¾ × 1½ × 44¼"	2	Pine
G	Stile	¾ × 1½ × 28½"	3	Pine
H	Horiz. cleat	¾ × ¾ × 20¾"	8	Molding
I	Vert. cleat	¾ × ¾ × 35"	4	Molding
J	Substrate	¾ × 30½ × 46½"	1	Particleboard
K	Top	¼ × 30½ × 46½"	1	Tileboard
L	Long edge	¾ × 1½ × 48"	2	Pine
M	Short edge	¾ × 1½ × 32"	2	Pine
N	Support	1½ × 7¼ × 7¼"	2	Pine
O	Shelf	⅝ × 20½ × 20½"	2	Pine panel

Materials: Wood glue, #6 wood screws (1", 1¼", 1½"), ½" tacks, 4d finish nails, 24" shelf standards (8), shelf standard supports, contact cement, finishing materials.

Note: Measurements reflect the actual thickness of dimension lumber.

Cut the toe board notches into the ends and divider using a jig saw.

Gang the cleats together while drilling countersunk pilot holes.

Directions: Kitchen Island

CUT THE ENDS AND DIVIDER.

1. Cut the ends (A) and divider (B) to size from pine panels, using a circular saw.

2. Measure and mark the 3"-wide × 3½"-tall toe board notches on the lower front corners of all three pieces using a combination square (see *Diagram*). This notch allows you to approach the cabinet without stubbing your toes against the bottom.

3. Clamp each piece to your worksurface, and cut out the toe board notches using a jig saw **(photo A).**

PREPARE THE CLEATS.

The cleats reinforce the internal joints of the cabinet. Countersunk pilot holes are drilled through each cleat in two directions, and are offset so the screws won't hit one another.

1. Cut the horizontal cleats (H) and the vertical cleats (I) to length from ¾ × ¾" stop molding.

2. Clamp the vertical cleats together so the ends are flush, and mark four pilot hole locations along the length of each cleat (see *Detail* for pilot hole locations). Drill countersunk pilot holes at each marked location.

3. Remove the clamps and give each cleat a quarter turn. Reclamp the cleats, then mark and drill the second set of offset pilot holes. Repeat the process for the horizontal cleats, drilling three holes through one edge of each cleat and two offset holes through an adjacent edge **(photo B).**

PARTS H AND I DETAIL

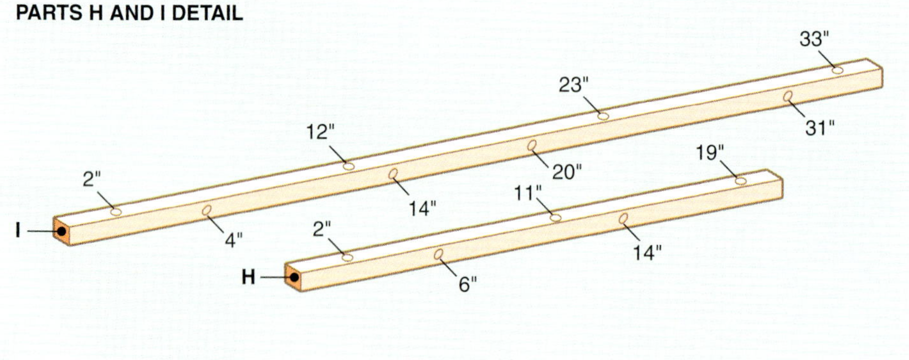

Center a marked template between the cleats to uniformly attach the shelf standards.

Clamp the back to the divider along the centerline, and adjust when attaching to the end.

ASSEMBLE THE ENDS AND DIVIDER.

1. Align a vertical cleat along the inside back edge of one of the ends. Align the pilot holes so the back can be attached through the offset holes.

2. Apply glue and fasten the cleat to the end with countersunk 1" screws. Attach vertical cleats to the inside face of the other end, and to both back edges of the divider. Attach the horizontal cleats to the ends and divider, using glue and 1" screws.

ATTACH THE SHELF STANDARDS.

1. Cut a 15 × 30" template from scrap particleboard or heavy-stock cardboard. Make sure the standards are properly aligned in the same direction so the holes for the supports line up.

2. Place the template on the lower horizontal cleat, and center the template between the vertical cleat and the front edge. Measure 2" up from the bottom edge along each side of the template and make a reference mark.

3. Place a standard against each edge of the template and adjust so the bottom of the standard is on the 2" mark. Nail the standards in place with the provided nails.

4. Repeat for the other end, and on both faces of the divider **(photo C).**

ASSEMBLE THE CABINET.

1. Cut the backs (C), bottoms (D) and toe board (E) to size, and sand the edges smooth.

2. Cut ¾ × ¾" notches in the back corners of each bottom to

TIP

The back, end, divider, bottom and shelf pieces used in this project are constructed from ⅝" edge-glued ponderosa pine panels, available at most building centers. This material, available in varying dimensions and thicknesses, is manufactured from small-width pine glued together under pressure. The result is a strong material that is slightly thinner than standard dimensional plywood. It features a distinctive paneled appearance, and since it is made entirely of one type of wood, exposed edges do not require veneer.

Arrange the toe board so the corners and edges are flush, and attach to the divider and ends with glue and 4d finish nails.

Sand the rails after the stiles to avoid cross-sanding marks on the rails.

accommodate the vertical cleats.

3. Stand one end and the divider upright on their front edges. Position a bottom piece against the lower horizontal cleats. Use bar clamps to hold the assembly in place, and attach the bottom with glue and 1" screws driven through the pilot holes in each cleat. Position the remaining bottom and end in place, and attach the bottom to the cleats.

4. Attach the back pieces one at a time, using glue and 1" screws driven through the vertical cleats inside the cabinet. Make sure each back piece is aligned with its inside edge flush against a marked reference centerline on the divider. Check frequently for square, and use pipe clamps to hold the pieces in position as you attach them **(photo D).**

5. Carefully turn the assembly over, and fasten the toe board in place with glue and 4d finish nails.

ASSEMBLE THE FACE FRAME.

1. Cut the rails (F) and stiles (G) to size, and sand them smooth. Position the top rail so the top edges and corners are flush, and attach with glue and finish nails. Attach the stiles so the outside edges are flush with the end faces and centered on the divider. Finally, attach the bottom rail **(photo E).**

2. Reinforce the joints by drilling pilot holes through the rails into the ends of each stile and securing with 4d finish nails.

3. Use an orbital sander to smooth the face frame and the joints between stiles and rails. By sanding the stiles before the rails, you can avoid cross-sanding marks at the joints **(photo F).**

BUILD THE COUNTERTOP.

1. Cut the particleboard substrate (J), tileboard top (K), long edges (L) and short edges (M) to size. Make sure the top fits perfectly over the substrate, and trim if necessary.

2. Miter-cut the ends of the long edges and short edges at 45° angles to fit around the countertop.

3. Apply contact cement to the substrate, and clamp the tile-

Clamp scrap boards to the tileboard to distribute pressure and establish good contact.

Attach the supports to the back from inside the cabinet using glue and screws.

board top in place, using scrap wood under the clamps to distribute pressure and ensure even contact with the cement **(photo G).**

4. Unclamp and flip the assembly on its top when dry. Arrange the long and short edges around the countertop, so the top surface will be flush with the tops of the edge pieces. Glue and clamp the edges in place. Drill pilot holes and drive 4d finish nails through the edges into the substrate.

ATTACH THE COUNTERTOP AND SHELVES.

1. Cut the shelves (O) from pine panels and the supports (N) from 2 × 8 dimensional pine. Round the cut corners at the long ends of each diagonal, using a jig saw or a sander to soften the profile of the supports.

2. Mark a line on the top edge of the back, 11" in from each end. Position the supports so they are centered on the lines. Drill pilot holes through the back and attach the supports with glue and 1½" countersunk screws driven from the inside of the cabinet **(photo H).**

3. Center the countertop from side to side on the cabinet with a 1" overhang on the front. Attach with glue and 1¼" screws driven up through the top horizontal cleats. Insert supports into the shelf standards at the desired height, and install the shelves inside the cabinet with the grain running left to right.

APPLY FINISHING TOUCHES.

1. Recess all visible nail heads with a nail set, and fill the holes with putty. Sand all surfaces, outer edges and corners smooth.

2. Finish the kitchen island with a light stain and apply a nontoxic topcoat. We used a traditional American pine finish.

PROJECT POWER TOOLS

Pine Pantry

Turn a remote corner or closet into a kitchen pantry with this charming pine cabinet.

Construction Materials

Quantity	Lumber
2	1 × 10" × 10' pine
3	1 × 8" × 8' pine
1	1 × 8" × 10' pine
1	1 × 6" × 8' pine
1	1 × 4" × 8' pine
5	1 × 3" × 8' pine
1	1 × 2" × 10' pine
1	¾" × 4 × 8' plywood
1	¼" × 4 × 8' plywood

This compact pantry cabinet is ideal for keeping your kitchen organized and efficient. It features a convenient turntable shelf, or "Lazy Susan," on the inside of the cabinet for easy access to canned foods. A swing-out shelf assembly lets you get the most from the pantry's space. Its roominess allows you to store most of your non-refrigerated food items.

But the best feature of the pantry is its appearance. The rugged beauty of the cabinet hides its simplicity. For such an impressive-looking project, it is remarkably easy to build. Even if you don't have a traditional pantry in your home, you can have a convenient, attractive storage center.

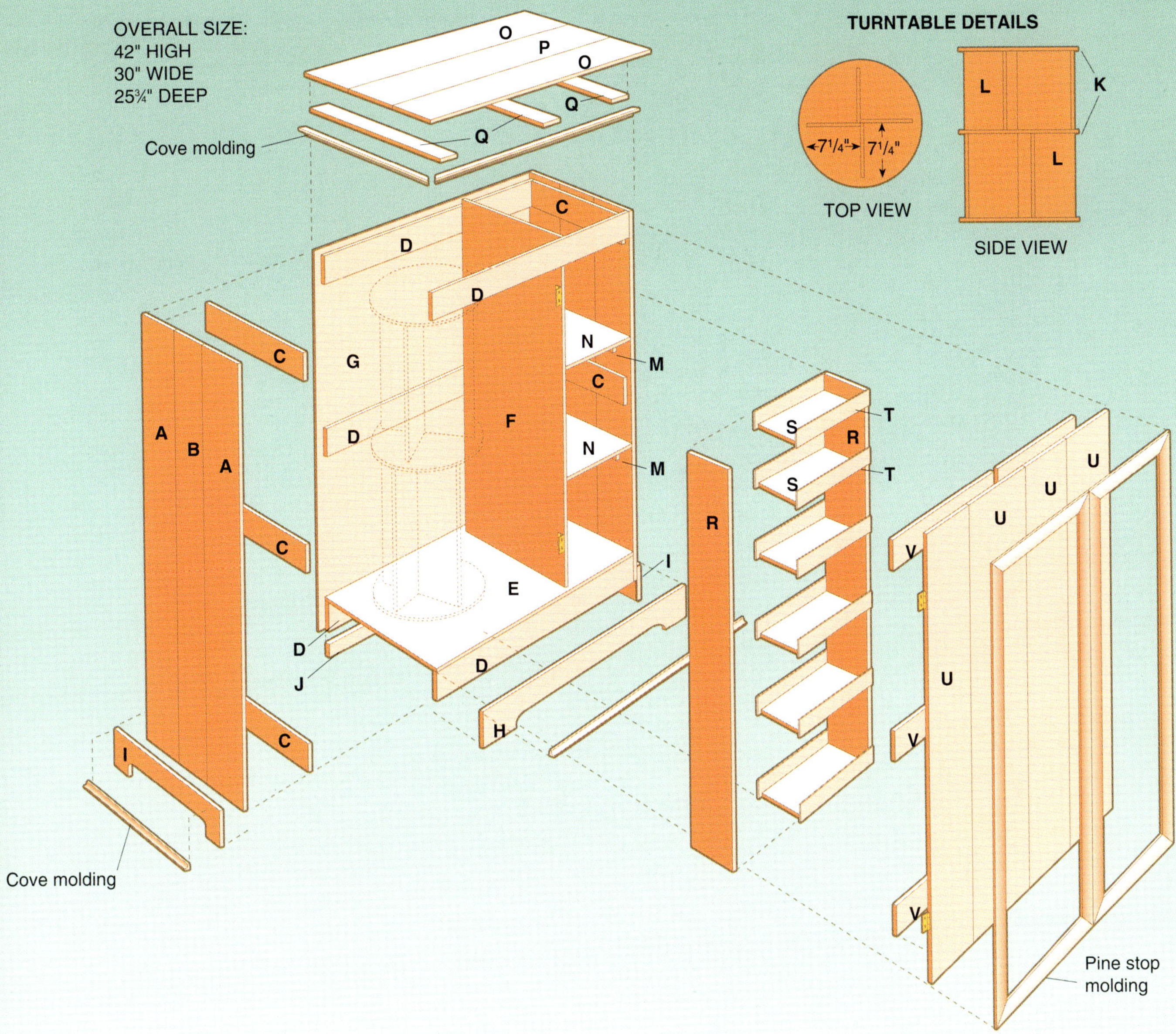

Cutting List				
Key	**Part**	**Dimension**	**Pcs.**	**Material**
A	Side board	¾ × 9¼ × 39¼"	4	Pine
B	Middle board	¾ × 5½ × 39¼"	2	Pine
C	Panel cleat	¾ × 2½ × 22½"	6	Pine
D	Stretcher	¾ × 2½ × 26½"	5	Pine
E	Floor	¾ × 24 × 26½"	1	Plywood
F	Divider	¾ × 22½ × 36"	1	Plywood
G	Back	¼ × 28 × 39¼"	1	Plywood
H	Base front	¾ × 3½ × 29½"	1	Pine
I	Base side	¾ × 3½ × 24¼"	2	Pine
J	Base back	¾ × 1½ × 28"	1	Pine
K	Turntable shelf	¾ × 16"-dia.	3	Plywood

Cutting List				
Key	**Part**	**Dimension**	**Pcs.**	**Material**
L	Supports	¾ × 7¼ × 12"	8	Pine
M	Shelf cleat	¾ × 1½ × 22"	4	Pine
N	Fixed shelf	¾ × 9 × 23"	2	Plywood
O	Top board	¾ × 9¼ × 30"	2	Pine
P	Middle board	¾ × 7¼ × 30"	1	Pine
Q	Top cleat	¾ × 2½ × 22¼"	3	Pine
R	Swing-out end	¾ × 6 × 32"	2	Pine
S	Swing-out shelf	¾ × 6 × 10"	6	Pine
T	Swing-out side	¼ × 2 × 11½"	12	Plywood
U	Door board	¾ × 6⅝ × 35"	4	Pine
V	Door cleat	¾ × 2½ × 11"	6	Pine

Materials: #6 × 1¼", 1½" and 2" wood screws, 2d, 4d and 6d finish nails, 16-ga. × 1" wire nails, turntable hardware, cabinet handles, 3 × 3" brass hinges (2), cabinet door hinges (4), ¾" cove molding, ⅜ × 1¼" stop molding, glue, finishing materials.

Note: Measurements reflect the actual size of dimension lumber.

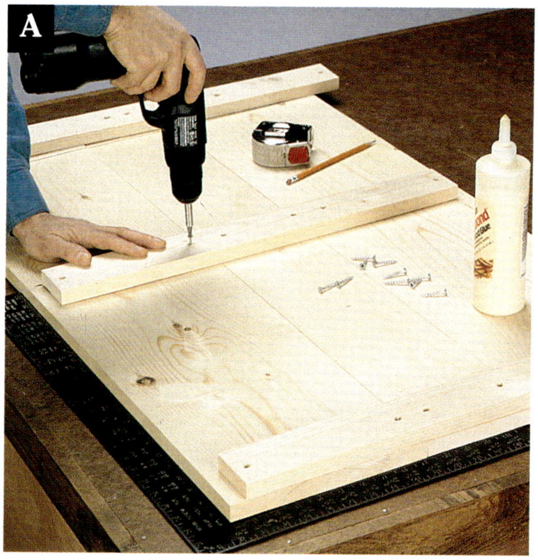

Fasten cleats to the side and middle boards, forming the cabinet sides.

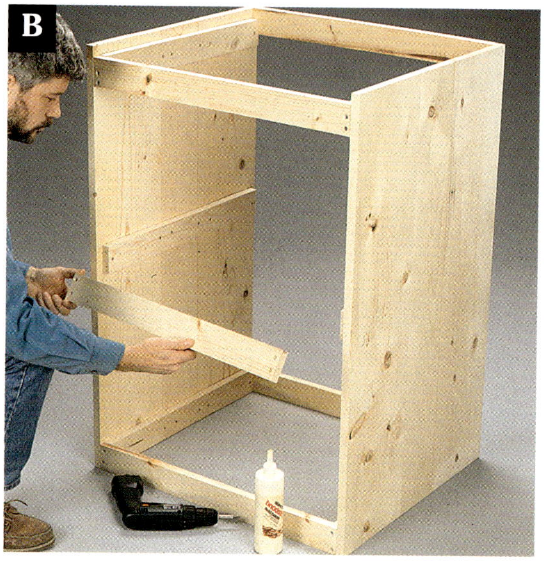

Attach front and back stretchers at the top and bottom, and a middle stretcher at the back.

Directions: Pine Pantry

For all screws used in this project, drill 5/64" pilot holes. Counterbore the holes 1/8" deep, using a 3/8" counterbore bit.

MAKE THE CABINET SIDES.

1. Cut the side boards (A), middle boards (B) and panel cleats (C) to length. Sand all of the parts smooth.

2. Position a middle board between two side boards with the ends flush. Butt the boards against a framing square to keep them in line. Position a panel cleat flat across the boards so the bottom edge of the cleat is flush with the bottom edges of the boards. The ends of the cleat should be 3/4" from the outside edges of the side boards. Fasten the cleat to the boards with glue, and drive 1 1/4" wood screws through the cleat and into the side and middle boards.

3. Attach the next panel cleat to the boards so its top edge is 21 1/2" up from the bottom edge of the first cleat **(photo A).** Maintain a 3/4" distance from the cleat ends to the board edges.

4. Install the top panel cleat with its top edge 1" down from the board tops.

5. Repeat these steps to make the other cabinet side.

ATTACH THE SIDES.

1. Cut the side stretchers (D) to length.

2. Connect the cabinet sides by attaching the stretchers to the ends of the panel cleats. Position bottom stretchers at the front and back of the cabinet, keeping their top and bottom edges flush with the top and bottom edges of the panel cleats. The top two stretchers are each positioned a little differently—the back stretcher is flush with the tops and bottoms of the panel cleats, and the front stretcher is flush with the top edges of the cabinet sides. Apply glue and drive 1 1/2" wood screws through the stretcher faces and into the ends of the cleats.

3. Attach the remaining stretcher at the back of the cabinet, flush with the panel cleats on the middle of the cabinet sides **(photo B).**

ATTACH THE FLOOR.

1. Cut the floor (E) to size. Sand the top face smooth, and fill any voids in the front edge of the floor with wood putty.

2. Position the floor on top of the bottom stretchers and panel cleats, with the floor's front edge flush with the face of the front stretcher. Glue the parts. Drive 1 1/2" wood screws through the floor and into the stretchers and panel cleats.

ATTACH THE DIVIDER.

1. Cut the divider (F) and shelf cleats (M) to size.

2. Draw a reference line across the floor from front to back, 9" from the right cabinet side. This line marks the position of the divider's shelf-side face. Measure and mark shelf cleat position lines on the right cabinet side, 10" and 20 3/4" up from the cabinet floor. Draw corresponding lines on the divider. These lines mark the top edges of the shelf cleats.

3. Use glue and 1 1/4" wood screws to fasten the shelf cleats

Install the divider 9" in from the right side of the cabinet.

Check for square by measuring diagonally between the corners to make sure the distances are equal.

to the divider and side with their top edges at the lines. Keeping all back edges flush, drive the screws through the cleats and into the divider and side panel.

4. Apply glue to the bottom edge of the divider. Insert the divider into the cabinet with its cleated face toward the cleated cabinet side. Drive 1½" wood screws up through the cabinet floor and into the divider edge. Drill ¹⁄₁₆" pilot holes through the top stretchers and drive 6d finish nails through the top stretchers and into the divider edges **(photo C).**

ATTACH THE BACK.

1. Cut the back (G) to size, and position it on the cabinet.

2. Drive evenly spaced 1" wire nails through the back and into the edge of one side panel.

3. Measure diagonally across the opposite corners to check if the cabinet is square **(photo D).** Square the cabinet, if needed, by applying pressure to opposite corners. When the diagonal measurements are equal, complete the nailing of the back to the stretchers and the remaining side panel.

ATTACH THE FIXED SHELVES.

1. Cut the fixed shelves (N) to size. Sand them smooth.

2. Position the shelves on the shelf cleats, with their ends butted against the cabinet back. Attach the shelves with glue, and drive 1½" wood screws through the shelves and into the cleats.

MAKE THE BASE.

Three of the four base boards have cutouts that create a foot at each corner.

1. Cut the base front (H), base sides (I) and base back (J) to length. Sand the parts smooth.

2. Use a compass to draw 1¾"-radius semicircles, centered 7¼" from each end of the base front. Hold the point of the compass as close as possible to the bottom edge. Using a straightedge, draw a straight line connecting the tops of the semicircles. Repeat these steps on the base sides, but center the semicircles 4¾" from the front end and 5½" from the back end. Cut along the lines with a jig saw.

3. Mark lines on the rear edges of the base sides, ½" from the bottom edge. These lines mark the position of the bottom edge of the base back.

4. Attach the base sides to the base front with glue, and drive 4d finish nails through the base front and into the ends of the base sides.

5. Attach the base back between the base sides at the reference lines, using glue and 4d finish nails.

Cut the round turntable shelves with a jig saw. Each turntable shelf has an 8" radius.

Assemble the turntable supports in three pairs, joined at right angles.

Using glue and 4d finish nails, attach the swing-out shelf sides.

ATTACH THE CABINET AND BASE.

1. Turn the cabinet on its back, slide the base over its bottom end until the base back meets the bottom cleats. The base should extend 2" beyond the cabinet's bottom edges. Drive 2" wood screws through the bottom cleats and side boards and into the base sides.

2. Drive 1¼" wood screws through the front stretcher and into the base front.

BUILD THE TURNTABLE SHELVES.

1. Cut the turntable shelves (K) to size. To cut the circular shape, mark the center of the turntable shelves, and use a compass to draw a 16"-dia. circle. Cut the shelves to shape with a jig saw, and sand the cuts smooth **(photo E).**

2. Cut the turntable supports (L) to length.

3. Attach pairs of turntable supports at right angles by applying glue and driving 1½" wood screws through one support's face and into the other support's edge, forming simple butt joints **(photo F).**

4. Use a straightedge to draw a line across the turntable shelves, directly through their centerpoints. Place one pair of turntable supports along the line with the joint at the centerpoint (see *Diagram*). Make sure the support pair forms a right angle. Then, draw the outline of the supports on the shelf. Position another support pair on the other side of the line and draw the outline. Drill pilot holes through the shelves, centered within the outlines, and fasten the turntable shelves to the turntable supports with glue and 1½" wood screws. The supports should have their spines meeting at the centerpoint of the turntable. Offset the upper and lower sets of supports on the opposite sides of the middle shelf to allow room for driving the screws.

5. Attach the turntable hardware to the bottom face of the bottom turntable shelf, following manufacturer's directions. The turntable must be centered on the shelf, or the assembly will not rotate smoothly. Install the turntable assembly after you apply the finish to the pantry.

BUILD THE SWING-OUT RACK.

1. Cut the swing-out shelves (S), swing-out ends (R) and swing-out sides (T) to size. Sand the parts smooth.

2. Draw lines 6" apart starting from the bottom of the swing-out ends. These lines mark the positions of the bottom faces of the swing-out shelves. Apply glue to the shelf edges. Then, attach them to the swing-out ends by driving 1½" wood screws through the ends and into the shelf edges. The bottom shelf should be flush with the bottom of the end edges.

3. Attach the swing-out shelf sides (T) on the edges of the shelves with glue and 4d finish nails **(photo G).**

MAKE THE TOP.

1. Cut the top boards (O), middle board (P) and top cleats (Q) to length. Sand them smooth.

2. Attach a top cleat across the inside faces of the boards, 1¾" from each end. Make sure that

Use a circular saw with a straightedge as a guide to rip-cut the door boards to size.

Attach pine stop molding to create a frame around the edges of the door boards.

the ends of the boards are flush and that the cleats are centered from front to back. Apply glue and drive 1¼" wood screws through the cleats and into the top and middle boards. Fasten the middle cleat so its right edge is 11½" from the right end of the top.
3. Position the top on the cabinet so it overhangs the front and sides of the cabinet by 1". Fasten the top by driving 4d finish nails into the cabinet sides and toenailing through the middle cleat and into the divider.

BUILD THE DOORS.
1. Cut the door boards (U) and door cleats (V) to size **(photo H).** Sand them smooth.
2. Lay the boards in pairs, with their ends flush. Center the top and bottom cleats, keeping them 2" in from the top and bottom ends. Apply glue and drive 1¼" wood screws through the cleats and into the door boards. Attach the middle cleat, centered between the top and bottom cleats.
3. Miter-cut ⅜" stop molding to frame the front faces of the doors. Fasten the molding with glue and 2d finish nails **(photo I).**

APPLY FINISHING TOUCHES.
1. Miter-cut ¾" cove molding to fit around the base and top (see *Diagram*). Attach the molding with glue and 2d finish nails.
2. Set all nails with a nail set, and fill the nail and screw holes with wood putty. Finish-sand the pantry, and apply the finish of your choice.
3. Attach two evenly spaced 3 × 3" butt hinges to the edge of the swing-out rack. Mount the rack to the divider, using ¼"-thick spacers between the rack and divider **(photo J).**
4. Install the turntable assembly on the floor of the pantry.
5. Attach hinges and handles to the doors. Mount the doors to the cabinet sides.

With spacers in place to help align the parts, attach the swing-out rack to the divider with 3 × 3" butt hinges.

PROJECT
POWER TOOLS

Recycling Center

Recycling is no longer a chore when this convenient recycling center is a fixture in your kitchen.

CONSTRUCTION MATERIALS

Quantity	**Lumber**
1	¾" × 4 × 8' birch plywood
1	1¼"-dia. × 36" birch dowel
3	¼ × 3 × 3" hardboard or scrap wood

Finding adequate storage for recyclables in a kitchen or pantry can be a challenge. Gaping paper bags of discarded aluminum, newspaper, glass and plastic are an unsightly nuisance. Our recycling center eliminates the nuisance and makes recycling easy. The recycling center holds up to four bags of recyclables, keeping the materials in one place and out of sight. Arches create four feet on the bottom of the cabinet and a bold detail on the front edges. The two spacious bins pivot forward on a dowel for easy deposit and removal of recyclables, and the broad top of the cabinet serves as a handy low shelf.

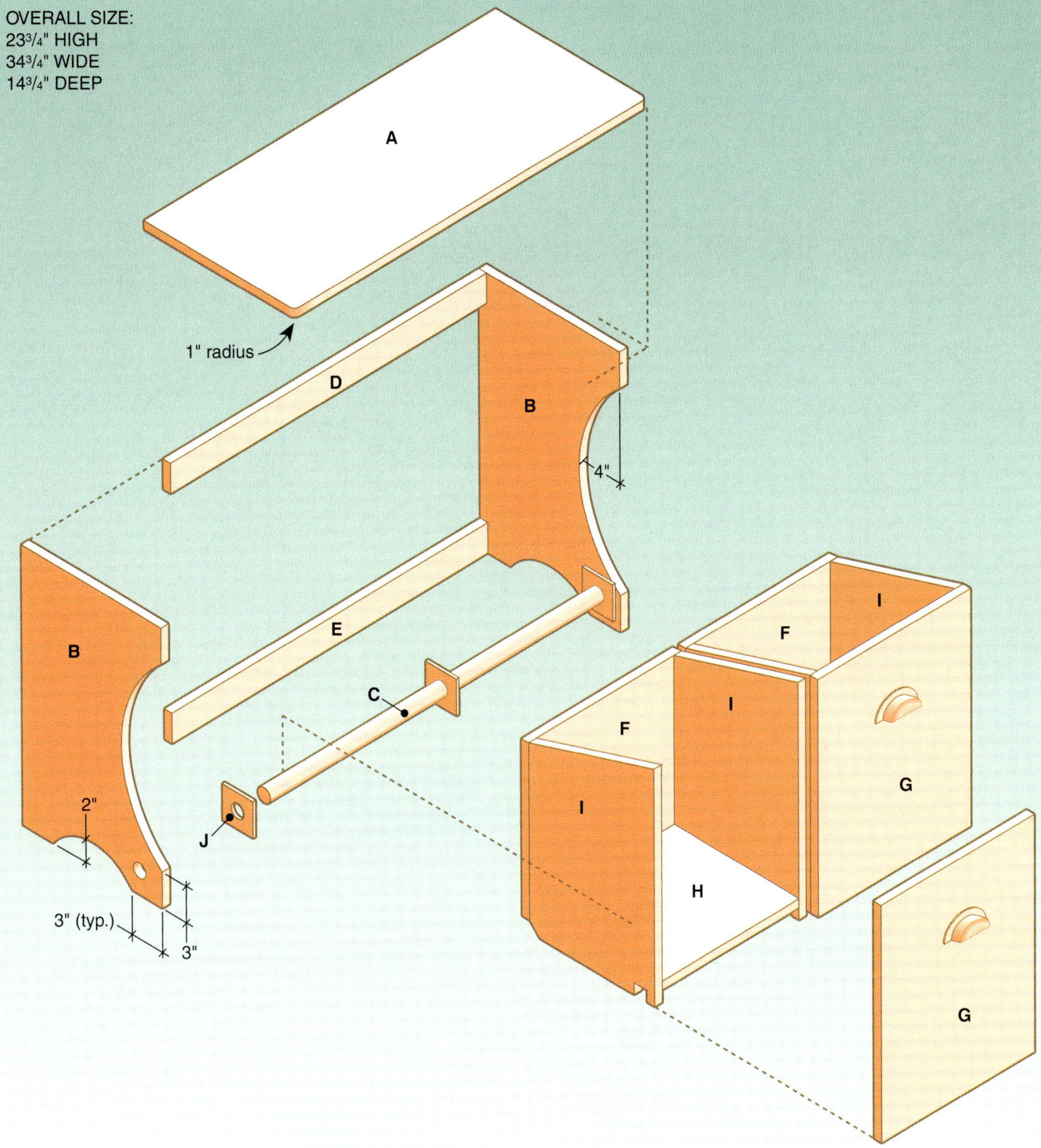

Key	Part	Dimension	Pcs.	Material
A	Top	¾ × 14¾ × 34¾"	1	Plywood
B	End	¾ × 13¾ × 23"	2	Plywood
C	Dowel	1¼"-dia. × 34"	1	Birch dowel
D	Top stretcher	¾ × 2½ × 31"	1	Plywood
E	Bottom stretcher	¾ × 2½ × 31"	1	Plywood

Cutting List

Key	Part	Dimension	Pcs.	Material
F	Bin back	¾ × 15 × 16½"	2	Plywood
G	Bin front	¾ × 15 × 19½"	2	Plywood
H	Bin bottom	¾ × 12¼ × 13½"	2	Plywood
I	Bin side	¾ × 12¼ × 19½"	4	Plywood
J	Spacer	¼ × 3 × 3"	3	Masonite

Materials: #4 × ⅜", #6 × 1½" and #8 × 2" wood screws, 4d finish nails, 10" metal chains (2), screw hooks (2), drawer pulls (2), paste wax, wood glue, finishing materials.
Note: Measurements reflect the actual size of dimension lumber.

Drill pilot holes for the anchor screws through the bottom edges and into the dowel holes.

Apply glue and drive screws through the ends and into the stretchers. Use pipe clamps to ensure square joints.

Directions: Recycling Center

For all #6 wood screws used in this project, drill ⁵⁄₆₄" pilot holes. Counterbore the holes ⅛" deep, using a ⅜" counterbore bit.

MAKE THE TOP AND ENDS.

1. Cut the top (A) and ends (B) to size. Sand the edges smooth with medium-grit sandpaper.

2. Create rounded front corners on the top by marking reference points 1" in from the side and front edges at each front corner. Set a compass to 1", and draw the roundovers, holding the compass point on the reference marks. Sand the corners down to the curved lines with a belt sander.

3. Draw the arches on the end pieces by using a thin, flexible piece of metal, plastic or wood as a tracing guide. Along the front edge of each piece, make marks 3" in from each corner. Make a mark on the side face of each piece, 4" in from the center point of the front edge. Tack small finish nails at these three points. Hook the flexible guide behind the center nail, then flex each end and set them in front of the edge nails so the guide bows in to create a smooth curve. Trace the arches with a pencil, and remove the guide and nails.

4. Draw the curves for the bottom edges using the same technique. Along the bottom edges, measure 3" in from the bottom corners and 2" up from the center point of the bottom edge. Tack finish nails at the marks, set the guide and trace the arches.

5. Make the cuts for the bottom and front arches with a jig saw. Sand the cuts smooth with medium-grit sandpaper.

6. Mark the location for the dowel hole on each end piece, 2¼" in and 2" up from the bottom front corner. Set the end pieces with their inside faces

TIP

When checking a cabinet for square, measure diagonally from corner to corner. If the measurements are equal, the cabinet is square. If not, apply pressure to one side or the other with your hand or clamps until the cabinet is square.

Draw reference lines on the top to use for positioning when attaching it to the sides.

Anchor the dowel by driving screws through the pilot holes and into the dowel.

down onto a backer board to prevent splintering during drilling. Drill the dowel holes, using a 1¼" spade bit.

7. Drill pilot holes for the dowel anchor screws, using a 3/32" bit **(photo A).** Align the drill bit with the center of the dowel hole, and drill through the bottom edge of the end piece and into the dowel hole.

ASSEMBLE THE CABINET FRAME.

Attach the stretchers between the ends to form the back of the cabinet frame.

1. Cut the dowel (C), the top stretcher (D) and the bottom stretcher (E) to size. Sand all of the parts smooth.

2. Apply glue to the ends of the stretchers and position them between the ends so they are flush at the back edges and corners. Clamp the parts together and measure diagonally between opposite corners to make sure the assembly is square (see *Tip*). Then, drive 1½" wood screws through the end pieces and into the ends of the stretchers **(photo B).**

3. Set the cabinet on its back. Lay the top piece flat on your worksurface, bottom-side-up. Butt the back edge of the top

TIP

Careful planning can prevent valuable wood from being wasted. With the exception of the dowel and the spacers, all of the parts for this project can be cut from a 4 × 8' piece of birch plywood (see pattern below):

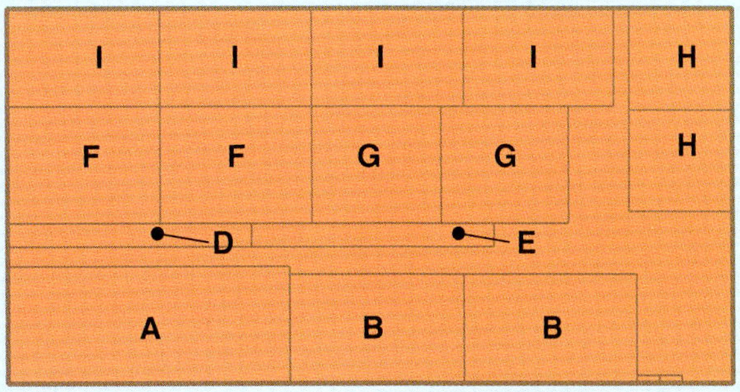

Clamp the bin sides to your worksurface, and use a jig saw to cut the notches and bevels.

Position the bin bottom flush with the dowel notch, and attach it with glue and screws.

against the top stretcher so the ends overhang the cabinet equally on both sides. Mark the bottom face of the top piece to indicate where it will rest on the cabinet ends **(photo C).**

4. Set the cabinet upright and position the top, aligning the reference lines with the outside faces of the ends. The back edge of the top should be flush with the back face of the top stretcher. Attach the top with glue, and drive 1½" wood screws through the top and into the edges of the ends and top stretcher.

INSERT THE DOWEL.

Place spacers along the dowel to separate the bins and ensure smooth operation.

1. Make the three spacers (J) by cutting 3" squares from hardboard or scrap ¼" material. Hardboard is a good choice because its hard, smooth surfaces create little friction.

2. Mark the center points of the spacers, and drill holes with a 1¼" spade bit to accommodate the dowel.

3. Apply paste wax to the dowel for lubrication. Slide the dowel through one end piece. Install the spacers, and slide the dowel end through the hole in the other end. Position the dowel so it protrudes an equal distance from both ends. Anchor the dowel in position by driving #8 × 2" wood screws through the pilot holes on the bottom edges of the ends and into the dowel **(photo D).**

MAKE THE BIN SIDES.

The bin sides have a notch near the bottom front edge so they can rock safely on the dowel. There are bevels on the top edges and at the bottom rear corners to provide clearance.

1. Cut the bin sides (I) to size. Sand the pieces smooth.

2. Use a jig saw to cut a 1¼"-wide, 1"-high notch, ¾" from the bottom front corner of each bin side (see *Part I Detail*).

3. Make the short bevel on the bottom by measuring and drawing marks along the bottom and back edges, 1" from the bottom rear corner. Draw a diagonal cut line between these two marks, and cut off the corner with a jig saw.

4. Make the long bevel on the top edge by measuring down 2" from the top back corner, and drawing a mark. With a straightedge, draw a diagonal cut line from the mark to the upper front corner, and make the cut with a jig saw **(photo E).** Sand all of the cuts smooth.

ASSEMBLE THE BINS.

1. Cut the bin backs (F), bin fronts (G) and bin bottoms (H) to size. Sand the pieces smooth.

2. Position a front over the ends of two sides so their tops and outside edges are flush. Attach the bin front to the bin sides with glue, and drive 1½" wood screws through the bin front and into the edges of the bin sides.

3. Position a bin bottom between the sides so it is recessed 1" and is flush with the top of the dowel notches. Attach the sides to the bottom with glue and 1½" wood screws **(photo F).**

4. Set the bin back over the edges of the bin sides, keeping the top edges flush. Attach the back with glue, and drive 1½" wood screws through the back and into the edges of the bin sides and bottom.

5. Repeat this process to assemble the other bin.

ATTACH THE CHAIN.

To prevent the bins from falling forward when adding or removing recyclables, our design uses chain and screw hooks to attach the bins to the top. The chains can easily be detached when the recycling center needs cleaning.

1. Center and attach the screw hooks on the top edge of the bin backs. Attach 10" chains with #4 × ⅜" wood screws to the underside of the top, 8" from the front edge and 8" from the inside faces of the ends.

2. Place the bins in the cabinet, with spacers in between and on both sides. For smoother movement, sand the notches as necessary.

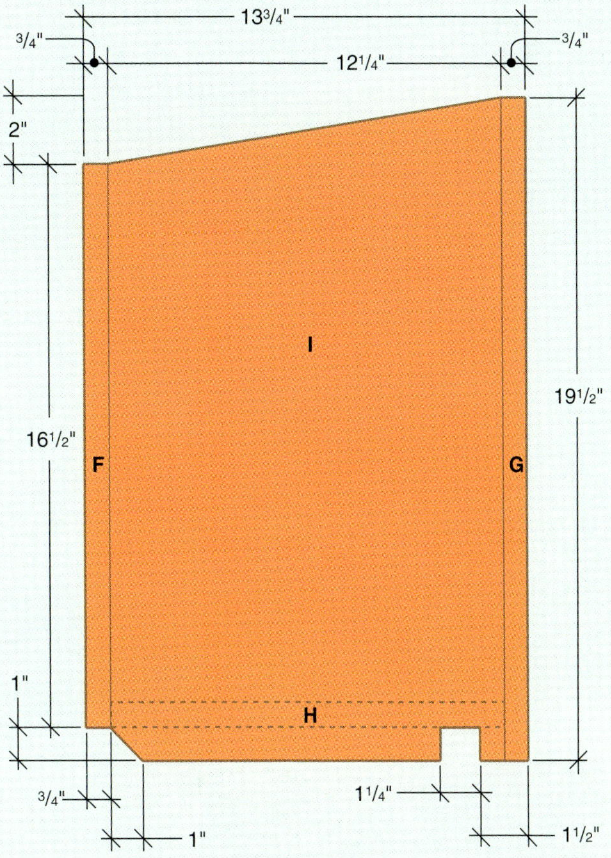

PART I DETAIL

Tip

Ensure a smooth finish by working in a well-ventilated, dust-free area. Airborne dust can ruin a painted finish. Avoid painting a project in an area where woodworking tools have recently operated, and wipe the sanded surfaces to remove all dust.

APPLY FINISHING TOUCHES.

1. Fill all screw holes with wood putty. Finish-sand the cabinet and bins with fine-grit sandpaper. Paint with an enamel with a medium gloss or eggshell finish to make clean up easy.

2. Install a metal drawer pull on the front of each bin when the finish is dry.

PROJECT POWER TOOLS

Utility Cart

Form and function combine in this richly detailed rolling cart.

Construction Materials

Quantity	Lumber
2	1 × 2" × 6' oak
2	1 × 4" × 6' oak
1	2 × 4" × 4' pine
1	1 × 4" × 6' pine
1	¾" × 4 × 8' oak plywood
2	⅜ × ⅝" × 6' dentil molding
4	¾ × ¾" × 6' stop molding
8	⅜ × 2¼" × 3' beaded casing
4	¾" × 2 × 3' melamine-coated particleboard

You'll appreciate the extra space, and your guests will admire the classic style of this rolling cabinet. The cart features decorative dentil molding around a scratch-resistant 22½ × 28½" countertop that provides additional work-surface for preparing special dishes. Two storage or display areas, framed by beaded corner molding, can hold food, beverages, dinnerware and appliances. Underneath, the cart has casters, so it easily rolls across floors to the preparing or serving area. Time and again, you'll find this versatile cart a great help in the kitchen, dining room or other entertainment areas of your home.

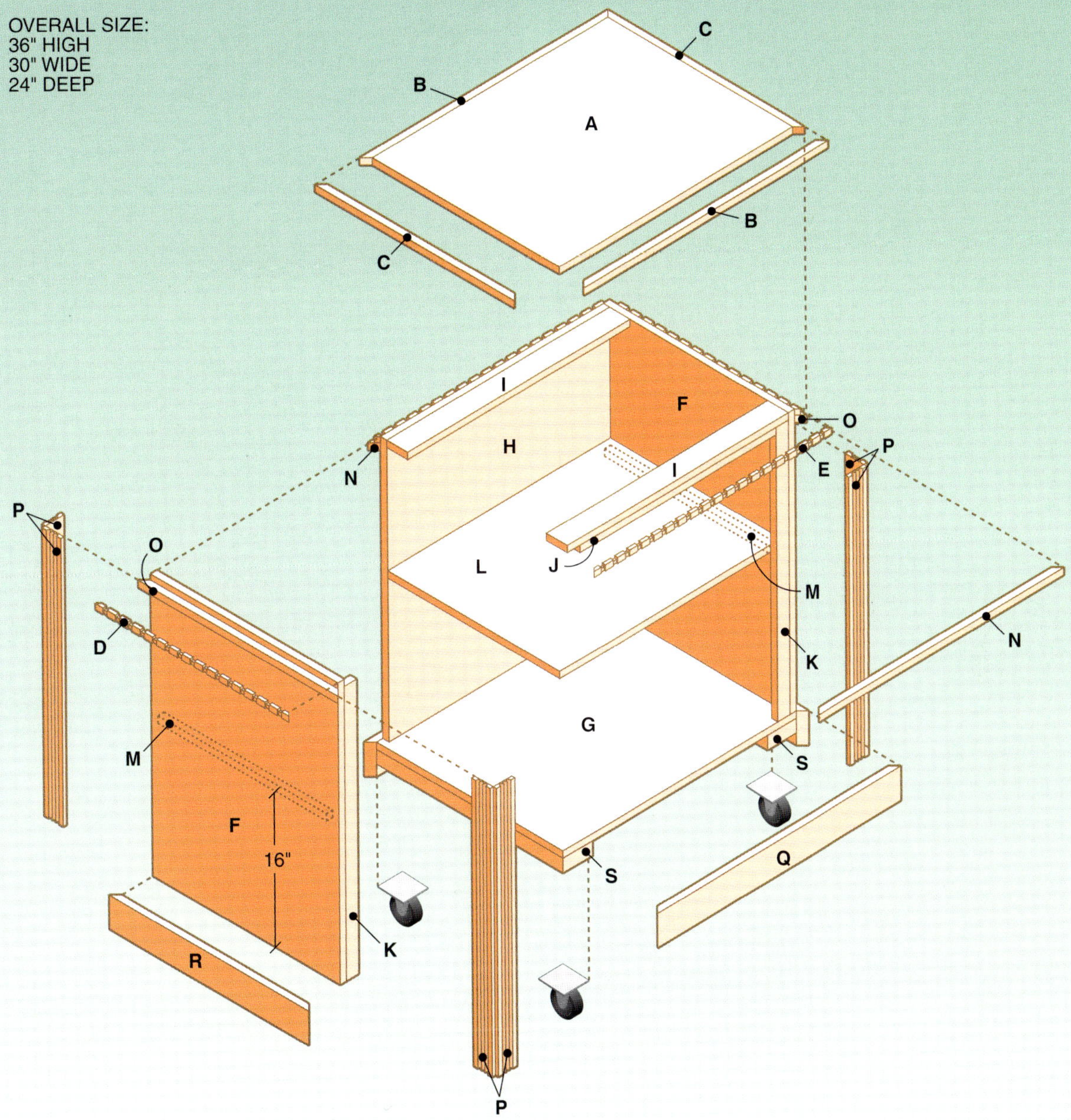

Key	Part	Dimension	Pcs.	Material
A	Top	¾ × 22½ × 28½"	1	Particleboard
B	Long upper trim	¾ × ¾ × 30"	2	Stop mld.
C	Short upper trim	¾ × ¾ × 24"	2	Stop mld.
D	Short dentil	⅜ × ⅝ × 23¼"	2	Dentil mld.
E	Long dentil	⅜ × ⅝ × 29¼"	2	Dentil mld.
F	Side panel	¾ × 22½ × 30⅞"	2	Plywood
G	Bottom	¾ × 22½ × 28½"	1	Plywood
H	Back	¾ × 27 × 30⅞"	1	Plywood
I	Stretcher	¾ × 3½ × 27"	2	Pine
J	Brace	¾ × 1½ × 24"	1	Oak

Cutting List

Key	Part	Dimension	Pcs.	Material
K	Post	¾ × 1½ × 30⅛"	2	Oak
L	Shelf	¾ × 20¾ × 27"	1	Plywood
M	Cleat	¾ × ¾ × 20¼"	2	Stop mld.
N	Long lower trim	¾ × ¾ × 30"	2	Stop mld.
O	Short lower trim	¾ × ¾ × 24"	2	Stop mld.
P	Corner trim	⅜ × 2¼ × 29½"	8	Bead. csg.
Q	Long base	¾ × 3½ × 30"	2	Oak
R	Short base	¾ × 3½ × 24"	2	Oak
S	Caster mount	1½ × 3½ × 22½"	2	Pine

Materials: #6 × 1", 1¼", 1⅝" and 2" wood screws, 16-ga. × 1" brads, 3d finish nails, 2" casters (4), ¾" shelf nosing or oak veneer edge tape (30"), ⅜"-dia. oak plugs, wood glue, finishing materials.

Note: Measurements reflect the actual size of dimension lumber.

Use a ¾" piece of scrap wood as a spacer to inset the cleats ¾" from the back edges of the side panels.

Drive screws through the top of the stretcher to secure the oak brace.

Directions: Utility Cart

For all screws used in this project, drill ³⁄₃₂" pilot holes. Counterbore the holes ¼" deep, using a ⅜" counterbore bit.

PREPARE THE SIDES AND BOTTOM.

1. Cut the side panels (F), bottom (G), back (H) and cleats (M) to size. Sand them smooth.

2. Drill four evenly spaced pilot holes along the long edges of each side panel, ⅜" in from each edge.

3. Flip each side over and, on the inside face, place a cleat so the bottom edge is 16" from the bottom of the side panel. Attach the cleats with glue, and drive 1" wood screws through the cleats and into the side panels. Make sure the ends of the cleats are inset ¾" from the back edges of the side panels **(photo A).**

4. Drill pilot holes along the side and back edges of the bottom, keeping the holes ⅜" in from the edges.

ASSEMBLE THE CABINET.

1. Position the back between the side panels. Attach it with glue, and drive 1⅝" wood screws through the pilot holes in the side panels and into the edges of the back.

2. Apply glue to the bottom edges of the side panels and back. Attach the bottom by driving 1⅝" wood screws through the bottom and into the edges of the sides and back. The side and back edges of the bottom piece should be flush with the outside faces of the side panels and back.

3. Cut the stretchers (I), brace (J), posts (K) and shelf (L) to size. Sand the parts smooth.

4. Position the front stretcher between the side panels, flush with the top and front edges of the side panels. Attach the stretcher with glue, and drive 1⅝" wood screws through the side panels and into the ends of the stretcher. Apply glue to the back edge and ends of the rear stretcher, and butt it against the back, flush with the

Use glue and brads to attach shelf nosing to the front edge of the shelf.

Fasten the dentil molding around the top edge of the cabinet with glue and brads.

top edge. Drive screws through the side panels and back and into the stretcher.

5. Set the posts in place, faces flush with the front side edges. Attach them with glue, and drive 1⅝" wood screws through the pilot holes in the sides and into the edges of the posts.

6. Apply glue to the brace, and clamp it to the front stretcher so their front edges are flush. Drive 1" wood screws through the stretcher and into the brace **(photo B).**

7. Clamp the shelf vertically to your worksurface. Cut a strip of shelf nosing to match the length of the front edge. Apply glue, and attach the nosing to the shelf with 1" brads **(photo C).**

8. Apply glue to the tops of the cleats, and set the shelf into place, butting the back edge against the back. Drive 3d finish nails through the shelf and into the cleats.

ATTACH THE UPPER MOLDING.

1. Cut the short dentils (D), long dentils (E), long lower trim (N) and short lower trim (O) to length.

2. Make 45° miter cuts on the ends of each piece of molding, always angling the cuts inward. When cutting the miters for the dentil molding, make sure to cut through the blocks, or "teeth," so the return piece will match at the corners (see *Tip*).

3. Fit the dentil pieces, with the gap edge up, flush to the top edge of the cabinet. Drill 1⁄16"

TIP

Instead of fastening shelf nosing to the shelf edge, an option is to apply self-adhesive oak veneer edge tape. Cut the tape to length, and press it onto the wood, using a household iron to activate the adhesive. When cool, trim away excess tape with a sharp utility knife.

pilot holes through the molding, and attach it with glue and 1" brads **(photo D).**

4. Attach the lower trim pieces snug against the bottom of the dentil molding, using glue and 3d finish nails. Set the nails with a nail set **(photo E).**

Attach the lower trim underneath the dentil molding, and set the nails with a nail set.

ATTACH THE BASE MOLDING.

1. Cut the caster mounts (S) to length.

2. Lay the cart on its back, and attach the caster mounts to the bottom of the cart, flush with the edges of the bottom. Apply glue and drive 2" wood screws through the mounts and into the bottom. Angle the screws slightly to avoid breaking through the top face of the bottom with the tip of the screw.

3. Miter-cut the long bases (Q) and short bases (R) to length.

4. Attach the trim to the cabinet, keeping the top edges flush with the top face of the bottom. Apply glue to all mating surfaces, and drive 1¼" wood screws through the trim pieces and into the edges of the bottom.

5. Cut the corner trim (P) pieces to length.

6. Apply glue to a corner trim piece, and clamp it in place over a post so the inside edges are flush **(photo F).** Drill 1/16" pilot holes through the corner piece, and nail it to the post and side panel with 1" brads.

Clamp the corner molding in place to ensure a tight bond with the posts as the glue dries.

7. When the glue is dry, complete the corner by attaching another trim piece with glue and brads. The edges of the trim pieces should touch but should not overlap. Attach the corner trim to the remaining corners.

MAKE THE TOP.

1. Mark the dimensions for the top (A) on a piece of melamine-coated particleboard. Apply masking tape over the cut lines, and mark new cut lines onto the tape. Use a sharp utility knife and a

Score the cutting lines on the melamine with a sharp utility knife to prevent chipping.

Apply glue and clamp the top in place. Then, secure it by driving screws through the stretchers.

TIP

The size of the "teeth" in dentil molding can vary, as can the gaps between the teeth. You might want to purchase extra molding to allow for cutting adjustments that may be necessary to form the corners properly.

straightedge to score the board along the cut lines. This will help prevent chipping and splintering from the saw blade **(photo G).** To minimize chipping when making the cut, use a sharp blade on your circular saw. Cut the top to size, using the straightedge clamped in place as a guide. Then, remove the masking tape.

2. Cut the long upper trim (B) pieces and short upper trim (C) pieces to length, mitering the ends at 45°.

3. Drill pilot holes through the trim pieces, and attach them to the edges of the top with glue and 1" brads. Make sure the tops of the trim pieces are flush with the top face of the top.

4. Center the top over the cabinet, and attach it with glue. Drive 1" wood screws up through the stretchers and into the underside of the top **(photo H).**

APPLY FINISHING TOUCHES.

1. Lay the utility cart on its back, and attach the casters to the caster mounts.

2. Set all nails with a nail set, and fill the nail holes with wood putty. Fill the screw holes on the base trim with glued oak plugs. Finish-sand the utility cart.

3. Finish the cart with the stain or sealer of your choice. We used a rustic oak stain to enhance the grain of the wood.

Conversion Charts

Drill Bit Guide

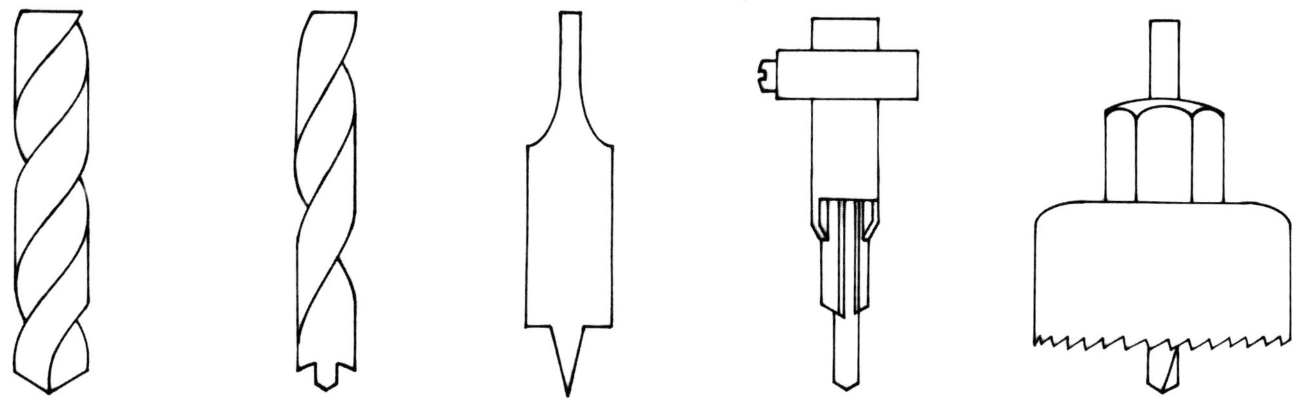

Counterbore, Shank & Pilot Hole Diameters

Screw Size	Counterbore Diameter for Screw Head	Clearance Hole for Screw Shank	Pilot Hole Diameter	
			Hard Wood	Soft Wood
#1	.146 (9/64)	5/64	3/64	1/32
#2	1/4	3/32	3/64	1/32
#3	1/4	7/64	1/16	3/64
#4	1/4	1/8	1/16	3/64
#5	1/4	1/8	5/64	1/16
#6	5/16	9/64	3/32	5/64
#7	5/16	5/32	3/32	5/64
#8	3/8	11/64	1/8	3/32
#9	3/8	11/64	1/8	3/32
#10	3/8	3/16	1/8	7/64
#11	1/2	3/16	5/32	9/64
#12	1/2	7/32	9/64	1/8

Abrasive Paper Grits - (Aluminum Oxide)

Very Coarse	Coarse	Medium	Fine	Very Fine
12 - 36	40 - 60	80 - 120	150 - 180	220 - 600

Saw Blades

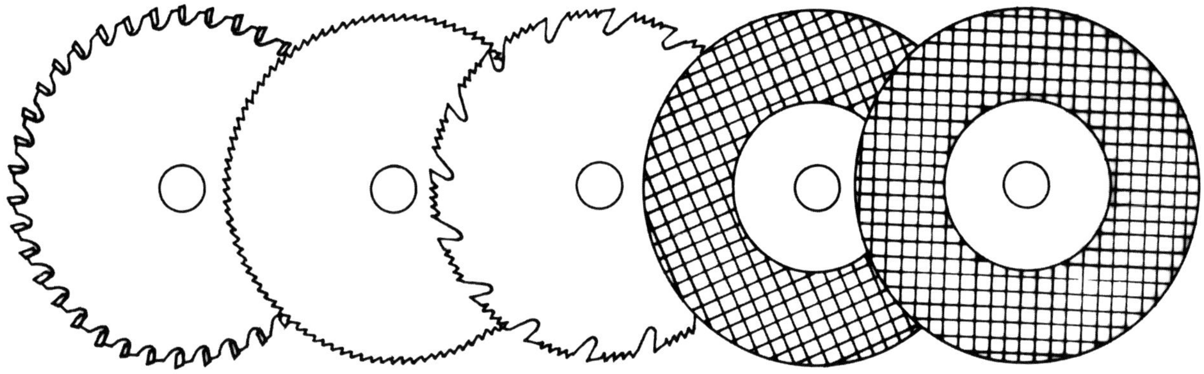

Adhesives

Type	Characteristics	Uses
White glue	**Strength:** moderate; rigid bond **Drying time:** several hours **Resistance to heat:** poor **Resistance to moisture:** poor **Hazards:** none **Cleanup/solvent:** soap and water	**Porous surfaces:** Wood (indoors) Paper Cloth
Yellow glue (carpenter's glue)	**Strength:** moderate to good; rigid bond **Drying time:** several hours; faster than white glue **Resistance to heat:** moderate **Resistance to moisture:** moderate **Hazards:** none **Cleanup/solvent:** soap and water	**Porous surfaces:** Wood (indoors) Paper Cloth
Two-part epoxy	**Strength:** excellent; strongest of all adhesives **Drying time:** varies, depending on manufacturer **Resistance to heat:** excellent **Resistance to moisture:** excellent **Hazards:** fumes are toxic and flammable **Cleanup/solvent:** acetone will dissolve some types	**Smooth & porous surfaces:** Wood (indoors & outdoors) Metal Masonry Glass Fiberglass
Hot glue	**Strength:** depends on type **Drying time:** less than 60 seconds **Resistance to heat:** fair **Resistance to moisture:** good **Hazards:** hot glue can cause burns **Cleanup/solvent:** heat will loosen bond	**Smooth & porous surfaces:** Glass Plastics Wood
Cyanoacrylate (instant glue)	**Strength:** excellent, but with little flexibility **Drying time:** a few seconds **Resistance to heat:** excellent **Resistance to moisture:** excellent **Hazards:** can bond skin instantly; toxic, flammable **Cleanup/solvent:** acetone	**Smooth surfaces:** Glass Ceramics Plastics Metal
Construction adhesive	**Strength:** good to excellent; very durable **Drying time:** 24 hours **Resistance to heat:** good **Resistance to moisture:** excellent **Hazards:** may irritate skin and eyes **Cleanup/solvent:** soap and water (while still wet)	**Porous surfaces:** Framing lumber Plywood and paneling Wallboard Foam panels Masonry
Water-base contact cement	**Strength:** good **Drying time:** bonds instantly; dries fully in 30 minutes **Resistance to heat:** excellent **Resistance to moisture:** good **Hazards:** may irritate skin and eyes **Cleanup/solvent:** soap and water (while still wet)	**Porous surfaces:** Plastic laminates Plywood Flooring Cloth
Silicone sealant (caulk)	**Strength:** fair to good; very flexible bond **Drying time:** 24 hours **Resistance to heat:** good **Resistance to moisture:** excellent **Hazards:** may irritate skin and eyes **Cleanup/solvent:** acetone	**Smooth & porous surfaces:** Wood Ceramics Fiberglass Plastics Glass

Conversion Charts (continued)

Lumber Dimensions

Nominal - U.S.	Actual - U.S.	Metric
1 × 2	¾" × 1½"	19 × 38 mm
1 × 3	¾" × 2½"	19 × 64 mm
1 × 4	¾" × 3½"	19 × 89 mm
1 × 5	¾" × 4½"	19 × 114 mm
1 × 6	¾" × 5½"	19 × 140 mm
1 × 7	¾" × 6¼"	19 × 159 mm
1 × 8	¾" × 7¼"	19 × 184 mm
1 × 10	¾" × 9¼"	19 × 235 mm
1 × 12	¾" × 11¼"	19 × 286 mm
1¼ × 4	1" × 3½"	25 × 89 mm
1¼ × 6	1" × 5½"	25 × 140 mm
1¼ × 8	1" × 7¼"	25 × 184 mm
1¼ × 10	1" × 9¼"	25 × 235 mm
1¼ × 12	1" × 11¼"	25 × 286 mm

Nominal - U.S.	Actual - U.S.	Metric
1½ × 4	1¼" × 3½"	32 × 89 mm
1½ × 6	1¼" × 5½"	32 × 140 mm
1½ × 8	1¼" × 7¼"	32 × 184 mm
1½ × 10	1¼" × 9¼"	32 × 235 mm
1½ × 12	1¼" × 11¼"	32 × 286 mm
2 × 4	1½" × 3½"	38 × 89 mm
2 × 6	1½" × 5½"	38 × 140 mm
2 × 8	1½" × 7¼"	38 × 184 mm
2 × 10	1½" × 9¼"	38 × 235 mm
2 × 12	1½" × 11¼"	38 × 286 mm
3 × 6	2½" × 5½"	64 × 140 mm
4 × 4	3½" × 3½"	89 × 89 mm
4 × 6	3½" × 5½"	89 × 140 mm

Index